GROWING UP CANADIAN

McGILL-QUEEN'S STUDIES IN ETHNIC HISTORY

Growing Up Canadian

MUSLIMS, HINDUS, BUDDHISTS

Edited by Peter Beyer and Rubina Ramji

McGill-Queen's University Press
Montreal & Kingston | London | Ithaca

© McGill-Queen's University Press 2013

ISBN 978-0-7735-4137-5 (cloth)
ISBN 978-0-7735-4138-2 (paper)
ISBN 978-0-7735-8874-5 (ePDF)
ISBN 978-0-7735-8875-2 (ePUB)

Legal deposit third quarter 2013
Bibliothèque nationale du Québec

Printed in Canada on acid-free paper that is 100% ancient forest
free (100% post-consumer recycled), processed chlorine free

This book has been published with the help of a grant from the
Canadian Federation for the Humanities and Social Sciences,
through the Awards to Scholarly Publications Program, using funds
provided by the Social Sciences and Humanities Research Council
of Canada.

McGill-Queen's University Press acknowledges the support of the
Canada Council for the Arts for our publishing program. We also
acknowledge the financial support of the Government of Canada
through the Canada Book Fund for our publishing activities.

LIBRARY AND ARCHIVES CANADA CATALOGUING IN PUBLICATION

Growing up Canadian : Muslims, Hindus, Buddhists / edited by
Peter Beyer and Rubina Ramji.

(McGill-Queen's studies in ethnic history. Series 2 ; 32)
Includes bibliographical references and index.
ISBN 978-0-7735-4137-5 (bound). – ISBN 978-0-7735-4138-2 (pbk.)
ISBN 978-0-7735-8874-5 (ePDF). – ISBN 978-0-7735-8875-2 (ePUB)

1. Children of immigrants – Religious life – Canada.   2. Muslim
youth – Religious life – Canada.   3. Hindu youth – Religious life –
Canada.   4. Buddhist youth – Religious life – Canada.   I. Beyer,
Peter, 1949–   II. Ramji, Rubina, 1967–   III. Series: McGill-Queen's
studies in ethnic history. Series 2 ; 32

BL625.9.I55G76 2013   200.86'9120971   C2013-901146-3

Set in 10.5/12.5 Minion Pro with Calluna Sans
Book design & typesetting by Garet Markvoort, zijn digital

CONTENTS

TABLES AND FIGURES

TABLES

FIGURES

ACKNOWLEDGMENTS

This book reports the results of a multi-year research project carried out at the University of Ottawa, Concordia University in Montreal, and the University of Toronto between 2004 and 2008. The project was funded by a Standard Research Grant from the Social Sciences and Humanities Research Council of Canada, and we wish to thank the SSHRCC for its generous support. Peter Beyer of the University of Ottawa was the principal investigator on the project, collaborating with the other authors as well as several others. Lori Beaman, at the time at Concordia University in Montreal but now also at the University of Ottawa, directed the research in Montreal, while John H. Simpson was principally responsible for the research on the three campuses of the University of Toronto. Nancy Nason-Clark at the University of New Brunswick in Fredericton took charge of important portions of the data analysis, and Leslie Laczko at the University of Ottawa provided important advice in the early stages of the project. Two postdoctoral fellows, Rubina Ramji and Shandip Saha, now at the Cape Breton University and Athabasca University, respectively, are especially to be singled out for having directed and carried out the lion's share of the data gathering in Ottawa and Toronto. Rubina Ramji is the principal co-author of this book. Three doctoral students played important roles throughout the project, Arlene Macdonald and Carolyn Reimer at the University of Toronto and Marie-Paule Martel-Reny at Concordia University. Wendy Martin and Kathryn Carrière, both of whom completed their doctoral degrees under Peter Beyer's supervision at the University of Ottawa, joined the team in the analysis and writing stages, as did Cathy Holtmann, a doctoral student with Nancy Nason-Clark.

Recruiting participants for this project proved at times quite challenging; the eventual success of the project in this regard is due to the tireless efforts of many of the people just mentioned, above all Ramji, Saha, Macdonald, Reimer, and Martel-Reny, but a number of people among the administrative staff of five of the six university campuses assisted greatly in our efforts at various stages. We would like to acknowledge especially the efforts of Professor Noel Salmond at Carleton University in this regard. A special thanks also to Bridget Beyer, Sarah Wilby, and Christina Nason-Clark, who helped with the transcription of the interviews.

GROWING UP CANADIAN

Growing Up Canadian:
Systemic and Lived Religion

PETER BEYER

FOCUS, CONTEXT, AND DELIMITATION

This book is about religion and global migration, with a specific focus on Canada. In today's world, the consequences and context of people relocating from one place with which they are familiar and in which they are embedded to another that is physically and culturally very different has taken on an abiding importance (Castles and Miller 2003; Papastergiadis 2000). Human migration is, of course, nothing new in history; rather, the opposite is the case (Lucassen, Lucassen, and Manning 2010). The question takes on specific qualities, however, depending on the particularities of different times, different places, and circumstances. The context of late twentieth- and early twenty-first-century global society has its salient peculiarities; some of the more significant include: (a) multidirectional and, in terms of sheer numbers, unprecedented migration flows that include almost all the inhabited parts of the globe, whether as places of origin, destination, or both; (b) rapid, thickly distributed, and intensively utilized global means of communication ranging from air travel to electronic connections; (c) the use of those means of communication for a very wide variety of purposes, such as economic, political, scientific, leisure, and religious; (d) a resulting thick social connectivity of virtually all parts of the world with all other parts; (e) significant processes of socio-structural and cultural homogenization across the globe; (f) but equally significant and simultaneous processes of social and cultural heterogenization, which manifest themselves across several levels ranging from the individual and group to the national and global–regional. Given the multi-dimensional quality of this global and globalized context, the question of migration and its transformative consequences becomes highly complex, because it will not be uniform around the world, varying according to place and the particular circumstances of different migrants, their personal characteristics, and social location above all. Thus, while one focus of this book is very consciously on migration in the broader contemporary global context, it is and must perforce be specific and localized, asking its questions of particular subgroups of migrants in particular places, and with respect to certain aspects or dimensions and not others. Whether the analyses we present can be generalized to other places, dimensions, and subgroups is an important question but one that must be examined separately, not simply assumed or deduced.

The specific focus of this book and the research that it reports is on late twentieth- and very early twenty-first-century migrants in Canada, on certain segments of the youth or young adults of these populations, and specifically on the question of religion among these immigrant youth in Canada.[1] This selectivity is to some extent arbitrary, reflecting the research interests and location of the authors, but it also takes its importance from the wider context just outlined. In the latter half of the twentieth century, patterns of migration that had been minimal before became far more commonplace. Prominent among these patterns are the movement for the first time of significant numbers of people from the regions of Asia, Africa, and Latin America to the regions of North America,[2] Australasia, and Europe, but these are not the only manifestations. Beyond the geographic fact of these new patterns of migration is that they have been one significant factor in bringing about or in signalling profound transformations in how people, whether migrants or non-migrants, whether dominant or marginalized, understand the world that we all live in. Symptomatic of this shift has been the concomitant rise of a series of neologisms that seek to express the awareness of living in a new context or of seeing that context in new ways, words like globalization, post-modern, post-colonial, and, perhaps more recently, post-secular (e.g. Habermas 2010). We seem to be no longer where we were before; we are in a "post" situation. Focusing on migration and its consequences in this period is therefore also a way of approaching these wider transformations in global social reality and in the discourse about or understanding of that reality.

The choice of Canada as the geographical focus suggests itself from a number of perspectives. On a per capita basis, Canada in the time period in question has received as many or more transnational migrants than any country in the world. Rates of immigration in the first decade of the twenty-first century averaged about 0.8% of the total population per year, immigrants thus constituting about 60% of the annual population growth in a country with a quite low rate of natural increase (figures available at www.cic.gc.ca). Moreover, although Europe still provides a disproportionate percentage of these immigrants relative to Europe's share of the world population, this percentage has been decreasing over recent decades (as has the percentage of immigrants who are Christians [Beyer 2005b]), with the result that by mid-decade, almost 20% of the population consisted of immigrants and, of these, 60% had come from non-European countries of origin (figures available at www.statcan.ca). And these figures do not yet include the Canada-born children of these immigrants. As important as the sheer volume, however, are the corresponding discourses and resulting transformations in how people in Canada understand themselves, their country, and the wider world in which they are situated. Concepts like diversity, pluralism, multiculturalism, accommodation, integration, tolerance, and inclusion have, since the 1980s especially, become constants in Canadian public debates and official policy alongside and in conjunction with the aforementioned globalization and "post" words.

A great deal of research that examines the consequences and context of global migration centres on those who have migrated relatively recently or at least within their lifetime. This first generation generally faces the question of relocation and having to reinvent oneself rather directly, and it is in the context of their arrival that the so-called "host" society most often exhibits the most emphatic reactions. This combination, likely because of the contrasts and the inevitable entry of the arising issues into public discussion, mass media reporting, and public policy considerations in various countries, also attracts significant scientific research attention. In both public debates and scientific literature on immigrants, however, the questions of generations and youth have also always been a common focus, in large measure because there are significant differences between these groups and their older first-generation relatives.[3] The second and subsequent generations *grow up adapting* to the "new" country and are, in that respect, formally as comparable to the long-established native-born as they are to their parents and grandparents. They provide a logical bridge between the "immigrants" and the "hosts," or at least speak more directly to longer-term implications. Those who arrive as immigrants at a young age, especially before puberty, are in most senses generally more like their native-born siblings than their parents and older siblings, and this feature points to the normally greater malleability of the young when it comes to adapting to new circumstances. In the context of the larger question of immigrant adaptation, integration, marginalization, assimilation, and transformation (of both them and their "host" society), native-born generations and the young are therefore of considerable interest inasmuch as they embody the longer-term consequences and implications of migration, in the present case of contemporary transnational migration in particular. In more theoretical terms, these 1.5- and second-generation populations are in a position to reconstruct boundaries and identities that their immediate forebears – both "immigrant" and "native" – may have taken for granted. These identities include the cultural, religious, gender, national, racial, class, and other identities through which people today understand the most important social differences in the context of the identity that is global society. Although their older relatives are in a similar position, they carry with them their lives both "back home" and in their "new home," whereas most of their children experience the former either only vicariously or through the intermediary of the "home away from home" that their parents may have managed to recreate. With respect to what their parents and the longer-established populations may take for granted, they are more likely to develop hybridized forms that, in the current globalized context, may claim a comparable authenticity or legitimacy to both the received religious, cultural, and other identities and those hybridized forms developed elsewhere in the heartlands and in diaspora (Beyer 2005a; Nederveen Pieterse 2003).

Focusing on religion in this context is on the one hand arbitrary, reflecting as it does the research interests of the authors. On the other hand, both the role that religion plays in the context of global migration and the consequences *for religion* are comparatively neglected topics, including as concerns Canada. Here as elsewhere, the greater part of research on migrants still ignores religion almost entirely.[4] This is also the case for research on the younger generations, where most of the research has focused on questions such as educational attainment, income, and cultural identity (see, e.g., Abada, Hou, and Ram 2008; Anisef and Kilbride 2003; Beiser et al. 1998; Corak 2008; Gosine 2000; Hanvey and Kunz 2000; Kibria 2002; for the United States, see, e.g., Portes and Rumbaut 2001). Moreover, research that has focused primarily on the role of religion has concentrated for the most part on immigrant religious institutions and the religious expressions of the first, adult generation (see Berns McGown 1999; Bramadat and Seljak 2005; Coward and Goa 1987; Coward, Hinnells, and Williams 2000; DeVries, Baker, and Overmyer 2010; Harding, Hori, and Soucy 2010; Israel 1987; Janhevich and Ibrahim 2004; McLellan 1999; Rukmani 1999). The great majority of extant research on immigrant youth in Canada also ignores religion, although that lack is gradually being rectified, not least in the form of the present volume.[5] While this fact does not detract from the value of the research that has been done – much of it is in fact quite useful and reliable – it does indicate that in certain areas a great deal of work needs to be done if we are to better understand the longer-term effects of the constant high-level migration to Canada and in particular the effects of this migration on the religious expression, the place of religion, and the religious diversity in this country.

Focusing on religion also raises the question of which religion or religions – of what, in the context of the research reported here, counts as religion. We have addressed this question in two ways. The first, and more important, is to follow a path of least resistance – namely, the research design simply accepted what was evident from the interviews that we conducted for this project: individuals in our society conceive religion in a great variety of ways, some of which are mutually contradictory, some of which are overlapping and mutually reinforcing. Yet there was also very broad acceptance of the ideas that (a) such a thing as religion self-evidently exists, (b) there is not only religion but also that there are religions, and (c) the list of religions, while variable, most often contains what one might call the R5: Christianity, Judaism, Islam, Hinduism, and Buddhism.[6] Although this set of understandings can be and has been challenged as too selective, too historically contingent, and therefore as excluding too much that by various criteria could or ought to count as religion (see, e.g., Knott 2005; Masuzawa 2005; McGuire 2008), we have rather accepted such "popular" understandings because they were most likely to provide a good entry point for data collection – most people would understand the "semantic region" that our research intended – without thereby determining or even restricting what our research would reveal. More specifically, while we recruited our participants through such popular understanding of what counts as religion, we did not then require or even overtly encourage them to abide by those conceptions either in the questions we asked or the responses that they gave. In this way, to a significant extent, the research design left open the question of what counts as religion, letting the participants' understandings prevail as much as possible.

On the basis of these assumptions, the second way we delimited the religious field was by recruiting for our interviews only young adults who self-identified as having either a Muslim, a Buddhist, or a Hindu background, letting them determine what that might mean. Above all, we excluded people who were only from other religious backgrounds, notably Christians and Sikhs, the other two religious identities that, according to census figures, are very strongly represented in the Canadian population.[7] People who identified with other religions could participate but only if they also considered that they had one of the three target religions in their background, meaning their family, their immediate forebears. We also excluded converts, people who have become Buddhist, Hindu, or Muslim in their lifetimes but who do not have these religions in their families or family backgrounds. This set of restrictions was entirely practical, responding to limitations in time and resources available to the project. A further project, in the process of completion at the time of writing, has endeavoured to address the same questions with respect to various excluded religious identities and backgrounds, notably second- and 1.5-generation Christians and Sikhs.[8]

THEORETICAL FRAMES

The central questions posed by the research reported here had two complementary aspects. On the one hand, we asked how the selected demographic groups relate to religion and the religions of their family heritages. What forms did this religion and these religions take in their lives, and what role did they play, what importance did they have in their lives and in relation to their families and social networks? On the other hand, we also wanted to know what effects their visions and performance of religion might be having or possibly will have on what religion is and what these religions are and are becoming in the Canadian and, by extension, global contexts. This combination of questions implies a double theoretical perspective with which we – severally and separately – came to the research. One observes religion primarily from the perspective of the individual, lending theoretical priority to how people construct religion for themselves. This comes close to what Hall, Orsi, McGuire, and others have called a "lived religion" approach (Hall 1997; McGuire 2008; Orsi 2005). The other theoretical perspective observes religion in somewhat the opposite way, looking to see what institutional arrangements, patterns, and social systems emerge as religion out of social action or communication, to some degree in abstraction from what individuals may intend or understand about what they are thinking and doing. This approach refers mostly to Beyer's efforts to theorize, on a Luhmannian basis, religion as a modern, constructed, and differentiated societal system on a glocal – that is, local and global at the same time – scale (Beyer 2006b; cf. Luhmann 2000).

The relation between these two theoretical approaches in the current context is complementary; they allow us to analyze different aspects of what is a single social reality without having to decide which one is, by whatever criteria, more correct or useful. To illustrate, McGuire defines lived religion as "how religion and spirituality are practiced, experienced, and expressed by ordinary people (rather than official spokespersons) in the context of their everyday lives" (McGuire 2008, 12). The participants in the research project are by most measures ordinary people, and it is their perspective on the core questions that we give priority to in our analyses. We wanted to see how they lived their religion, or not, as the case might be. The majority of the chapters seek to have the participants' voices heard, to have their accounts of religion count. What others, such as scholars of religion or theologians, might think is the proper way to do religion is put into the background and not used as the putative standards to which the religious orientations of the research participants are compared. The voices of official spokespersons, however they might be identified and to the extent that they are heard at all, appear only through the accounts of the participants. The lived religion approach allows for easier recognition of possibly unexpected and hybridized constructions of religion. This is the theoretical orientation that is most visible in what follows; it is front and centre.

The religious system approach takes these same individual accounts but shifts the context of analysis away from their everyday lives to ask how what these people do and say contributes to the broader societal construction of religion or religions – or not. It takes as its point of departure the core sociological observation that when individuals engage in social communication, they are contributing to the ongoing generation of a social reality that is more and even other than what they may think, intend, or experience. Just as, for example, using money to buy a product or service may contribute to the satisfaction of personal wants and needs while at the same time helping to reproduce a global capitalist economic system, so may prayer, meditation, or religiously intended fasting, however understood individually, be elements in the reproduction of a larger, possibly global, religious system. Social systems, in this theoretical perspective, are emergent social structures that require and assume the participation of individual human beings in the communication that (re)produces them. All societies exhibit such differentiated systems that are not simply the aggregates of individual action. What characterizes modern and now global society is the historical construction and perpetuation of dominant social systems that centre not, for instance, on status groups or locality but on particular functions, such as economic, political, scientific, or religious functions.[9] The religious system is the one that is of particular interest in the current context. It is a modern social system. It is the product of historical development and not some sort of essential analytic component of any society. Its features in contemporary global society are therefore contingent in the sense of not being necessary. They could be other than what they are, and we may be in a period – symptomatic of which are the above-mentioned discussions of living in a "post" context – in which key features of this system are in the process of important transformation (see Beyer 2012). The correlates of this transformation include the sorts of factors already mentioned, including greater and more intense global communicative connectivity of which global transnational migration is a key part. The second- and 1.5-generation Canadian population that is our focus here can be expected both to manifest and to contribute to these transformations in religion as in other dimensions of society.

In this second theoretical context, therefore, it is also not a matter of adding, prioritizing, or even comparing what religious experts, authorities, or officials might say or do with respect to what our participants contributed. The particular situations of the second- and 1.5-generation Canadians from transnational migrant families and what they may reveal about the (re)construction – again, or not – of a globalized religious system is what is of interest. In terms of comparison, what is for our purposes more important than the actions and perspectives of institutional authorities like theologians, priests, ulama, or monks are the possibly parallel situations and contributions of such second- and 1.5-generation people in other regions such as the United States and Europe.

The issue of comparison points to another aspect of the religious system orientation. In the contemporary globalized circumstance, globalized structures, ideas, and social patterns do not exist globally in a straightforward way, meaning that global commonalities also and only manifest themselves in terms of local differences. Continuities appear only and also as discontinuities. Following especially Robertson's theory of globalization as glocalization (Robertson 1992), the universal in global society is always a particularized universal, a localized version of what is in other respects a social singularity spread around the world. Applied to the participants in our research, we therefore looked to their particularizations of their received religions as possible manifestations of and contributions to the reproduction of what is globally speaking universalized as a single but multi-centred religion and more broadly of a global religious system still characterized in the main by a series of constructed and imagined religions (cf. Beyer 1998). It is for this reason that we asked them not only how they saw religion in their own lives but also how religion and, if applicable, their religion related to religion and religions in the larger generational, Canadian, and global contexts.

These theoretical perspectives are important for understanding the form our research took and the emphases of the analyses reported here. The theories' role, however, is primarily to provide the orientation for the project, and only in an extended sense is it intended to test portions of the theories. In that regard, and somewhat in contrast, although the broad question of "immigrant adaptation" does inevitably also inform the research, this is more because so much of the literature on transnational migration, and religion in that context, focuses on this issue,[10] not because it provided a primary theoretical orientation in addition. One consequence is that the religious and social situation of our participants' parents, including of course that situation in the latter's countries of origin, occupies more of a background and contextual place in our analyses, as it did in the research design itself. The "generational gap" is important but as part of the effort to understand the religion of the Canada-raised generation and only in the context of the adult first generation. Our research did not engage in a deliberate intergenerational comparison.

OUTLINE OF THE PROJECT

A detailed presentation of the research design, data gathering, and participant sample characteristics is given in the next chapter. However, a brief outline at this point will serve to show how the more abstract issues discussed to this point were operationalized in the project itself. To represent the core issue of religious (re)construction in the context of transnational migration, the project recruited about 200 participants from three Canadian cities, Ottawa, Toronto, and Montreal, through six university campuses in those cities. These participants were of self-declared Muslim, Hindu, or Buddhist background, were between the ages of 18 and 27, and came from recent immigrant families. One-on-one semi-structured interviews were conducted with them, lasting anywhere from forty minutes to two-and-a half hours and thematizing above all their relation to and involvement in religion and the religions of their family heritages, as they understood what these terms meant. Also included were contextual questions relating to family and social networks, their place in Canadian society, attitudes on a range of issues, and assessments of the larger

Canadian and global context. The majority of the participants were women in all three religious categories, and the single largest religious-background group were Muslims, constituting almost half the sample. The interviews were conducted between fall 2004 and spring 2006.

Post-secondary institutions were chosen as the sites of recruitment for a number of reasons, including that 2001 Canadian census data showed that, depending on the religious identity subgroup, from 75 to 95% of the population with the target characteristics was engaged in or had received post-secondary education. The fact that all recruitment ended up being done through four universities and six campuses was more accidental than deliberate. The three cities were chosen because, again according to 2001 census figures, from 65 to 80% of those with Muslim, Hindu, or Buddhist religious identity lived there. The aim of the project included avoiding recruitment through religious institutions or religiously identified organizations so as to access a reasonably broad segment of the second- and 1.5-generation population that was not skewed toward religiously involved people more than was unavoidable. This aim also excluded any deliberate form of snowball sampling.

SUMMARY OF MAIN FINDINGS

As one might expect from a large group of in-depth interviews, the participants in this project gave a great variety of responses and showed a great amount of variation in terms of the central questions posed. Any conclusions and generalizations that we were able to draw from the data had to be made with caution, carefully nuanced, and always with the proviso that "there were some exceptions," usually exceptions that went in the exact opposite direction of the generalization at issue. In other contexts, this observation might just be a way of referring to the inevitable "messiness" of reality; here, it already points to one of those conclusions about which one must be careful. With few exceptions, this sample of young adults considered themselves individually responsible for and capable of building their own, personal relation to religion. They did not, for the most part, simply receive their family traditions as something that was essentially to be carried on as a matter of tradition, with little emphasis on reconstructing it for oneself and above all understanding what one was doing and why. There was a consistent expectation that beliefs and practices had to make sense, to fit into a larger context of meaning, to have a reason other than that this was simply the way things were done. At the same time, it was up to the individual to discover this meaning from whatever sources each found authoritative or trustworthy, whether that be family, religious leaders, books, friends, the Internet, school, or other media.

From this finding it follows that the lived religious lives of the participants varied a great deal, as did perforce their contributions – of lack of them – to the construction of religion and religions in the wider context. There were nonetheless a series of important broad patterns of variation, including, especially, according to which religious background was at issue and, in a somewhat more subtle way, according to gender and the city in which they grew up. More specifically, those of Muslim background showed clearly different patterns from those of Hindu or Buddhist background, as did the latter two from each other. Women showed somewhat different patterns from men's, within particular religious backgrounds and across them, especially as concerns the importance and structure of religion in their lives. And living in the greater Toronto region, with its much more intense multicultural and religiously diverse reality compared to the situation outside this urban region, especially Ottawa,[11] enhanced the options for practising religion for the more than half of the participants who grew up there.

The differences between Muslims, Hindus, and Buddhists were sufficiently remarkable that the classification schemes we derived from the data in order to understand the commonalities and differences within each group had to be different for each one. Muslims could be understood as varying along a relatively clear continuum from completely non-religious to extremely devout and practising. Applying the same continuum to those from Hindu and Buddhist families would have made most of them appear as at best somewhat involved and more than half as completely non-religious, and it would have missed the rather different, one might even say "characteristically Hindu or Buddhist," ways of relating to religion and the religions of their family heritages that these participants exhibited. In that context, a great many of the Muslims shared a standard conception of what exactly constituted Islam, and often their general definition of religion reflected this Islamic understanding as well. To a large degree irrespective of whether or not they were "practising" Muslims, Islam was for them centred on the "five pillars," an ethical/behavioural code that featured tolerance, benevolence, sexual discipline, dietary restrictions, and the core sacred sources of the Qur'an and the Sunna. In contrast to this clear "global" model (cf. Roy 2004) of Islam, such a convergent understanding of religion and the religion of their heritage was absent among those from Hindu or Buddhist families. The former gravitated toward an understanding of Hinduism as flexible and varied in what constituted it – that is, as religion it was precisely non-convergent. They also tended to meld or at least draw a very indistinct line between Hindu as culture and Hindu as religion: Hinduism was most often understood as the religious aspect of their culture. They could as a result appear as either generally quite practising or as quite cavalier about religion, depending on the analytic perspective. Buddhists, by contrast to the other two, drew an indistinct line not only between Buddhism as religion and the culture of their families but also between Buddhism and what others outside their cultural groups would likely identify as non-Buddhist religious traditions. Their view of Buddhism as religion tended to be syncretic across possible religious identities, except with respect to Christianity, a religion to which a great many of them also had significant exposure.

Overall then, for all the central questions that our research asked, the answers and even the meaning of the questions varied according to which religious background one has in view. From a lived religion perspective, the patterns and styles of personal religious construction that were most frequent among Muslims were for the most part very different from those found among Hindus, which in turn differed from those prevailing among Buddhists. "Which religion" made a difference. And these differences were just as important from a religious system perspective. Based on our sample population, Islam, Hinduism, and Buddhism are constructed in today's global society very differently, and it makes little sense to use the criteria that apply to one – for instance, Islam – to try to understand the others. None of the modern religions that together are the major features of today's global religious system can act as the putative model for all religions or even religion more broadly and however conceived.

The differences that gender makes were somewhat more subtle but nonetheless significant, again depending to a degree on which religious background was at issue. Overall, women were more likely to be religiously involved, meaning that on average what they understood as religion tended to play a more important role in their lives. They were better represented among the highly involved, not as easily found among the non-religious, and included a higher proportion of people who were somewhat or moderately involved. The precise contours of such involvement, of course, varied according to religious background, but even taking a blanket measure such as frequency of ritual practice of any kind, women were more likely to report higher involvement than men. That does not mean that there were not a significant number of highly involved men and non-religious women; it is only in terms of relative distribution that this difference manifested itself.

A further important gender difference that emerged is rather more difficult to put in clear and simple terms; it concerns what one might call a relational as opposed to quest approach to what religion is all about. The women among our participants were more likely to see religion as something that gained its importance and manifested its contours primarily in the context of social relations, especially family and intergenerational relations. Religion was performed individually, but it was important that this be done in social connection with others, whether friends, family, or with a view to passing it on to one's (eventual) children. Although such a perspective was certainly not absent among men, one was more likely to encounter the view that religion was a set of ideals that one sought to enact in one's own life, a kind of challenge through which one tested oneself according to a defined and ideal model for being a good person and making the world a better place. Here again, however, the difference was one of frequency and degree, not a matter of clear and consistent distinction between male and female ways of being religious. Where such a clearer difference was manifest, by contrast, was in the differing expectations that the three historically patriarchal religious traditions had of the two genders, although in this case, quite a number of participants expressed discomfort with such distinctions, denied their importance, or explained them in terms of cultural norms that had distorted what the religion actually intended. Relatively few overtly accepted gender inequality – for the majority, including the idea of gender complementarity – as an integral aspect of "their" religion.

The intensity of the multicultural environment in the greater Toronto region often had clear reflections in the religious lives of our participants and in three principal ways. Greater presence of people similar to oneself means greater and more varied resources to enact one's religion: more and greater variety of temples and mosques, of co-religionists – including in one's own generation – who think or do in similar ways, of foods (e.g., halal meat, specialty ingredients for ritual food preparation). Growing up in the Toronto region means being less remarkable, less "visible" as a minority in a context dominated by a (white Christian) majority. Depending on where one lives in the metropolitan area, one's own group might be, if not the majority, then possibly the single largest group, or the locally largest group might be another "visible minority." Moreover, and somewhat in reverse, in Toronto it is far less likely that any given individual and their individual style of doing religion will be taken by others as the "typical" Muslim, Hindu, or Buddhist, because so many others in the same place with the same identity will live and construct the same religion differently. Or, put somewhat differently, there is less contextual pressure to do one's religion as others do, because whatever one chooses will not "stick out" as much and it is, as noted, easier to find like-minded souls.

Moving from patterns of difference to broadly based commonalities among participants with the three religious backgrounds, a string of characteristics and attitudes emerged. They include that almost everyone was accepting of religious diversity in their midst, and a great many celebrated it, seeing it as desirable and an advantage, because, for instance, it allowed one to express greater tolerance and learn from the other. In this context, the decided majority of participants were supportive of the idea of multiculturalism, even if they were often also critical of the fact that it was, for them, not being put into practice properly. Multiculturalism, like religious diversity, meant for the majority more than "peaceful coexistence"; there had to be mutual interaction and positive exchange among the different religious and cultural identities. In that context, the great majority declared that they felt comfortable living in Canadian society; a great many declared that they felt they were full and equal members of that society. For the clear majority, religion as such was a good thing – if not necessarily for oneself – and the religions were equal and equally good; the only unfortunate circumstance was that some of the adherents of any religion distorted it and thereby could produce extreme, intolerant, and violent versions. Correspondingly, practically no one was favourable – or would admit to being favourable – to politicized religion, religion of whatever stripe that sought to impose its views on others by whatever means, including not just violence but, for a good number, any overt proselytization. Religious equality and tolerance of differences meant that it was fine and even important to share one's religion, provided that it was invited and then done in the spirit of sharing and mutual understanding and not aggressively with the intention of converting the other. In connection with this feature, religion was for most people in the first instance a personal affair, very much within the community, but it was also something that one should be able to live visibly and in public, an orientation that one should be able to carry into public life without fear of discrimination or admonition.

Two final conclusions are worth noting at this point. The first is there was among the interviewees a strong correlation between religious socialization as a child and current levels of religious engagement. In particular, people who did not grow up in a religious household in which parents deemed it important that their children carry on the traditions were very unlikely to be religious adults. Our sample contained no one who was self-professedly religious but grew up in a non-religious household. In reverse, however, while a good many of those who grew up in just such religious households were themselves religious adults, a sizable number were not. Religious socialization, one might say, appeared to be almost a necessary but not sufficient condition for arriving at adulthood as a religious person. The second conclusion is somewhat related. A great many of the interviewees reported change in their orientation toward religion from the time that they were children to the present, a sizable number reporting such change, often dramatic in nature, within the one- or two-year period before their interviews – that is, quite recently. This pattern made it apparent that many of our participants found themselves at a point in their lives when they were in flux; what they were two years previously was in many cases not what they were then, meaning that they could change again in the not too distant future. Their average age was between 21 and 22. It is entirely possible that, interviewed five to ten years later, a significant number might give somewhat different answers to our central questions. Their generation in the early part of the last decade was on average quite young; it remains to be seen what their final adult stories as a generation will be.

These major conclusions of our study can thus be summarized as follows:

- Most participants took individual responsibility for building their own, personal relation to religion or their religion.

- Most participants insisted that beliefs and practices had to be defensible and have a reason; few just "followed tradition."
- Women showed patterns somewhat different from men's:
  - women were more likely to be religiously involved;
  - women were more likely to see the contours of religion primarily in the context of social relations;
  - men were more likely to see religion as a set of ideals to be pursued, a kind of challenge through which one tested oneself;
  - few men or women overtly accepted gender inequality or complementarity as an integral aspect of "their" religion.
- Living in the Greater Toronto Area (GTA) made a difference:
  - the available resources for enacting one's religion were greater and more varied;
  - growing up in the GTA meant being less of a minority within a (white Christian) majority; it was likely that one's own group constituted the local majority or plurality and that the largest group would itself be a "visible minority";
  - in Toronto, it was far less likely that an individual would be seen as the "typical" Muslim, Hindu, or Buddhist, because so many others in the same place with the same identity lived and constructed the same religion differently;
- Which religion was at issue made a difference:
  - those of Muslim background showed clearly different patterns from those of Hindu or Buddhist background, as did the latter two from each other;
  - a great many of the Muslims shared a standard, even global, conception of what exactly constituted Islam;
  - Hinduism tended to be seen as flexible and varied; the line between Hindu as culture and Hindu as religion was mostly quite indistinct;
  - Buddhism as religion tended to be syncretic across possible religious identities and understood in rather vague terms, whether culturally or religiously.
- Almost everyone was accepting of religious diversity in their midst, and a great many celebrated it:
  - the clear majority saw religion as a good thing and the religions as equal and equally good;
  - religion was for most people a personal affair, very much within the community, but it also was something that one should be able to live visibly and in public without fear of discrimination or admonition.
- The majority of participants were supportive of multiculturalism, although also often critical of its insufficient implementation in Canada. The great majority felt comfortable and accepted in Canadian society.

- Practically no one was favourable to politicized religion, religion of whatever stripe that sought to impose its views on others by whatever means, including not just violence but for many even any overt proselytization.
- Religious socialization in childhood appeared to be a necessary but not sufficient condition for becoming a religiously engaged adult.
- A great many participants were still in a stage of flux, including as concerned religion; what they were at the time of the interviews was often quite different from what they had been sometimes even only months before, and what the future held for them was often uncertain and malleable.

AN OVERVIEW OF THE CHAPTERS

The content and order of the twelve chapters that follow correspond to both the research design and the main findings as just outlined. The overall aim is, first, to detail the nature of the project and contextualize it in the specifically Canadian context; second, to present the findings in some detail and from the various perspectives discussed; and third, to situate the findings in the broader context through a comparison with research in select other countries.

The structure of a research project, from its initial conceptualization and design to the ways it was concretely carried out and the resulting data interpreted, already says much about what sort of conclusions can be drawn from it, including both the strengths and limitations of those outcomes. The above general discussion of the literature on religion and transnational migration in Canada and the theoretical considerations gives insight into the rationale for this project.

Chapter 2, on data and methods, looks in some detail at the particular recruitment strategy that we adopted for the participants, including why we recruited in major cities and on post-secondary campuses and not in other places. The possible impact and implications of recruiting on university campuses is the subject of particular attention. In that context, the chapter examines what techniques were used to solicit participation and what effect both of these factors may have had on the nature of the data gathered. There follows an examination of the interviews themselves, their structure, in what conditions they took place, and the nature of the questions asked. The chapter then provides an overview of the participants thus recruited, looking at them specifically in terms of their religious background, the gender and age distribution among them, and the cities in which they were recruited. Unsurprisingly, even this preliminary look already points in the direction of some of our main conclusions concerning what difference religious background, gender, stage in life, and city of upbringing make. The chapter concludes with consideration of how the data was analyzed and what effect this might have had on the character of our results.

Chapter 3 tackles the difficult question of how representative our sample of participants was of the larger subpopulations that the project envisioned. Because the project relied on qualitative methods, there is of course no claim that our sample was representative, but a comparison with that larger population is nonetheless instructive, especially since it supports the conclusion that it was also not totally unrepresentative. To this end, using descriptive statistical data drawn mainly from the Canadian census of 2001 and the Ethnic Diversity Survey carried out by Statistics Canada in 2002, the chapter presents demographic profiles of the various subgroups to which our participants belonged, principally Muslims, Hindus, and Buddhists, especially and as much as possible in the targeted age group of 18 to 27. It also looks at a number of attitudinal measures that roughly correspond to a number of the interview questions we asked, including a feeling of belonging in Canada, degree of life satisfaction and trust, and experience of discrimination and on what basis. In all cases, we make comparisons with the overall Canadian population to help situate our sample among the overall age group from which it was drawn and not just in comparison among the three religious identities.

Chapter 4 presents an overview of the three subgroups, discussing some of the main characteristics that they had in common and outlining the three different classification schemes that emerged from the data, which crystallize what difference religious background made. Those from Muslim backgrounds arranged themselves relatively clearly along a continuum from non-religious to highly practising on the basis of a fairly consistent understanding of what constitutes Islam as religion and how one practises it. Those from Hindu backgrounds could be seen as arranging themselves according to the relative importance given to Hindu as a cultural and Hindu as a religious category. There were those who gave neither much importance, those who gave the religious a high degree of importance, and those, the single largest group, who by and large favoured Hindu as a cultural identity but with a variable admixture of the religious as an expression thereof. Those of Buddhist background showed yet a different pattern, which included those for whom Buddhism, however understood, had little to no importance – among them some explicit Christians; those who were in some sense religious, or at least spiritual, seekers on what they understood as a Buddhist basis; and those who saw matters viewed as Buddhist as part of their "ethnic" (most often, but not exclusively, Chinese) identity. The chapter therefore focuses on the differential (re)construction of religion as a contribution to the theoretical notion that these differences were a reflection of the different ways that these three religions are constructed systemically and globally.

Chapters 5 to 10 are elaborations of the overview chapter, the purpose of which is to show in some detail exactly what these generalizations look like in the actual responses of the various participants. They are divided according to religion and gender, with one each for female and male Buddhists, Hindus, and Muslims. These chapters, to a greater or lesser extent, use the classification schemes introduced in chapter 4 but also go beyond them, above all in that each includes more detailed individual profiles of selected individuals, the purpose of which is to move the presentation clearly to the level of individual lived religion. The individuals chosen for profile are therefore not so much representative as both typical and atypical in the sense that each person is shown in their uniqueness but also as they reflect some, but by no means all, of the general and overall patterns. A main purpose of this mode of presentation is to juxtapose the concrete variety and the general analytic patterns, the lived and the systemic religion.

Chapter 11 takes out and makes explicit what is implicit in the previous six, and that is the differences that gender makes. It includes six "composite" profiles of Muslims, Hindus, and Buddhists of each gender that emerged from analysis of the data and then distills some of the most important differences, while not discounting various cross-gender continuities. Just as the differences of religious background make a difference, but certainly not all the difference, so it is with the category of gender: whether one is female or male often makes a significant difference when it comes to how religion is constructed and lived, but it also does not make all the difference.

Chapter 12 then adds and overlays the factor of geographical location and context, focusing on participants who grew up in the Greater Toronto Area. Similar to the intra-religious classifications, the inter-religious differences, and the gender distinction, the unique (in Canada) social and cultural context of the GTA conditions how religions are constructed and how they are lived. Again, the chapter shows that the Toronto context is an important factor in terms of the greater variations that it facilitates and the degree to which it mitigates the experience and reality of "being a minority religion," but there are nonetheless strong continuities that can be generalized across geographical locations and thus, at least implicitly, across Canada.

The final chapter, chapter 13, widens the lens again to look more closely at the Canadian example as revealed in our – but also others' – research in a partial global context. Given Canada's status as a rich Western country that has experienced high levels of post–World War II transnational migration, the most obvious countries are those that are very similar but also clearly different. In principle, those would be Western European countries, the United States, and the two Australasian countries. Since, however, such a comparative analysis depends on research carried out in these countries among the corresponding 1.5 and second generations, the current state of the literature permits a meaningful comparison only with the first two, to some degree because more research has been done in Europe and the United States but also because of the timing of postwar transnational migration of Muslims, Hindus, and Buddhists. Australia and New Zealand changed their immigration policies somewhat later than Canada and the United States and much later than several Western European countries. The result has been that the relevant 1.5 and second generations in the former are on average still quite a bit younger, making research on young adults somewhat premature and therefore comparatively rare. That said, the comparison in chapter 13 between Canada, the United States, and some Western European countries shows a similar combination of commonalities and differences, as does the analysis according to religion, gender, and geography. Each of the comparator countries is different, in spite of similarities, meaning, among other conclusions, that simple generalizing in these questions from one to the others is highly problematic and must be done with great care.

A WORD ABOUT APPROACH AND STYLE

This book is a multi-authored effort, as was the research project at its base. Six of the thirteen chapters are co- and, in one case, multi-authored; the remaining seven are single-authored. This collaboration reflects itself both in stylistic differences among the chapters and to some extent in differences of analytic approach as well. Thus, the nine chapters (including this introductory one) authored or co-authored by Beyer sometimes betray not only a difference in emphasis and style from the other four but also slight differences in analytic perspective, including in the consistent concern with the systemic portion of the above-discussed theoretical frame. The other four chapters, two of which are also collaboratively written, display comparable differences among them. Although every effort has been made to write the chapters as a coherent whole and not simply as individual contributions, we have also not attempted to paper over, let alone eliminate, our somewhat differing concerns and perspectives. Research data are subject to a certain range of interpretations, and it is best to let some of that ambiguity remain in this report; this is what we have done.

Data and Methods: University Settings in Toronto, Ottawa, and Montreal

JOHN H. SIMPSON AND PETER BEYER

RESEARCH DESIGN AND CONTEXT

The context for this research was Canadian society of the early twenty-first century but within a global society that has featured as one of its determinative features substantial and ongoing global migration. That migration has, among other consequences, been instrumental in creating the multicultural and religiously diverse society that Canada has become and in developing both the official and popular discourses of multiculturalism that interpret this new social reality. The participants in the research represent within themselves– "embody," as it were – this combination of migration and changed social context. They and their families have physically linked and continue to link spaces outside Canada with Canada. They are what one might call the material substrate of human restlessness. The materiality of population movement, however, is not divorced from the languages and cultures borne by bodies that move. The geographic mobility of humans entails the transfer from one place to another of cultures and languages and the conditioning of cultures and languages that have not moved.

The resources, structures of security, cultures, and languages that are present in the places of migration define one side of population movement. On the other side are the languages and cultures of the migrants themselves, including structurally linked expectations operative in emigrant spaces – the lands left behind. Both sides – the expectations and cultures of entrants and occupants – must be taken into consideration in order to understand what occurs when individuals, families, or other groups from one population move into the space of another population. In that regard, the state, today, uses its authority not only to count the primordial properties of individuals within its jurisdiction (e.g., sex, age) but also to construct and use cultural categories such as ethnicity, language, and religion, filling them with counts in order to grasp the prevalence and incidence of differences in its population at various levels of aggregation – e.g., municipal, regional, provincial, national.

This book explores a cultural element: the religion of three subsets in the Canadian population among those who were 18 to 27 years of age in the period from 2004 to 2006. The sampling frame for the study was limited to persons of self-attributed Hindu, Muslim, or Buddhist background who were either born in Canada to at least one immigrant parent or entered Canada as an immigrant before their eleventh birthday. Limiting the study to these three religious identities was done for purely practical purposes relating to the amount of research funds available through the Social Sciences and Humanities Research Council of Canada's Standard Research Grants program. A subsequent research project, in the process of completion at the time of writing, has included the same populations but also individuals from other, notably Christian and Sikh, religious backgrounds.

Besides the focus on these three religious identity backgrounds, recruitment of the project was carried out exclusively in the three urban areas of Toronto, Ottawa, and Montreal. The choice of researching in urban areas is rather obvious, because that is where most of the target population lives in Canada; more than 90% live in urban areas and most of them in the six largest cities that include the above three plus Vancouver, Edmonton, and Calgary. Limiting ourselves to the three central Canadian cities was a purely practical decision reflecting the limits on resources and the physical location of the researchers. The most consequential exclusion in this regard is Vancouver and mainly concerning those of Buddhist background: while almost 75% of Canada's Hindus and 67% of its Muslims live in the three target cities, less than 40% of its Buddhists live there. Put in reverse terms, excluding the large western cities eliminates only about 17% of Canada's Muslims and 14% of the Hindus but 35% of the Buddhists (Beyer and Martin 2010). Only further research will show whether this limitation of our research was consequential.

A similar mix of convenience, purpose, and budgetary constraint led to the recruitment of participants almost entirely among students enrolled in the University of Ottawa, Carleton University (in Ottawa), the University of Toronto, and Concordia University (in Montreal). These institutions are located within large urban catchments containing significant proportions of persons of Hindu, Muslim, and Buddhist identity according to the 2001 census of Canada. The proportionately high level of the regional densities of the study's subpopulations facilitated the recruitment of participants and reduced research costs attributable to spatial distance between potential participants and the researchers.

Using spatial density as a property of the sampling design also increased the likelihood that organized forms of the selected religious backgrounds were available to potential participants. Self-attributed religious background implies a range of involvement in religious activity and the organized contexts where it occurs. The scale runs from self-attribution of religious background with no involvement – and even rejection of the religious identity concerned – to intense levels of activity that most often include spatially specific contexts for their expression. By locating the study's catchments in regions where there were significantly high proportions of the targeted subpopulations (and, hence, organized religious contexts), the likelihood that there would be variation in religious involvement among study participants was enhanced. The aim of the study to include a full range of variation from the entirely non-religious to the very religious meant that recruitment could not be restricted to venues with a clear religious identity, such as religious organizations or, in the case of universities, religious student associations. Even so, because the recruitment text used to inform potential participants of the project had, for ethical reasons of free and informed consent, to mention that the project was about religion, it is likely that the resulting sample of participants was somewhat skewed to those who either were religious or at least felt that religion was an important or interesting topic to talk about. Recruitment on the campuses of public and secular universities nonetheless was intended to reduce this bias.

Recruitment among the population of university students likely also had the effect of reducing the gap between researchers and subjects, since they shared an institutional environment, thus potentially increasing trust or at least not creating an extra problem in this regard. Moreover, most of the interviews were conducted by Ramji and Saha, who but for their age would have qualified as participants in the project. They thus potentially shared more characteristics with our actual participants, again possibly reducing bias and increasing trust between participant and researcher or at least reducing the possibility that the interviewer would be regarded as someone from the dominant (white, Christian) majority whom one must be careful not to offend. Nonetheless, it is also the case that this tactic might only have changed the kind of bias between participant and researcher. For instance, in the case of Ramji, we cannot know what effect (if any) her status as a Muslim woman might have had when she was interviewing Muslim men or women or what effect (if any) Saha's status as a practising Hindu would have had when he was interviewing fellow second-generation people from Hindu families. Research on interviewer and respondent bias based on race and ethnicity is extensive, but it fairly consistently shows that such bias exists: participants tend to respond differently depending on the perceived racial or ethnic identity of the interviewer (see, from among many, Weeks and Moore 1981). This sort of bias does not, however, necessarily mean that participants will respond more fully and "honestly" to someone whom they perceive to be of their "own group." It is just that the responses will be affected by this factor.

The specified age range and immigration history limited the sample to those in the late adolescent/early adult phase of the lifecycle with no less exposure to the immigrant experience than having at least one immigrant parent if a participant was born in Canada; for those not born in Canada, it also included a maximum of ten years spent in the country of origin and often the personal experience/memory of immigration. The purpose of the study design in that regard was to obtain (a) participants for whom immigration was either a lived event (participants who were immigrants and old enough to remember coming to Canada) or a family "story" (participants born in Canada or arriving at a very early age) and (b) participants who had experienced socialization in Canada in the childhood, teen, and early adult years, in particular some time before they had reached puberty. Our assumption was that there would be little to no difference between 1.5-generation people (arrived at age 10 or younger) and those who were "true" second-generation, an assumption entirely borne out by the results. We specifically excluded persons who had arrived in Canada only in their teen or high school years and later. The fact that all the participants spoke English (or, in three cases, French) with the locally dominant accent and the typical styles and usages of this age group in Canada is an indicator of the difference this distinction makes. Listening to the interview recordings, one could not tell from the spoken language that they were of recent immigrant families except from the content of what they said in answer to our questions.

Recruiting on university campuses enabled the use of established means for communicating with students. It also provided natural controls for (a) academic ability (minimum requirements for university admission), (b) exposure to career possibilities in occupations requiring university education and having higher than average economic returns over the life course, and (c) experience in the university milieu that is the common base from which most of those who achieve elite status in Canada are drawn. Given the purpose of the study – the exploration of religion among immigrant youth – the use of universities as recruitment sites not only provided quasi-controls for academic ability and other things related to mobility and career paths, it also exposed study participants to the varieties of religious and ethnic presence and expression that exist within the organizational context of contemporary Canadian universities. And by the same token, it brought into play the differences between new immigrant cultures – in this case, mostly those of so-called "visible minorities" – and the cultural strands of the receiving population, including the cultures of apprehended dominant elites and long acculturated ethno-religious groups with an established niche in the Canadian "mosaic." In the context of recruiting in three of the major and most multicultural urban areas in Canada, areas that similarly exhibit this more intense juxtaposition and interaction of religious and cultural differences, focusing the study on university campuses in those urban areas had the effect of greatly intensifying these factors: our participants grew up in, lived in, and studied in the most intense multicultural and religiously diverse environments in the country.

Using universities as recruitment sites was further suggested by the educational characteristics of the overall Canadian target subpopulations. As of

2001, the vast majority of persons in Canada who identified with one of the three religions and were in their late teens or early adult years had at least some post-secondary training, and the clear majority either had university degrees/ diplomas or were enrolled in university degree or diploma programs (see chapter 3). Given the intent to recruit as broadly as possible in these subpopulations and, above all, not to privilege religious venues as recruitment sites, resource limitations for the project led to the decision that university campuses would yield the best sample, even though it inevitably left out minorities without post-secondary exposure. The results from such minority segments would likely have been somewhat different from those obtained here; finding out will require additional research that specifically targets them.

Population movement always triggers some degree of perceived cultural difference. The fit between the culture of an immigrant source and the culture(s) of a receiving population mediates the ease of integration – the looser the fit, the greater the potential for discord. Canada's immigration history does not lack what might be called "civilization differences," but until the latter part of the twentieth century, most immigrants were drawn from the imperial centre – the United Kingdom – or various parts of Europe. Thus, source and receiving cultures tended to be matched at a high level of aggregation in terms of religion (Christian). When immigration rules were relaxed in the 1960s, there was a proportionate decline in the overall match between entrant and host subpopulations, especially in terms of self-attributed religious background. Proportionately, many more non-Christians were coming to Canada than had been the case in the past, and many of them were from places that had been subjected to colonial rule, especially British colonial rule (Kelley and Trebilcock 2010).

About the same time that new types of immigrants were entering Canada and thereby creating a new mix in the Canadian population, the post-secondary education system was changing too. Old foundations were renovated, and new universities were added. The capacity of the system was expanded. Women and immigrant youth increasingly took up the available places. The role of educating an elite cadre was not abandoned, but it was repositioned in a system pointed in the direction of mass post-secondary education and – noteworthy for this study – a system that had undergone a "quiet revolution" of its own in the matter of religion.

RELIGION IN THE CHANGED CONTEXT OF CANADIAN UNIVERSITIES

Had the participants in this study entered university sometime before the early 1960s, they would have found themselves on a campus where Christianity in one form or another had a significant presence. Roman Catholic and Protestant colleges and universities were under the financial, administrative, and cultural control of their founding orders or denominations. Prestigious campuses with religious roots such as Dalhousie University, McGill University, and Queen's University and non-denominational public foundations such as the University of Alberta and the University of British Columbia were in the hands of the liberal Protestant establishment whose sensibility dominated post-secondary education in Anglo-Canada.[1] The goal of higher education was the transmission of the Judeo-Christian tradition strengthened by the wisdom of the Greco-Roman tradition. The objective of higher education was to form leaders who would understand their role in terms of the principles of liberal Christianity: tolerance of diverse viewpoints (within a framework of relative intolerance of racial and cultural diversity), an emphasis on religious experience (rather than religious doctrine), and zeal for a better society on earth, all framed by behaviour that was morally "pure."[2]

By the end of the 1960s, the operating budgets of the universities were provided by provincial governments, the morally strict regime of *in loco parentis* was in disarray, students were challenging university governance and the authority of administrators in various ways, and the purpose of higher education could no longer be credibly framed as the transmission of Western culture defined in terms of the Judeo-Christian and Greco-Roman traditions. Knowledge was specialized and functionally pragmatic. Instruction in the liberal arts unified by Christian ideology was no longer deemed to be the foundation of leadership.[3]

Government funding came with certain conditions, but once received it brought with it increased enrolment. The four universities in Montreal, Ottawa, and Toronto from which all the participants in this research were recruited present variations on the outcome. The University of Ottawa was, until the mid-1960s, a Roman Catholic institution; to take advantage of the new situation, it effectively secularized, transferring its religious degree-granting powers to a newly created St Paul's University.[4] Carleton University, which had only achieved that status in the 1950s, required no such transition but ironically ended up absorbing another Roman Catholic degree-granting institution, St Patrick's College – previously associated with the University of Ottawa – and dissolving it altogether in 1979 (MacDougall 1982). Concordia University in Montreal was the outcome of a similar process: when in 1974 Sir George Williams University, founded by the Montreal YMCA in 1929, became Concordia University, it absorbed and effectively dissolved Loyola College, a clearly Jesuit institution, keeping only the latter's campus and its theological studies program. These formal changes were, however, only part of the picture: accommodating a rapidly increasing number of students provided an unobtrusive measure of the secularization of the post-secondary system. The University of Toronto, from which more than half of our participants were drawn, is a case in point. Prior to the 1970s, the undergraduate arts and science programs of the University of Toronto involved an arrangement with colleges controlled by denominations with one exception. St Michael's College (Roman Catholic), Victoria College (United Church of Canada), and Trinity College (Anglican), together with University College (non-denominational), were the admitting units for undergraduates seeking a degree in arts and science. There was a division of extension for part-time students. To accommodate enrolment increases, the University of Toronto established five new colleges: Woodsworth for part-time students; Innis and New (St George campus); Scarborough (eastern borough of Toronto); and Erindale (west of Toronto in an area that was eventually incorporated into the City of Mississauga). None of these colleges had a religious tie. Each was founded as a secular unit by the central administration of the University of Toronto. The architecture of these colleges is revealing. Unlike the buildings of the so-called "federated colleges" (St Michael's, Trinity, Victoria), there is no display of religious symbols. None of the new colleges has a significant segregated internal space – a chapel – designed to accommodate the rituals of a specific religious tradition. The new colleges encompass secular, religiously neutral space.

When religion ceased to be a significant source for the justification and legitimacy of the post-secondary education system, religion did not disappear from university campuses. Roman Catholic and conservative Protestant foundations maintained religious expressions that were no longer set against the hegemony of liberal Protestant Christianity. Voluntary participation in student groups devoted to various forms of Christianity and Judaism had a presence. Bramadat (2000) notes that evangelical Christianity in particular attracted followers.

Notwithstanding these expressions of religion, the secular culture of knowledge, self-governing forms of student life, freedom of expression flowing from the counterculture of the 1960s, and toleration (as a stand-alone value sheared off from the other principles of liberal Christianity and stated in a positive form as support for much more substantial diversity) were the bedrock of campus life by the time the new wave of immigrants began arriving in Canada in the last quarter of the twentieth century. Students of non-Christian background with no roots in Western culture did not find it difficult to mark and defend ethno-religious "turf" on religiously neutral university campuses, something that could be seen as a contribution to the development of Canada as a multicultural social formation in a global world.[5] Participants for this study were recruited in that context, and their responses were arguably influenced by this context. Indeed, they would be entirely unrepresentative – or only of a privileged minority – of the second- and 1.5-generation population if it were not for the fact that such a high percentage of this population has significant experience in these post-secondary environments.

RECRUITMENT OF PARTICIPANTS

The aim of reducing bias as much as possible toward religiously engaged people also affected the recruitment strategies used on the university campuses. The universities that came under consideration were those located in the three cities where the research took place – Montreal, Ottawa, and Toronto. Within these cities, the original intention was to recruit both French- and English-speaking participants at as many post-secondary institutions as possible, including community colleges in Ontario and CEGEPs in Quebec. The reasons that participants came only from the select four universities are instructive for understanding the sample that was eventually obtained. They also illustrate the well-known difference between research design and the practical and often unforeseen barriers to its implementation.

Initially, the recruitment techniques included various forms of advertisement, on bulletin boards in various university buildings, in student newspapers, and even once or twice on university radio stations. Attempts were also made to recruit in large introductory undergraduate courses and by asking various student associations to send our recruitment text to their lists. These techniques proved to be very time-consuming and not very productive. In effect, the subpopulations we were targeting, although demographically relatively concentrated on university campuses, are still minorities on most of those campuses. These standard techniques of recruitment were not effective in finding these minorities, to a large extent because, unlike (for instance) international students, they do not appear to concentrate more in some venues than in others, with the possible exception of student associations dedicated to Muslims, Hindus, Buddhists or the ethnic identities more typically associated with them – for example, South Asian, Arab, or Chinese student associations. Even in these cases, however, the response proved to be quite minimal, and in any case we were trying to avoid recruiting only in such venues or to do so using "snowball" techniques. The main reason that the final sample of participants included only eleven people from Montreal and only three French-speakers is that we were unable to go beyond these relatively neutral recruitment techniques at the post-secondary institutions in that city and, for the purposes of the research design, we were unwilling to skew our sample more than practically necessary. It is for this reason that the possible difference that living in Montreal or more broadly in French-speaking Canada and in Quebec makes, including with regard to our central research questions, could not be included in our results, analyses, and conclusions. Our eventual sample of participants did not permit this. In the cases of the universities in Toronto and Ottawa, however, a single additional technique proved very effective for recruitment: having various university administrative units send out mass emails to *all* the students on their contact lists, irrespective of identity. The vast majority of students who received these emails would not have met our criteria for inclusion, but the small percentage that did amounted to substantial numbers of our target populations. More than 80% of the participants for this project were recruited in this way.[6]

The mass emailing technique was highly effective in yielding a broad and varied group of participants. It contributed greatly to the aim of the project to avoid as much as possible recruitment with biases toward particular types of students, particular networks, and particular organizations. Unfortunately, it also proved to be difficult to use consistently, mainly because university staff and administrators responsible for the mailing lists were quite inconsistent in their responses and often highly resistant to requests to use them for our research purposes. Officials at three Montreal-area universities refused repeated requests outright, and that included Concordia University, where the research was primarily being conducted. Carleton University agreed without question the first time, and then six months later refused. The University of Ottawa was generally the most cooperative institution in this regard, and the University of Toronto was also cooperative, depending on the subunit. The reasons for refusal were diverse, ranging from concerns over privacy and overburdening students with emails from the administration to the view that such use of mailing lists was inappropriate. Generally, the higher the administrative official involved, the more likely refusal was. Ethical concerns should not have been an issue, since the project had research ethics clearance from four university research ethics boards and no official had raised this as a concern. A number of colleges and universities, when contacted, did not even reply to our requests. In several cases, members of the research team were given to believe that our request was considered equivalent to a request to use the email lists for marketing or soliciting purposes and that to allow such use would open the door to a flood of such requests. The fact that universities are research institutions, one of the main purposes of which is to pursue and encourage research, and that the research in question was being conducted by researchers at the universities concerned did not seem convincing. Needless to say, these difficulties forced the researchers to use a higher than foreseen portion of the project's resources on the recruitment of participants. While the situation is in general quite understandable and these sorts of practical challenges are always part of the research environment, it is just a bit ironic that the same administrations that put great pressure on their faculty members to bring in external research funds – which, when they arrive, are dutifully touted as a sure indicator of the superior performance of the institution – then, perhaps inadvertently or for lack of having established a positive policy, force the inefficient use of those funds in carrying out the research.

CHARACTER OF INTERVIEWS

The initial aim for the sample was to have an equal number of Muslim-, Hindu-, and Buddhist-background participants and, within each of these, an equal number of men and women. As discussed below, neither aim was achieved, although that result, as will become clear in subsequent chapters, says as much about the outcomes expressed in the interviews as it does about the technical challenges of recruiting for this sort of qualitative research. In the end, the project conducted 202 semi-structured interviews in three cities, Toronto, Ottawa, and Montreal, and on six university campuses, the University of Ottawa, Carleton University, Concordia University, and the University of Toronto's three campuses in downtown Toronto, in Mississauga, and in Scarborough. Of these, 197 were valid within the parameters set. These interviews lasted anywhere from thirty minutes to two-and-a-half hours, for the most part depending on how engaged the participant was with the questions posed and how loquacious individuals proved to be.

The individual face-to-face semi-structured interviews were conducted on campus, thus framing them within the environment of academic/student life space. The semi-structured form of interviewing involves constructing a range of themes that encompass a research objective. The list of themes guides the interviewer. The interview is not a fixed progression through a predetermined set of specific questions. The interviewer steers the conversation by taking into account the responses of the participant in order to develop the interlocution in ways that are consistent with the objective of the research. The interview process is open-ended in the sense that the overall pattern of an interview and information pertaining to particular themes can vary widely over participants. The natural course of semi-structured interviews (their history) may display very different sequences of communication from one interview to another. Nonetheless, in order to maximize the comparability of the interviews, interviewers were given a list in which the themes to be covered were each broken down into a series of specific sample questions, it being understood that no interviewee would actually be asked all of these questions, let alone necessarily in the precise form that they took on the list. The purpose was to make sure that themes were covered thoroughly and as much as possible with a good degree of uniformity (see the appendix for a list of themes and questions).

The form of interviewing affects the properties of the knowledge that can be constructed from the information obtained in an interview. Semi-structured interviewing is an exploratory "journey" to discover the range of semantic categories that participants use in responding to the thematic inquiries of the interviewer. The emphasis is on qualitative variation. Other forms of qualitative research such as focus groups may emphasize consensus and saturation – that is, the presence of central tendencies in the use of categories within a group and over groups and closure or the presence of a point in the process of communication within a group when new categories cease to be introduced.

Neither semi-structured interviews nor focus groups provide counts or scores for all participants that represent internal options within semantic categories. These are obtained from the type of interview done in survey research. The interview schedule is a set of fixed, ordered questions with predetermined response categories. Questions and response categories may be set up to test a hypothesis, assess a theoretical perspective, provide information for a population-based inquiry such as a census or the investigation of an epidemiological question, or serve a pragmatic goal – for example, political polls and market surveys.

Each of these methods produces its own tranche of knowledge, no one a replica of another and each specific to an identified purpose. In a thematically focused research program, each method provides a complementary "take" on the phenomena of interest and contributes to the development of an understanding of the phenomena as a unity of multiple realities. The research reported in this book uncovers the stories about religiosity that selected individuals (participants) constructed in the context of scientific enquiry.[7]

DISTRIBUTION AND CHARACTERISTICS OF INTERVIEWEES

As noted above, the final number of interviews conducted was 202. Five of these were excluded from the analysis because the person did not qualify in terms of one of the main selection criteria: they either did not have one of the three religions in their background or they had arrived in Canada only as teenagers. Their interviews were nevertheless completed, because we only found out about the mismatch after their arrival for the interview. We also kept them for possible inclusion in subsequent research projects. Table 2.1 presents the number, gender, religious background, and city of recruitment for the 202 interviews.

Some of the details in this table are worthy of note. The low numbers from Montreal have already been explained and the consequences of this low number pointed out. Although Ottawa is a much smaller city than Toronto, the difference between the student populations of the two Ottawa universities and the multi-campus University of Toronto is not as great, hence the relatively high number of participants from Ottawa compared to Toronto. The proportionately higher population of Muslims in Ottawa in relation to Toronto probably explains the near equal number of Muslims recruited in the two cities. While not in themselves conclusive, these proportions do support the idea that the sample was drawn more or less neutrally in both cities, without additional skewing factors such as would be introduced by tapping into specific social networks, recruiting in specific locations, or recruiting through organizations.

Table 2.1   Participants by gender, religious identity, and urban region

	Total	Muslims	Hindus	Buddhists	Others
Women	127	58	39	28	2*
Men	75	35	18	19	3**
Totals	202	93	57	47	5
Urban region					
Toronto	109	44	36	27	2
Ottawa	82	41	20	19	2
Montreal	11	8	1	1	1

* 2 Muslim women arrived as adolescents.
** 2 Sikhs, 1 Baha'i

A further salient detail resides in the male/female and cross-religious bal-ances. Women from each identity responded more readily than men; Muslims were more enthusiastic than either Hindus or Buddhists. The first is a com-monplace for research on religion and likely reflects the likelihood that women will be more interested in religion than men.[8] The second is subject to the same explanation. For people from Muslim families, religion has an on average greater salience than it does for people from Hindu or Buddhist backgrounds. This is so much so that the total number of Muslims in the sample was not that far below the total number of Hindus and Buddhists combined. Since we asked for people interested in talking about religion, people for whom religion was important would be more likely to respond, especially since we provided no other incentive for participation than interest. These conclusions are en-tirely borne out by the content of the interviews, as subsequent chapters show in some detail. The proportion of interviewees in each subcategory already tells us something important about the average role of religion in their lives.

The average age of the participants was between 21 and 22, a clear reflection of the fact that most of them were undergraduates at the four universities. Somewhat over half of them (about 54%, or 106 of 197) were born in Canada, the rest having arrived before the age of 11. The origins of their families were from all over the world, as one would expect, with heavy concentrations of South Asian, East/Southeast Asian, and to a lesser degree North African/West-ern Asian origins. Relatively few of their families arrived in Canada as refu-gees, most coming as independent immigrants. Correspondingly, their parents were mostly well-educated and middle-class, although quite a few came from families that had experienced significant downward economic mobility in the years after they settled in Canada. A not insignificant number came from fam-ilies of mixed ethnic or religious parentage, although the great majority had parents of uniform ethno-religious origin. Virtually none of the participants were married or had children, as one might expect among undergraduate university students. There were some impressionistic differences between those in the earlier part of the age range, 18- to 20-years-olds, when compared to those over the age of about 24. The younger ones seemed more likely to portray unsettled identities, as one might expect, with the older ones having on average a clearer sense of who they were and where they were going. There appeared to be no difference in level of religiosity across the age range. These differences were, however, as noted, impressionistic, and in the final analysis they were not consistent or clear enough to enable us to venture an extrapolation of what this group of participants might be like as they enter the stages of life when they start families and embark on careers. This research is therefore entirely preliminary in terms of this question, but given the age of the overall population from which they were drawn, more definitive answers will have to wait until the bulk of them reach those later stages of adult life.

DATA ANALYSIS

Analysis of the interview data proceeded heuristically, iteratively, and somewhat intuitively. Upon preliminary analysis as interviews were being completed, interviews were assigned for detailed analysis to specific researchers according to religion, Muslim, Hindu, or Buddhist. The aim of this exercise was to identify, to the extent that the data suggested them, patterns of responses to the different themes that structured the interviews but according to religious background. This was done because the preliminary analysis suggested that this distinction of religious background made a significant difference in terms of how participants related to the central question of the research project – namely, how Canadians from the target populations related to the religion of their heritage. Although there were also evidently strong similarities in certain respects across "traditions," a classification of interviews according to religion, and within religion according to particular typologies, appeared consistently warranted. Subsequent stages of analysis only reinforced this preliminary finding. A further very significant category of difference that emerged early on was gender. Although not as consistently evident as differences according to religion, patterns of responses according to gender were strong enough to warrant a further breakdown, a decision that expresses itself in this book in the form of the six core chapters devoted to each of the six religion/gender subgroupings, Muslims, Hindu, and Buddhist. Each of the interviews was analyzed by a minimum of two members of the research team, and there were numerous discussions among members comparing our results in order to minimize the possibility that the primary divisions according to religion and gender would prejudice the overall results.

The interviews yielded very rich data on the various themes that structured the interviews. In this book, we have limited our reporting to only what we felt were the main patterns of difference and similarity within each subgrouping and across them. We have focused on the differential construction of religions, including on how people understand the idea of religion, but also on how the participants see themselves and their lives in the Canadian context, how they see Canada and its situation in the wider world, how they relate to their families and their co-religionists or co-ethnics, intergenerational issues, their family backgrounds, their attitudes to questions of gender and sexuality, how they see their futures, and other themes. There are, however, a number of threads of analysis that we could have followed but did not with any thoroughness, including the above-mentioned possibility of finding patterns of change over time, especially from childhood to adolescence to adulthood; possible relationships between educational area of specialization and religion or ethnicity; possible correlations between various factors and physical, as opposed to virtual and media, transnationalism; and possible differences between "later" 1.5ers – for example, those who arrived after the age of 8 compared to those who arrived before the age of 5. While our analyses did not show there to be any evident patterns along these lines, further and more detailed analysis might have revealed otherwise.

In a strong sense, this research project is only the first phase of a two-phase project, the second being well underway at the time of writing. This second project, mentioned above, includes focus on religious backgrounds and identities not included in the current one, notably on varieties of Christians and Sikhs in young adulthood and of immigrant families. It also includes a few additional Hindus, Buddhists, and Muslims. While the design of this second-phase project is somewhat different, it does include about another 100 semi-structured in-depth interviews with comparable participants of these other religious backgrounds, interviews with a parallel thematic structure to the ones about which we report here. With this additional data in hand, we intend to engage in a more detailed analysis of the entire set, Christians, Muslims, Buddhists, Hindus, Sikhs,[9] and the sizable number of those with no religion who ended up being recruited in the context of these other religious categories.

3

Young Adults and Religion in Canada: A Statistical Overview

PETER BEYER AND WENDY K. MARTIN

A DEMOGRAPHIC PROFILE OF MUSLIMS, BUDDHISTS, AND HINDUS IN CANADA (2001)

The focus of the research reported here is on the population of young adults, aged 18 to 27, who self-describe as having either a Buddhist, a Hindu, or a Muslim background, whether they identify with, adhere to, or practise these religions or not. Canadian census and other Statistics Canada data do not precisely track this population, but they come reasonably close in counting those who identify with these religions, including within specified age groups. It is therefore possible, at least up to 2001–02, to gain an approximate appreciation of the portion of these religious populations that falls within the targeted age group, what portion of them were born in Canada or are themselves immigrants, where in Canada they are geographically concentrated, what their level of education and income is, what sorts of families they tend to inhabit, and the income levels of these families. For these sorts of variables, the data give us points of reference for judging how representative or unrepresentative our participants might be on such measures.

Two Statistics Canada datasets inform the following analysis: the 2001 census of the Canadian population and the 2002 Ethnic Diversity Survey. We draw much of this analysis from previous work that the authors of this chapter did in the context of a research project conducted under contract to the Department of Canadian Heritage and the Department of Citizenship and Immigration (Beyer and Martin 2010).

POPULATION DISTRIBUTIONS: AGE, GENERATION, AND GEOGRAPHICAL CONCENTRATION

The age structure of Canada's Muslim, Buddhist, and Hindu populations at the beginning of the century varied significantly from one religious identity to the other and in comparison with the overall Canadian population. Table 3.1 shows the age distributions in 2001. Muslims had a very high percentage in the under-15 and a relatively low percentage in the over-45 age groups; Hindus

Table 3.1   Age distributions, three religions, Canada, 2001

	Total (all ages)	Under 15	%	15–24	%	25–44	%	45+	%
Muslims	579,640	168,120	29.0	94,490	16.3	202,525	34.9	114,505	19.8
Hindus	297,200	69,955	23.5	42,830	14.4	106,905	36.0	77,505	26.1
Buddhists	300,345	46,610	15.5	42,760	14.2	103,870	34.6	107,105	35.7
Canada	29,639,035	5,737,675	19.4	3,988,200	13.5	9,047,175	30.5	10,865,985	36.7

Source: Statistics Canada, Census 2001

conformed more to the national averages but were still somewhat younger, again with higher proportions in the under-15 and lower in the over-45 categories. Buddhists, by contrast, were the opposite with respect to the other two religious identities, with relatively few in the youngest group and rather more in the oldest one. When one looks at the young adult proportions, however, the target ages for the current research, the three groups and the overall population were far closer to each other: the 15- to 24-years-olds (our research was conducted from two to five years after the Statistics Canada studies, so this is more or less exactly our target age group) constituted from about one-seventh to one-sixth of each of the three religions and the population as a whole. Of course, given the larger overall population of Muslims compared to the other two religious identities, the former naturally outnumber the latter substantially, in this case in the order of more than two to one. There were somewhat fewer than 100,000 Muslims in the 15- to 24-year-old age group as compared to only around 43,000 for each of the Buddhists and Hindus. This ratio may be one, but only one, of the reasons that Muslims were so much easier to recruit for this project than either of the other two identities.

Looking at the immigrant status of this subpopulation, essentially what proportion was born in Canada or not, one notes the disproportionate number that were immigrants, born in another country. Table 3.2 gives the statistics. From 26 to 39% of the 15- to 24-year-olds were born in Canada, and one notes the significant percentage of Buddhists and Muslims who were non-permanent residents, meaning mainly that they were in the country on student visas. None of the latter was included in our research, the chances of this happening being very slight given our requirement for second- or 1.5-generation status. The situation reflects the relatively recent arrival of these immigrant populations in Canada – mostly after the 1960s – and therefore the relatively young age of their second generations in 2001. A main reason why the present research project could not easily have been carried out much earlier than it was (2004–06) was that too much of the target population would have been too young. As it was, we included the 1.5-generation population (those who arrived in Canada

Table 3.2   Immigrant status, three religions, 15–24-year-olds, Canada, 2001

	Totals	Non-immigrant		Immigrant		Non-permanent resident	
Buddhist	42,760	13,620	31.9%	26,125	61.1%	3,015	7.1%
Hindu	42,830	16,715	39.0%	24,895	58.1%	1,215	2.8%
Muslim	94,490	24,505	25.9%	63,640	67.4%	6,345	6.7%
Canada	3,988,200	3,466,825	86.9%	470,335	11.8%	51,035	1.3%

Source: Statistics Canada, Census 2001

Table 3.3   Buddhist, Hindu, and Muslim populations in Toronto, Ottawa, and Montreal, 2001

Numbers and percentages of total population group in all of Canada

	Total population		Buddhists		Hindus		Muslims	
Montreal	3,380,640	11.4%	37,835	12.6%	24,075	8.1%	100,185	17.3%
Ottawa	1,050,755	3.6%	9,980	3.3%	8,150	2.7%	41,720	7.2%
Toronto	4,647,955	15.7%	97,165	32.4%	191,300	64.4%	254,110	43.8%

Source: Statistics Canada, Census 2001

under the age of 11) in order to bolster the numbers from which we could recruit, and the large presence of 1.5ers in our sample is a reflection of how necessary that was.

The recruitment for this project took place on university campuses in Ottawa, Montreal, and Toronto. As discussed in chapter 2, for technical reasons a disproportionate number of our participants ended up being recruited in Ottawa, with most of the rest coming from Toronto. In terms of the overall distribution of Muslim, Hindu, and Buddhist populations in Canada, the latter result makes a great deal of sense. About one-third of Canada's Buddhists, about two-fifths of the Muslims, and almost two-thirds of the Hindus resided in the Toronto urban area in 2001. Table 3.3 compares the three census metropolitan areas of Toronto, Ottawa, and Montreal in this regard. The high number of participants in the project from Ottawa would therefore seem to be disproportionate, but one must take into consideration that university campuses have different proportions – generally higher – than the urban areas in which they are situated. And indeed, a significant number of those recruited on the two Ottawa campuses were in fact people who studied there but came from Montreal or Toronto, or at least their immediate families lived in those cities. Still, undoubtedly the main reason for the disproportionately high num-

Table 3.4   Ethnic origins* of Muslims, Hindus, and Buddhists in Canada, 2001

	Muslims	Hindus	Buddhists
Totals	579,640	297,200	300,345
African	18.1%	–	–
North African	7.8%	–	–
East African	7.6%	–	–
Middle Eastern	14.5%	–	–
Lebanese	7.5%	–	.–
West Asian	16.3%	–	–
Iranian	10.3%	–	–
Balkan	3.5%	–	–
South Asian	37.3%	90.5%	2.4%
Indian	21.2%	61.0%	–
Pakistani	11.1%	–	–
Sri Lankan	–	13.2%	1.6%
Guyanese/Caribbean	2.2%	7.1%	–
Southeast Asian	–	–	33.6%
Vietnamese	–	–	24.2%
East Asian	–	–	60.1%
Chinese	–	–	54.0%
Japanese	–	–	4.5%
Korean	–	–	1.3%
Canadian	4.4%	3.3%	4.8%

* Includes single and multiple origins. Therefore, total percentages may exceed 100%.
– = less than 1%

Source: Statistics Canada, 2001 Census

bers from Ottawa lies in the fact that we were able to use the most effective recruitment technique there more than in either of the other two cities.

ETHNIC ORIGINS

The ethnic origin compositions of Muslims, Hindus, and Buddhists in the targeted age groups are not appreciably different from those of these religious populations as a whole. Most Buddhists have East or Southeast Asian origins, dominated by those of Chinese origins. Hindus, not surprisingly, are dominated by people with South Asian origins, although significant minorities also claim Caribbean or Guyanese roots. Muslims, by contrast, have several dominant origins. Good percentages originate in North and East Africa, the Middle East, and West Asia (mostly Iran). South Asia is the single largest region of origin, about 37% of all Muslims. A small but significant number has Balkan origins.

Table 3.4 demonstrates these distributions through selected data taken from the 2001 Canadian census. The participants in the current research reflected these distributions for the most part, the one significant exception being the heavy presence of Trinidadian and Guyanese among the Hindus. We cannot account for this one difference, except to say that a qualitative sample such as ours will never be entirely representative of the populations from which it is drawn and therefore such anomalies are to be expected.

FAMILY STRUCTURES AND INCOMES

One of the abiding questions in this research was whether and how the parents of immigrant families were successful in passing on their religious identities and, where relevant, their religious practice to their children, the next generation. One way of approaching this question statistically is to ask what percentage of children share the religion of their parents, depending on the religion involved, and conversely, what percentage of children with a given religious identity have parents with the same religious identity. Simply put, the results show that if a child in Canada grows up identifying with one of the three religions that are at issue in our research, then it is almost certain that that child will have had that identity transmitted from one or both of his or her parents. Yet it is also the case that, from the parent's perspective, a smaller percentage of one's children will end up having the parental religious identity. We will express this idea in subsequent chapters as follows: being socialized in one of these three religions comes close to being a necessary but not a sufficient condition for becoming an adherent to that religion in adulthood (see the discussion in chapter 5). Table 3.5 expresses this difference using some census statistics in this regard, comparing the situation for parents and children who are Buddhist, Hindu, or Muslim. What one notices immediately is that the Buddhists differ significantly from the other two religious identities in that substantially fewer Buddhist parents pass on their Buddhist identity to their children than is the case for Hindu and Muslim parents. On the other hand, children who do identify as Buddhists will almost always have Buddhist parents, just as is the case for Hindu and Muslim children. The comparative lesser degree of socialization of children as Buddhists in Buddhist or mixed religious families where Buddhism is one of the religions, as will be seen, is very evident among the Buddhist-background participants in our research. And the relatively greater success among Muslims in this regard is equally evident. What these figures hint at, but do not actually reveal, is the ambiguous situation with Hindus. While it appears that Hindu parents are almost as successful as Muslims in socializing their children as Hindus, they are not quite as successful, and, as we will see, what constitutes passing on Hindu identity is more ambiguous: it is not nearly as often the passing on of an explicitly religious

Table 3.5   Religion of parents and children for Buddhist, Hindu, and Muslim families, couples, and lone-parent families, Canada, 2001

	Families based on couples				Lone-parent families	
	% Child religion same as Parent 1 (father)*	% Parent 1 (father) with same religion**	% Child religion same as Parent 2 (mother)*	% Parent 2 (mother) with same religion**	% Child religion same as lone parent*	% Lone parent with same religion**
Buddhist	66.0	92.7	63.5	94.5	68.3	91.2
Hindu	91.2	97.6	93.1	96.9	91.2	97.7
Muslim	94.1	97.7	96.6	96.1	94.0	96.1

* If the parent is of this religion, the percentage of this parent's children who are of the same religion
** If the child is of this religion, the percentage whose parent is of the same religion

Source: Statistics Canada, 2001 Census

Hindu identity, but more often one of passing on Hindu cultural or religio-cultural identity. In addition, it cannot be assumed that these differences are a reflection of differing efficacy in religious socialization – that, for instance, Muslim parents have more effective means of religious socialization than do Buddhist (or Hindu) parents. Rather, as we suggest on the basis of the analyses of our own data below, it is more likely that the differences have to do with the self-conceptions of these religions in the modern circumstance. One might suggest that for Muslims, Islam requires that every effort be made to ensure that one's children become (good) Muslims, but Buddhism is less "pushy" and will be there for the children when they are ready.

Turning now to the question of income, or the relative economic success of people with these three religious identities in Canada, we find what one might call the opposite situation. In a nutshell, if Muslim parents are highly effective in passing on their religious identities to their children, they are not nearly as effective as the other two in attaining anything close to the sort of income level that the average Canadian has. Table 3.6 presents one set of data that illustrates this rather stark difference. On average, Muslims in Canada receive only something in the neighbourhood of 60% of the income of Canadians as a whole. This percentage descends to as low as a half in some cities like Ottawa and Montreal and is below the national average in Toronto as well. Although both Hindus and Buddhists also do not come close to the national average, their situation seems somewhat better, with median incomes at two-thirds or higher in Canada as a whole and in the different cities. Hindus especially fare significantly better. The explanation for these overall disparities cannot detain us here and requires further research;[1] their importance in the present context

Table 3.6   Median individual total incomes, overall population, three religions, Canada and three metropolitan areas, 2001

| % of total population median total individual income | | | | |
	Canada	Montreal	Ottawa	Toronto
Muslims	63.1%	53.4%	50.2%	58.7%
Hindus	86.2%	65.8%	80.3%	77.5%
Buddhists	73.7%	69.6%	70.2%	70.3%
Median total income	$22,120	$21,888	$28,956	$25,591

Source: Statistics Canada, 2001 Census

is whether or not they were reflected in the experiences of our participants. The answer, of course, is yes. A significant number of our interviewees told of the negative experiences of their parents in this regard, working in low-paying jobs for years because their credentials were not recognized, because they did not have the education, language abilities, or experience necessary, because of discrimination, or for other reasons. What did not emerge from our data, however, was the Muslim disadvantage. Although we did not ask for or receive precise figures on family income and status, we did ask all our participants a general question in this regard: most felt that their families were middle-class or higher, relatively few pegged their families as at a serious economic disadvantage. These results may indicate that our sample was economically unrepresentative, but it should be noted that the level of post-secondary educational attainment among Muslims is not inferior to that of other religious identities and is on an overall basis significantly higher than the Canadian population average (see next section). Other factors are therefore likely also at issue, one of which may be that objective income levels do not necessarily correspond to subjective experience of being below, at, or above average, let alone being privileged or disadvantaged. Another possible factor is that many of the participants in this research project might have considered their own situation and prospects more important than the experience undergone by their parents. And in this respect, both objectively and subjectively, the economic disadvantages of being Muslim, Hindu, or Buddhist were not nearly as evident. An intervening factor in this regard is of course educational attainment and its relation to income. It is to this that we turn next.

EDUCATIONAL ATTAINMENT

In the context of Canada's post-1967 immigration policies, newcomers to the country have, on average, arrived with a higher level of formal education than

Figure 3.1 Educational attainment among Canada-born according to religion and gender, select ethnic identities*

Adults, 21–30-year-olds, Canada, 2001 (%)

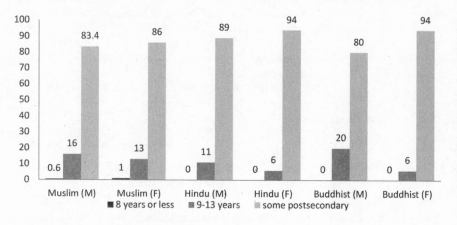

* Excludes ethnic identities in which a large majority does not stem from post-1970 immigration

Source: Statistics Canada 2003a. See also Beyer 2005c.

the population as a whole (Beyer 2005c). This greater degree of education has not, for the most part, translated directly into corresponding levels of income. Since the early to mid-1990s especially, new immigrants have experienced significant downward mobility (Hiebert 2009; Picot and Sweetman 2005) and indeed, the stories that our interviewees told often featured parents who were highly educated but struggled for years after arriving in Canada to find employment commensurate with their expectations and their formal qualifications. Yet, after economic and political reasons, a main – and frequently the primary – motive for these parents to come to Canada was so that their children would have better opportunities and richer lives. In key respects, their hopes and expectations appeared to be being fulfilled as concerns the education of their children and, at least thus far, as concerns economic well-being. The next generations were with few exceptions achieving higher levels of formal education than even their parents did, and they were receiving it in Canadian institutions with credentials that are not downgraded or dismissed the way those of their foreign-educated parents were.

As discussed in chapter 2, a main justification for recruiting our participants on university campuses was that such a high percentage of Canada-born Muslims, Buddhists, and Hindus in the targeted age group received some form of post-secondary education. Using 2001 census data, the figures for

Table 3.7   School attendance by gender, 15–24 year-olds, Canada, 2001, %

	Gender	Canada	Muslims	Buddhists	Hindus
Not attending		36.9	25.0	25.8	25.7
	Female	35.0	27.2	24.1	25.7
	Male	38.7	22.9	27.4	25.8
Attending full-time		57.1	68.8	67.1	67.7
	Female	58.8	66.5	68.8	68.2
	Male	55.4	70.9	65.5	67.3
Attending part-time		6.0	6.2	7.1	6.5
	Female	6.1	6.3	7.1	6.1
	Male	5.9	6.2	7.1	6.9

Source: Statistics Canada, 2001 Census

Canada-born 21- to 30-year-olds with these religious identities are from 75 to 94%, depending on the religion and the gender. Figure 3.1 illustrates this result. If one looks more closely at the nature of this post-secondary exposure, the prevalence of university-level exposure becomes evident.

Tables 3.7 to 3.9 present 2001 census results from various angles.[2] Table 3.7 shows that Muslims, Buddhists, and Hindus between the ages of 15 and 24 were overwhelmingly still attending school, either full- or part-time; approximately 75% did so. This percentage was significantly higher than for this age group in the overall Canadian population. Table 3.8 presents educational attainment – namely, the highest level of schooling attained at the time of the census and for the same age range. It again shows higher levels for the three religious identities than for the overall population. In addition, one notes that a greater percentage of women as compared to men in each case had attained a bachelor's degree, a pattern that was evident in the general population as well. Finally, Table 3.9, although it does not distinguish according to gender, does separate the 15- to 19-year-olds from the 20- to 24-year-olds. Our participant sample had an average age of between 21 and 22, and therefore the second group came closer to the sample than the first. For the 20- to 24-year-olds, one notes not only the tendencies seen in the other tables (namely, the significantly higher levels of attainment when compared to the general population) but also that fully two-thirds of the Muslims, Hindus, and Buddhists were attending post-secondary institutions, had already completed some post-secondary education, or had qualified for either a university or non-university diploma. That this represents in large measure university exposure is verified by other research, which, while not focusing on religion, shows that by the time they reach the age of 35, second- and 1.5-generation people with family origins in

Table 3.8   Educational attainment, 15–24-year-olds, by gender, Canada, 2001, %

	Gender	Canada	Muslims	Buddhists	Hindus
Less than high school diploma		42.7	40.2	39.9	36.4
	F	39.7	39.5	38.5	34.1
	M	45.5	40.9	41.2	38.9
High school diploma		15.5	16.6	13.9	16.5
	F	14.5	16.9	12.4	16.2
	M	16.5	16.2	15.3	16.8
Some post-secondary		20.8	23.9	27.4	25.9
	F	21.8	23.1	27.6	26.4
	M	19.8	24.6	27.2	25.5
Non-university diploma		14.4	9.1	9.8	8.9
	F	15.6	9.1	10.5	9.3
	M	13.2	9.1	9.2	8.4
Bachelor's degree		4.9	6.8	6.1	8.4
	F	6.1	7.8	7.4	9.3
	M	3.7	5.9	4.8	7.5
Master's or doctorate degree		0.2	0.5	0.3	0.7
	F	0.2	0.4	0.3	0.7
	M	0.2	0.5	0.2	0.6

Source: Statistics Canada, 2001 Census

the regions/countries from which Canada's Muslims, Hindus, and Buddhists typically come – Africa, the Middle East, South and East Asia – complete high school at rates over 90% and attain bachelor's degrees at rates ranging from 44% (West Asia/Middle East) to 65% (India) to 70% (China), much higher than the non-immigrant population as a whole (28%) or the second and 1.5 generations from all origins taken together (38%) (Abada, Hou, and Ram 2008).

EDUCATIONAL ATTAINMENT AND ECONOMIC SUCCESS

An important contextual question with regard to the educational levels of the target populations for the present study is whether the typical economic downward mobility of their immigrant parents will carry over into the next generation. It is an important question, because it speaks to how the participants in this study might judge their situation living in Canada and thus how optimistic they might be for their future in the country as Muslims, Buddhists, Hindus, or non-religious. One could expect that the disadvantage would not carry over, given that they will have no trouble having their Canadian educa-

Table 3.9   Educational attainment, 15–19- and 20–24-year-olds, Canada, 2001, %

	Age Group	Canada	Muslims	Buddhists	Hindus
Less than high school diploma	15–19	67.7	64.2	66.3	62.3
	20–24	16.3	14.3	14.4	13.2
High school diploma	15–19	16.0	18.6	15.8	20.6
	20-24	15.0	14.3	12.1	12.8
Post-secondary, no degree or diploma	15–19	12.7	13.8	15.4	14.4
	20–24	29.3	34.8	39.0	36.3
Non-university with diploma certificate	15–19	2.2	2.1	1.7	1.8
	20–24	20.2	16.5	16.9	15.9
Bachelor's degree	15–19	0.1	0.4	0.1	0.2
	20–24	9.9	13.7	11.8	15.8
Master's or doctorate degree	15–19	0.03	0.1	0.1	0.1
	20–24	1.2	2.1	1.3	2.5

Source: Statistics Canada, 2001 Census

tional credentials recognized, that they are at home in the local languages, and that they have been culturally raised in Canada. Yet overt and subtle forms of continued discrimination are definitely possible in Canada, and therefore one might instead expect that they will experience a comparative disadvantage with relation to their generational peers. Research on this question has generally tended in the optimistic direction, showing that the income of the second generation in Canada is by and large commensurate with their high levels of educational attainment (Boyd and Grieco 1998; Corak 2008). One must nonetheless be careful, because as in all other questions concerning the fate of immigrant populations, much depends on which subgroup one is discussing. Integration, if that is what we wish to call it, is always to some degree "segmented" (Zhou and Bankston 1998), meaning quite specifically that the experience of all immigrants and their children is not the same. It therefore makes sense to ask whether religion makes a difference in this regard.

To some degree, the question of the economic fate of the second and 1.5 generations is premature in Canada, given how young those generations still are. At the time of the 2001 census, more than 80% of the second generation we are examining here were still under the age of 20. This does not, however, prevent a comparison with other people in the same age group, all the while admitting that the future on this question remains undetermined. Table 3.10 presents 2001 census data that compares the relation between educational attainment and income for two sets of groups: the entire Canadian population accord-

Table 3.10   Median employment income by age and educational attainment,
Canada, 2001, % relative to Canadian median employment income

	Population as a whole		Aged 20–24	
	Bachelor's degree	Postgraduate degree or certificate	Post-secondary, no degree or diploma	Post-secondary with degree or diploma
Muslims	51.0	49.3	74.1	83.8
Hindus	71.1	76.1	80.2	89.8
Buddhists	68.9	64.7	86.1	93.6
Sikhs	65.1	58.6	98.6	102.7
Jews	117.3	116.0	75.9	88.3
No religion	92.6	95.5	110.6	105.2
Canada	100.0	100.0	100.0	100.0

Source: Statistics Canada, 2001 Census

ing to various religious identities, including Muslims, Hindus, and Buddhists, and those between the ages of 20 and 24 according to the same identities. In the first case, educational attainment is limited to all those with a bachelor's degree or higher; in the second, the distinction is between those who have post-secondary education but no degree or diploma and those who do have a degree or diploma. Using different educational measures is warranted, because many of the 20- to 24-year-olds will not have completed their education and therefore it would be too limiting to restrict the view to only those with degrees. For each group, their relative median employment income is reported, in each case expressed as a percentage of the median income for the population as a whole. Several observations are of note from this table. The most obvious is that all the religious identities that consist in a great majority of post-1970s immigrants – all but Jews and those with no religion – are at a distinct income disadvantage, a result that represents the comparative downward mobility of the "parental" generation after coming to Canada. Just as evident is the greater degree of disadvantage experienced by Muslims (and, to a lesser extent, Sikhs) when compared to Hindus and Buddhists. On the side of the 20- to 24-year-olds, the immigrant/non-immigrant differential largely disappears, but one notes that the Muslims seem still to be at a disadvantage, albeit a lesser one among the "children" than among the "parents." In light of the fact that Jews are the religious identity closest to the Muslims at the lower-income end and that those with no religion and Sikhs are at the top, the reasons for these figures are somewhat difficult to determine without further detailed analysis. What is clear is the stark contrast between the younger age group with its heavy presence of the 1.5 and second generation and the larger immigrant population dominated by the parental generation. As with other research on this overall question, the results are not unequivocally in the direction of the income differences disappearing, but the trend seems very much to be in that direction. This statistical trend is consistent with our research results insofar as the interviews revealed virtually no one who, upon observing the difficult time their parents may have had economically after arriving in Canada, gave any indication that they expect or fear that they will be facing a similar problem. Economic prospects are, however, not the only factors important in assessing the way this young generation is finding its place in Canadian society. Attitudinal questions are just as important.

ATTITUDES TO LIFE IN CANADA: BELONGING, TRUST, AND LIFE SATISFACTION

In a 2007 publication, Jeffrey Reitz and Rupa Bannerjee raised the alarm that second-generation youth from immigrant families showed signs of not fitting well into Canadian life, of in fact being less integrated and comfortable in Canadian society than their immigrant parents or older siblings (Reitz and Bannerjee 2007). They based their conclusion on data from the 2002 Ethnic Diversity Survey (EDS), the same dataset that we are using here. As usual, they found that the question was different depending on which subgroup one was observing, but they did not use religion as a variable for identifying subgroups. On the qualitative level, as will become evident in later chapters, our research did not support these findings for any of the three religious subgroups; if anything, we found the opposite to be the case among the subpopulations of young adults of Muslim, Hindu, and Buddhist families. To be sure, we did recruit our participants among the elite at Canadian universities, and even if they do constitute the majority of the young adults in question, it is possible that our sample was skewed toward those who might be expected to have fewer problems with finding a positive place in the society in which they grew up. An analysis of the EDS data in fact reveals that our qualitative results are in line with what that survey revealed but with one or two "surprises."

The EDS included questions probing participants' subjective feelings of belonging, trust, and life satisfaction; it also asked about experiences of discrimination, both as they were growing up and in 2002, the time of the survey. Table 3.11 presents the overall results from the first three sets of questions for 18- to 24-year-olds in Canada as a whole and among those who identified with one of the three religions at issue. They reveal that the three religious identities have a generally stronger sense of belonging than the Canadian average for this age group, the one exception being Buddhists' sense of belonging to their families, which is somewhat lower than others'. Life satisfaction varies a

Table 3.11   Senses of belonging, trust, and life satisfaction, Canada, 18–24-year-olds

	Canada	Muslims	Buddhists	Hindus
Belonging to Canada[1]	4.03	4.38	4.36	4.23
Belonging to family	4.55	4.71	4.40	4.65
Belonging to ethnic group	3.36	4.08	3.65	4.08
Satisfaction with life[2]	4.16	4.15	3.96	4.23
Trust: "People can be trusted" (%)	45.4	34.5	40.6	41.9
Trust: "You can't be too careful" (%)	50.9	60.1	55.4	55.0
Trust in people in family[3]	4.77	4.85	4.79	4.77
Trust in people at school/work	3.65	3.44	3.58	3.64
Trust in people in neighbourhood	3.39	3.25	3.29	3.61
Sample size (N)	5,548	171	99	128

1 Figures in first three lines are averages on a 5-point analog scale from "not strong at all" (1) to "very strong" (5).

2 Figures in this line are averages on a 5-point analog scale from "not satisfied at all" (1) to "very satisfied" (5).

3 Figures in last three lines are averages on a 5-point analog scale from "cannot be trusted at all" (1) to "can be trusted a lot" (5).

Source: Statistics Canada. 2002. Ethnic Diversity Survey

bit, with Buddhists again being the only ones with somewhat lower levels on this measure. In terms of trust, however, there is a difference: Muslims, Buddhists, and Hindus were all less trusting of people than was the overall Canadian population – in the case of Muslims, significantly less. Not surprisingly, perhaps, that comparative caution referred more to outsiders like people at work, school, or in their neighbourhoods than it did to family members. The one significant caveat with respect to these results is that the sample sizes were really quite small; one should not make too much of these results, even if they do confirm our qualitative findings.

It is possible to break down these figures according to gender and places of birth (Canada/outside Canada). The sample sizes, however, become so small when one does this that the results are more or less completely unreliable. We therefore do not report them, except to say that the majority of the small samples for all three groups consist of people born in Canada. Given that the portion born outside Canada includes the 1.5ers such as constituted a good portion of the participants in our qualitative research project, it may be safe to say that the overall figures roughly represent the segments of the population from which they are drawn.

ATTITUDES TO AND EXPERIENCES OF DISCRIMINATION

As noted, of the three religious identities, Muslims in the EDS were significantly less likely to be trusting, particularly of people outside their families. That contrasted with their sense of belonging, which was as high as or higher than that of the Hindus, Buddhists, and the overall population in this age group. It is then perhaps not surprising that Muslims were more likely to feel that discrimination existed in Canada, to have experienced such discrimination, and to consider that this discrimination included religious discrimination. In all these senses, the participants in our project confirmed the EDS findings: Muslims felt that they belonged in this country, but they were also more likely to be aware of and to have experienced discrimination against themselves, including on the basis of their religious identity.

The Ethnic Diversity Survey asked a series of relevant questions in this regard. It asked whether people had felt uncomfortable before the age of 15 and at the time of the survey (2002, from two to four years before our interviews). It asked for the reasons for this discomfort, if experienced. It also asked whether discrimination occurred in Canada and what the reasons for this discrimination were, irrespective of whether or not they had experienced such discrimination. Together, these questions tackled the issue of discrimination from various angles, and therefore it is likely significant that in all cases among the 18- to 24-year-olds in the survey, Muslims distinguished themselves in consistent ways: they were more likely to feel uncomfortable before their mid-teens and after; they were more likely to think discrimination occurred in Canada and to attribute it to religious discrimination. Table 3.12 presents the results with respect to feelings of discomfort and the reasons for it. One notes that while Muslims were less likely to feel uncomfortable as they grew older, the decline in this figure was less dramatic than for the other two religious identities and the overall population in this age group. In addition, the likelihood of attributing this discomfort at least in part to religious difference was not only higher than for the other groups but it increased rather than decreased with age. Since the survey was conducted in 2002, it is possible that this higher figure reflects the effects of 9/11. In this regard, it should be pointed out that the Muslim participants in our research generally felt that discrimination against Muslims and Islam in Canada had decreased after the initial upswing in the wake of 9/11. They were, however, well aware that such discrimination existed; many had experienced it themselves or knew fellow Muslims who had; many averred that the portrayal of Muslims in Canadian mass media was particularly problematic; but few felt that overall discrimination was a larger problem in Canada or for them personally.

Table 3.13, then, shows the percentages of respondents who felt that discrimination exists in Canada, along with the percentages of those who thought

Table 3.12   Feelings of discomfort and reasons for discomfort, Muslims, Buddhists, and Hindus, Canada, 18–24-year-olds, %

	Canada	Muslims	Buddhists	Hindus
Discomfort before age 15				
uncomfortable from sometimes to always	14.4	31.6	26.8	20.1
reason: race*	15.7	25.9	30.7	38.8
reason: religion*	5.9	19.0	6.9	8.5
Discomfort in 2002				
uncomfortable from sometimes to always	8.4	23.0	11.9	8.5
reason: race*	13.2	20.1	16.8	28.7
reason: religion*	4.6	21.3	5.9	2.3
Sample size (N)	5,548	171	99	128

* % of total sample, not % of only those who reported feeling uncomfortable; includes multiple responses

Source: Statistics Canada. 2002. *Ethnic Diversity Survey*

Table 3.13   Discrimination and reasons for discrimination, Muslims, Buddhists, and Hindus, Canada, 18–24-year-olds, %

	Canada	Muslims	Buddhists	Hindus
Discrimination exists in Canada				
often or sometimes	9	19	14.9	15.5
rarely or not at all	91	81	75.1	84.5
reason: race*	14	24.7	27.7	21.8
reason: religion*	3.2	19	5	3.1
Sample size (N)	5,548	171	99	128

* % of total sample, not % of only those who indicated that discrimination occurred; includes those who gave multiple responses and those who said that discrimination occurred only rarely

Source: Statistics Canada. 2002. *Ethnic Diversity Survey*

that the reasons for such discrimination were either racial or religious. The results mirror those for personal discomfort. Muslims were more likely to say that discrimination occurred in Canada, although one notes the general reluctance in all categories to say that it occurred more than rarely. Moreover, in sharp contrast to the Hindus, Buddhists, and all 18- to 24-year-olds, Muslims were at least four times as likely to say that the basis of discrimination included religion. One notes, however, that, as Reitz and Bannerjee confirm in a more recent analysis, the dominant reason for discrimination given by all groups was race or skin colour, not religion (Reitz et al. 2009).

Again, as with the EDS data on belonging and trust, the sample sizes for all three religious identities are too small for one to break the responses down further, especially according to gender and place of birth. Doing so only yields unreliable results that are due as much to chance as to actual differences.

CONCLUSION

Participants in most qualitative research projects are not statistically representative of the overall populations from which they are drawn. Ours were no exception in this regard: they were almost certainly skewed toward those who:

- are more religious or at least interested in matters religious;
- have a higher level of educational attainment even in a population that has very high levels of educational attainment when compared to the overall population;
- are female rather than male;
- live or grew up in large Canadian cities, Ottawa and Toronto in particular.

On the other hand, the statistical profile that we have drawn of our target Canadian populations in this chapter shows that the participants in this project were not noticeably skewed toward those who:

- are better integrated into Canadian society, including a range of measures of such integration such as economic (level of income and employment), social (composition of social networks), or cultural (values and world views);
- have had, for whatever reason, fewer experiences of religious or other discrimination than the average of their population group;
- with the exception of Guyanese and Trinidadian Hindu men, come from "minority" ethnic origins within the three religious identities;
- come from economically better-off families;
- have better educated parents than the average person in their category.

Taking all the comparisons between the statistical data and our research participants into consideration, it is probably safe to conclude that although the latter were not statistically representative, they very likely did reflect the majority situation among people in their age group and with their family backgrounds. In other words, this may not be a representative population, but it is also far from an unrepresentative one. As such, it is highly unlikely that there is in the target population a significant presence of profiles of young Muslim, Hindu, and Buddhist adults that are not present in our sample, and, to the degree that there are, those profiles will constitute only a tiny minority in the overall population of the second generation of immigrants from these religious backgrounds. To be sure, only further research can determine, first, whether this is definitively the case and, second, even it if is, whether our sample of participants will continue to reflect what is happening in their generation. In the meantime, we can safely suppose that what we report in the remaining chapters is reflective of the general or background situation with young adult Muslims, Buddhists, and Hindus of immigrant families, the inevitable exceptions notwithstanding.

4

Islam, Hinduism, and Buddhism: Differential Reconstruction of Religions[1]

PETER BEYER

THE COMMON CONTEXT

The ways that the Canadian young adults who participated in this research were relating to the religious heritages bequeathed to them by their families were first of all very varied. In most of the following chapters, we put a great deal of emphasis on describing and documenting this variation, even dividing the main chapters according to important axes of variation – namely, religious background and gender. And within these chapters, we analyze further dimensions and characteristics of variation within each subgroup, all the way to the profiling of representative individuals whose stories demonstrated such difference as much as possible in specific and "lived" biographies. The variation, however, does not negate that there were also a significant number of important commonalities, most of which were related to common contextual factors such as the following:

- the shared Canadian state and societal context of the 1990s and 2000s and within that the central Canadian large urban contexts of Toronto, Ottawa, and Montreal;
- growing up in families of recent transnational migration;
- growing up "Canadian," meaning the shared and formative experience of "Canadian culture" (however conceived) and including having (Canadian) English or (Quebec) French as their mother tongue or main first language;
- being part of the same age cohort and therefore sharing a similarity of life stages and being part of the same "generation";
- the already discussed (see chapter 2) similarity of a post-secondary educational environment;
- the shared globalized context that includes not only ongoing and even increasing levels of transnational migration but also the ever denser network of communicative possibilities most visibly concretized for these participants in the globalized media of transnational travel, telephone, television, and the Internet.

In this common context, however, a further, and highly consequential, aspect is also a significant difference. This concerns religion itself and the three religions of Islam, Hinduism, and Buddhism in particular. How these youths and young adults were relating to these three religions and to religion more generally had also to do with how these religions and religion have been and are being reconstructed globally – that is, their character as historically contingent global religious systems. We hypothesize that the wider global reconstructions of Islam, Hinduism, and Buddhism – another way of saying what these religions, sociologically speaking, currently are – are having a significant influence on and are exemplified in how these youths engaged in their own understandings of and participation in religion and these religions. The particular roles that these religions played or did not play in the lives of these youth varied as a function of the global differences between these religions, in addition to being a reflection of their common experience as the Canada-born or -raised children of post-1970 migrants to Canada and the proclivities of individuals in their life-worlds. Given that none of these three religions has a significant history in the Canadian context, the appropriation of Islam, Hinduism, and Buddhism, as influential categories within the society and as lived social realities, by these Canadian youth should therefore be seen as an exemplification of glocalization, the simultaneous and non-contradictory globalization of these religions through their localization in Canada (Beyer 2006b). What the participants in this research project did was localize globalized forms, in this case the very idea of religion and these three religions specifically. The manifestations of this commonality of difference will become evident as we proceed in this and the following chapters.

COMMON CHARACTERISTICS OF 1.5- AND SECOND-GENERATION IMMIGRANTS IN CANADA

In earlier chapters, we noted that the level of education among the Canadian second generation varies to some degree according to the subgroup one is talking about. For instance, there is a fair amount of variation according to ethnic origin, with the people of some origins showing significantly higher educational attainment than others. In terms of religious background, however, the three research groups of Muslims, Hindus, and Buddhists showed hardly any differences at all (Beyer 2005c). That was as concerns level of education. In terms of religion, however, it was a different matter entirely. Although all three subgroups showed very high levels of educational attainment, their relation to and style and level of practical involvement in the religions of their respective heritages showed rather different profiles when we compared one group to another. A major aim of this chapter is to outline these differences and to suggest some of the reasons for them. To contextualize those differences, however, it is important nonetheless to begin by looking at some of the things that these participants had in common, religiously and in related respects. Three general areas of commonality are particularly evident from an analysis of the research data and salient for understanding the differences.

To begin with religion, whether one is looking at those who were involved and practising their religion, those who had only a general identification with it, or those for whom religion had little to no relevance in their lives, the dominant evaluation of religion across the sample of participants overall was positive, as were the attitudes toward religious diversity in Canada and around the world. Although a minority felt that religion was a regrettable illusion or a psychological crutch that some people seemed to need – and they were mostly among Buddhist and Hindu men – very few expressed the idea that the world would be a better place without it. The vast majority declared not only that religion was a good thing but that there were no bad religions. A great many felt that all religions were pretty much equal in value, although if they identified strongly, theirs was clearly the best for them. Even and especially among those who were highly practising, exceedingly few showed any intolerance toward other religions, and a good number celebrated both the fact of religious diversity in Canada and the prevailing religious pluralism. As Maryam, one of the female Muslim interviewees, stated when asked her opinion about religious diversity in Canada,

> I think it's a good thing for Canada. I mean it's always more exposure, more ideas, more – even … if you don't necessarily believe in another religion, you can always take certain aspects of what they practise or what they do if it's a really good thing. I mean, I see it as a good thing, it's just more diversity and more exposure to ideas you never would have considered before had you been living in a small tiny bubble. (MF14)[2]

Moreover, with few exceptions they all considered that people in Canada were free to practise their different religions, although the majority also maintained that Christianity was clearly the dominant and privileged religion demographically, culturally, and legally. The reverse side of this prevailing attitude was a virtually unanimous rejection of religious extremism and politicized religion in particular. The "bad" in religion was correspondingly attributed to practitioners who distorted their religion through violence and intolerance; it was generally not regarded as an attribute of religion or a particular religion as such. As Ahmed, a Muslim male whom we profile in chapter 6, put it, "I don't think any religion itself is dangerous, it's just the people in the religion that can distort it. I think in every religion there are bad people and there are good people, just the people, but no religion is bad" (MM13).

In tune with these orientations, most participants also did not think that religions or a particular religion should have more influence in Canadian society or elsewhere except as several and equal players. A great many thought that religion was and should remain a private affair but one that people should be able to display and practise publicly. In all these matters, of course, there were a few interviewees who differed, but they were a very small minority of the sample.

Far from distinguishing these participants as exceptional, this prevalent attitude toward religious diversity and the place of religion in Canadian society is actually quite typical in Canada more generally. These young adults reflected in their attitudes the general and, one might add, changed attitude in Canada toward religious and cultural diversity, one that is perhaps not completely accepting and unproblematic when it comes to religion in particular but one that is generally tolerant and "accommodating." Indeed, one indicator of the degree of "integration" of our participants was how many of their commonalities they appeared to share with the general population and particularly the overall age group of which they were a part.[3]

Another strong commonality among all three groups was the very high percentage of participants who were highly individualistic in terms of what they felt was important in life and how to go about achieving the goals of life. Even and especially for those who were highly religiously involved, this involvement was individually driven: most participants felt that it was their responsibility to work their religious lives out for themselves – and they were very often willing to let their eventual children do likewise – most often learning from their parents and relatives in many respects but ultimately being responsible for their own religious choices. There was very little evidence of the attitude "I do this because we do this" and much more of "I do this because I have decided for myself (or have discovered for myself, through my own efforts) that this is the correct thing to do." In general, being from an immigrant family, regardless of specific background, did not mean that they had failed to absorb key values of most Western societies, including Canada, here an acceptance of the individual as the authentic centre of personal life-construction (for similarities with Muslims in Europe, see Vertovec and Rogers 1998 and chapter 13). While group belonging, whether religious or cultural, was quite important to the majority, it was always based in individual choice. The fact that they belonged to particular cultural and religious groups was something they were born with and raised in; the importance they gave to such belonging and what specifically they did in terms of it was their own individual business. Radhika, a Hindu woman participant, put this in terms of growing up:

> Hinduism wasn't really something that I questioned … it was automatic, it was a given, right? But then, after that, I [started asking] … is Hinduism really the right way or is it not … I'm still [in a] confused phase, there are certain things I have decided, like I do believe there is some form of higher form or some form of God, but I really don't know if … this fixed form of religion is the best way to go. (HF32)

Finally, connected with the preceding, is a generally high level of integration into the dominant Canadian society. Integration, in this case, is structural, psychological, and cultural. Aspects of the latter I have just outlined. With respect to the structural integration, the high levels of post-secondary education are indicative, as are the so far promising signs in terms of economic integration, both of which were discussed in the previous chapter. The second generations overall have even higher levels of education than their parents – whose level is already higher than the national average – but also tend to earn a higher income than their parents or the population as a whole. To be sure, there are significant differences from one immigrant subgroup to another – the idea of "segmented assimilation" has some validity in Canada as it does elsewhere (Portes and Zhou 1993; Zhou 1997). There is also at least some indication that the Muslim second generation, whether the men or the women, fares somewhat less well than do the Hindu or Buddhist (Beyer 2005c). Overall, however, the current trend is clear: the educational integration is thus far resulting in economic integration (Boyd and Grieco 1998; Corak 2008; Geschwender and Guppy 1995; Gosine 2000; Halli and Vedanand 2007).

What I am calling psychological or identity integration was also evident, and clearly so, from the data analyzed here. We asked all our interviewees questions such as whether they felt accepted as a full member of Canadian society; whether they had experienced discrimination on the basis of their religious, cultural, or physical differences and, if so, how they interpreted that; whether they felt that Canada was accepting of immigrants like themselves or their families; whether Canada was succeeding or not in its officially avowed aim of constructing an inclusive and multicultural society. The aim was to see how much they felt integrated. As it turns out, they rarely felt like outsiders, and very few indeed expressed the desire to live somewhere else, such as the country of origin of their families. To be sure, they usually recognized their effective "minority" status, and many had known in their own lives or in the lives of others like them a certain amount of discrimination, but this they more often than not attributed to the ignorance of individuals, not to a general characteristic of a culture and society that would not accept them as equally belonging in Canada. A great many, in fact, averred that Canada was the best or one of the best countries in the world, warts and all. As Darren, one particularly positive interviewee, put it in response to the question of whether he thought Canada was welcoming of immigrants,

> Yes, very much so ... My family immigrated here because of all the opportunities that lay here ... The way my parents have explained it to me, they've always looked to Canada as a place of miraculous opportunity. And I know people who came up here from China just like three years ago, same thing, like they came up here for the opportunity. People who came from Korea like last year ... they're here for the opportunity

to make something of themselves, be better than they could have been back home. [Q: Do you think that Canada is religiously tolerant?] Yes, I do believe that. There's always gonna be the odd person who's not tolerant of people who aren't like him or her, but yeah, I do believe that we're tolerant of religions. (HM04)

As with all these common characteristics, it must be emphasized, there were of course notable exceptions, people who did not feel comfortable, who considered Canada a hypocritical, racist society that did not welcome immigrants and only pretended to do so. Out of 202 interviews, however, these can be counted on one hand.[4]

While these commonalities are thus important, they only serve as background for many of the remarkable differences that different participants and different groups of participants also exhibited. It is to some of these in relation to religion that we now turn, looking first at the Muslims in our sample, then the Hindus, and finally the Buddhists. As we attempt to show, in spite of the individualism, in spite of the sometimes low level of involvement, which religious background one is from seems by itself to make a significant difference in how one constructs one's religious/spiritual life and identity.

MUSLIMS

Broad comparison of the three religious subgroups requires a kind of global categorization or typology, which serves to orient the general pattern of commonality and variation within the subgroup. This categorization must to a significant degree emerge from the data itself. One of the notable features of our data is that this exercise could not be done effectively by using one typology or continuum for all three religious subgroups. To do so would merely miss the main characteristics of one, two, or all three of the groups. For the Muslims, however, a rather commonly used prime axis of variation worked quite well, largely because the Muslim participants themselves tended to use it. It was to distinguish them according to their level of practice of Islam and identification with Islam according to what one may call a "five-pillars orthodoxy" model (Roy 2004). We thus arrived at a 10-point scale where 1 was assigned to people who were non-religious and rejected a Muslim identity and 10 to participants for whom Islam was central, who were highly practising, who avoided all forbidden moral behaviour – especially rules regarding sexual behaviour and relations – who restricted their social circle to Muslims, and who generally led a highly "sectarian" lifestyle. For the purposes of the current analysis, however, we group these categories into three, those who were highly involved (categories 7–10), those who were somewhat to moderately involved (4–6), and those who were in effect non-religious (1–3).

A closer description of the category groupings reads as follows, beginning with those Muslim participants who were deemed *highly involved*. They adhered to a rather consistent standard of Muslim orthodoxy that locates the five pillars of confession, prayer, almsgiving, fasting, and pilgrimage at the very centre of what it means to be Muslim and that emphasizes restricted sexual behaviour, endogamy, dietary regulations, and a moral emphasis on peace, tolerance, justice, caring for others, and a compassionate social order. Dina, a highly involved female interviewee, expressed it like this when asked what the chief characteristics of Islam were:

> I would say it's modesty and being humble. Those are one of the main characteristics ... And there's of course the five pillars where you have to pray five times a day, to believe in God, and Mohammed was the last prophet of God, fasting during the month of Ramadan, paying charity which is zakat, and going for *hajj* ... if you can afford it. So those are the five pillars which you should follow, but there's also things about being humble, being modest, being honest ... personally to me, honesty's a huge thing. (MF05)

Dina and the others in the highly involved categories thus contributed to the reproduction of Islam along the lines of this rather standard orthodoxy. They put great emphasis on the idea that Islam was one unified religion with clear defining characteristics, that Islam was a clear and systematic (or systemic) religion that was the same everywhere, whether in Canada or elsewhere around the globe. In this regard, however, one should note a virtually total absence of political Islamism in this group or among any of the Muslim subcategories. As far as militant Islamism especially is concerned, there was nearly unanimous distancing and quite often outright condemnation. It was not seen as a legitimate part or expression of global Islam.

Most often, these Muslim participants would locate Islam at the very centre of their lives, at least claiming that it determined everything else in their lives, even though they might guiltily confess that their actual behaviour in various ways strayed from this ideal. In tune with the general characteristics of all participants that I emphasized above and like Muslim participants that we classified in the other categories, the way that these highly involved Muslims came to their vision of what constituted this ideal Islam was highly individualistic, not in the sense that they would decide whatever they wanted but rather in the sense that the search for authentic Islam was in most cases ongoing and derived from a variety of sources that they accessed individually and directly. These sources included most especially the Qur'an and to a slightly lesser extent the Sunna, the opinions of their parents and other close relatives, and a variety of sources both printed and accessed through cyberspace. Local imams and specific Islamic organizations rarely had any influence, unless indirectly through these other means. Corresponding to this highly individualistic as opposed to communal or group-oriented style, the highly involved Muslims showed great variation on virtually every one of the details that composed their otherwise common "orthodox" model of Islam. Their lived religion was not subsumed entirely in the common global model that they all espoused. Many details could illustrate this variation,[5] including the relative importance given to the different components, which of the physical observances (e.g., with respect to clothing, social life, and eating) were seen as essential and which more optional, and how the "rules" were to be applied in daily life. In only a very few cases – clearly only in four cases, one male, three female – among the highly involved did the combination amount to a classification of either 9 or 10, those who tended toward a "sectarian" lifestyle. The vast majority, by contrast, insisted that their strong identity as Muslims should in no way hinder them from full participation in the surrounding society, whether this meant socially, culturally, politically, or in terms of profession. Although many had difficulty with certain features of that surrounding society, ranging from personal sexual issues to geopolitical ones, this only induced them to be selective in what they did; it did not amount to a feeling of being an outsider and therefore keeping to one's own group.

The second category of Muslim participants, what we are calling the *moderately to somewhat involved*, used the same standards but did not feel that they had to conform to them as strictly. They did not contribute to the construction of a different systemic Islam so much as they more selectively incorporated the common model into their lived religious lives. For people in this category, Islam and Muslim identity were often important, but they were not deemed to be what oriented their lives at the most fundamental level; it was more one factor among several, others of which might include career, personal taste, friends, and so forth. This group included everyone from those who aspired to highly involved status and "tried their best" in the meantime to those who did little more than identify as Muslims and engaged, if only occasionally, in specific religious practices such as prayer or fasting during Ramadan. In comparison to the highly involved, this group lacked the high level of Islamic practice and the assertion of Islam as central in their lives. As a concrete example, no women in this category wore the headscarf, but all could understand and even admired women who did. Correspondingly, quite a number of the highly involved wore the headscarf, but next to none would condemn those who didn't as "bad" Muslims.

The third category consisted of those who were clearly non-religious, including those who rejected identification with Islam or as Muslims. From the perspective of religious reconstruction, this group could not even be said to be involved except insofar as they failed to construct an alternative. Although

Table 4.1   Religious involvement of Muslims according to gender

	Men	Women	Total
Highly involved	15 (43%)	29 (50%)	44 (47.3%)
Moderately to somewhat involved	9 (26%)	19 (38%)	33 (33.3%)
Non-religious	11 (31%)	10 (17%)	21 (22.6%)
Totals	35	58	93

some in this group lacked an explicitly Muslim upbringing, just as many came from practising Muslim families, rejecting Islam, and not infrequently religion more generally, for various reasons, including, as in the case of most of the Iranians in the sample, a negative association of religion and Islam with its authoritarian and often politicized versions.

Overall, among the 93 interviewees of Muslim background in our sample, just a little less than half fell into the highly involved category (see Table 4.1). This is a much higher percentage than one would find in the general 18- to 27-year-old Canadian population, even accounting for a sample that is skewed in favour of the religiously interested.[6] Some of these participants were relatively more involved than their parents, some less, but in general there was a high correlation between the importance of Islam for them and for their parents. In the vast majority of these cases, the parents seemed to put a high importance on the religious socialization of their children; in most cases, this effort bore fruit but, as noted above, not in all. One might say that religious upbringing was something close to a necessary condition for being religious in adulthood, but it was not a sufficient one (see chapter 5, 78–80). In addition, there was evidently no relation between level of involvement or practice among these Muslim young adults and their integration into Canadian society, whether one is looking at the psychological component as in the subjective senses of belonging and acceptance, concrete structural indicators like educational attainment, or the sharing of cultural core values like individuality or a positive orientation to religious and cultural pluralism.

As for the rest of the Muslim participants, a little less than one-third fell into the somewhat to moderately involved category and the remaining one-fifth were non-religious. Of particular note with regard to the non-religious category is that a very high proportion of it consisted of participants from Iranian background. Of 11 participants of Iranian origin (6 women and 5 men), 5 of the women and 4 of the men were non-religious, most of them not even considering themselves as Muslims.[7] The other two were only somewhat involved. Relatively few of these Iranian participants had a religious upbringing, quite possibly reflecting the emigration patterns from Iran after the 1979 revolution.

The gender division for the three categories was slightly skewed toward women being in greater proportion in the more practising categories, but not too much. The main difference was that women were less frequently in the non-religious category and correspondingly more in the somewhat to moderately involved category. Beyond that, the relation of the women and the men to Islam was not all that different. Attitudes to questions of gender and sexuality, for instance, were not that different; they did not differ noticeably in terms of how many had restrictive attitudes toward sexual relations or "traditional" attitudes about gender roles in religion or society.

Overall, then, using level of involvement according to five-pillars orthodoxy standards as the prime axis of the Muslim continuum worked quite well. For these participants, Islam was a clear religious system, which most of them helped to reproduce. It speaks not only to the very often high importance that Islam has in the lives of the Canadian Muslim second generation but also to the prevalence of that standard vision of what constitutes Islam among Muslims of all stripes. In other words, the reason that the classification worked as well as it did is that the participants themselves had adopted it, irrespective of whether they put themselves inside it and to what extent. The reconstruction of Islam in the Canadian context, it seems, is very much aided and influenced by a globally spread and globally available model of Islam that our participants generally accepted. The situation contrasts markedly with the Hindus and Buddhists in our sample.

HINDUS

If we were to use the same continuum for the Hindu and Buddhist subgroups, the result would be that most would hardly appear on the continuum at all, clustering at the non-religious to only somewhat involved end. Rather than applying a classification continuum that used some standard of orthodox involvement to find the patterns of relation to their religious heritage in these two groups, much more could be gained by finding a different continuum, or at least a different set of criteria. For the Hindus, the category that seemed to work far better than orthodox religious involvement according to some standard of orthodoxy (for which the subjects themselves were also not forthcoming in their own self-descriptions) is, tellingly, that of culture. When we pursued this strategy, the bulk of the Hindu-background participants fell under what we are calling ethnocultural Hindus: they considered their Hindu identity to be important for themselves but more as a cultural identity that had a religious dimension and only sometimes including what one might call standard Hindu practice or belief, such as temple worship, the regular performance of *puja* and other rituals, adherence to some form of Vaishnava, Saivite, or other sub-identity, having a personal god/goddess or following a specific

Table 4.2   Orientation to religious and cultural identity among Hindu participants by gender

	Women	Men	Totals
Ethnocultural Hindus	25 (64%)	5 (28%)	30 (53%)
Non-religious	8 (21%)	11 (61%)	19 (33%)
Highly practising	6 (15%)	2 (11%)	8 (14%)
Totals	39	18	57

guru, believing in the reality of the pantheon, and so forth. Hinduism as a religious system, in other words, was present but far less consistent or uniform, less clearly separated or differentiated than was the case with Muslims, and inherently selective. As one of the Hindu women put it, "see, the beauty of Hinduism, you can pick and choose … It's a very flexible religion" (HF27). In this regard, the Hindu participants more consistently valued their Hindu family connections, cultural practices relating to art (e.g., classical dance), music, film (e.g., Bollywood), food, and sometimes language (see the more detailed discussions in chapters 7 and 8). Explicitly religious practice was not absent from their profile; it was in fact fairly consistently present but embedded in familial-cultural practices. Just over one-half of our 57 Hindu participants were comfortably slotted into this category (see Table 4.2): being Hindu was more of a cultural feature and in that context only sometimes the substantive practice of a clearly delineated and coherently constructed religion. An intriguing example of this "cultural" way of understanding what counts as Hindu was the frequent admission from these participants that their source of knowledge about matters Hindu was not just or even primarily their family, certainly not the priests at the local temple, and only occasionally sacred texts directly and as such. Much more prevalent were precisely the cultural productions: Bollywood films; stories told by older family members, especially mothers, grandmothers, and "aunties"; the television versions of the Mahabharata and Ramayana; and Hindu comic books relating the same stories. As one participant succinctly put it, "When I was younger, I was hooked on those Mahabharata tapes and Ramayana. That's how I learned about [Hinduism], and when I wanted to learn more I would look up stuff and we had books at home and I would just flip through them" (HF09).

Exposure to these "cultural" sources meant a reasonable level of what one might call Hindu mythological familiarity, but it did not translate very consistently into regular "involvement" in especially ritual life as was the case with the majority of the Muslims. Another way of putting the same conclusion, only from the other side, is that although most of these Hindu participants, like almost all participants across the three religious categories, distinguished clearly between religion and culture, they did so in favour of the cultural side, considering the religion less important for themselves but identifying the cultural explicitly as Hindu.

For the rest, one-third of the Hindu interviewees were completely non-practising, whether religiously or culturally, but the remaining one-seventh was highly involved in ritual practice. These two categories would have fit nicely in a scale like the Muslim one, divided according to level of religious involvement. The small number of highly involved engaged in regular religious practice such as the kind just mentioned – temple worship, the regular performance of *puja* and other rituals at domestic shrines, having a personal god/goddess, or following a specific guru – and they adhered to some form of Vaishnava or Saivite identity and a corresponding belief in the various important gods and goddesses of these traditions. The cultural dimensions, of course, were also important for them, but unlike among most of the Muslims, there was little practical dividing of religion and culture so as to identify a "pure" religious tradition in contrast to the "cultural" admixtures typical of others, especially their parents. The line between religion and culture was there but far less precise and far less important, and thus the contribution to the reproduction of a systematized religion was less clear, albeit not absent. In fact, the prevalence of this religion/culture continuity, along with the very high internal variety from one participant to another – that is, the "components" of what constitutes the Hindu – is what prevents us from considering the highly involved, ethnocultural, non-religious distinction among the Hindus from being effectively parallel to the highly involved, moderately involved, non-religious distinction among the Muslims.

In connection with this vagueness, of particular note among the Hindus is that both the ethnocultural Hindu and the religiously involved Hindu categories were heavily dominated by women. By contrast, the non-religious category consisted in majority of men. Thus, of the 39 female participants, 25 were in the ethnocultural and 6 in the highly practising categories, but only 8 were in the non-religious/non-cultural. Of the 18 males (note the low number that was even interested in participating in a project about religion), 11 were in this latter category, 2 in the practising, and 5 in the ethnocultural categories (see Table 4.2). What seems clear is that the women, much more than the men felt a responsibility for carrying on and carrying forth the Hindu traditions and identity, even if for most this was not a matter of perpetuating religion but more one of culture, or at least both at the same time. Many of the ethnocultural Hindu women in particular tended to view it as their specific responsibility to ensure that the Hindu cultural traditions and identity were passed on to the next generation – and this well before any of them was seriously considering producing and raising that next generation. As Sheena replied when asked about future marriage and children:

> *Culture first and foremost.* I want to marry someone who's Indian. I want somebody of the same culture because there are things I want to be able to share with them, and I want to be able to pass on if I have children, like the language, the silly things like the movies ... the clothes and the customs ... I would like to marry somebody who's Hindu though because *I have about a dozen versions of my religion* and if I were to marry somebody who's not Hindu, that version would be further diluted because I would want to teach my kids what's involved with Hinduism ... and then give them the freedom to take it to whatever level they're comfortable with. (HF13; italics added)

It is almost as though the traditional Hindu concept of *stridharma* – namely, the religious duties assigned specifically to women – was manifesting itself in this sample. Women, traditionally religiously and especially ritually responsible for assuring the cosmic welfare or "spiritual health and well-being" of the family, maintain this sense of gender-specific duty even without the religious world view in which it has traditionally been embedded. They (and eventually their children) may have less appreciation for what they themselves recognize as the explicitly religious aspects of their inherited traditions, many – unlike the participant just quoted – may have no difficulty marrying outside their group, but they feel it is their responsibility that their cultural and religious identity and the appreciation for their cultural–religious traditions be passed on to their children, irrespective of who, culturally and religiously speaking, their father is.[8] A more unequivocal example of this orientation comes from Seema, an 18-year-old woman born and raised in Toronto in what she said was a "strict" family. She had this exchange:

> SEEMA: And my friend he's from Delhi, so he was born there and raised in Germany and here now ... He's got that culture, and so that's what I want. He can speak Hindi perfectly.
> INTERVIEWER: So you know that marriage to someone from that background you won't lose your own culture.
> SEEMA: Exactly. I won't be like my cousins who do not know the language ... I'm sorry, I can't do that to my kids ... And I can't do that to my mom ... So, if I was to marry him, it would be perfect because he knows his culture, he knows my culture. He knows the Indian culture, and he knows the language, and ... the most important thing for me is the language.

INTERVIEWER: More than religious traditions?
SEEMA: Yes. (HF24)

In general, one could conclude from the Hindu subsample that the second generation of Hindu background *thus far* is not contributing meaningfully – or at best only ambiguously – to the Canadian reconstruction of Hinduism as religion, very much in contrast to their Muslim fellows. Whether this continues into their more mature adulthood, as they pursue careers and found families of their own, remains to be seen. In particular, given that so many of the women, at least, felt a strong sense of responsibility for perpetuating a highly valued religio-cultural identity, we will have to see whether the explicitly religious aspects become more important as these passing-on-to-the-next-generation tasks become more of a concrete reality. They may. On the other hand, given the lack of a clear and authoritative model for what it is that, religiously speaking, is supposed to be passed on, there may be no exemplary path, or at least no widely present exemplary path, to follow in this regard. It could be, of course, that one develops among them, perhaps a neo-Vedantic path that does not require the belief in supernatural beings and the practice of regular ritual. There were traces of such an attitude in the explanations of several of the Hindu participants. What was almost completely absent, however – and not just less present like the sort of *bhakti* devotionalism that some of them do represent – was the sort of politicized Hinduism that has recently been so visible among Hindus in India and in segments of the first and second generations of migrants in North America and Britain (see Jaffrelot and Therwath 2007; Kurien 2007; Raj 2000). Only one participant was overtly sympathetic to the sort of Hindu nationalism espoused by such organizations as the Bharatiya Janata Party or the Vishwa Hindu Parishad. And she, like the two or three who vehemently rejected politicized religion of any sort, was not among the religiously practising.

Looked at from another angle, however, the relation of these Hindu youths to the religious heritage of their families also paralleled that of the Muslims. It is at least arguable that the global reconstruction of Hinduism in the modern and global era resonates quite strongly with what these young adults were doing, as much as was the case with the Muslim participants and global Islam. What counts as Hinduism in today's world does not have a clear and coherent centre or a discursively and practically dominant version. There is in fact not a very clear dividing line that those who consider themselves Hindu make between Hindu religion and Hindu culture, even though the sense that Hinduism is a religion is clear for them (if not for some scholars [Balagangadhara 1994; Fitzgerald 1990; Frykenberg 1989; Smith 2000]). This seems to apply not only in the Hindu heartland but also in the "diaspora." In this light, the dominance in our sample of Canadian Hindu youth of "ethnocultural" Hindus is

Table 4.3 Orientation to religious and cultural identity among Buddhist participants by gender

	Women	Men	Totals
Religio-culturally based religious seekers	12 (42.9%)	7 (36.8%)	19 (40.4%)
"A little bit Buddhist"	10 (35.7%)	12 (63.2%)	22 (46.8%)
Imitative traditionalists	3 (10.7%)	0 (0%)	3 (6.4%)
Christians with Buddhist background	3 (10.7%)	0 (0%)	3 (6.4%)
Totals	28	19	47

a good reflection of a global situation. In this context, it will be indeed very interesting to see what happens religiously in the lives of these youth as they move into the "householder" stage of their lives.

BUDDHISTS

If the Hindu subgroup needed the substitution of a culture-oriented continuum to make sense of their internal religious continuity and variation, an altogether different classificatory scheme emerged from the Buddhist-background group. Very few of our participants from Buddhist backgrounds were in any sense "involved" in Buddhism if by that is meant regular religious practice and the adoption of a world view centrally informed by traditional Buddhist precepts and concepts. However, we did not therefore write off these subjects as a-religious, because analysis of the data from their interviews suggested another approach, focusing on the indirect implication of Buddhist religious tradition in the world view construction of these participants. Accordingly, a closer examination of what these participants had to say about matters Buddhist showed that although they very often did not identify as Buddhist and knew very little about Buddhism, they were frequently engaged in what one might call a broadly "spiritual" search, or at least spiritual interest, but on a self-described Buddhist basis. This subgroup among the Buddhists we therefore called "religio-culturally based religious seekers." Parallel to the Muslim and Hindu groups, about 40% of the Buddhists could be classified in this category (see Table 4.3). Specifically, of the 47 Buddhist participants, 28 were women and the remaining 19 were men. Of these 47, 19 fell into this first category, 12 women and 7 men. In terms of ethnic background, a little more than half of them were of Southeast Asian (11) origin, the rest of Sri Lankan (3) or East Asian (5: Chinese and Japanese) origin. How did they manifest this "seekership" on a Buddhist basis? First, it should be noted that, in keeping with using this different approach to understand the patterns among the Buddhists, these 19 included one or two who by other criteria would be considered "highly involved," but only one or two. Therefore, rather than giving this tiny minority its own category and thereby privileging an understanding of religion and Buddhism that did not really emerge from the data, it made more sense to put them in with the religio-culturally based spiritual seekers, because that is precisely what they also were; they just did it in a more institutionally Buddhist mode. The rest might or might not consider themselves Buddhist but perhaps expressed the wish to "check it out in the future": to be positively oriented toward Buddhism and to wish to explore what their family sub-tradition had to offer. One participant put it like this: "Y'know ... after I finish my BA, I want to travel, first across Canada ... and then ... to Cambodia. And I'm thinkin' that it might be fun to get initiated as a monk, maybe just for a year, just to learn and see what I have to offer" (BM03).

They might have a strong secular sense of values and morals, including advocacy of social justice, sustainability, freedom, equality, peace, and tolerant goodwill, but they would see a connection between these, their basic value orientations, and their barely inherited Buddhism. As one Buddhist participant put it,

> I definitely consider myself an atheist, [but] I do believe in the precepts and the value system of Buddhism. I find, because I have a Buddhist upbringing ... like all the precepts and values of Buddhism, I find I like to follow or want to follow because it's just good moral value, like don't kill, don't steal, don't lie ... So that's where I consider myself only in the core idea of Buddhism which is mindfulness, like y'know, respect everyone, value life. (BM08)

As with the ethnocultural Hindus, one may speculate as to whether this openness to Buddhism will translate into more active and explicitly institutional religious practice and involvement as Buddhist as this group gets older. That remains to be seen, but one may also speculate that if something like this happens, it will definitely be on a more "Western" Buddhist model, one emphasizing individual and engaged seekership and personal spiritual practice rather than a "traditional" one emphasizing ritual practice, master/disciple relations, and a clear distinction between monastic and lay Buddhist responsibilities and practices.[9]

The other three-fifths of the Buddhist participants must also be understood by different criteria. Accordingly, we isolated three other subcategories. First, there were those we called "imitative traditionalists," people who, in express contrast to the seekership group, laid great stress on simply continuing the traditions handed on to them by their families, without much real reconstruction and noticeable adaptation. There were very few of these, however – 3 women, 2 of Sri Lankan and 1 of Southeast Asian origin (see chapter 10, 226–8). Of the remaining 25, 22 we classified, adopting a phrase from one of them, as "a little bit Buddhist."[10] These participants were mostly of Chinese ethnic background, including ethnically Chinese from Southeast Asia. They did, believed, or even knew very little that was specifically Buddhist. They nonetheless claimed that it was there in their identities in some indirect, perhaps cultural, way. Most of them, very typical for people in Canada of Chinese ethnic origin, claimed to have no religion at all but recognized that aspects of several religious traditions, including Buddhism, were included within their inherited cultural traditions.[11] They gave no centrality to the Buddhist aspect, however, in contrast to the religio-culturally based seekers. About 47% of the 47 Buddhists fell into this category, 10 women and 12 men. One notes that almost two-thirds of the men fell into this category and that it is the one that best corresponds to the non-religious in the other two classification grids for Muslims and Hindus. The remaining three Buddhists were not Buddhists at all but rather Christians and that for at least one generation before them. They were also of Chinese ethnic origin. Buddhism for them was little more than a bunch of superstitious practices carried out by one of their grandparents; Christianity was the real religion (see chapter 10, 228–9). As far as this category is concerned, it is notable that, first, neither the Muslim nor Hindu subsamples captured people whose adherence was actually to another religion and, second, that these participants still came forward because they recognized themselves of Buddhist background.

Overall, then, the Buddhist subsample showed a rather high correlation between religious orientation and ethnocultural origin: most South and Southeast Asians found their way into the first two categories, the East Asians mostly into the latter two. Rather than pointing to some unique feature, however, it must be underlined that this was actually a feature of all three subgroups but in different ways and less clearly in the other cases. The Muslims did vary to some degree according to ethnocultural origin: Iranians were almost entirely non-religious, Somalis generally very religious (but there were only 4 in our sample), and South Asians on the whole more highly involved than those originating from the broad belt from North Africa to the Middle East. The Hindus also showed internal ethnocultural variation, especially those who came to Canada as twice-migrants from East Africa or the Caribbean in contrast to those whose families came directly from India. Yet here there does not seem to be a good correlation between such differences of origin and the category into which an individual Hindu participant fell. Only the Buddhists showed this relatively consistent correlation, the only ambiguous ones being those of Southeast Asian Chinese ethnic origin. This group crossed the boundaries, finding their way into three of the four categories that we isolated.

Another important common feature that applied to all the Buddhist sub-groups except the three who were in fact Christians was the way that the participants were exposed to Buddhism as they grew up. In most cases, their parents enjoined them to participate in what the family considered Buddhist practice – e.g., temple visits, commemorating the ancestors – but did not place much emphasis on explaining the reason for these practices. Nor, when it came to it, did the parents in most cases insist that the children keep up these practices except in the family context. Buddhist explanation was minimal; Buddhist practice was desirable but ultimately optional. Leading a morally good life and making a success of oneself were much more important. This was combined with the attitude expressed by many interviewees that, in effect, Buddhism is not – and religion in general should not be – pushy or aggressively trying to assert itself but rather act as a background good, as a source of morals and good life practice, and only for those who felt the need for or were inclined toward a defined set of practices and philosophy in which one engaged "religiously" (see chapter 10, 216–17).

Looked at in a broader context, these various features can again, as with the Muslim and Hindu cases, be seen as a reflection of what Buddhism is globally. There is no clear and "orthodox" model of Buddhism that dominates globally. Only in a very few states such as Sri Lanka and Thailand does Buddhism have the status of a "national" religion, and in the areas from which the vast majority of Canada's Buddhists originate, Buddhism for most people is woven into the broader religio-cultural fabric as a dimension of popular belief and practice. Only for the minority is it a question of explicit and exclusive "adherence." There may be in process the construction of a global Buddhism in the form of various movements ranging from what is sometimes called "Western" Buddhism to organizations like the Fo Guang Shan, Xiji, and Soka Gakkai,[12] but most carriers of Buddhism do not (yet) participate in this process, just as these Canadian second-generation Buddhists did not in any meaningful sense.

CONCLUSION

A number of conclusions can be drawn from the analysis just presented, but perhaps the most important and most obvious is that the relation of second-generation immigrants in Canada to religion and to the religions of their family heritages depends in no small way on the specific religion that is involved. Muslims, Hindus, and Buddhists showed different patterns of variation and similarity within each group based on aspects of each religion. In theoretical terms, these three religions in Canada (and also globally) are being constructed rather differently, one not serving as the evident model for the others. Thus, the contemporary global dominance of an "orthodox" model of what Islam is supposed to be is having a direct effect on how the second generation of Muslims in Canada is relating to that religious tradition. A great many of them have adopted the model and judge themselves in terms of it. By contrast, Hindus and Buddhists have no such dominant model upon which they can draw. Another factor is that the two religions have a different relation to that other broad category, culture, different from that of Islam and different from one another. All of our participants drew a line between religion and culture. Most recognized that religion and culture nonetheless were very much related in concrete social reality. The Muslims, however, tended to use that distinction to clarify what they meant by Islam, what was and was not a core part of Islam: unnecessary additions or accretions were deemed "culture," not religion. Hindus, on the other hand, made the distinction far less sharply and, to the extent that they did, tended to favour the "cultural" end as more important and closer to what identified them. In this case, rather than accepting that culture inevitably had an effect on how religion was practised – the Muslim pattern – religion was seen as at least an occasional, if not usually centrally important, aspect of cultural practice. It would probably be going too far to assert that a neo-Vedantic vision of Hinduism was behind this orientation, meaning that the "essence" of Hinduism does not require the elaborate edifice of devotional Hinduism but is rather located at a philosophical level. Yet the conception of Hinduism as culturally bound while still being an identifiable religion was definitely present. Buddhists, finally, largely had what one might call a "secularized lay" orientation to their religion: "real" Buddhist practice was the domain of, if not just monks and nuns, at least people who felt the need or were so inclined; for the rest, it was a kind of background resource that was always available when needed and somehow informed aspects of life practice in an indirect but still avowed way.

If these conclusions speak to the differences among the three groups, just as important is what emerged with respect to their commonalities. For all three groups, religion was something distinct, if at times hard to define precisely. Religion was also a "privatized" matter, not in the sense of being restricted to some sort of "private sphere" but rather in the sense that its role was to give the lives of individuals and groups meaning, structure, and purpose, not to impose itself on everyone as some kind of authoritative system of belief and behaviour. Almost all of our participants were not just tolerant of religious pluralism, they more often than not celebrated it. Even those who were simply tolerant had no wish to impose their religion on others. This to a large extent was reflected in the absence of politicized religion among all three groups; most went in the exact opposite direction: religion that was politicized was bad religion, if it still qualified as religion at all. On the whole, one might conclude that to the extent that these youths were representative of the second-generation immigrant populations in Canada, and to the extent that these populations represent the future directions for religion in Canada, this bodes well for the continuation of not just the ideal but also the reality of a multicultural and multi-religious society, one in which religion is nonetheless a private and optional matter, one in which religion is less a force for division and conflict and more an actual medium for the integration of diverse populations. This applies to the Muslims as well as to the two other groups: Islam for the vast majority of Muslims is not a force for setting people apart, let alone for radicalization, but rather, if these participants have anything to say about it, a way of being religiously Canadian. Whether such conclusions are in fact warranted over the longer term remains to be seen. Our research needs to be repeated as these generations reach mature adulthood; we need to keep an eye on changing patterns of subsequent migration, and the research needs to be expanded to include other religious and cultural groups such as Sikhs and Christians, the missing groups of significant importance in the Canadian religious and immigrant landscape (this, as noted, our group of researchers is currently doing). Only on that ongoing and wider basis will we be able to know what present trends actually exist and which of them will continue.

There is, finally, before we move on to a more detailed analysis of the six main subgroups, the question of how the Canadian situation compares to that in other Western countries that have experienced significant immigration and religious diversification in the post–World War II period. As noted at the outset, this sort of comparison must be done with caution, because the patterns of immigration as well as the ways of understanding and responding to immigration in these countries are often quite different. In certain respects, the Canadian situation might be most comparable to that in the United States and Australia, the other major historically European settler societies. Although migrants to the United States who are Muslim, Buddhist, or Hindu share most of the characteristics of their counterparts in Canada, the patterns of incorporation in the two countries are in many senses quite distinct, an impression that was shared by many of the participants in our Canadian research (see Bloemraad 2006). Something comparable can be said for Australia (cf. Bouma 2007). As for Western European countries, the composition and socio-economic class of migrants has been quite different, as has the political and cultural receptivity to them. In that context, it is therefore likely that there will be similarities and differences across these countries as concerns the central question posed here – namely, how the second generation of migrants is relating to the religions of their heritages. We postpone a more extended discussion of this question to the final chapter (13), but the little research that has thus far been done – mostly on European Muslims (see, e.g., Khosrokhavar 1997; Vertovec and Rogers 1998) – shows precisely that the Canadian case is similar in some senses to those elsewhere but also sufficiently different that possible generalizations are few and the need for comparative research high (cf. Kurien 2007, especially chapter 10). The reconstructions of religion in the contemporary global context depend not only on which religion one is discussing (if any particular religion at all) but on the particular circumstance. The Canadian case illustrates the idea that general, global, or universal models in today's global society cannot be properly understood except as glocalizations, as also dependent on local context.

With all that said, the next six chapters take these summary discussions as starting points, delving into all aspects in greater detail and introducing a number of additional discussions. In this regard, the following chapters also shift the dominant theoretical focus from that of the religious system and the three different religions to an emphasis on the lived religion approach, how all these matters and others actually operate in the individual lives of our participants.

From Atheism to Open Religiosity:
Muslim Men

PETER BEYER

It is by now almost a truism in the study of religion, and so in the study of the religion of migrant populations, that gender makes a significant difference, that the religious orientations, lives, and profiles of men and women diverge. So much is this the case that, as already discussed, the current research project was structured in anticipation that gender would be a primary variable. Thus, the following six chapters are divided according to gender, and a separate chapter (11) looks specifically at the gender variable across the three religious-identity groups. That acknowledged, it is perhaps just a little bit surprising that, looking specifically at the 93 Muslims in our sample, there were some broad differences between the men and the women as concerns our central questions but these differences were somewhat muted, the commonalities between them standing out more than the differences. Where the differences were stark, by contrast, is between all the Muslims and the Hindu and Buddhist portions of our sample. More specifically, the ways in which men and women from Muslim families related to the religion of their heritage, the way that they were going about reconstructing Islam for themselves was, in most senses, very similar, including the role of gender and sexuality in that religion. In that light, most of what we relate in the next two chapters about the Muslim women also applies to the Muslim men. Where there were differences, of course, they will also be highlighted and discussed.

We begin with a demographic profile of the Muslim males and then look in greater detail than in chapter 4 at their distribution across the 10-point scale of involvement. That section examines what the Muslim males had in common and how the scaling allows one to appreciate the areas of significant difference across the sample. The final section focuses on particular individuals who were representative of the broader categories, again allowing one to get a more con-crete appreciation of what these categories reflect at the individual level, at the level of "lived religion."

A DEMOGRAPHIC PROFILE OF 35 MUSLIM MEN

In Canada at the time of the 2001 census, almost 84% of Muslim males born in Canada and between the ages of 21 and 30 had some form of post-secondary schooling (Beyer 2005c; Corak 2008). It is from this large segment of the Muslim population that our sample of 35 Muslim males was drawn (see the discussion in chapter 3). All of them were at the time of their interviews either enrolled in university or had already graduated.

In age, they ranged from 18 to 27, with an average age of 21.4 years. Only 5 of them were 25 or older, whereas 11 of them were under 20. As such, they were on average a very young group. This feature of the sample is also reflective of the overall population in the sense that the vast majority of the second generation of Muslim immigrants in 2001 were still quite young: 86% of them were still under the age of 20, and 96.5% were under the age of 30. Even among the overall Muslim population, which includes the 1.5 and second generations of our sample, 45.3% were under the age of 25 (Statistics Canada 2003b; 2004). As a reflection of their young age, the Muslim male participants, for the most part, had not settled into a definitive adult identity, including quite possibly as concerns religion. None of them was married (2 of the Muslim women were), and relatively few had full-time jobs or were already actively engaged in pursuing careers.

Our selection criteria included that participants had to have been born in Canada or had arrived when they were younger than 11 years old. For the sake of recruitment, we were a bit flexible on this last criterion, and therefore the sample includes a couple of men who were 11 when they arrived and a couple whose families went first to the United States and then later to Canada. Our reasoning was that the latter had nonetheless grown up in North America and that the difference between 10 and 11 was probably not significant. Accordingly, the sample of 35 consisted of 15 males born in Canada and 20 whom we counted as belonging to the 1.5 generation. As anticipated, there was no detectable difference between the two subgroups, especially as concerns their relationship to Islam.

Like the Muslim women, the men and/or their families had their origins in a wide variety of countries around the world. The vast majority came from Muslim majority countries, especially the countries of North Africa and the Middle East (12) or Pakistan and Bangladesh (13). One gave India as his country of origin, 5 Iran, 1 Guyana, 2 East Africa, 1 Somalia, and 1 Sri Lanka. The only country-of-origin subgroup that was different from the others was the 5 whose families came from Iran. As with the 6 Muslim women with the same origin, these 5 were uniformly very little involved with religion, and 4 out of 5 were expressly non-religious, even anti-religious. In spite of the fact that a few participants averred that South Asian Muslims were on average more "extreme" in their Islam than, for instance, those from North Africa and the Middle East, this sample of 35 men did not show any pattern in this regard.

Again, as with the Muslim women, while the clear majority of the men were Sunni or from Sunni families, a significant portion were one variety or another of Shi'a. Twenty-one were Sunni, 10 were 12er Shi'a[1] (including the 5 Iranians and 1 Sunni who had converted to 12er Shi'ism), 2 were Ismaili, 1 Ahmadi, and 1 came from a mixed Shi'a/Sunni family.[2] None indicated that they or anyone in their immediate families was an adept of Sufi forms of Islam. Again with the exception of the Iranians, the subdivision of Islam was not a reliable predictor of religious involvement, understanding of Islam, or importance of religion in the lives of individuals.

In sum, then, as concerns these cultural and demographic characteristics, the 35 men were very similar to the 58 Muslim women, and the only one of these factors that proved to be in any consistent way relevant was country of origin and then only as concerns Iran. Thus, with the exception of Iran, we can for the most part abstract from variables like age, generational status, type of Islam, and country of origin. They did not show themselves to be in any sense relevant except, of course, in the context of the individual stories.

CLASSIFYING THE MUSLIM MALES

To repeat what was said in earlier chapters, the function of the overall classification schemes for each religion is as heuristic devices that give points of reference for comparing the different individuals to one another. The various categories within them are also not ideal types in a Weberian sense but rather descriptive labels of convenience, the sole purpose of which is to assist in the comparison. In the case of the Muslims, the 10-point classification scheme running from non-believers/express atheists to the most sectarian and highly practising should, on the one hand, be seen as a kind of continuum of involvement from low to high and, on the other, as a rough grouping into the non-involved, the somewhat to moderately involved, and the highly involved, with gradients according to certain criteria within each of these broader categories. The 10-point gradient also allows different ways of dividing the group into low, medium, and high. In addition, the classification scheme was not theoretically derived but rather emerged from the analysis of the data of the interviews. Others doing the analysis might well have come up with a different and potentially just as valid scheme. Its justification is in how and what it helps us to see, not because there would have been no other way of seeing.

Figure 5.1 depicts how the 35 Muslim men fell along the 10-point scale, comparing them with the Muslim women. The comparison with the Muslim women shows both differences and similarities. Regarding differences, proportionately more men than women were in one of the three non-religious categories: 31% of the men compared to 17% of the women. Correspondingly, more women than men were in the somewhat to moderately involved middle three categories: 26% of the men compared to 33% of the women. On the high end of the scale, categories 7 to 10 included 43% of the men and 50% of the women. If we group the categories somewhat differently, into lower (1–5) and higher (6–10), the distinction being the presence or absence of self-described

Figure 5.1   10-point classification distribution of Muslim participants, men (35) and women (58)

In numbers

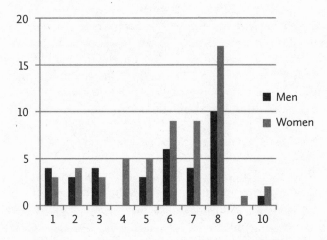

In percentages

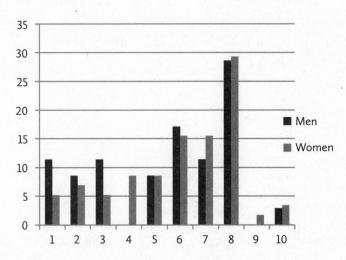

regular practice, then the outcome is again similar, slightly in favour of the women. With this grouping, 60% of the men but 65% of the women engaged in regular Islamic religious practice.[3] On the whole, then, the data appear to be consistent with the common conclusion that women are somewhat more religiously involved than men. In this case, however, what is particularly significant is the greater polarity among the men between the non-religious and the highly involved and the very high percentages of both sexes that are significantly or highly involved, from half to two-thirds of the sample depending on how one groups them. On the higher end of the scale, the difference between men and women is not that large. As noted in earlier chapters but worth repeating here, the nature of the participant recruitment process would favour people who cared about religion and therefore were more likely to be involved in religion, but given that this process was not different for the Buddhists and the Hindus in the overall sample, the high proportion among the Muslims of the highly involved in all likelihood means that, on average, young Muslim adults in Canada are more religious by their own standards (and those of most others in society) than those of the other two religious identities.[4]

Non-Muslims and Non-religious Muslims

We distinguished the three non-religious categories (1–3) for Muslims on the basis of whether or not the person identified as a Muslim and on whether or not they displayed interest or openness to, broadly speaking, "spiritual" questions such as the existence of a transcendent reality, the search for universal meaning in life, and the possibility of continued existence after death. Thus, category 1 was for those who denied Muslim identity and had no professed spiritual interest; 3 Muslim men fell in this group. Category 2, with 4 of the men, was for those who denied Muslim identity but did profess spiritual interest in some way. Together, categories 1 and 2 consisted of those with Muslim background but who did not consider themselves Muslim. Of note is that none of the 7 men in these categories professed another religion. They were all non-religious and non-Muslim by their own declaration. Category 3, with another 3, was for those who declared themselves to be non-religious but maintained a Muslim identity and showed interest in spiritual matters. What unified them was that essentially they neither professed Islamic belief nor engaged in anything that they considered Islamic practice.

Since the non-religious Muslim males constituted a significant portion (as noted, around 30%) of the sample, it is important to understand what conditions and factors are behind this non-involvement and even lack of interest. After all, if, just for the sake of argument, we were to extrapolate this figure to the entire Canadian Muslim male population, this would mean that roughly 100,000 of Canada's Muslim men are non-religious Muslims.[5] Just as many wonder what the conditions and factors involved in young Muslim male "radicalization" in Western countries are (see Al-Lami 2009), in terms of sheer numbers it may be just, as if not more, important to understand what leads in exactly the opposite direction.

Among the factors that were apparent from the interviews with the 11 Muslim males in these low-involvement categories, two stand out. First, there were those who did not have a religious upbringing and who more or less carried forth the non-religiousness or the weak religiousness of their parents.[6] Second, there were those who, although they received religious socialization as children, never showed much interest in or attraction to religion and increasingly rejected it as they went through adolescence and into adulthood. Only one of the latter was ever highly practising after about the age of 8 and then only for a couple of years in his mid-teens. For most, Islam as religion never "took," even if their families often tried to greater or lesser degrees to instill the faith in them. As Osman, one participant, put it during the interview, "my mom would always try to make me pray five times and ... observe all the practices and stuff. I guess that is one of the things that turned me off about religion. There was too much" (MM01). Another, Masoud, simply remembers religious practice as boring and pointless: "I remember it vividly because it was – quite frankly, and I don't mean any disrespect – it was a very boring time for me ... I could understand what was being said, but I didn't understand the significance of it ... I didn't understand why these words are making people react in a certain way" (MM26).

Seven, or a majority, of the 11 grew up in households where religion was important at least until they reached puberty and often thereafter. Several of them hid their rejection of Islam from their parents, while in the case of those who did not hide it, their parents were deeply disappointed in the outcome. The other 4 experienced an effectively non-religious upbringing, or their families drifted away from religious involvement when the children were at an earlier age. Of the 11 in these non-religious categories, there appeared to be no correlation between the socialization and whether one retained Muslim identity or whether one was spiritual or not. Participants in categories 1, 2, and 3 were equally likely to have grown up with religious socialization as not. Although research tends to show that a person is significantly more likely to be a religiously practising adult if he or she grew up in a religiously practising household than if brought up in a household where religion and religious practice were not that important (see, e.g., Bibby 1993; 2002), as these results show, religious socialization in no way consistently yields this result. For a good number of people, it seems, including these young adults from Muslim families, religion is just not that attractive; unless they live in an environment with significant social pressure to appear religious, they are likely to drift away or reject religious involvement. In tune with Max Weber, one could count them among the religiously "tone-deaf."

Since 4 of the 11 non-religious participants were from Iranian families (the fifth Iranian male was classified as 5), it is well to look at whether there was some internal consistency in this group that might point to their clear difference. The immediate suspicion, of course, is that direct or indirect (through their parents) experience of the Islamic Republic with its often authoritarian

and so-called theocratic government might have led them to reject Islam or religion for themselves. One commonality in support of this proposition is that
all four of the Iranian non-religious men considered themselves to be open to
spiritual questions, even though two of them did not identify as Muslims and
the other two were not religiously practising. All four were in categories 2 or
3, none in category 1. In terms of socialization, the father of one of them was
a communist, a member of the Tudeh party in Iran; religion never played an
important role in this family or in the life of its children. Two of the other 3
grew up in families where religious practice was regular in childhood, but the
children and the parents drifted away from it later on, especially after they
came to Canada. The fourth grew up in a religious household, even went to
elementary school in Iran, but had rejected Islam and did not have fond memories of his religious upbringing. Moreover, all four of the families left Iran
for political reasons; they did not like or were in trouble with the regime. A
possible way of understanding this combination is to assume that people who
left Iran after the revolution were generally those for whom either religion
or Islam as understood by the regime and its supporters was never entirely
central and they disliked having it imposed on them. As one of the Iranian
women in our sample put this idea, "Iranians don't seem to be extreme people
in terms of religion. I mean, sure, there are some, but they're not the ones that
leave the country; they tend to like where they are" (MF34). An idea like this
would make sense of the fact that not only were the 5 Muslim males of Iranian
origin either non-religious or only somewhat religious (no higher than category 5, which includes occasional religious practice and basic beliefs), so were
the 6 women, without exception. None of the latter grew up in households that
were religious or where the parents placed high importance on their children
practising Islam, and all of them also left Iran for political reasons. Again, our
sample is not representative, and what it is most likely to miss is examples of
people who represent a tiny minority in the corresponding population, devoutly religious Iranians from devoutly religious families.

From Minimal to Regular Involvement: Categories 5 and 6

From one perspective, it may seem that relatively few Muslim men fell into the
middle three categories, a total of only 9 out of 35. That we classified them all
as either 5 or 6 – that is, in the higher gradients of the middle range – might
also be taken as evidence of a rough polarization in the sample between the
non-involved and the highly involved, given that the difference in our scheme
between moderate and highly involved, between the 6s and 7s, is that the latter
considered Islam to be at the very centre of their lives whereas the former did
not. Both groups engaged in quite regular practice and therefore could, from
that perspective, be labelled as highly involved. Then, as Figure 5.1 shows, all

but three of the Muslim male participants would be either a non-believer or a devout Muslim; only 3 of 35 would be of the sort that identify as a Muslim but practise only rarely or occasionally, the equivalent of Easter and Christmas or major-rites-of-passage Christians. This impression, however, would be incorrect, because the Muslim males who we decided belonged in categories 5 and 6 were in fact a much more clearly defined group, really quite different from either the non-religious or the highly religious and showing a correspondingly different way of relating to religion and Islam. Put in terms of the lived religion approach, these in-between Muslims did not fit that easily on the non-religious to highly involved continuum, or at least what was religiously specific about them was not captured by their position on this scale.

All the categories were, of course, to some degree judgment calls on the part of those of us who analyzed the interviews. Sometimes participants could have been put either in the category to which we assigned them or in one of the neighbouring ones: people are usually complex and not easily pigeonholed. In the case of the middle-range Muslim males, that was even more the case than it generally was across the sample. Specifically, all three of those whom we classified as 5 – people with solid Muslim identity who shared core beliefs and practised occasionally but not regularly – could also have been classified as 4 – minimal belief and practice – depending on how one judged the degree of their belief and practice and also their "orthodoxy" when compared to the highly involved, who consistently followed that global five-pillars-orthodoxy model of Islam so widespread today. As an example, Khalid was raised in a highly religious household in Calgary and felt firm in his basic Islamic beliefs; he tried to pray regularly and felt that one should observe Muslim dietary and behavioural norms. Yet his level of involvement at the time of the interview was quite low, because he lived in Ottawa, away from his parental household; he felt that he shouldn't eat pork but at the same time stated that "on pizza, honestly, I need some pepperoni ..." (MM22); he knew his parents wanted him to marry an Egyptian Muslim, but unbeknownst to them, his current girlfriend was a non-Muslim, and he did not think that the religion of his eventual spouse was all that important. Moreover, when asked about eventual children, he said that he would want to raise them as Muslims as he had been, but that if it came right down to it, they could choose to convert to another religion or have no religion at all: "say my children would want to convert or something like that. I wouldn't be for it, but at the same time I would be, 'do as you wish'" (MM22). This sense of flexibility, of other criteria and circumstances often taking precedence over what they recognized as the Islamic way of conducting one's life, was common to all those in the middle categories.

The 6 Muslim men of category 6 were somewhat varied but showed analogous features. Three of them were at the time of the interviews regularly practising but also stated that their involvement had been and was decreasing, that they weren't as observant as in the past. Like the Muslim of an Iranian family who was judged to represent category 5 and who felt attracted to aspects of Zoroastrianism, the ancient Persian religious tradition, two of those in category 6 either felt attraction to another religion – Roman Catholic Christianity in one case – or had family members who had in fact converted to Judaism or Christianity. They were not as religiously single or exclusive as most others. Moreover, all of those in this category, when they expressed an opinion, were more "liberal" in their socio-moral attitudes, including not only regarding dietary regulations such as prohibition of pork and alcohol but also on sexual questions such as intimate relations before marriage or homosexuality. What also characterized them, however, was that they considered Islam both important in their personal lives – even when they also thought that their actual behaviour did not always reflect this fact – and that it had a great deal to offer the world. As an example of the latter, two of these men believed that, ideally, Islam could form the basis of very good government but that reaching this ideal was difficult. Referring to the Islamic Republic of Iran, Rashad said that "Iran actually is a really funny case where, you know, if you take away the Ayatollah, it's a perfectly democratic country" (MM21). Farouk averred that he partially agreed with those who said that "Islamic law is the perfect form of government" but qualified this by adding that "at the same time, you can try to institute Islamic law, but once someone is in power inevitably that person will become corrupt." Typically for this group, Farouk also added that although Islam could provide guidelines for laws, it also enjoined "that you have to move with the times or you have to make laws that are contemporary to what's happening" (MM12).

A further way of understanding the contrast between the Muslim men in category 6 especially and those in the higher or lower categories is to look more closely at this combination of the importance of Islam with flexibility or malleability of interpretation. Clearly, what separates the 9 men in categories 5 and 6 from those in 1 to 3 is that Islam for the former, in belief and practice, was important even though they might not engage in that much regular practice. What separates them from the high involvement categories is that they did not treat Islam as a systematic and complete package that could be understood in terms of a clear and largely unequivocal set of rules, virtues, obligations, and orientations. In theoretical terms, their systemic Islam was not as self-referentially complete. Or at least, to the extent that they did understand Islam that way, they took more of an à la carte attitude, picking and choosing what they believed to be proper and important while ignoring the rest. To illustrate, Bilal, after stating that Islam was very important in his life, also related how he started questioning Islam when he was about 15 years old. This did not mean questioning in the sense of doubting but rather questioning in the sense of verifying for himself and, critically, as he stated, "determining what I want to do" (MM19). The centre of religious construction, as it were, was in himself as an individual, and thus, in lived religion style, the important goal was to reconcile Islam with his own basic value orientations. As he put it,

> I started researching, and that gave me hope that perhaps there are alternative views that fit with my understanding. But I was also conscious [of] not just trying to make everything fit into my view just so I could be Muslim. I think I was as honest as I could be about the material that I found, that if at the end it didn't fit with my beliefs, then I would have to leave it or at least leave parts of it alone. (MM19)

In a similar vein, Taha, who stated that his Islam was starting to "fade away," claimed that although he would like to learn more about his religion, he couldn't believe everything that was told him, including whether "the Prophet Muhammad exists ... People could have just made that up" (MM07). Farouk, who considered himself a Muslim and religious "because religion is what I use to determine morals and values and what is right and wrong" (MM12), also felt attracted to aspects of Roman Catholicism, sometimes attended mass with his friends, and even went to Catholic World Youth Day in Germany, but not to the extent of considering conversion. He stated at one point, "Catholicism is always talking about the love of God; Islam it's always putting fear into ... your head ... So I am kind of stuck in between what [the imams] say and what Catholicism would say about the eternal love of God" (MM12). Clearly, religious exclusivity was not that important a criterion in his way of thinking.

What becomes particularly evident from many of these interviews is that many of the Muslim men were clear about what they thought and felt at the time of the interview but also considered themselves to be in a state of transition, the endpoint of which was usually uncertain. This was the case for quite a few of the 35 participants, irrespective of how practising or religious they were. With the category 5 and 6 participants, however, this transitional quality was not only more consistently evident, it was also part of a more general fluidity in the way they related to Islam. Many of them were uncertain but also open to being convinced, to a more Islamic future, as well as to a possibly greater distancing from Islam.

The category 5/6, together with the non-religious participants in categories 1 to 3, constituted almost 60% of the Muslim male sample, 20 out of 35. In comparison to the 15 highly involved men, to whom we shall turn in the next section, they can be considered the less religious in the conventional, institutional, and systemic sense. Given the nature of the recruitment process that we used, it could also be argued that they were under-represented in the sample in comparison to the total Muslim male population from which they self-selected. This leads us to conclude that the non-religious-to-somewhat-to-moderately-involved might well constitute the clear, but not overwhelming, majority of the

Canadian population of Muslim men in these age and generational categories, 1.5 and second generation in early adulthood. In all likelihood, however, they will have less influence on the future of Islam in Canada than their highly involved co-religionists. It is the highly involved in this demographic who will probably be the carriers of this future, and it is to them that we now turn.

Islam as Central to Life: Categories 7 to 10

Like the other classification groups, the men of the four highly involved categories displayed both an internal continuum and individual and qualitative differences among themselves. What centrally distinguishes them is that they considered Islam not only important but central, as the axis around which their lives were organized and in terms of which they took their meaning. One could say that systemic Islam and lived religion (Islam) overlapped to a high degree with these participants. All the participants in this group believed and practised regularly along the five-pillars model already discussed above and in previous chapters. This included above all praying regularly every day, usually trying to do so at the five (sometimes three) prescribed times or more often, and attending Friday communal prayers at a mosque. A further consistency was fasting during Ramadan along with the core dietary restrictions of avoiding pork and alcohol. *Zakat* and *hajj* were intentions limited by their stage in life and the fact that few of them had much of an income, since they were mostly full-time university students. Their profession of faith comprised principally the *shahadah*, other variously described core belief items, including above all the centrality and truth of the Qur'an and the Sunna or Traditions of the Prophet Muhammad. Their moral code included refraining from sexual activity outside marriage and dating before marriage, disapproval of homosexuality, insistence on marrying either a Muslim woman or one from a religion of the book (which men could do but not women), and determination to raise their eventual children as Muslims. Azim, who stated that Islam was "the most important thing in my life" and who defined religion as "a set of laws in order to live your life," put what he thought were the principal teachings of Islam like this:

> The main thing is believing in one God and not ... having any other God ... mixed in with it. Believing in all the messengers that he sent in order to pass down the message. Just keeping good moral character ... Fasting and prayer are all mentioned [in the Qur'an and] are important [and] will make you more righteous and better, but it's things to help you to stick to the one pillar of Islam, which is to believe in one God. (MM27)

Zohair put it much more simply: "if someone was to ask me ... about Islam then I would tell them about ... the five pillars and ... the six articles of faith" (MM20). In terms of the main sources of authority, of what to believe and what to do in Islam, those who expressed an opinion were unanimous that the Qur'an was central, followed immediately by the Traditions of the Prophet and, for 12er Shi'is, prominent scholars of this tradition. For many, trusted family members and websites were important intermediaries for helping to interpret these sources but rarely local leaders such as the imam at a mosque. As Abdul put it, "most of my religious knowledge comes from my dad ... When I got older, I did a lot of it on my own, like I read on the Internet, I read books and stuff like that, but my basis comes from my dad" (MM28).

This last quote points to a strong commonality among those in categories 7 to 10. Without exception, the 15 Muslim men in these highly involved categories grew up in households where Islam was important; they received a religious upbringing, or their parents presented devout models for them. Although in some cases the participants said that they were somewhat more observant than their parents, at least one of the parents in each case was still highly observant. None grew up in the sort of non-religious environment that some of the non-religious participants experienced in their childhood or had what two or three of the moderately involved described as "liberal" parents. If this sample of 35 men were to be seen as representative, they support the idea that, with minor and inevitable exceptions, religious socialization may be a necessary but not sufficient condition for religious offspring, at least among immigrant Muslims in Canada.

Again, these features are defining for these categories because they emerged from the data: so many of the participants displayed this combination of features that they clearly constituted a distinct grouping. What distinguishes the categories internally is that the 7s professed these beliefs, engaged in most of the ritual, but fell short on actual behaviour according to the moral norms. The 8s claimed to observe all aspects in their own lives. What distinguished these two categories from the highest two was that the former were fully involved in society, including above all regarding their circle of friends, which was almost always mixed: Muslims and male friends along with non-Muslim and often female friends. Although Islam was their self-professed complete way of life, in only one or two cases did the interviewee claim that it determined all aspects, such as, for instance, their voting behaviour or their choice of career. Although none of the men ended up in category 9, two came close; its distinguishing feature was that, in addition to all the characteristics found among the 8s, a 9 would opt for a sectarian lifestyle, including deliberately limiting his social circle to Muslims. The one person in category 10 went one step further by also avoiding as much as possible contact with women outside the close family, including at school, at work, and in everyday life, and by leading a consciously sectarian lifestyle in excess of that of category 9. This would include political and professional orientation.

These highest categories show the extent to which some participants might seek to express the centrality of Islam in their lives; they show the extremes of involvement and dedication. The main analytic reason for creating these categories, however, was to help bracket and define the single most common category, the number 8s, who constituted something of a dominant model for the highly involved young Muslim adults of this research. As Figure 5.1 above shows graphically, while the minority of participants (both men and women in this case) followed and sought to embody what was meant with category 8, they were by far the single largest category and in that sense presented a kind of standard, even more so if one adds the number 7s, who espoused the standard without necessarily claiming to embody it in all the key aspects. There was somewhat of a continuous and gradual numerical build-up to this category (more clearly among the Muslim women) and then a sudden drop thereafter. Beyond the 8s, there were only tiny minorities, and they would exhibit the sort of radicalized political Islamist stance that some observers in current debates worry might be spreading among the second-generation Muslim youth[7] but which, as it turns out, none of our participants actually revealed. The 9s and 10s were not political Islamists. That said, because the classification system was generated inductively, from the data, it might be that the high number of participants in category 8 is merely an artifact of that analytic process, that it shows a lack of refinement at that point in the scale more than it does a commonality in the role and character of Islam in these participants' lives. Although other researchers analyzing these data might indeed have come up with a different sort of heuristic classification, the cogency of the one we offer here lies in a set of observable characteristics that together demonstrate significant aspects of what it might mean to be a young devout Muslim in today's Canadian society. Adapting an expression that is becoming popular in French and Quebec debates about the "accommodation" of religious diversity – namely, the idea of laïcité ouverte (Bouchard and Taylor 2008) – we suggest that what the number 8 participants – and the number 7s to an extent but not the 9s and 10s – embody could be called a religiosité ouverte.

The religiosity in this phrase refers to the global five-pillars model already outlined. Among the 15 participants in categories 7 to 10, none deviated significantly from this model, although they did put emphasis on different aspects. Najib, a Canada-born 18-year-old of Pakistani origin, was very rule-oriented; practising Islam meant not doing forbidden things. He put it like this: "This world is just a test; if I do well in it, if I do everything that I'm given … then I'll go to heaven. And I try my best now, and I know everything I did wrong before, the haram that I've done, Allah will forgive me, I hope He does … So that's how I view everything, I try not to do anything wrong" (MM17). Karim, 20 years old and also Canada-born from a Pakistani family, put the emphasis on broader moral principles. He stated, "Most important teachings? As a philosopher, the one thing I can't give up is belief in God. Everything else is debatable ... If I give that up, then I fear my whole philosophical system would be nonsensical ... Most important practices: the way in which you treat other people, kindness and things like that ... Those are the primary objectives, and then secondary objectives would be praying, fasting, the rituals" (MM05).

A critical aspect of this Islam-centredness, however, what makes it an "open religiosity," is how these Muslims saw themselves and Islam in relation to and in the context of the surrounding society. Relevant aspects of this situatedness are the attitudes to other religions, which is to say religious diversity, to the secular nature of Canadian society, to their own place as devout Muslims in that society, and to the role of religion/Islam in political life, including in relation to militancy and the political expression of Islam in the state. Summarizing these aspects, those in category 8 accepted religious diversity and, in that context, were generally positive about the idea of Canada as a multicultural society; they accepted or had few problems with living in a secular or nominally Christian country; they participated and expected to participate fully; they wanted to be thoroughly woven into the life of that society through their studies, their careers, and their social relations, and almost uniformly rejected any direct political role for religion and Islam in Canada, although they had mixed opinions on this question in Muslim majority countries. On each of these items there were, of course, exceptions and significant variation.

A closer look at how some of the interviewees expressed this combination of strong religiousness with openness to full participation in the wider, largely secular society can put some flesh on these basic ideas. Shabib, another 20-year-old from a Pakistani family, put the combination succinctly with relation to the second generation that he represented:

I'm noticing here in the university, a lot of young Muslims, especially ... second-generation immigrants, second-generation Canadians, they're responding to the initial, I guess, ghettoization of the community by asserting their place in this society ... We have this tradition [Islam] ... this total package ... [and] what we're seeing is that this package can be applied right here, right? And part of this package is this feeling of belonging, this feeling that this is my home too. (MM02)

Implied in this statement is the idea that Islam or the Muslim identity not be restricted to a compartment of life, that, for instance, the way to be religious was to be Muslim in private while keeping that aspect hidden or bracketed in public. Abdul, a 22-year-old Shi'a man from an Indian family, put his opposition to this orientation and his acceptance of a religiously pluralistic society like this:

> The problem with Canada I find [is] that the religious aspect or the spiritual aspect ... is totally gone in our society ... You can't have a Christian government or a Muslim government because we have a multicultural society, but you shouldn't have an anti-God society either, where even mentioning God is kind of like taboo. I don't agree with that; I think we have to become more spiritual in our society. (MM28)

Hussain, a 19-year-old Shi'a participant, put it another way: "right now, personally I don't think that a lot of Canadians are religious; a lot of them don't care about religion, which I find is really sad, whether it's Christianity, Judaism, or Islam, or whatever religion, I think that more people should be ... more caring for religion" (MM06).

The explicit attitude to other religions in this society was generally accepting without thereby weakening the central status that Islam had for individuals. As an example, the same Shi'a participant replied to the question of whether some religions were better than others, saying, "No. I don't think so. They're all doing the same thing, basically." He elaborated later:

> I don't judge a person by their religion or their background, because ... if people aren't going to do that to me, I'm not going to do that to them. I have a lot of friends that are Christian, friends that are Jewish, I don't mind it ... It doesn't conflict with me. I'm talking to the person, not to the religion itself. I have nothing against the religion. I'm Muslim, I chose that religion on my own. (MM06)

Others put the same idea in somewhat different ways. Bahir and Hakim said:

> I don't know what God's plan is for [people of other religions]. Like, everyone has their own life and ... everyone's judged accordingly, right? So whether you're spiritual or not ... there are a lot of good people. You know, there are good people, being Hindu or Muslim or even within Muslims there are bad people, it's just the way they are ... like, their character alone is good ... And I can't just tell them, okay, you're going to hell. (MM23)

> You got to understand that since the last 30 or 40 years, Islam has absolutely exploded, right? Absolutely exploded. So I wouldn't say that there's one [religion] better than the other, but if it continues this way, then it's going to be the dominant religion ... so let's leave it at that. (MM16)

The issue of living this Islam in what is largely a secular, at most nominally Christian society was also understood in variable ways, but it included the idea that people were free to practise their religion as fully as they wished. These Muslim men felt that freedom of religious practice was a reality in Canada for themselves and others; the secular or non-Muslim context could nonetheless be seen as a challenge. Bahir, whose life was so centred around Islam that he might possibly have been classified as a 9 rather than just an 8, put it this way: "[In Canada] you're free to practise and do what you want to do ... It's a very good country for that, you're able to practise your own religion ... you're able to be a Muslim ... The only thing is you're also surrounded with all the other influences too, which makes it harder for a Muslim to be a Muslim" (MM23).

Hussain, the 19-year-old Shi'a, felt that in terms of religious tolerance, Canada was "perfectly fine" and averred that "right now Canada, it's basically taking care of all religions at the same time, which I think it's doing a very good job at it" (MM06). Abbud, however, a Somali Muslim, was somewhat less sanguine, stating that he could practise Islam to its fullest in Canada but "that it's tough. It takes a lot of determination, it takes a lot of energy ... You can practise your religion, but you're going to have to face a lot of hurdles and downright discrimination against you, especially if you're a woman" (MM08).

Although the general attitude toward the relation between religion and politics was to the effect that the two should be separated and there was unanimous rejection among the highly involved participants of religiously inspired violence and what many described as religious extremism, several participants held a nuanced view of the religio-political relationship. One exception even negated the general attitude in wishing that religion and politics could be united in Canada as elsewhere. He was the other participant who could have been classified as a 9 if his sectarian orientation had not been accompanied by his having a religiously and culturally quite mixed circle of friends. Najib, a recent convert to Shi'a Islam from a Sunni family, declared outright that religion and politics should be fused and even declared that "if Ayatollah [Sistani][8] was running the country, like, well, not running it, but if he was the leader of the country, he would make laws and tell everybody that this is in the Qur'an and this is how you should act upon it. So, I think that would be ideal" (MM17). Not surprisingly, this participant approved of the government of the Islamic Republic of Iran. He was not the only one, but the others who did so (none of whom were Iranians, of course) qualified their approval by stating that Iran had gone too far or was not living up to the ideal. Abdul, the 22-year-old Shi'i who thought that Canada should be more spiritual, also had this opinion about Iran:

> The thing I like about Iran, but the thing that's not done properly, is that there's two bodies, of the people and there's the religious[9]... In Iran right now, the religious overrules the people, which is not right ... In my ideal

Islamic society, there should be a democratically elected representative, but there should also be a council of learned scholars, Islamic scholars who can decide … whether or not the laws proposed by the house are in accordance with Islamic law, but they shouldn't be able to overrule them. It would be like an equal [relation], like the House and the Senate in the States. It has to pass in both houses before it can be law … In our [Canadian] society the religious is overpowered by the secular and in Iran … it's the religious [that] overpowers the secular, but it has to be a balance because you have to respect people who are following [other religions or other versions of Islam]. (MM28)

In that context, he also said that "Islam in government, if it's done correctly, I think is good, but I haven't seen it done correctly, ever." A stronger negative opinion was expressed by Hussain, the 19-year-old Shi'i quoted above. He felt that religion should have more of an influence in Canadian society but not a specific religion, and he thought that in countries like Saudi Arabia and Iran, where religion had a strong role in the political sphere, it was "people who are misinterpreting religion governing" (MM06). Beside these qualified opinions, there were also those among the highly involved who, unlike the convert to Shi'ism, were convinced that religion and politics should not mix. Abbud, the Somali Muslim already quoted, was quite unequivocal. He stated that "when religion's applied to politics, or when religion is applied with nationalism or racism, a lot of evil things happen." Elaborating, he said,

Unfortunately … even in countries where they have Muslim Islamic movements that are political, it's never good to have the dominant religion in power or influencing over minorities. It's just not. I hate to say this, it's just not. That doesn't mean you should restrict religious people from politics … But to have a religious party … aligned so much with religion is not a good thing for society, especially when you have minorities, especially when you have racial minorities that don't belong to that dominant religion. (MM08)

Of note in most of these opinions, as in the last one, and consistent with the attitudes of the great majority of the highly involved Muslims, is that their situation as highly religious people in a religiously diverse society where their religion is a minority influenced how they see this question of religious influence in any society: they could not be and were not against such influence but mostly wanted it to be non-specific, not tied to a particular religion such as their own or that of the nominally Christian majority. Their generally positive evaluation of religious diversity, or at least their acceptance of that diversity, correlated with this way of seeing religious influence. It was an important aspect of their "open religiosity."

SOME DETAILED LIVES

Although a discussion of the common threads across these interviews gives a necessary general picture, much else that is important in understanding how these Muslim men reconstructed or failed to reconstruct Islam in their personal lives remains hidden from view. One of the methodological strengths of qualitative research projects such as the one being reported here is that it allows one to see beyond general patterns and their multiple possible interpretations to the specific and concrete situations that generate them, at least to an extent. The method allows the application of a lived religion approach, which can show aspects of how religion operates in Canadian society that more institutional and generalized approaches are more likely to occlude. Here, in order to look at the data at this more individual level, we select the interviews of 6 of the 35 Muslim male participants, representing the different regions of the overall classification. These include 2 in the non-religious categories, Hasan (MM24), who is a category 1 and a non-Iranian, and Ali (MM14), a category 3 Iranian. From the moderately involved, we examine Mohammed (MM29) from category 6. And from among the highly involved, we select 1 category 7, Ahmed (MM13), and 2 category 8s, Karim (MM05) and Ibrahim (MM10).

Hasan (MM24)

Hasan is a self-declared atheist who at the time of his interview in October 2005 was 22 years old and a humanities major at the University of Toronto. His father was a well-to-do businessman in Idi Amin's Uganda when he, along with all other South Asians, was expelled from the country in 1972. His mother was born in Tanzania, also of South Asian origin but from another part of India. In Canada, both parents had average white-collar jobs, together earned a middle-class income, and lived with Hasan in a single-family house in Toronto. Both parents were devout Ismaili Muslims, followers of the Aga Khan. Hasan therefore grew up in a religiously practising household, as was the case for the majority of non-religious Muslim men in our sample.

Hasan's orientation to religion quickly became evident when he was asked to define religion. He immediately drew a distinction between religion and spirituality, declaring religion to be an institutional form of social control centred around what he called a "moral didacticism" based in the interpretation of a source "like the holy book" and involving a higher power. Spirituality, by contrast, was "more of a self-enlightenment ... like a Buddhist achieving nirvana." It was "more of an understanding of nature than [of] God." In spite of making such a clear distinction, he considered himself neither religious nor spiritual. As he put it, "pretty much anything to do with metaphysics, I would reject." This negative orientation to religion, he remembered, went back to his childhood. He never wanted to go to *jamatkhana* (Ismaili equivalent of a mosque) with his father, he resented having to go to the Ismaili equivalent of Sunday school, and he devised a variety of strategies to avoid these experiences when possible. More critically, however, he could never accept what he was being taught religiously: "[It was] just a lot of things that would ... be said. Like ... you know, what God would want you to do, like it's just ridiculous, it just seemed utterly, utterly ridiculous."

As an adolescent, Hasan reached a point where he refused to continue. He tells a poignant story of the night he insisted his father let him leave an import- ant religious celebration at the *khana* early: "as he [his father] was driving me home, he was doing his absolute best ... I think very few people could have done it better, but he made his best attempt to get me to go back, to be an Is- maili, everything that he wanted, and I did not go back. And that was the first time I actually saw my dad cry." Hasan's mother hoped that one day he would return to his faith, but he insisted that "I don't think I ever will. I'm certain I will never, ever be religious again ... I will never ever again have any kind of faith in a higher being."

Hasan also did not have a strong cultural identity, although he by no means rejected his family's cultural roots. The closest thing he had to an alternative community was his circle of mostly white and like-minded friends. He real- ized that he was part of the "visible minority" population and recognized that a certain amount of prejudice existed in Canada against people who were not part of the majority, but his experience was greatly attenuated by living all his life in the Greater Toronto Area: "in Toronto ... you have to accept other cultures. You can't be an explicit racist in Toronto" (see the fuller discussion in chapter 12). He was optimistic that with time, such prejudice as existed would disappear as his environment became more and more multicultural. Even though he was himself not religious, he had nothing against religion and did not think it was a particularly outstanding source of problems and conflict, just as it was not necessary in order to be a good person.

In sum, Hasan was a person who was raised in a family where Islam, where religion, was important, but he had never found any resonance with it. Like a few others in his category, and almost all those in category 1 especially, it was not a question of falling off from religious faith and involvement; he was never in a place from which he could fall. Hasan's experience and orientation is un- doubtedly not peculiar to people from immigrant, let alone Muslim, families. He did not so much reject Islam as what he understood as religion/spirituality: either as moral code, ritual practice, felt community, and system of belief or as anything like a "spiritual quest." Although from the perspective of the recon- struction of Islam in the Canadian context he was unlikely to make much of a contribution because he had excluded the material with which to do that from his personal lived reality, he did appear to represent a significant minority of young men from Muslim families in Canada. In that regard, he also presented somewhat of a contrast to others in the non-religious categories, those who, while not considering themselves religious or sometimes even Muslims, were more open to matters deemed spiritual in their lives. Ali was one such person.

Ali (MM14)

Ali came from an Iranian Shi'a family that left Iran in the years after the Islamic revolution of 1979. He arrived in Canada at the age of 1 and therefore is for all intents and purposes a member of the second generation. In 2005, at the time of the interview, he was 21 years old and completing a natural sciences undergraduate degree at the University of Ottawa, although he had grown up in Toronto and most of his experience of Canada was in that city. Both his parents came from upper-class Iranian families that were very well connected in Iran both before and after the revolution. Both sides of the family were in general quite religious, but neither of his parents was religious in any conventional Islamic sense; his father was a declared atheist and communist,[10] and his mother was a self-professed rebel with a spiritual bent whom Ali likened to James Dean's character in the 1950s film *Rebel without a Cause*. His mother and father had been separated for many years but cooperated in running a business out of Tehran, where his mother lived, and Toronto, where his father lived. Ali visited Iran and his extended family with some regularity. He and his family had strong transnational connections.

In this context, Ali was not in any sense raised in a religious household and even declared himself to have been "indoctrinated against [Islam] like any other religion." When asked, he stated that he was "not very religious," but this had little to do with being disillusioned by the theocratic and authoritarian role of Islam in Iran. As he put it,

> I think for someone in my position … I don't not like Islam because it
> was forced upon me. I don't like Islam because I don't relate to it much
> and because I've been indoctrinated just the same against it like any
> other religion. I mean, most people, you say Islam, they think funda-
> mentalism, they think Al-Qaeda. So … if I'm not obliged to be that reli-
> gion by my family, why would I associate myself to that? That's more the
> reason I would reject Islam than what's going on back home [in Iran].

Accordingly, Ali had never been a practising Muslim and observed none of the rituals or personal behaviour typical of the more highly practising men in the sample. Yet even if he did not consider himself religious, he declared himself to be spiritual. His lived religious life did not observe the boundaries of constructed religions, and he was therefore not specific or exclusive in his identifications. As he put it, "to me religion is spirituality, there is something there, and I'm not sure what there is … I do believe in a higher being, but I shy away from admitting it." In this light, he had throughout his young life dabbled in various religious/spiritual directions and professed to having frequent extraordinary experiences of a quasi-mystical nature, such as having dreams that then came true, going into a trance-like state in St Peter's Basilica, or using a ouija board and accurately predicting a future event with it. In one exchange with the interviewer, he described his spiritual journey like this:

> INTERVIEWER: So you've gone from a little bit of Islam, Catholicism, Native religions …
> ALI: And the list goes on … Sufism, somewhat meditation, somewhat just spirituality, somewhat just a science background even. And I've blended this all together to get a big question mark. That's where I stand now.

Like Hasan, Ali did not think religion was in any sense necessary, considering it more a source of division and conflict. With regard to religion's supposed role in making people good, he stated that

> I don't believe that religion gives you a good heart. I think that's humanity. I think people use the fact of religion or apply religion as a label to it in order to maybe advertise for the religion. But I think it's nothing less than human to want to help each other and be a Mother Teresa … My view is, you don't need religion as a moral code. A moral code is almost biological … I mean, my dog knows when he does something right, when something's wrong, it's a very biological thing, he doesn't have a religion.

One of the consistencies among the 35 Muslim men was that religiousness did not correlate with how much a person approved or was critical of Canadian society and with the extent to which they felt comfortable and accepted in that society. Ali illustrated this lack of correlation well. He was in many senses a very secular person, but he was also fairly critical of aspects of Canadian society. With regard to multiculturalism as policy and reality, he was one of those who felt that multicultural policy was either an exercise in Canadian self-deception or simply subtle racism. In tune with John Porter's thesis from the 1960s that Canada managed its cultural diversity through the establishment of a vertical mosaic (Porter 1965), he felt that "Canada likes to play the multiculturalism card a lot, but, I mean, look at the classes in Canada: whites on top." To an extent, this opinion was a reflection of the discrimination that he felt he and his father had experienced, his father because of "his accent and his name," he himself because he wasn't white.

In spite of these doubts, Ali did not seem to have felt particularly out of place or marginalized in Canada and certainly had no desire to live somewhere else such as his native Iran, where he said that the younger generation was becoming a lost generation without a future. He was confident about the future and ambitious in his goals and prospects. Most of his circle of friends was white or Iranian (largely his relatives), and he experienced no prejudice from them. He considered himself to be "both Canadian and Iranian" but Iranian first from a cultural perspective. His pride in Iranian culture and history was as strong as his inability to relate to Islam or religion. He was not so much "caught between two worlds" as someone who was secure in his cultural identity as Iranian living in Canada.

Ali's story makes for intriguing reading; he was clearly a complex personality with a complex family history. His profile helps to demonstrate that even among participants who were clearly not religious, there was a fair amount of variation in the way the men of Muslim background related to Islam and to the society in which they lived. That said, no more than Hasan was Ali and those like him likely to be among those who contribute meaningfully to the construction of Islam in Canada or in the world. In this regard, Ali did, however, have an opinion about those in his generation who were more involved in Islam than he was. He felt that even among the religiously involved, the Canadian environment militated against the maintenance of a strict and traditionalist Islam, and, perhaps remarkably, he found this depressing. In spite of rejecting Islam for himself, he nevertheless felt that it had value and that compromising it for the sake of fitting into Canadian and Western society would be a tragic outcome. To illustrate his perspective, he referred to the commonly observed phenomenon in Canadian cities of young Muslim women who combine hijab on the head with more "fashionable" clothing on the body. What he said when asked whether he thought the Muslim second generation of which he was formally a part would fall away from their religious heritage is worth quoting at some length:

> I think they're already starting. I think … most second-generation Islamic people I have seen in Canada are very hypocritical. They'll wear the veil, but then they'll wear the tightest clothing you've ever seen. I mean, if … you're … going to wear revealing clothing and then a veil, that's just hypocritical. I think that's the kind of internal conflict many people run into. Essentially [it's] "I want to fit into society," and [in this society] sexuality is what is considered a plus, you know, being beautiful and blah, blah, blah. Whereas my original culture is one where women should be judged based on her mind and her personality rather than her appearance … I've seen the conflict many times. My cousins who came from Iran when they were 8 or 10 … went to public schools … and they

were ostracized for wearing the veil ... They still believe in Islam and
everything, but they don't wear the veil, and they've loosened up a lot
and very much become Westernized in order to fit in and to be able to
make friends ... [Islam and Western ways are] two completely different
ideologies, and when you try to merge them, it just doesn't work. And
if you try, you're going to have to really make some severe compromises
... Historically, Islam was the religion of the people because it was such
an easy religion, it was fair to everyone. Relatively. And if you look at the
West, it's selling another dream, you know, the American dream they
sell us. Forget who you are, join who we are, essentially sell your soul in
order to be successful ... And I find a lot of people are coming here and
trading that off.

To what extent Ali is correct about his Muslim generation in Canada is difficult to tell from our data. Suffice it to say that the larger number of our participants disagreed.

Mohammed (MM29)

In certain senses, Mohammed presented a kind of mirror image to Ali: he also
considered himself more spiritual than Muslim but pursued his spirituality in
what he regarded as a very Muslim way, and his attitude to living in the Greater
Toronto Area was much more positive. Where Ali saw a hypocritical and
somewhat racist society that peddled a shallow and delusory dream, Mohammed saw something closer to the opposite, although not uncritically. We classified Mohammed in category 6, because he was more than occasional in his
practice and took Islam rather seriously, even though, as for all the middle
three categories, it did not constitute the centre of his life, nor did he practise
it along the lines of the standard, globalized five-pillars model outlined above.
Mohammed might have been exhibiting precisely the sort of "serious compromises" and hybridity that Ali thought did not work. His lived religion could
be described as both Islamic and more, as both spiritual and religious.

Mohammed was a Sunni Muslim from a Bangladeshi family; he arrived in
Canada at age 6 and was the youngest of three children. At the time of the
interview he was 19 years old, in his first year at the University of Ottawa,
pursuing a degree in international development and globalization studies.
His father was an engineer and his mother an early childhood educator. They
lived in Toronto and came to Canada expressly so that their children would
receive a better education. Mohammed was a member of a middle-class family
in which Islam and Islamic religious practice was a regular and constant part
of his upbringing. That had resulted in a strong Muslim identity on his part
but one that did not manifest itself in the simple carrying on of the traditions

and beliefs that he received as a child. Mohammed was, in fact, actively and selectively reconstructing Islam for himself. As he put it,

> I follow the Islamic faith, and I might not be as devout as my parents, but ... I'm starting to find religion for myself ... and I've started thinking critically of my religion, so instead of having everything in a religion inherited like a lot of people, I've started to start all over again for myself, 'cause I wanted to find out why I believe in this religion ... find out the reasons behind the practices ... and find meaning for myself.

This effort to appropriate his received faith for himself was reflected in the way he distinguished religion from spirituality. He said, first of all, that "I don't consider myself an extremely religious person, but I consider myself spiritual." When asked what he meant, he indicated that being religious was adhering to the beliefs and practices of a particular religion whereas being spiritual was "being connected with the world ... realizing that you're part of a larger concept, something more grand." Being spiritual involved belief "in a higher being, whether you call it a god or whether you call it Buddha or call it Allah," a being that is "in charge of everything in this world." In other words, Mohammed felt that he had to take a step back from his imitative childhood religion, centre himself in his spirituality, and find his own way back to religion eventually. In this regard, he had stopped reading the Qur'an, because although he had been taught to read it imitatively, "I don't understand any of it ... I've ... pulled away from it just because I actually want to learn Arabic first and then ... study the context and then maybe go back to the Qur'an one day." This reversal of what one might see as the usual orientation was reflected in his concept of what a Muslim is:

> A Muslim is someone who sees people as their brothers and sisters. They see themselves equal to others. So there's no boundary between race, colour, gender ... just a person that's connected to the world, connected to the earth, connected to nature. Someone who's environmentally conscious. I'd say the ideal Muslim [is] a person who is just aware of the world and not too focused on the superficial things and also not too concerned on just getting themselves into heaven ... I think we all have to work together, and so the ideal Muslim is someone who incorporates that, incorporates other people to help them, help them help everyone else and help the world too.

Correspondingly, he did not place great emphasis on the sort of orthodox and regular practice that the more highly involved did. He did not try to reproduce the orthodox five-pillars model. He prayed but said, "in our religion you're supposed to pray five times a day; I do not pray five times a day, but certainly when I feel it ... I do it more for meditational and spiritual purpose." Mohammed fasted during the entire month of Ramadan, but he observed few of the other associated practices that, for instance, his parents would insist upon. He went to Friday prayers with some regularity when he as at home in Toronto but not assiduously. In fact, although he highly valued the Muslim style of communal prayer with people praying lined up shoulder to shoulder as a mark of their equality before God, he did not like other aspects of the atmosphere in his Toronto mosque, because too much emphasis was put on imitation instead of inspiration, on rules for what is permitted and forbidden: as he put it, "it's do this you'll go to heaven, do that you'll go to hell." Interestingly enough, he attributed this emphasis to the fact that the mosque leaders were all of Indian and Pakistani origin and displayed what he called an "old school ... subcontinent mentality." He was not the only participant who voiced the opinion that Indian and Pakistani Muslims tended to be more "extreme" than those from elsewhere – although it should be noted again that our data does not in the least point in this direction.

The selectivity implied in Mohammed's attitude to religious rules and standard religious practice manifested itself in the realm of moral questions as well. Thus, to take two important examples, on homosexuality, he stated that "I've grown up in a society where ... I've had friends that were homosexual [and] ... I'm not sure where the actual Qur'an stands on that issue, but personally I don't have a problem with it, but my parents do." Then, on other questions of sexual behaviour, he had similar attitudes, considering that dating and other meaningful contact and relations with women before marriage were in principle quite all right, but again this was an attitude that his parents, to say the least, did not share. Nor did he talk to them about such issues.

Turning now to Mohammed's opinions about the Canadian society of which he felt himself to be a full and equal member, they, as noted, were by and large quite positive. Asked about the multi-religious and multicultural situation in Canada and about Canada's multicultural policy, his response was similar to that of a number of other participants:

> Just being in the ... same atmosphere with so many different people ...
> I've grown so much as a person, especially in Scarborough, it's so multi-cultural, and now in Ottawa ... you know, Canada's open immigration, I think they should not only do that, but I think they should also further explore the religions and the cultures that come into this country, because ... that's what makes this country great.

One notes in particular that in consonance with his open attitude toward Islam, he did not just advocate the side-by-side toleration of different religions and cultures; the value of having them all in the same country was precisely that if they "talk to each other," they could learn from each other. And this in no way undermined his strong identification as a Muslim. That said, Mohammed was not uncritical of Canadian and Western, even global, society. In part echoing Ali, he felt that one of the biggest challenges facing the world today was too much materialism and concentration on what he called superficialities. A long response on his part contained the following bit: "I mean, just the fact that there's so many people that are like, 'Oh my God, J-Lo broke up with Ben!'[11] and then at the same time, there are children dying, not only African, children dying in our own countries ... Just like I said with religion, we should stop concentrating on all these trivial things so we can concentrate on the bigger problem."

Unlike the two previous participants profiled, Mohammed was much more the sort of person who might contribute to the meaningful construction of Islam in Canada. As an individual, of course, he has little influence, and at this point it is rather uncertain where even his own efforts to understand his tradition will lead, but he might well represent a significant portion of the younger Muslim generation in the hybridity evident in his efforts and his openness to diverse ways of being religious and being Muslim. His insistence that religion – beliefs, practices, rules for behaviour – be grounded in a spirituality based on guiding ethical principles means that the principles determine the nature of Islam and religion, not only, or even in the first instance, the standard sources of authority such as the Qur'an. The Islam to which his way of living religion might be contributing is one of more fluid boundaries, where the distinction between "orthodoxy" and "heterodoxy" might not be that clear. Religious diversity by such standards would be characterized less as a collection of distinct and exclusive religions and more a matter of emphasis of one identity over others but in the process of mutual influence and interaction. In this regard, among the involved Muslims of his generation, he differed substantially from others, including the plurality of Muslim males whom we put into the higher involvement categories. Even among them, however, there was significant variation and complexity.

Ahmed (MM13)

Ahmed represented the category 7 Muslim men,[12] meaning that he followed the orthodox and globalized five-pillars model of what it means to be a Muslim, but his actual behaviour deviated somewhat from that norm. In certain ways, he was like Mohammed; in others, he was like the two category 8 men whose stories follow. Understanding this "in-between" status is important for gaining a good appreciation for the range of orientations that the moderately to highly involved Muslim men represent.

By his own description, Ahmed was a regularly practising Sunni Muslim: he said that he prayed five times a day, he fasted during the entire month of Ramadan, he went to Friday prayers at his local mosque regularly, he founded a Muslim charitable organization with his cousin, and he had every intention of performing the pilgrimage to Mecca at least once in his lifetime. As he said when asked if *hajj* was important, "yes, definitely, I mean, it's one of the five pillars." He read the Qur'an in Arabic, which he had learned, and he consulted both the Qur'an and the Hadith when he had a question about what Islam enjoined. Parallel to this, however, his description of what made a good Muslim was in a certain way reminiscent of what Mohammed had said: "I would say someone at peace with themselves; someone who is ... devoted and committed, because it takes quite a bit to follow Islam; someone who respects others regardless of whether they are Muslim or not or what culture they are; that is what a true Muslim would be in my mind." Ahmed felt that religion was a "personal thing," but he also stressed the communal aspect: "community is really big in the religion [Islam] as well ... They stress [that] community is brotherhood and sisterhood, so I think community strengthens your own personal resolve in your faith."

Born in Canada to Muslim parents of Pakistani and Indian origin, Ahmed was at the time of his interview 21 years old, in third year studying political science and international relations at the University of Toronto. He lived with his parents, who had been in Canada for about 30 years; most of his extended family lived either in the Toronto region or elsewhere in North America. He said that he grew up in a moderately religious household, and, indeed, several of his cousins and other near relatives, unlike him, were not particularly practising at all; his sister considered herself an atheist. Again, the relationship that the Muslim men of our sample had to the religion of their heritage bore little to no correlation with whether they were born here, where their parents came from, and how long their family had lived in Canada. Although all the highly involved had a religious upbringing, this was clearly not a straightforwardly causal relationship. Even field of study – since all our participants were attending university or university-educated – says little: Ahmed might have been specializing in a field that dealt directly with religious and other diversities in the contemporary global world, but overall, devout Muslims in our sample were no more likely to specialize in the humanities or the social sciences than in the natural and applied sciences or in business, and the same can be said for the less devout and the non-religious.

Although in terms of practice Ahmed was what one might call a standardly devout Muslim, his was not a rigidly orthodox Islam closed to alternate interpretations and flexibility in certain areas. For instance, rather than account for internal Islamic divisions between Sunnis, Shi'is, and Ismailis (the three he mentioned when asked) by saying, as others did, that the differences were insignificant, that they were unfortunate, or that the non-Sunnis were just wrong, he respected them in their difference even if he felt his version was correct: "Would I consider them to be as authentic? I guess I believe that what I follow is the correct way, but that is not in any way to demean them or think less of them, it's just that they follow something different."

In terms of specific social behaviours often considered un-Islamic by orthodox Muslims, Ahmed also showed a kind of hybrid flexibility: he interacted with women regularly and personally; he dated, but she had to be Muslim. His last girlfriend at the time was Ismaili. He very occasionally drank alcohol and went to bars and clubs with some of his friends but hoped to reduce and eliminate such behaviour over time. As a Muslim, he could not approve of homosexuality, but this issue would not be decisive, for instance, when it came time to choosing which party to support in elections. In some sense, Ahmed felt conflicted precisely on issues where his personal attitude did not mesh with what he understood that Islam taught. Here is part of an exchange on the question of the equality of men and women:

INTERVIEWER: How do you understand the differences between men and women?
AHMED: I think they have different roles, obviously; there's different emotional needs, physically and biologically, they have different roles, but I think at the same time they are equal and women should have more rights, especially in Islam … In the Qur'an it says women are equal but … the cultural … aspects come into play and then they get relegated, so I think that's a big misinterpretation of the religion. I think women should have a more prominent role than they have right now … I think women should be just as involved in society as men.
INTERVIEWER: Okay, how about as leaders of the mosque?
AHMED: Personally, I don't find anything wrong with it … I'm always torn because it's like my Western education conflicting with my religious background … I'm sure everything we've been prescribed in Islam, there's been a reason behind it, and I think it's been justified in some ways, so I would go with that, but at the same time, I wouldn't be against a woman taking the lead.

Ahmed's overall tolerance and flexibility was also reflected in his attitudes toward Canadian society and to religious diversity and multiculturalism in that society. Pluralism for him was healthy, homogeneity was dangerous. On both these issues, his opinions were in consonance with what one might call official Canadian policy:

I think [having many religions represented in Canada] it's definitely healthy … If everyone's homogeneous … it's just looking for danger … and I think Canada's a good representation of people being tolerant of

one another ... I 100% agree with [Canada's multiculturalism policy] ...
I think multiculturalism is definitely something that's really important; I
think ... you could say it's part of the Canadian identity.

There is a strong sense in which Ahmed displayed many of the "typical"
features of the entire Muslim male sample in our research. He was clearly religious and in a highly orthodox fashion. He did not find it easy to be this
way in a secular, "Western" society such as exists in Canada, but his cultural
identification with that society was strong. He felt himself to be a full and equal
member of Canadian society; he considered himself Canadian; he would not
want to live elsewhere. He identified with most of what one might call its core
values such as the equality of all human beings and the goodness of difference.
He was sufficiently strong in his orientations that he was unlikely to move his
Islam either into a rejectionist, sectarian direction or into an assimilationist
one in which religion remained but a private proclivity without broader social
relevance. In the terms used above, he presented a good example of an "open
religiosity." Moreover, his was a variant of most of those in category 8, and it is
important to understand him in that context, because while his understanding or construction of Islam was highly orthodox according to the five-pillars
orthodox model, his openness and, to an extent, flexibility showed that his
lived religion (potentially) consisted in more than what, strictly speaking, is
found in this model. The systemic and the lived were not identical, but they
were certainly not in contradiction with one another.

Karim (MM05)

Like Ahmed, Karim is a Canada-born Sunni Muslim whose family emigrated
from Pakistan between two and three decades ago. He was 20 years old at the
time of the interview but also one of the most reflective and one could also
say mature participants in the entire sample of 202. He was studying for an
undergraduate degree at the University of Ottawa, majoring in ethics and philosophy. That choice of specialization says much about how he thought about
Islam, religion, Canada, and the world around him. He was one participant for
whom the university context appeared to be highly relevant for his orientation
to religion (and vice versa).

We classified Karim as a number 8 because he followed the standard global
five-pillars model of Islam and did not deviate from it in any significant way in
his own behaviour. His circle of friends was mostly Muslim. He was a regular
member of his campus Muslim Students Association. His definition of religion
was as "something that guides your actions ... For me, it's a way of life." His
parents were religious and practised regularly, and so did he. He said that there
was no significant difference between the way he practised Islam and how his

parents did. On more than one occasion during the interview, he declared that he had inherited his religion from his parents and that that was why he was a Muslim. He was far from an unreflective imitator, however.

At the heart of Karim's uniqueness was the consistent way that he drew various distinctions, between the essential and the secondary in Islam, between religion and culture, and between the Islam of his generation and that of his parents'. In each case, these distinctions helped him to define the specificity of Islam and showed how he had appropriated his inherited religion for himself in his Canadian context. These three areas of distinction were intertwined.

With regard to the difference between religion and culture, Karim drew this rather more strongly than did many others in the sample. Like others, however, he felt that the difference was less clear in the case of his parents, leading to an amalgam of Pakistani culture and Islamic religion, an amalgam that he felt he was in a better position to undo as a Muslim in Canada. Here is how he put the matter in terms of multiculturalism and his own "in-two-worlds" position within Canadian society:

> We have a fairly good multicultural model here in Canada, whereas in Pakistan, I think there's more racial polarization … I think I have an advantage over people who live in Pakistan all their lives, because I can see from the dominant culture, which I consider to be the Christian Canada; I can see from their vantage point as well as what happens at home and what my parents believe. So there's much more of a basis of comparison, and I think that makes my choice more genuine.

Far from extending his "advantage" to the rest of his Muslim generation in Canada, however, he also felt that many of them had taken a wrong turn, one that ended up emphasizing what he considered secondary and even superficial aspects of Islam rather than what was essential and important. He put it in terms of the "rebellion of youth":

> I think I may be echoing other people when I say that every generation has its rebellion, and the rebellion in my generation has been something called the Islamic Revival Movement, the movement that says that our parents' way of following religion was not strict enough … I see it just as adolescent rebellion … It's a trend towards going back to the sources, things like that, specifically things like the hijab and the beard, those are more prevalent in the new generation than in the older one … I've seen in my generation a lot of protesting the Pakistani culture and protesting things like music, dancing, wearing of suits and ties is considered to be copycat emulation of British culture … But I dissociate myself. I don't protest.

Commensurate with this criticism of his own generation, Karim also felt
that this trend might be more widespread and that it resulted in emphasis in
Islam being put on what was superficial:

> INTERVIEWER: What do you think are the main challenges facing your
> religion today?
> KARIM: The trivializations ... Islam is supposed to be something sig-
> nificant ... something that transcends throughout the world. And if you
> go to Muslim lectures today, they're all about how Muslim men should
> grow beards. And I find it difficult to believe that that's why the Prophet
> Muhammad was sent down, that that is the noble purpose of mankind,
> that that's why God created the world. I think we're focusing too much
> on the little things, and we're forgetting the big things.

In light of these criticisms, it is perhaps not surprising that Karim wished
to participate in a reform movement within Islam that would correct these
imbalances. Such reform included a reemphasis on the ethical core of Islam
and this in an atmosphere of collaboration with other people, other religions,
and indeed toward what he himself called a "global ethic." He tied his choice of
undergraduate specialization to this task:

> I'm majoring in ethics, so I'd like to be something of a leading moralist
> of my time [small laugh], something of a reformer. Job number one .
> would be to give some kind of moral accountability for the things that
> happen in the Islamic world, put back in the morality that is missing
> in so many implementations of Islam ... then after that perhaps to par-
> ticipate in a global ethic ... I think the trend in the world today is to
> form some kind of unified world view, and I think that Islam should
> participate in it, and that means that Islam first needs to take a good
> look at itself and see if it's any good [laughs], so to speak. So, correcting
> ourselves, and then participating in the correction of humanity, if that's
> not too presumptuous.

At least as much as any of the other highly involved participants, Karim exemplified that combination of a strong Islamic faith with an openness to the world
around him. He was highly practising and liked to stick to his inner circle of
Muslim friends and family. He wanted to marry within Islam and not lose
his Pakistani culture. He felt comfortable in Canada but not quite as equally
accepted as others. And yet all these things formed the basis of his willingness and eagerness to participate more fully and make a difference. He did not
think that one religion was superior to another, except that he had by cultural
inheritance and by personal choice opted for Islam. He approved of Canadian

multiculturalism but felt it should be deepened, that at the moment different people – he mentioned Hindus, Muslims, and Sikhs living in Toronto, for instance – were just living beside one another without actually engaging each other. He thought multiculturalism was important, "but it isn't easy. Yeah, you have to work hard to really tolerate people." He ended the interview with these words: "in Islam we have a saying, it's that you should correct yourself and then go out and correct the world. And job number one is that you love it. So, I'll do what I can."

Ibrahim (MM10)

In a sense, Ibrahim was one of those that Karim talked about: a second-generation member of the "Islamic Revival Movement." Ibrahim put great stress on the punctilious practice of Islam in ritual performance and moral strictures. He said that in these terms he was more practising than his parents and mildly criticized them for, in his mind, confusing what was cultural and what was enjoined by Islam. Yet, contrary to what one might therefore think, Ibrahim was also among the most insistent in the group of the highly involved that he was thoroughly integrated into life in Canada, felt he belonged here, and felt comfortable in that belonging as a devout Muslim. Here is one brief exchange from his interview:

INTERVIEWER: Are you able to fully practise your religion in Canada?
IBRAHIM: Yup.
INTERVIEWER: Do you feel as if you're an accepted and equal member in Canadian society, as a Canadian?
IBRAHIM: As a Canuck, ya, for sure.
INTERVIEWER: You're a Canuck.
IBRAHIM: I'm a Canuck.

Ibrahim was 27 years old, one of the oldest participants in the sample. He had finished his university education, specializing in economics, and was working for the federal government at the time of the interview. He was the eldest of four children, all born in Canada to parents who had emigrated from Egypt in the late 1970s. Unlike practically every other interviewee in the entire sample, he did not grow up in a large city but rather in a small village in eastern Ontario. Only when he attended university did he move to larger centres. The university environment evidently had an effect on him. It was after he moved away from his parental home that he began to become a more and more seriously practising Muslim and this by what he felt were the only truly Islamic standards. His understanding of Islam was very unequivocal, highly orthodox in the sense we have been describing of a global five-pillars model. From his description of what Islam was all about, one would think that he would be precisely the sort of Muslim who would end up classified higher than 8, but the way he situated himself as a devout Muslim in Canadian society prevents this conclusion. He was religiously a Muslim but culturally a Canadian. It is this, not juxtaposition but hybridity, that is worth examining more closely, because it tells us much about the range of possibilities for an "open religiousness" among these 35 Muslim male participants.

Ibrahim's definition of religion was very Islamic and his description of the essence of Islam very orthodox Sunni. He defined religion in terms of spirituality: "I would say it's a spirituality; it's a way of living that allows the person to get closer to their creator ... to communicate with their creator, to submit to their creator, so that's what I think religion is." One notes that spirituality for him was the larger way of life informed by what the religion enjoined. This is how he saw Islam as well: it was a set of prescriptions that informed all of life, directly or indirectly. The core of Islam was the five pillars:

> God doesn't ask any more of any Muslim. He says that you are to pray
> five times a day; you are to fast the month of Ramadan; you are to testify
> that there is no God but God, the one true God, and that Muhammad
> – may the peace and blessings of God be upon him – is his messenger;
> and pilgrimage to Mecca once in your lifetime; and you have to give to
> charity, annually two-and-a-half per cent of your wealth.

In actual fact, however, for Ibrahim, God did ask for more. Here are a few of the points about which Ibrahim felt strongly: God forbade usury. Ibrahim had disagreements with his father about this, his father being a successful entrepreneur who had invested in real estate and set up businesses. Ibrahim was not rigid but would not buy a new car because the interest rates were almost always beyond what he felt God permitted. On Karim's two items, "hijab and the beard," Ibrahim had this to say:

> Women should wear the veil because it stipulates it in the Qur'an
> [which] very strongly encourages that women are to cover ... their hair
> once they reach the age of puberty. Men, the beard part, comes from
> the prophet himself having a beard.[13] So men are encouraged to have a
> beard. Mind you, you see tons of men with no beard who are Muslim
> and practising, so it's really just an extra reward if you have the beard.

Moreover, when asked to what branch of Islam he belonged, Ibrahim would only say, "I follow the Qur'an and the teaching of the Prophet and that's it. There's no innovations above and beyond that."

A dozen times during the interview, Ibrahim talked about Muslims, particularly himself, being integrated. Integration meant, in a nutshell, being Muslim but, within the strictures set by this identification, doing what any other Canadian might do. After describing how he was taking "the faith a lot more seriously" since childhood, he talked about some of the challenges that this presented:

> All the social activities that I have, all the friends that I have, I have to include everything and just package it all together and just get it all done. So, you know, because I go snowboarding with non-Muslims,[14] I play hockey with non-Muslims. I have more non-Muslim friends than Muslim friends, just because I was raised here and with non-Muslims. I can get close to non-Muslims much more quickly than Muslims ... I prefer hockey more than soccer, even though I'm of Egyptian descent.

The issue of his sports and hobbies came up several times. When he was a university student, he went to clubs and bars with his friends, although he did not touch alcohol, nor did he try to strike up relationships with women. Rather than seeing this sort of experience as a failure to live up to the requirements of his religion, he saw it as another way of being more integrated; it showed his non-Muslim friends the strength of being Muslim and thus increased their acceptance of him. Here is how he put it:

> I was fairly integrated. Because at the time, I was into music, and I was into going out and things like that ... but I just didn't drink. So they [his friends] thought this was a huge thing ... And they get to see, well, there's a guy who can do all these things, just without this one ingredient, which he thinks is bad ... So when you see all these things and you see the faith, the faith gets exposed. So their perspective on it changes. And the way they treat you changes. They start to see that you have a spine, and it's firmly embedded in the roots of what was taught you. So, you see a tree and your roots are firmly stuck, planted into the ground; no one can rip them out. But the tree can sway. So, they see this, and they're like, "he's different."

With regard to his relationships with women while at university, he made an analogous observation:

> Because, when you get to university ... you're off on your own ... no one is going to slap your hand if you commit a sin ... When I went to [my first university], they always would look at me a little differently.

The girls used to get close to me, just because I wouldn't have anything –
you can't have premarital relations. So they wouldn't feel threatened
anymore. They would be like "well, he can't do anything, so I can talk
to him, I can get close to him" ... They feel comfortable around me obviously.

In Ibrahim's experience, people ended up accepting him more and respecting
him because he manifested such a strong faith; it did not isolate him but rather
gave him his individuality: "So, that's when it hit me: the religion has an impact
on the way people see you, and for me the impact has generally been positive."
There was, however, another side to this equation – a cost, as it were. As a
Muslim, Ibrahim wanted eventually to marry a Muslim woman. Yet Muslim
women, he claimed, generally did not understand him because of his degree of
integration as a "Muslim Canuck." Comparing non-Muslim women to Muslim
women as marriage partners, he saw problems with both. Non-Muslim women
might engage in un-Islamic behaviour like drinking or not accept that their
children would have to be raised Muslim. Then,

there are other issues that come with non-Muslim women, like previous
relationships and things like that ... These are all issues that I'd never
have to look at with a Muslim woman. Muslim women know half of ...
you already. Half of you is your faith ... The problem lies in their lack
of integration. I'm very integrated. I go to hockey games all the time ...
I snowboard. I work on my car. I'm a car fanatic ... I'm going to go to
car shows ... When I'm not worshipping God, I'm going to do whatever
interests me. Can you handle that? Some women can't, some Muslim
women ... So I'm trying to find that mix, and I'm not having any success
on either side.

Irrespective of whether Ibrahim's perception of his situation was accurate or
not – if we were to take on the role of matchmakers, we might be half-tempted
to introduce him to a dozen or so of our Muslim women participants (see
chapter 6) – the core of the issue for him was his identity as occupying "two
worlds" at the same time, or at least as reconciling in his own life with "ways
of life" that others, like Ali above, consider antithetical. He considered such
"hybridization" a straightforward outcome of growing up in Canadian society
as a Muslim, as personally unproblematic but as something that others around
him did not always understand. In that context, Ibrahim's attitude to the fact of
Canadian religious diversity and to multiculturalism as both reality and policy
is probably not surprising. The latter he saw not only as beneficial but beneficial to himself in particular:

I understand that you do take away in some respects opportunity for people who ... are Canadian and grow up here. Because if a seat is filled by an immigrant child, someone who's from ... foreign descent, that's a seat that could have been filled by a Canadian. But in essence, that guy will grow up and have family and have them as Canadians ... and you have this salad bowl mix [that] starts up ... It's been beneficial to me. I don't see why anyone would want to change it, unless they feel threatened by it.

Religious plurality he saw in a similar and very personal vein:

I think Canada has a really good foundation when it comes to this multicultural, multi-faith society. I think it's really helped the general public open its eyes and realize that there's a vast variety of people who are out there doing all kinds of different things ... So, I mean, my working at this [government] agency, I'm the only one there who's a practising Muslim, so these people have gotten to know what I do ... how I treat people, what my views are ... and yet I'm integrated, I work with these people, I get things done ... everybody has to work together. In the process, they get to know what kind of person I really am: go-getter, ambitious, determined ... they get to see this, and faith becomes secondary when they know everything ... that says, well, I'm satisfied ... with the information he's given me about his faith. I can move on.

In essence, Ibrahim was saying: I'm different, I'm Muslim, and I'm just as much a part of this society as you are.

CONCLUSION

If one had to say what dominant patterns emerged from the sample of the Muslim men, then these patterns would have to include the very consistent way in which they understood what Islam was as religion and the degree to which they felt it possible to live this faith more or less fully within Canadian society and, in most cases, fully identifying as a Canadian – but often not only as Canadian. If this sample of 35 men from Muslim families were to be taken as representative of the future of Islam in this country, then there seems to be no significant barrier to this religion becoming as regular a part of the religious landscape as any other minority religion, even more so in the larger urban centres like Toronto and Ottawa where almost all of them lived or studied. To be sure, the 1.5- and second-generation individuals profiled here as a group currently only constitute a small minority of all of Canada's Muslim population, and many of them were still in a state of flux with regard to what their orientations and identities would be as fully mature and older adults. Yet the consistency of what they were showing, in spite of all the significant variations among them, would support the conclusion that these core characteristics will continue and will become more widespread as their younger siblings join them in adulthood and as more young Muslims swell their numbers through continued immigration.

In light of the probably skewed nature of our sample, it is likely that the overall population of young Muslim men is in majority rather lukewarm in their involvement in religion, and a very sizable proportion of this majority can hardly be counted at all among practising Muslims in this country. The latter are correspondingly unlikely to have a serious influence on what Islam will become in Canada over the next decades, but they could have a sizable influence on how others in the population see Muslims in general: like Christians and Jews, as a mixed group that includes a sizable minority of the highly devout and usually socially conservative, a great variety of ways of being religious or not, and a good proportion of people who have a religious identity but for whom religion is at best only one dimension of life and one that they do not often visibly manifest in public. The lived religion of nominal Muslims, like others, in majority includes other orientations and behaviours than those prescribed by a constructed and orthodox model; their religious or spiritual selves probably include selectively and other than what these models contain.

On the other hand, the very significant number of highly involved individuals in the sample points to a large minority of Muslims in the second generation who are not only likely to have a significant influence on what Islam becomes as a systemic religion in Canada but who are busily constructing a way of being Muslim that may make this religion as regular and as unproblematic a part of the public religious landscape of this country as are various forms of Christianity and Judaism. To some degree, this will be the Islam of the first generation of immigrants, of their parents, since few of them deviated substantially from the model taught to them as children and some portrayed the parental model with what they saw as even greater fidelity. From another angle of view, however, their way of situating their Islamic orthodoxy within Canadian society appeared to be much more melded with the everyday cultural habits and values that dominated in the rest of the population. It accepted without too much difficulty the status of Islam as one religion among others that were equally to be welcomed and tolerated and as a minority religion as well. It generally saw the growing religious diversity and multicultural reality of Canada, to which they saw themselves as consciously and incontrovertibly contributing, as a positive value to be encouraged, as something that made Canada a good place in which to live. Theirs was in that sense an "open religiosity" in parallel with what they saw – in practice or in principle – as the dominant "open secularism" around them. The Islam that they represented was anything but a foreign religion to be tolerated or accommodated in Canada; they saw it as an increasingly regular part of the Canadian social fabric, as regular and as "at home" as they were themselves.

As we shall see in the following chapters, the Muslim men in our sample were quite similar in a great many ways to their female counterparts, although there were also differences. Both genders of this religious background, however, were markedly different in their relation to religion from those of Hindu and Buddhist background. Nonetheless, there was also important continuity, principally in the degree and in the ways that they considered themselves full members of Canadian society and shared key value orientations that were dominant in that society. These values included a stress on the individual as the centre of authenticity, including in matters of religion; a positive orientation to religious and cultural diversity; and insistence on the inclusion of this diversity in the power structures and benefits of that society and criticism to the extent that this goal was perceived as not having been achieved. The strong religious differences must be seen against this common background.

6

A Variable but Convergent Islam: Muslim Women

RUBINA RAMJI

As the religion of Islam becomes increasingly transnational, the "authoritative use of the symbolic language of Islam" has become fragmented and contested (Shafiry-Funk 2008). Although many Muslims explain their lives through the normative language of Islam, to be Muslim does not have the same meaning for all followers of the faith. This is one of the conclusions that emerge from the previous chapter. Muslim identity politics takes on many forms, including class interests, nationalism, family networks, and furthermore, these identity formations differ vastly in Muslim-majority states in comparison to states where Muslims form a minority within a population (Eickelman and Anderson 1999). The Canadian situation is one of the latter, and in this chapter we look at how the Muslim women – including in comparison to the Muslim men just discussed – among our participants addressed and contributed to this identity and religion-formation process.

DEMOGRAPHIC PROFILE

Fifty-eight young women, sometimes known as second-generation Canadians,[1] stepped forward to share their meaning of Islam as interview participants in this project. They ranged in age from 18 to 27. Twenty-six participants were under the age of 20, and only 7 women were 25 or over. The mean age for all participants was 21.8 years. Only 2 women were married, and given the young age of the group, most of them were still pursuing a higher education degree rather than working. Their families came from a wide variety of countries all over the world: 16 were from Pakistan, 7 from East Africa, 6 from Iran, 4 from Lebanon, 4 from India, 4 from Egypt, 4 from Bangladesh, 3 from Somalia, 2 from Trinidad, 2 from Algeria, and 1 family each from Sudan, Guyana, Morocco, Afghanistan, Turkey, and South Africa. The only consistency found among the participants geographically was that those whose families originated from Iran maintained no religious or only a somewhat religious identity: 5 were non-practising, and the other was only moderately involved in her faith (this trend, as discussed in the previous chapter, was also found among the male Muslim participants with Iranian origins). The participants' parents immigrated to Canada, thereby bringing their cultural form of Islam with them.

Yet these women were either born or raised in Canada from a young age, so the ethnic and national dimension of their parents' faith had changed for them dramatically.

DATA-GENERATED CLASSIFICATION SYSTEM

For this particular study, it was imperative that the interviewees' own self-presentation be utilized in any comparative classification. Within the interviews, "some kind of balance between the interviewer and the interviewee can develop which can provide room for negotiation, discussion, and expansion of the interviewee's responses" (Hitchcock and Hughes 1989). Examining orthopraxis (actions of obligation), intentions, and familial and institutional influences, as well as levels of belief, leads to an understanding of the way unorthodox and nonconformist views, by whatever standard, exist side by side with orthodox views, not to "relativize" the so-called "truth" of a religion but to add to the constructed and pluralistic nature of religious expressions found among many people who hold the same faith. This points to the core of the lived religion approach. With the information provided by the participants during the interviews, these women can be located along a 10-point classification system starting from non-believers to the highly involved on the basis of self-definition and identification.

NON-INVOLVEMENT TO HIGH INVOLVEMENT

Ten female participants ranked within categories 1 to 3: they defined themselves essentially as atheists or people without a religion, although they admitted to being Muslim by family and cultural background. These participants fell into the non-religious grouping. Those who fell into category 1 professed no religious beliefs whatsoever (3 participants). Category 2 participants did not identify with the faith of Islam but displayed a curiosity towards the notion of spirituality (4 participants). In category 3, participants maintained a belief in a creator and linked it to a Muslim identity. They acknowledged a Muslim identity by virtue of family and cultural background (3 participants).

The 19 participants ranked within categories 4 to 6 can be considered moderately involved in their faith (see Figure 5.1 in the previous chapter). They were generally knowledgeable about Islam, engaged in some practices such as high feast days like the Eids, and identified clearly as Muslims, but otherwise Islam did not form the central practical part of their identities and lives. Many of them were like a large portion of the Christian North American and Western European population, who adhere or identify and believe but only practise occasionally. The Muslim women in these categories often admitted to smoking, dating, drinking, and clubbing but felt a sense of guilt about it, because they understood that they were not being "good" Muslims. Many expressed an inner struggle to balance their lives as Muslims and Canadians: to maintain a Muslim identity while at the same time fully participating in Canadian culture.

The 27 participants who ranked within categories 7 to 9 could be considered highly involved Muslims who deemed their form of Islam central in their lives, almost always centring on the importance of the five pillars as the core Islamic practices. They prayed five times a day, followed halal regulations, and fasted during Ramadan. Those in categories 8 and 9 wished to be more religious: by thinking of God regularly and immersing themselves in the teachings of Islam. In comparison to those ranked in category 10, these women were less insistent on the unique validity of their own understanding of Islam, were significantly more irenic in their attitude to others and other lifestyles and world views, and correspondingly were internally more varied in the specific ways that they constructed their Islam.

Two participants fell into the highest level, category 10. These participants believed that the only reliable guides for living and practising Islam were the Qur'an and Hadith. These, they insisted, should not be viewed in innovative ways, and therefore many of their views about Islam were highly conservative or restrictive. They not only put Islam at the centre of their lives, they put a highly demanding and conservative form of Islam there.[2] Although the category 10 and the category 7 to 9 participants shared many characteristics, those in category 10 separated themselves in terms of a strict adherence to practice. The central features of those in category 10 involved a strict observance of what they considered religiously obligatory acts such as following halal.dietary and sexual regulations, fasting during Ramadan, and a minimum of five daily prayers. These two women found it difficult to live in a society that was not segregated by sex. In keeping with these injunctions, both women wore hijab. The majority of their friends were Muslim (and they only had female friends) who shared their beliefs, their behaviours, and their decisions. Of the utmost importance was the remembrance of God at all times. We begin with a more detailed look at one of these two participants, because they set what one might call an "upper limit" to those who see themselves and their religion as operating strictly within the boundaries of systemic religion, here Islam. In other words, here lived religion and systemic religion overlapped, if not perfectly, then virtually indistinguishably. In that context, however, these two women were also still forming "their own" Islam.

FRAGMENTS OF VARIANCE – FORMING ONE'S OWN ISLAM

The first category 10 participant, Sonia (MF29), 20 years old, was born in Egypt and spent four years in Saudi Arabia before coming to Canada. All of her free time was used for supplication – remembering God constantly. All actions could be considered a form of worship of God, as long as it was performed with the right intention: be it washing dishes or studying for an exam. Every free moment of time could be spent in devotion to God. Islam defined her whole life: "everything, the way you act, your values, your morals, in every circumstance, whether you're at work or at school or at home or alone, totally isolated, you would be ... you would follow your religion. So it's a complete and total way of life for me." Islam fed her soul – it offered contentedness and peace. She considered traumas in life to be tests from God, testing her faith and patience. Sonia's mother began teaching her daughters to recite the Qur'an from a young age, and eventually she learned to understand daily events through the teachings of the Qur'an and Sunna. She also attended an Islamic summer camp for girls and then became a counsellor. While performing all of the religious acts she considered obligatory, such as praying daily, participating in family Eid festivals, and fasting during Ramadan, she was also a member of the Muslim Students Association (MSA) at her university. She was responsible for the da'wa table for the association, which gives out weekly information to the student body. She was also a host on an Islamic radio program at her university (she considered herself to be following in the footsteps of her father, who was one of the first MSA members at his university in 1969). She began wearing the hijab when she was 10 years old, because at puberty it was required: she then consciously only chose female Muslim friends, because she could no longer socialize with Canadian youth (who went to bars, drank, and dated). Sonia did not attend mosque, since she could pray anywhere: in a hallway, stairwells, a classroom, or a park. In fact, for Sonia there were benefits to praying in different places, because "there's a saying by the Prophet, Peace Be Upon Him, that basically the more places you prostrate, so your head touches the ground ... all these places that you've ever prostrated on will be there on the Day of Judgment to testify for you that you've prostrated." But community was also important to Sonia, because "people are weak on their own, they need the support of others." The idea of congregation in a foreign land was a necessity to Sonia, so she often volunteered to organize Eid events and enjoyed congregational prayers during Ramadan.

Sonia had a very close relationship with her parents: she would agree to an arranged marriage with an appropriate Sunni Muslim who shared her understanding of Islam when the time came. But at the same time, she practised a higher level of Islam than either of her parents, given their country of origin. Sonia stated that for her, it was actually easier to be a Muslim in Canada than in Egypt. In Egypt, everyone is assumed to be Muslim, although many do not follow the teachings of Islam (because they drink and go to bars). It is a cultural definition. In Canada, she could be as religious as she wanted, and because Canada was a tolerant society, people would understand her beliefs when she stated that she did not drink or go to bars or when she stopped to pray in a park. In essence, Sonia felt freer being Muslim while Canadian than her parents ever could. As discussed in the previous chapter, she shared this attitude with some of the more highly involved Muslim men in the sample.

While just two women were ranked at the highest end of the classification scale, the largest number of the Muslim women fell within categories 7 to 9. The 27 women at these levels were highly involved in their faith. To show the variances within their constructions of Islam, greater detail on their beliefs and practices is required. Thus, for example, Sultan (MF08) was 18 years old and prayed daily but did not always do it on time. She fasted during Ramadan regularly. Although she did not wear the hijab, she wished to in the future. She believed that honesty was an essential part of her religious practice. She could only marry a Muslim man because of her religion and stated that Islam had affected her career choice in that she wished to help others by working for the United Nations.

A slightly different example was presented by Sufia (MF35). She was 19 years old and read the Qur'an on a regular basis. She learned about Islam from her father when she was very young. He taught her the *namaz* (prayer), how to observe Eid, and how to fast during Ramadan. Sufia prayed every night before going to sleep (four to five *suras*). She also recited a *sura* when leaving the house in the morning and when starting a meal. She prayed regularly during Ramadan and tried to attend Friday *jum'ah* prayer at the university. In terms of dietary restrictions, she began by avoiding pork products and then became a vegetarian based on a childhood story of the Prophet Mohammed. She took the idea of not hurting ants to include all animals. Sufia dressed modestly but did not wear the hijab. She also wore an "Allah" pendant on a necklace for good luck during exams. When she was 8 years old, her parents began isolating her from boys to create sexual segregation. She was discouraged from playing with boys and had no male friends. Dating was forbidden. Sufia's future aspirations were also affected by her faith. She believed that the act of charity was the most important element in her life and participated in Amnesty International because it was important to help other people.

In relation to the highly involved participants, the 19 women in categories 4 to 6 showed a much lower degree of involvement and belief, their faith therefore having less impact on their lives. As an example, Mona (MF10), 23 years old and born in Lebanon, did not consider herself "religious enough," because she did not practise the religion to the level she would like to. She considered herself religious but not as a good practising Muslim. She learned of Islam at a young age but did not practise the religion as a child. Around the age of 15, she learned to pray from her cousin, not her parents. She found herself lost and wanted something to look up to, so she started reading and praying to feel guidance in her life. She also began using the Internet as her source of authority to learn more about Islam. Mona did not spend time in Muslim groups, because she didn't want to be manipulated by the views of others: she wanted to learn about her faith herself. Mona began praying five times a day at home to "acknowledge what's in your life, to thank God," but she did not attend mosque. She used to practise her faith more before she began university but then found it hard to keep it up because of her school schedule. She was an example of how the university environment can have different effects on different people; whereas others found the means there to increase their practice, identification, and involvement, Mona was one of those who had a somewhat opposite experience. Regarding other religious practices she performed daily, Mona did not eat pork, she was respectful to her parents, she did not gossip, and she gave back to her community through charity – "if you give your parents something, you get it back ten times" – and she had experienced this firsthand. Mona gave money to charities and fasted during Ramadan when she was in high school. She felt guilty for doing things she was not supposed to do, such as clubbing with her friends: "God watches over you, everything you do." Mona smoked but did not think that this was against her religion. She had issues with Islamic inheritance laws and cultural inequalities that existed between Muslim men and women. She believed that it was a good thing to wear the hijab, because men and women were biologically different, so she wanted to wear the hijab when she got older.

In contrast to Mona, Alia (MF23), 21 years old, felt religious even though she didn't practise much, because she believed in all the values and tenets of Islam. Important religious practices for Alia were to be humble, polite, and pious. Although she learned about Islam in her childhood, she did not practise her faith as much as her mother wanted her to. She had performed the *shahadah*, and she fasted as much as she could during Ramadan (about two to three weeks during the month). Alia did not pray or attend mosque regularly except during the Eid celebrations. She prayed once in a while with her roommate. She did not attend mosque, because she found it too "gossipy and more community-oriented" rather than about faith. Alia did not give to charity at that time because she had no money, and she wanted to go to Mecca to perform *hajj* one day. She used the Internet to better understand her religion.

The 10 women in the non-religious categories varied from being spiritual to being atheist, from affirming their Muslim identity to having no religious identity whatsoever. An example was Salima (MF40). She was 21 years old and was born in Canada, her parents having immigrated from Pakistan and India. Her father went to Friday *jum'ah* services, and her mother prayed five times a day. In comparison to her parents, Salima wanted to distinguish between faith and following a religion. She believed that "there has to be something out there. Religion is what you make of it." She was on a path to find spirituality but did not follow the religion of her parents. In contrast to Salima, Begum (MF34), who was 25 years old, was born in Iran. Her grandparents were religious, and she felt that she was shielded from the faith by her mother. She believed that religion was not logical, "especially as a woman – it closes doors for women." Begum did not believe in a higher being and saw religion as flawed, therefore not having any divine inspiration. Begum did meditate but did not see any benefit in prayer. She acknowledged that she performed meditation to calm herself down and for introspection, "to live in the moment. Prayer is to get somewhere which you never will get to." Begum, typical of those who considered themselves non-religious but still spiritual, was one of those for whom lived religion (here spirituality) and systemic religion overlapped very little.

MAJOR THEMES

All of the women in the highly involved and highest categories declared that their involvement in the faith had begun in childhood and that their level of involvement had increased since then. Twenty-six of the 58 interviewed stated that they continued to practise and believed at the same level as their parents. Twenty-one women felt that their level was lower than that of their parents, but quite of few of them said that they hoped to increase their level of practice after completing their education. From the interviews with these Muslim women, several major themes emerged for each grouping.[3] These themes concerned gender relations, the role of religious institutions compared to individualistic ideas, the types of religious practice, parental influences, moral questions, and religious versus non-religious activities.

Being Muslim and Being a Woman

Since these women had varied ethnic and national origins, they all had comprehensive but different identity negotiation processes based on these contexts. Taking into account that these identities shift, we examined how this specific cohort negotiated "hyphenated identities" (Sirin and Fine 2008, 16). Gender relations is a common theme in the process and negotiation of identity formation. This was especially the case for the Muslim women in our sample. Based on their religion, a majority of these women discussed the various restrictions placed upon them in terms of dating, having friendships with men, and wearing the hijab. The two category 10 women did not date but were highly involved in volunteering activities in their communities, through the Muslim students associations, by being counsellors at summer camps for girls, and even being part of the university campus radio show on Islam. But on the whole, the women in this group had few extracurricular activities that led them to interact with non-Muslims outside of their school environment. That feature was a primary basis for their separate classification. They found ways to maintain a boundary for themselves that kept them from the male gaze and that also allowed them to pass the faith on to other young Muslim girls. Only 5 of the highly involved participants had dated, and all of them admitted to hiding it from their parents. Although the no-dating rule was not enforced among the women in the moderately involved levels, many of them nonetheless refrained from sexual contact because of religious ideals. These women took on the gendered responsibility of the requirement of sexual segregation expounded in Islam. Some of them also illustrated how, as women, they felt that they were culturally responsible for segregation. For instance, Alia described her culture as difficult for women because it was assumed that all women were to conform to strict rules of sex segregation, otherwise rumours would spread about the girl and her family. Her mother also would not let her have male friends, but for religious reasons:

INTERVIEWER: Would you say that the difference of opinions that you have with your parents, is it religious or cultural? Is it like a clash between Somali culture and Canadian culture, or is it specifically religious?
ALIA: Um, I think it's a little bit of both. Uh, because my mom, on top of her wanting me to be religious, she also wants me to be more Somalian. Um, and I think for her, the two are a lot more linked than they are for me. Um, so when she's talking or yelling at me, um, it's more of a "let's try and get her to be more like me and be Muslim and religious, I mean Somalian and religious." (MF23)

Many of these women had to negotiate between cultural and religious values, which often overlapped, and in both circumstances they often found themselves in the position of representing not only themselves but their families, faith, and communities as well.

Understanding the intention for wearing the veil in Islam is a complex endeavour. Unlike the first generation, who brought the tradition of veiling with them from their countries of origin, these women needed to find ways of negotiating with others who were within their faith and those from outside their faith. As they navigated the space between the self and other, they entered into what Pratt calls "contact zones," "social spaces where disparate cultures meet, clash, and grapple with each other, often in highly asymmetrical relations of domination and subordination" (Pratt 2008, 7). Contact zones here were the spaces and situations encountered by these women, which required them to decide more precisely what kinds of personal religious and cultural identity lines they would draw and how. Although the stereotypical image of a woman wearing a veil is that she is subordinated by her culture and her faith, the hijab in personal practice can have many meanings: it can be used as a barrier between these spaces and also as a claim to recognition. For the two category 10 women as well as the highly involved participants in this study, the hijab played a central role in the structure of their religious identity. Both of the females in the highest category wore the hijab out of a sense of obligation as Muslims but also as a way to help them maintain a barrier to cultural influences. The 12 highly involved women who wore hijab gave a variety of reasons for doing so. One woman felt that it was part of her identity, another for reasons of modesty. A few of them met with parental opposition to wearing the veil. One woman said that her father considered it "backward-minded for women to wear it." Another woman stated that her mother believed that by wearing the veil, she was losing her rights as a woman and a Canadian. Another woman began wearing the veil because her aunt bought it for her, even though her mother felt it too restrictive. 9/11 also played an important role in her desire to identify as a Muslim in Canada. She considered herself a "Muslim trying to figure out how to live life as a regular Canadian teen and do all the regular 'fun' stuff but trying to keep Canadian culture enough at bay so I will not stray from Islam." Five of the other highly involved females expressed a desire to wear the hijab in the future. One woman was a dancer and felt that she needed to stop dancing in order to fully commit to the meaning of wearing the veil – a responsibility came with choosing to wear it. Another woman felt that "there's too much crap living in Canada" that comes with wearing the veil, although she desired to wear it. She believed that if she wore the veil to a job interview, she would be denied the job because of racism. The practice of veiling, even though complex and varied among these women, was strongly correlated with intensity of practice and belief and was not a matter of simple conformity to parental or community pressure. In many instances, the hijab played an important role in delineating boundaries and helping them negotiate their private religious identities in the public sphere.[4]

Creating a Religious Identity

Just as new immigrants recreate religion in a new homeland based on the way their religious communities are shaped, second-generation Muslim Canadians are recreating their religious identities in new and meaningful ways. Scholarship has shown that the religions that immigrants bring with them "carry the distinctive traits of the culture in which they were practiced" (Foley and Hoge 2007, 185). While first-generation immigrants in particular are often nurtured by religious communities in their new homeland, this was not true for the second-generation Muslims females (and males) in this study. Most of the highly involved and category 10 women constructed their religious identities individually rather than having strong ties to any particular religious congregation or community.

Their religious identities were not shaped or nurtured primarily or all that directly by their religious communities, but a significant number of the most highly involved youths considered themselves deeply religious. This group of women, who practised what they felt was a fundamental understanding of Islam, were inclined to keep their style of Islam to themselves rather than practising it within a worship community. Instead of finding comfort and a sense of belonging in these congregations, they found institutional outlets at their university Muslim students associations or through chat groups in cyberspace.

The role of university MSAs for the women in fact appeared to be stronger than even for the devout Muslim men. Rather than searching for the ethnic or linguistic connections to which their parental generation were drawn, these women did not associate with what they labelled the cultural values of their parents, who, like many new immigrants, did indeed carry distinctive traits of their culture in the way they practised their religion. They did not consider the mosque of their parents a significant or natural location in which to learn about their faith. In fact, rather than relying on immediate family members as a source of religious information or wisdom, the category 10 and many of the highly involved women embarked upon personal searches to better understand Islam and made a clear distinction between the so-called ethnic practices of their parents and the practice of Islam. For instance, Irshad (MF09; a Salafi) did not attend mosque, because she believed it was not obligatory for women to go there for prayers, but she also stated that the mosque gave her community a sense of "brotherhood." Therefore, it was, for instance, important for her father to attend community worship.

The parental ethnic and cultural practices that many of these highly involved youths often criticized focused on issues such as having extravagant weddings, listening to music, and encouraging the idea of a good career over marriage for their children. Irshad not only claimed that Islam influenced her career choice but felt that her parents focused too much on career, whereas, to Irshad, Islam placed importance on family, and so she wished to get married rather than pursue a high-paying career. She also searched out Islam individually, first reading the Qur'an in her youth and then using the Internet. She first learned the practices and beliefs of Islam from her parents but felt that she had to pursue it independently, because they were busy integrating into Canadian society, something which she did not feel was necessary, since she was already a Canadian.

At the same time, none of these women considered their own level of belief and practice of Islam as exceeding that of their parents; they just considered their Islam to be "purer," because it did away with the cultural attachments that their parents carried with them from the homeland. This is a prime indicator of how they were reconstructing systemic Islam, albeit with the common understanding among those who reform religion that they were "purifying" and not changing (Beyer 2005a). Moreover, since they considered themselves detached from their parents' homelands and cultures, these women felt that in their purer form of Islam, they were thereby full and participating members of Canadian society. Their ethnicity was distinct: they were truly Canadian and truly Islamic. On the whole, these women carried out their religious identity by dressing modestly, not dating, and wearing the hijab or planning to in the future, and they were convinced that they were free to practise their religion as freely as they would like, living in Canada. They saw themselves as "full and equal members of Canadian society." Although the majority of the highly involved and category 10 (Salafi) women thus distinguished between their parents' culture and Islam, some of the highly involved (categories 7 to 9) nonetheless continued to follow their parents' way of practising Islam and incorporated aspects of their parents' homeland culture into their lives while at the same time actively participating in Canadian society.

In comparison to the highly involved participants, most of the moderately involved women continued to follow the Islam they were taught by their parents, who were also moderately involved practitioners. Participants who learned about Islam from extended family members rather than from their parents tended to practise their faith at a higher level than their parents. For the few participants who had parents with mixed religious backgrounds, if they practised Islam, it was also because they had learned their faith from extended family members. Mona (MF10), whose parents were not very religious, learned from her cousin how to pray properly as a teenager. She eventually took religious classes by herself and went to spend time with her grandmother in Lebanon to learn more about her faith. Yet she too did not join a community of worship but searched the Internet to read about and better understand Islam. In fact, she claimed that she did not spend time in Muslim groups because she did not want to be manipulated into believing something that was not truly Islamic – she wished to search for the answers herself. In general within this subgroup, very few participants affiliated with religious institutions: they only went to mosques for special events such as Eid, breaking fast during Ramadan, and sporadically for Friday jum'ah prayers. The participants within the moderately involved group also considered themselves Canadian first, but the reasons for not feeling truly Muslim lay in the fact that they behaved in ways they considered to be un-Islamic. In fact, they characterized these behaviours as "Canadian": some of them admitted to drinking occasionally, smoking, and dating. Aminah (MF12) was 19 years old and was born in Canada. Her father was a Muslim from Algeria, and her mother was non-religious and from Holland. Her father taught her and her two siblings the basics of Islam but did not practise the faith much when she was young. In fact, Aminah attended Catholic school as a child but said she knew she was a Muslim. So in her teens she attended Islamic classes. She began praying, fasting, and attending mosque with friends and their families. But Aminah did go clubbing, so she did not feel that she could wear the hijab, because wearing it comes with a responsibility in that it "symbolizes Islam." Aminah also dated, although she said that she did not date casually but for marriage prospects. For the bulk of the practising participants in this study, there was a sense of civic engagement, which intertwined with their understanding of Islam. Unlike many new immigrants, a majority of the participants demonstrated high levels of interest in community development programs (several of the highly involved volunteered at Islamic summer camps), they participated in social service programs and wanted to work in foreign countries as aid workers, and they also displayed high levels of interest in civic affairs. These participants had also experienced a new aware-ness of their religions: in response to the stereotyping that occurred after 9/11, quite a few of the women who were moderately involved or highly involved began researching Islam further in order to better understand their faith and to find responses to constant questions and reactions to Muslims. For these respondents in particular, the understanding of their faith in relation to Can-adian culture had helped form their personal and community identities. They were not rooted to the heritage of their parents, nor were they turning to re-ligious communities to maintain their culture or their faith. Yet, at the same time, they felt connected to a wider Islamic community, a universal under-standing of the faith that transcended any linguistic or ethnic identities their parents might carry.

"Contact Zones": Negotiating Social Influences

In order to understand how second-generation Muslims negotiate the space between themselves and others, it is important to examine what social relations are important in nurturing and shaping these identities. Pratt's (Pratt 2008) notion of "contact zones" helps to explain how these youths were creating and recreating their identities: these identities were informed by family, friends, the media, politics, and gender. Each of these areas represents a contact zone that can have different kinds of influence on identity formation, including, of course, religious identity. The majority of the female participants acknow-ledged that they had been shaped by their family's religious background. This influence directly affected the quality of the relationship they had with their parents. Both of the category 10 (Salafi) participants and the majority of the highly involved group agreed that they had inherited their religious values from their parents in childhood, but as young adults they did not expressly seek out their parents to further discuss religious issues. Because of their desire to disconnect the cultural aspects of their parents' homeland from their understanding of Islam – to understand a pure Islam, as it were – they often held opinions different from those of their parents as to what constituted the practice of "authentic Islam." The other highly involved members of the group regarded their parents as role models for religious expression and behaviour. But all of the category 10 and highly involved women had strong relationships with their parents. The moderately involved group acknowledged that they tended to quarrel with their parents much more regarding religious practice, or their lack of it, if their parents were at a higher level of practice. The major-ity of the non-believers had poor relationships with their parents, particularly those whose parents continued practising the religion regularly.

Social relations with peers played a key role regarding religious involve-ment. The sources of social identification networks could be found in their schools, in Muslim students associations, in the mosque, and on the Internet.

Most of the category 10 women's friends (up to 90%, if not all) were Muslim females who shared their beliefs, practices, and judgments. Both Irshad and Sonia stated that they tried to remember God constantly, prayed every day wherever they were, were counsellors at Islamic summer camps, and were active members of their Muslim students associations. They co-ordinated all their "contact zones" to reinforce their strong identification with an adherence to Islam. This trend was not evident in the highly involved group, but many mentioned that their friends had many of the same values and family rules to follow. Although the mosque was part of their lives in one way or another, the worship community played an insignificant role in shaping and nurturing their faith. While the category 10 females prayed five times a day (if not more often), they only attended mosque in order to participate in the festivals with their families. Each made a point of noting that it was not obligatory for women to attend *jum'ah* services but performing prayer was of utmost importance. Irshad, in university, would use the university prayer room and would leave a class if it was prayer time. A majority of the highly involved women attended mosque on a regular basis with their parents or at the university but also went to religion classes on weekends or had tutors to learn to read the Qur'an and Hadith, with the approval of their parents. Unlike the women in category 10, more than half of the highly involved group said that they would go the imam of the mosque if they had religious questions. This is in contrast as well to the majority of the highly involved men, as we saw in the last chapter. Only half the moderately involved participants went to mosque, and it was usually for special occasions or sporadically to pray. Many of the female participants at all levels, when asked whether they went to the mosque for prayer, pointed out that it was not mandatory for women to attend mosque: many prayed with the family in the home, and quite a few highly involved and the category 10 women prayed specifically at the designated prayer time in whatever location they were in.

In terms of personal faith, the Internet has turned out to be of particular use in shaping individual religious identities. Although it has been argued that patriarchal Islamist discourse has led to the objectification of Muslim women, many Muslim women use information technology to "master" or appropriate that discourse through language, law, and metaphor (Karim 2005). In this study, at least 18 female participants acknowledged that they used the Internet as a religious forum and a source of information. Farida (MF15), a 20-year-old moderately involved participant, used the Internet as a form of "soul searching." In fact, her mother also watched religious programs on the Internet. Rather than just using the Internet as a way of mirroring one's offline religious expression and experience, these women used it to provide them with new articulations of faith (Bunt 2004). The category 10 participants and some of the highly involved group stated that they often used the Internet and electronic chat rooms as sources for understanding Islamic values and practices and as religious organizations. This practice added to the notion of eliminating (their parents') cultural values in order to find a true understanding of Islam for themselves. The highest-category participants and many of the highly involved participants were encouraged by their parents to learn more about their faith on their own. Interestingly, the category 10 women were very specific about the content they looked for on the Internet. They searched only for articles dealing with the Qur'an and Hadith and often avoided forums and chat rooms to stay away from non-believers. Irshad maintained that Western values and thoughts had corrupted some people who claim to be Muslims on the Internet and therefore had compromised the true teachings of the religion. She used the Internet to read a lot of lectures and speeches, but she was very precise in whom she listened to: "Like, before I was just 'oh, he's Muslim whatever' and just listen to it, but now I'm like, okay I have to listen to the one that I know will not lead me to any other path, you know; that will lead me you know, to pure, the way Islam, pure Islam basically. So there's only certain speakers I listen to, you know, and whatnot" (MF09).

Highly involved female participants who used the Internet claimed to spend time reading religious articles and listening to lectures about Islam online. Noor, a 22-year-old highly involved female, began learning about Islam on her own when her father starting becoming more religious. Her mother was a convert to Islam before marrying her father and was not as highly practising as her father. Noor began surfing the Internet more often in university to better understand her faith. She used it specifically to better understand the Qur'an and Hadith, so she spent much of her time specifically on Sunni websites, because that was their focus. She also did not find it necessary to follow just one particular authority on the Internet. "There's just difference of interpretations and there's different scholars that they go by and, for me personally, I'm against going like following one scholar and just being like, 'Okay, whatever he says goes.' Because I don't – I like looking into things and I think it's better to get the whole realm of opinion rather than just like following this one thing" (MF04).

In trying to better incorporate Islam into her daily life, Noor found that she disagreed with her university professors in classes on women and Islam so turned to the Internet to better understand the arguments out there. For this reason, she decided to start wearing the hijab. Another highly involved female felt that there was nothing to be gained by approaching the imam of her mosque, so she used the Internet to research areas that were pertinent to her life at the moment, in this instance marriage and children. She basically admitted she was "shopping around." When asked about her views on the imam, she stated, "I wouldn't go to the imam in the mosque or anything in my mosque, because I've heard him speak and I don't agree with half the things he says. I suppose if I did have any questions, I love the Internet, so I'd probably look it up, or you can email a scholar like some scholar at a university or an academic" (MF04).

Eight moderately involved female participants also searched for answers on the Internet, because they did not feel comfortable enough becoming members of organized associations in light of their own perceived differences from what they considered highly involved practitioners. For instance, they didn't dress modestly enough, or they were more culturally oriented than those in the associations or mosques. Alia (MF23) stated that in terms of meeting the needs of youth, the mosque and the imam were only for the very, very religious youth, not for people like herself (only moderately involved). She believed that if she approached the imam, he would give her a hard time for not wearing a headscarf. Therefore, she turned to the Internet to better understand the rituals and practices of Islam (usually when someone would ask her about it – for instance, what is Eid, and how many are there? She said two). Another moderate female said that she would also not approach the imam to seek answers about elements of the faith. She would rather look up her faith on the Internet if she had questions relating to it. In fact, she was currently reading an English translation of the Qur'an online. Within our study, we found that the Internet was a valued resource that accommodated individuals who were being religious outside the control or authority of an organized religious institution (cf. Helland 2004). Nonetheless, as has been noted more than a few times, this fluidity and variety of sources had not resulted in a wide variety of constructions of Islam but rather a consistent convergence on what we have been calling the five-pillars global model of Islam.

One specific contact zone, rather than supplying support and influencing the shape of the religious identities of these women, has played a contentious role. Some Muslim immigrant youths have been angered by controversial aspects of popular culture, specifically the way Islam has been stereotypically portrayed since 9/11. The study of Muslim youth in the United States by Sirin and Fine (Sirin and Fine 2008) found that young Muslim men found contact with American media "dangerous, offensive, engulfing and annihilating" (171). On the other hand, their focus group of young Muslim women were ambivalent yet felt an "embodied invitation to engage and struggle" (171). Among the category 10 and highly involved women in our study, media representations of Muslims after 9/11 had a very specific effect on their identities. In reaction to the "terrorist" image bandied about in portrayals of Muslims on television and popular films, many of these young women began "wearing" their Islamic identity with pride and more openly. Noor started becoming more serious about her faith after 9/11. She even began wearing the hijab six months prior to the interview, against her father's wishes (he claimed that the hijab was worn by backward-minded women). The tragic events of 9/11 made her want to learn more about her religion in order to answer constant questions. Her search for religious understanding led her to begin attending Friday *jum'ah* services at the mosque and university and also to start praying at home with her father. Moderately identified Muslims also felt that the image of Islam had been tarnished after 9/11, and some acknowledged that they actually began studying Islam to better understand it and to explain it to others. Aminah declared that she became more proud of saying that she was a Muslim after 9/11 in order to defend her faith. Rather than feeling alienated or isolated, these young women felt impelled to better educate themselves about Islam in order to challenge the stereotypes that surrounded their faith. For those who donned the veil in response to this contact zone, it became a marker of their pride in demonstrating their religious identity in Canada (see also Haddad 2007).

SOME DETAILED LIVES

In moving now to the lived religion approach, it is necessary to get a more detailed understanding of how individual women in our sample are reconstructing or rejecting their faith within a Canadian context. We have selected four voices to represent the different categories in the classification system outlined in this chapter. These snapshots include one in the non-religious region, Meena (MF27), who was a category 2 Iranian. In the moderately involved region, we examine Dilshad (MF43), who was in category 5. Aisha (MF49) was in the highly involved region at category 8. We also include a detailed description of Irshad (MF09) to illustrate how she fitted into category 10, the highest category, in comparison to those in the highly involved categories.

Meena (MF27)

At the time of the interview, Meena was 26 years old, completing a graduate degree in psychology at Concordia University in Montreal. Her parents left Iran in 1988 because of the political situation. Meena's parents chose to immigrate to Canada on the advice of a friend who had already immigrated to Canada and informed them that it was one of the better countries in which to live. They chose Canada as their home, even though they had no relatives living in Canada at the time, and had never returned to Iran. Her father owned a landscaping company, and her mother was a nurse. Meena had three siblings.

When asked about religion, Meena, much like many of the other Muslim participants from Iran, drew a strong distinction between religion and spirituality. For Meena, religion was organized and structured, whereas spirituality was a personal relationship with God; it did not require particular rituals. Prayer did not require bowing down to God five times a day as Muslims do but was more of a private conversation. Although Meena did not follow any organized religion, she did acknowledge that there were positive elements to religion: it taught the value of life, caring for and loving others. When it came to being spiritual, Meena stated that she did believe in God, and this belief was very important to her. But she was clear in stating that she was not religious. "I don't follow religion, I may have when I was younger, but at this point I don't. I believe there are certain things that I don't agree with that the Muslim religion preaches, and there are certain things that I hold as, it's my view and it's also shared by a religion." These views, as taught to her by her parents, included being kind to others and respecting family. Although her parents were more religious than she was in that they openly followed Islam by praying sometimes (not daily), fasting often during Ramadan (as much as possible but not the whole time), and sometimes observing Islamic rituals, they also had a spiritual relationship to God and were very open to other ideas and religions. "I can say on a scale from 1 to 100, with 100 being very religious, my parents are about 50. They do believe in certain things, but they don't preach Islam and the fundamentalist stuff." Meena also drew a cultural distinction in relation to Islam in that it was part of her heritage and country: she self-identified as Muslim on census forms "because I have to, I mean, I don't want to lie about a religion that I grew up in and that I come from, but it's hard to say what they are really asking you." She saw herself as Muslim by birth but not by practice. In fact, Meena pointed out that many Iranians did not attend mosque because of prior history in Iran but culturally socialized through the Iranian community centre. One notes that Meena would therefore "count as a Muslim" on the census and probably if she were asked, but her actual "religious" (i.e., spiritual) identity and practice was outside that systemic whole for the most part. In being "spiritual but not religious" she, like a good number of the non-religious and not a few of the somewhat involved, did not fit with any clarity in an exclusive and single category.

As Meena grew older, her religious views began to change, especially through contact with friends who had different ethnic and religious backgrounds. Interestingly, Meena's sister shared the same perspective on spirituality and religion, while her older brother converted to Christianity and became a devout follower. But Meena thought that through integration, many youths who come to Canada from other countries lose their religion: "You cannot necessarily be, in one sense, a Muslim, practise Islam the way you do in your country, and hold your own cultural beliefs you have learned and call yourself Canadian and be here, go to school like everyone else ... I don't know, associate with your friends. It's different." She found this a positive element, because she did not see the youths who held on to their faith and country heritage as fully integrated and therefore saw them as unhappy.

Although Meena grew up in a Muslim household and had a Muslim heritage, she did not consider anything she did to be Muslim. She was religious in that she believed in God but did not follow any structured or institutional format of practice. Even though she felt guilty for having moved away from the religion of her parents, she felt that she could not believe in some of the aspects of religion (such as the concepts of heaven and hell) and tried to allay her guilt through prayer with God – private conversations in which she let God know that she believed in the existence of God but not in the practice of Islam. "Like, I feel like I have abandoned God, is what I feel like. Because, unfortunately, your religion sometimes teaches you that if you let go of this religion that you have now, then you are abandoning God. And I think with Muslims it is the same." Much like others in the non-religious category, Meena declared that she was spiritual but saw religion as sometimes problematic. Her friends came from disparate backgrounds, and she had experienced no prejudice living in Canada. Although she was quite happy living in Canada and agreed that Canada treated different religions and ethnicities with respect, she acknowledged that people who did follow their faith from a country that was religious had a harder time practising their faith fully living in Canada. "There are certain things that you do [in your country], certain ceremonies or rituals that people practise which you can't practise here."

Dilshad (MF43)

Dilshad was 22 years old and in her final year, completing a degree in chemical engineering in Montreal. Her parents came from Egypt. Her father chose to come to Canada to complete his graduate degrees, also in chemical engineering. Once he had attained his PhD, he brought his wife and first daughter to Canada. Although Dilshad's mother took some typing classes when she arrived in Montreal, she stayed home to raise the children. Dilshad and her younger sister were born on the south shore of the Montreal area, and her family still resided there. She and her siblings went to both English and French schools, so they are fully bilingual. All of her extended family lived in Egypt, and they visited them often until school and work began to interfere with free time. Dilshad had not been back to Egypt in eight years, although she would like to return for a visit after she graduated.

In contrast to Meena, Dilshad considered herself to be both religious and spiritual, and in her case the religious included the spiritual. Religion, to Dilshad, was about faith and morality, whereas spirituality included cultural history and tradition. She was a Sunni Muslim and believed that this is the truest form of Islam. Religion offered Dilshad hope in bad situations and included the notion of forgiveness. There was always a goal to aspire to, no matter how difficult life became. In terms of regular practice, Dilshad stated that she used to pray more often when the prayer room at Concordia was conveniently located, but since it had moved she did not pray as often. "I feel bad because my family is religious ... Well, when I do more activities with Muslim people and talk to my Muslim friends, then I get more into praying. It's pretty much the praying. Like, I don't drink and I don't eat pork and all those things, but praying is very important in my religion. It's really, really important, and I don't do it often enough." Her faith was important to her, and she knew this because she felt guilty when she did something that was not acceptable in Islam. In fact, at the time of the interview, she did not consider herself religious, because she had a boyfriend (which leads to other non-religious activities). Although Dilshad thought she was not religious because of the boyfriend, she fasted and prayed as much as she could. "I think a person who can say that they're religious, it would be on a 24-hour basis and not an intensive all the time praying, just a constant uniform basis, and going to school, going out eating, but I'm not ready, not constant."

When asked what a practising Muslim does to be religious, Dilshad responded that honesty to anyone and everyone was of great importance. Also, Muslims helped people in need, "and not just the poor but their friends, their enemies, your classmates, your teachers, your elders." Other important characteristics of a Muslim included fully applying oneself to the work that one was doing, "whether it is studying and work or cutting your carrots, cut them right; you do a good job of everything." And finally, the most important element was cleanliness. "Being clean is very important, because obviously when you pray five times a day you have to be clean when you pray. Another characteristic of a Muslim is to tell God all the time – I know Christians do that too – when you're about to eat or leave the house." In essence, a Muslim must remember God all the time.

Dilshad believed community was important in maintaining one's faith. "Say that you stop praying or stop fasting; then you're doing other things, and you become disconnected from the religion. So I think that the community is very important, the overall connection is very important." Dilshad's father attended mosque in Montreal every Friday, but the rest of the family did not, because it was not essential for women to pray in the mosque. She prayed at home when her parents reminded her to pray (the women in the home do not pray together). As a family, they all went to the mosque during parts of Ramadan. Although Dilshad found it difficult to have a strong community in Montreal, because there were very few mosques there in comparison to Egypt, she used to attend an Arabic school when she was younger. She was happy to have attended, even though it was difficult to have an extra day of school, because she could now read and write a little in official Arabic (she considered Egyptian Arabic, which her family spoke, a less proper form of the language). She hoped to read the Qur'an in Arabic someday but was currently reading it in English.

In terms of learning about the faith, Dilshad saw the Qur'an and Hadith as stories that taught the message of Islam and helped her stay connected to God.

But this learning was as important as "everyday living and having fun." Dilshad also had issues with certain aspects of Islam in terms of male–female relations:

> I've never had any problems with the beliefs or the praying and every-
> thing, those things are fine. The alcohol or anything never bothered
> me either, it's the relations. Some people take it too far, some are like
> "don't look the man in the eyes," and that I reject, because it's 2006.
> Some things in Islam are of a very old mentality, so things like that. Um,
> there's also another thing. With marriage in Islam, the man can marry
> four women at one time. There are a lot of rules and reasons, if the
> person can't reproduce then they can marry more. But I don't think it's
> very fair to the women.

One notes in this quote how Dilshad considered that there was a clear and orthodox model of Islam – and she sometimes felt guilty when she did not observe it – but she was not above "editing" that model when she saw fit. She was in this way someone who, while generally faithful to what is inside Islam, did practise a certain "religion à la carte," picking and choosing (cf. Bibby 1987).

Dilshad did not wear the hijab, by choice, but her younger sister began wearing it when she turned 18. "It was her choice, and what happened, I guess, was when we went to high school we went to a very French high school and had a lot of Muslim friends. She's very quiet, she's different than me; she's quiet and serious, and that's good for her, and so it's a good step for her." Her mother and older sister did not wear the hijab either, but her parents were happy when her younger sister began wearing it, because many of their female family members in Egypt wear the hijab.

In comparison to Meena, who did not feel she did anything Muslim, Dilshad saw herself as a Muslim but less so than her Muslim friends, because they were more involved in the faith through the Muslim Students Association on campus and their friends were all Muslim. Dilshad chose her friends by how comfortable she felt with them. In her free time, she did not really attend religious events, so most of her time was spent with non-Muslims. She also considered herself less of a Muslim than her friends because she had a boyfriend. He was Muslim as well, and they planned to get married, but her parents did not approve of dating, so they did not know she had a boyfriend. "I just hope we can get along with my parents, because if it goes good, then we can get married. I agree with that, with seeing someone if you're being serious, and I wish that Islam would too; but it's just not …" Dilshad shared the same religious views as her parents but considered herself less practising because of this secret. Part of her change occurred when she was allowed to spend six months away from home in England on an exchange program and found people more relaxed there. For instance, she and her parents often argued about clothing, because she liked to wear tank tops in the summer to stay cool but her parents did not want her exposing too much "flesh" in public. Before her trip to England at the age of 20, she considered herself more conservative. Now, if her parents were to ask her to change, she might argue with them, or she would put on a jacket and remove it when she became warm. But Dilshad wished she could find a way to be honest with her parents about the one thing that kept her from feeling Muslim "enough": her boyfriend. She hid the truth and planned to continue to do so, because some of her other Muslim friends who had been upfront with their parents lived with tension and she wanted to avoid that. Even though Dilshad hid the truth about her boyfriend, it was of utmost importance that she marry a Muslim, since it was "forbidden to marry anyone else" in Islam. "Islam is very community and very family, and if she's marrying a non-Muslim, it would be hard for the children ... You know, the father might not be involved and they might get influenced, and that's how the religion becomes divided and decreases and all that." She would insist on raising her children as Muslims.

Unlike Meena, Dilshad continued to follow her parents' practice of Islam. She shared their views and endeavoured to be a good Muslim. She felt guilty for breaking the "no-dating" rule but hoped that her parents would understand when the time came to get married. She freely practised her faith in Canada but did not feel that religion dictated all aspects of her life. She also saw Canada in the same way she practised her faith. "I think that religion and society should stay separate, because there are so many religions so you do your own thing and still you can mingle with who you want, like work, school." Dilshad had Muslim and non-Muslim friends. She aspired to pray regularly but didn't. She followed halal rules and fasted during Ramadan and then liked to hang out with her friends and have fun. She was the epitome of a moderately involved Muslim and paralleled quite well, in many respects, the Muslim males in this category whom we examined in the previous chapter.

Aisha (MF49)

Aisha, at the time of the interview, was 19 years old and was studying life sciences at the University of Toronto with plans to become a doctor. She was born in Afghanistan and came to Canada at the age of 4. She had five younger siblings: two were born in Afghanistan and the other three were born in Canada. Her parents left Afghanistan for a better life, because there was a lot of conflict taking place in their home country. Her father was a teacher in Afghanistan and was a driving instructor in Canada; her mother stayed at home. Most of her extended family ended up leaving Afghanistan for Canada, but her parents often travelled back to Afghanistan to visit family. In terms of language acquisition, the entire family had to learn French first, because they initially lived in Montreal, then they moved to Toronto and had to learn English: Farsi was their primary language.

Aisha defined herself as a Sunni Muslim. To her, religion was "very important because … it keeps me going every day." It affected every single aspect of her life. On a scale of 1 to 10, the importance of religion was a 9 for Aisha. Her parents were not as religious as she was, but she learned the rituals and practices from them. "Like, every child learns it from their parents, but there were some things that umm … In Afghanistan it's kind of culture that takes over and they think that's religion and it mixes the basics of religion with the culture. So I guess to me I had to learn those other things, and I learnt it from people."

Around the age of 15, in order to better understand why her parents told her to pray (occasionally), she began researching it on her own to make sense of it. As a result, she became much more regular in her practice of Islam and a stronger believer: "Because if you don't believe it, then there's no point of practising it." Aisha had also taken it upon herself to make her younger siblings practise the faith more regularly. She always fasted for the whole month of Ramadan, but it had more significance for her now. As for her siblings, "I try to get them into it, and they do fast for probably I'd say half of it. You know, sometimes I give them these speeches about it and why it's good and all of that, and then they'd be like 'okay, okay, I'll do it.'"

After acknowledging the basic five pillars of Islam as the important aspects of the faith, Aisha continued to explain that for her, it was necessary to read the Qur'an on a daily basis (even though she was working up to this), do the five daily prayers, and do good things: "it's just a part of you, every day." These particular practices helped her to become close to God. In order to understand the Qur'an, Aisha took Arabic classes and had read it in both Arabic and in translations. Her sources of authority were the Qur'an and Hadith. If she had questions about her faith, she probably wouldn't ask her parents but would turn to books and religious friends at university or discussion groups through the Muslim Students Association (in which she was also a volunteer). Asking an imam was not really an option for Aisha, because she did not regularly go to mosque, since she could pray at home. She did readings on the Internet as a further source, but in a sense, the MSA had become a community for Aisha, and she saw doing service for the members as doing something good for her religion. It was at the MSA that Aisha found other youths who practised at the higher level she did in comparison to her family. One notes how the university environment for some, like Aisha, allowed a more faithful practice of her religion, whereas others, like Dilshad, found the overall secular atmosphere there more of a reason not to practise as much. Although she found a community in the MSA, Aisha also noted that some of her friends (not many) were not

Muslim but they all shared the same social behaviours, such as not drinking, clubbing, or hanging out with boys. Having Muslim friends was very important to Aisha:

> Yeah, it is important because let's say my friend is a Muslim and if she understands me then ... let's say if she were going, I don't know, going to a club to drink or whatever and she'd be like, "hey do you want to celebrate with me and go have a drink?" and I'd be like ... "What do you say? – I don't drink and stuff." So it's important for them to understand, and it'd be important for me to understand theirs too, that there are certain things that they can't be doing either, right.

In terms of practice, Aisha made sure to pray five times a day and would go out of her way to take time out to conduct afternoon prayers, even leaving a class for fifteen minutes. She performed the ritual cleaning of hands and face before praying. She also prayed at work, since her boss is also Muslim. If she knew a prayer time was coming up, Aisha made sure that she was not busy at that time: "like, I pray, then go to the mall ... So that I wouldn't miss my prayer." Aisha also prayed before leaving the house and after eating a meal. She did not drink alcohol or smoke and only eats halal. Her parents made sure that all the meat in the house was halal, but sometimes she would throw away certain things in the house that she found haram (such as candy with gelatin). Aisha began wearing the hijab when her family moved to Toronto. "When I came here in Grade 7, my Dad's like, 'why don't you wear it?' and stuff, because there's not much racism [compared to Montreal]. I'm like, 'sure I'll wear it.'" She began by wearing it to certain places such as school but not openly in the mall. When she began researching Islam for her own personal interest, "I got more information and started truly believing in what I was doing. Then I wore it everywhere, except let's say a wedding [laughs]. But that was it ... Other than that, it was everywhere." Even though her mother did not wear the hijab regularly, her parents were proud that she began wearing it daily until she entered university:

> The thing is, they're also afraid that people might judge you because of that. Like your professors or ... let's say you're trying to get into med school, and you go to your interview, you know. There are people who are racist. But that doesn't mean everyone is or anything. So they're kind of scared of that, so they told me, like, "it's okay, you don't have to wear it anymore," and I'm, like, "no, I want to."

Aisha also tried wearing the abbaya[5] for a while, but her parents didn't permit it. She dressed modestly with the hijab, making sure to wear long sleeves and pants, no short skirts or low necklines. But if her future husband wanted her to wear such clothing, that would be fine.

Aisha also made a strong distinction between culture and religion. She found that her parents followed more cultural aspects, which Aisha considered unimportant. She found that her parents had a double standard in the way they allowed her brother to go to bars and date. Her parents would tell her that she did not have to be "so religious," but she said she wanted to be: "That's what I think is right, and what you think is right is what you'll do." She was comfortable with the way she practised her faith: the only aspects she would change would be to read the Qur'an every single day and attend mosque for the informational lectures. But for Aisha, the most important aspect was one's intention to do more even if it wasn't possible: "I think if my intentions are okay then, you know, it shouldn't really be too much of a problem." Religion had also influenced her choice of career, since she wanted to be a doctor because it meant helping people. She would only marry a Muslim, as dictated by her religion, and she would not date before marriage – she could spend time with a boy as long as she was with a group of girls – but this was a hypothetical situation for Aisha, since she had not done it yet. She would not mind if her parents found her a marriage partner, as long as she agreed to it. It would also be very important to raise her children as Muslims and teach them aspects of Islam that her parents were unable to teach her when she was growing up.

Although Aisha found it difficult to practise some aspects of her religion (such as wearing the hijab or abbaya), she was happy that Canada was a multicultural country, because that reduced racism and allowed people to learn from each other. Canada had allowed her to maintain her faith. "Like, what's the point if I can't just be me, if I can't have my faith with me when I'm going anywhere and everywhere, right? So I think Canada is doing a good job."

Aisha fell within category 8 in that she followed the orthodox teachings of Islam but would like to be a better practitioner. She did the obligatory prayer five times a day, fasted during Ramadan, and followed the dietary laws. She wore the hijab and wished to perform the *hajj* in the future. She had read the Qur'an completely in Arabic and consulted Hadith and readings to help her better understand certain aspects of her faith. However, what was of greatest importance to Aisha was to publicly practise her faith, even when it defied the norm (again by wearing the hijab and perhaps the abbaya in the future), because the challenge built one's faith: "It's sort of like the prophets, right? They went out and they, you know, they tried to follow their religion in a society and try to deal with it that way. It's much harder that way, it's more challenging that way. It kind of tests you, you know."

Without question, for Aisha religion was entirely subsumed with orthodox Islam as she had come to understand it. She was, however, still quite open about her involvement in Canadian society, including as concerns her social circle. In this and several other ways, in spite of being so highly involved, she contrasted notably with those in category 10, of which Irshad is one.

Irshad (MF09)

In many ways, Aisha emulated Irshad in terms of orthopraxis. Yet Irshad displayed a rigid understanding of Islam that distinguished her from the highly involved Muslim participants. Diversity in belief was unacceptable; thus, non-Sunnis were not really Muslim. Socially, Irshad did not interact with men, to the point where she averted her gaze from all males. She was striving to build a stronger barrier to maintain the male–female segregation requirements of Islam. Tolerance for a multicultural Canada was based on following the example of the Prophet.

At the time of the interview, Irshad was 21 years old; she was born in Mogadishu, Somalia, the homeland of her parents. She spent two years in Saudi Arabia before coming to Canada at the age of 5. Irshad had three siblings, one older sister, a brother who was 16, and a sister who was 13. Once in Canada, she had only ever lived in Ottawa. Her father chose to come to Canada so that his children could pursue university degrees and therefore be able to work anywhere in the world they wanted. Her father and mother both worked in Somalia, but her mother was unable to transfer her skills to Canada so chose to be a stay-at-home mom. She had relatives living in both Canada and the United States, so the family did not travel to Somalia.

In defining religion, Irshad was quick to explain that it was a way of life, not just for herself but for everyone who is religious:

> For me as a Muslim, it affects everything I do in my life, that's why I consider it a way of life. It's not just something that I remember once a week. It's not something that, you know, I do sometimes on religious holidays. It's the way I live, like from the way I eat, from the way I go to the bathroom even, the way I do everything, it affects it. You know, the way I talk to people, the way I'm talking here right now, the way I talk to people of opposite genders, you know, it just affects absolutely everything I do.

In defining the difference between religion and culture, Irshad said she believed that Somali culture allowed people to behave in a certain way: men and women could be around each other and "hang out," but Irshad considered this to be "non-religious." Therefore, she did not follow the cultural practices of Somalia, which she considered to be the practices of her parents as well.

When asked to explain how different religions compare to each other, Irshad explained that the only way she could answer that question was as a Muslim.

So as a Muslim, you know, I think Islam is the perfect way of life. I think it outshines every other religion there is because … I have studied other religions before, and I have friends who, like two, three of my best friends, actually they're Catholic, they're all Catholic Canadian girls. And I try that, and the way their lifestyle is and the way my lifestyle is, it's completely different. I find that we just live a life that's more [pause] better [small laugh]. I don't want to sound superior, like that's not my, that's not what I'm trying to do. But I just feel, like it's the way of life, it's just better.

Irshad felt that being Muslim was of the utmost importance to her. It affected every aspect of her life, all the time. Rather than explaining the different ways one could be Muslim (halal, fasting, praying), Irshad took it one step further: "I'm constantly conscious of it every single time." When she passed a man, it was necessary to lower her gaze and to remain humble about it as well. "I know that there are times that I don't, and I try and remember and be, like, conscious of that and try to lower my gaze, especially when I'm with, like, the opposite gender." Although she found this practice extremely difficult, because she was surrounded by males constantly at university, she tried her best to be vigilant. In fact, Irshad had taken this vigilance to include modest dress.

And the way that I do everything, like the way I dress even, like we're supposed to dress modestly, and I dress as modest as I can. I know I wasn't always like that, because you know, growing up in Canada, and I've always been going to predominantly white schools, it's been difficult 'cause I've been trying to be so much like them, but then now I'm like, I'm very comfortable with who I am, and I'm very comfortable with dressing the way I am.

She completely covered her hair, neck, arms, and legs. Only her face and hands could be seen. Irshad began wearing the hijab in Grade 11, and even though her mother wears the hijab as well, Irshad wears it "the proper way": "The way I wear the hijab and it goes over my neck, my mother doesn't. She just wears it from behind her neck. And I mean, like she knows that's not the correct [small laugh] way of doing it. But she says 'I'm not strong enough to wear it that way,' you know, she admits that she's not strong enough."

When Irshad was younger, she would actually try to fit in with her "white" friends, since she went to a predominantly white school and lived in a white neighborhood. She admitted that she had been ashamed to let people know that she was Muslim when she was young. In fact, she used to wear makeup when she was in school, without her parents' knowledge. She began to rebel against the image of the subjugated woman. In Grade 8, she began learning more about her religion and realized that Muslim women were supposed to behave differently: not worry about fashion and makeup.

> You know, in Islam, the woman is supposed to cover, the woman is sup-
> posed to, and that brings us dignity, and that empowers us, you know.
> It's a complete opposite of what I've always been taught, that a woman's
> empowerment is her body and to constantly show your body, and
> Islam's the complete opposite. Like, empowerment was covering your
> body and not being, you know, obsessed with looking good all the time,
> the way it is here.

Irshad grew up in a Muslim family. Her parents taught her how to practise her faith from a young age, teaching her to pray and fast, but she wished
that her parents had taught her more. "I've always known about my religion,
you know. But things like this, you know – I found my parents – I wish they
had taught me more about it when I was young. But now I understand it was
difficult for them, you know, coming to a new country and being constantly
busy and trying to adapt to this, like this completely different world." So Irshad
began her own quest to understand Islam. She found a copy of the Qur'an in
her school library. "So I just took it out and I read it and it kind of changed
me, you know, it really affected me. And I was like 'I really need to start learning more,' and from then on I started learning more and learning more and
reading. And it didn't happen overnight, it took me years to become who I am
now." Irshad considered herself responsible for the Muslim she became.

Irshad's understanding of Islam was based specifically on the Qur'an and
Sunna. When asked if she was Sunni, Irshad was very clear in stating that
she was "just a Muslim ... because Islam is based on the Qur'an and it's based
on the Sunna, which is like the way of the Prophet, Peace Be Upon Him, you
know, his sayings and his actions. So automatically, like, that's what the word
Muslim is, you know." Anything else in Islam (i.e., Shi'a) was not authentic and
therefore not Islamic: they were deviations and innovations from the true path
of Islam.

Irshad's search for a true understanding of Islam had been a private endeavour. Although accepting of her parents' understanding of Islam, she felt that
she had to explore the true meaning of the faith herself, thus not imitating her
parents or family members. Incorporating Islam into her daily life began with
prayer.

> Prayer is *the* most important thing ... Because through prayer you're
> acknowledging that there is only one God and you're giving praise and
> thanks to God who, like, created you, you know, like created you when
> you were nothing. So that's why we pray five times a day, we even stop

everything we're doing, everything we're doing, to stop and pray those five times during our day. And so to me prayer is, like, it's like breathing, you know. Like, if I don't pray, it's just like I can't breathe. That's how important it is to me, it's almost like you can't breathe without praying.

Irshad would pray wherever she was. When she was on campus, she would go to the prayer room at Carleton University, or if it was too far away from her classroom, she would leave class and take her prayer mat and find an empty hallway (in contrast to Dilshad; see above). She had it with her at all times so that she would not miss prayer time. She would also not make plans to go somewhere if it overlapped with prayer time. Prayer, to Irshad, was not restricted to five times a day. She constantly remembered God: "It's just in my mind, you know, just thinking about it, just thinking about God and talking to God and stuff in my mind."

Irshad did not pray at a masjid (mosque),[6] because it was not obligatory for women to pray there. Yet it was very important for men to pray at the masjid whenever possible, even for every single prayer throughout the day. It was also important for the men to maintain a sense of community for the whole family, including women, because announcements were usually made about events that were taking place for both men and women. "It is a place where people are supposed to bond, you know, a sense of community, a sense of brotherhood, sisterhood." Although she did not go to the masjid, she considered the role of the imam important for "marriage counselling and all sorts of counselling, even if people are trying to find a suitable husband or wife," they could go to the masjid and ask the imam for suitable partners and families. But when it came to looking for religious information, Irshad turned to scholars based in Saudi Arabia, because they were able to answer questions about "new things." For example:

People are asking about the Internet, and like how should we go about the Internet, because the Internet, there's a lot of bad things in it that, you know, that are against our religion. And they would make such rules like the Internet is okay as long as you do not go on these things that are, you know, not allowed in Islam. You know, things that are modern-day things that people just wouldn't know how to handle, they wouldn't know how to connect it with Islam. They would tell them how to connect it.

It was also extremely important for Irshad that she be a role model for young Muslim girls growing up in Canada. She did this by volunteering at a Muslim girls' camp during the summers. "I think it's so important for them to see like older girls, because most of the girls who are the camp counsellors are like university, college students or not even at all. But like I really like being a role model to kids, and I hope I can be a positive one to them."

Although she wished to spend more time with the Muslim Students Association, she could not dedicate time to it at that moment. She enjoyed going to the campus prayer room so that she could meet up with her friends. Almost all her friends were Muslim as well, and they all shared the same religious views and level of practice. They were all female. The few who were not Muslim had the same religious values as Irshad.

When asked about the role Islam played in her life, Irshad reiterated that Islam affected every aspect of her life.

> Like, I can go on forever, every single way. Like, the way that I treat my parents ... treating your parents with respect is really something that is huge in Islam. And I know that before I might have been like, "psst-uh" [sounds of frustration], then just like "uhhh" with my parents or "ooph," you know, and now as I learn about Islam, that's not even allowed. So it's like sometimes I have to control myself and say, "okay, you can't do that" [lowers voice like a whisper].

In terms of her own education, her faith had also changed the way she saw her future. Her parents wanted her to pursue a medical career, but after embracing an orthodox understanding of Islam, she would prefer to go to a Muslim country and learn all that she could about Islam.

> And if I went to medical school, I'd basically live out my life, the rest of my life to it because medicine it's just you have to devote, it never stops. So, you know, that's something I was going towards, now I just really really want to learn about my religion, and I really want to go to a Muslim country and study, and so I've, I forgot about med school, and now I'm in Human Rights and Sociology, and I find that's something that I like.

Irshad acknowledged that her parents came to Canada to ensure that their children would be university-educated and gainfully employed. Although her father had a well-paying job in Saudi Arabia, he felt that the society there would be restricting for his daughters. In contrast, Irshad believed a career went against the teachings of Islam as she now understood them.

> It's better for a woman to be at home and be with her family. Like, that is considered something that is *more* um, that's like more, I don't want to say honourable, but it's something that is preferred ... Family is such an important thing in Islam, and the woman is considered like the core,

like the essence of the family. And when she's missing from the home and, you know, she's out, you know, all day working and then spends only a few hours with her children a day, it's something that people, there's something really missing from the family. Like, that's how Islam views it.

Therefore, Irshad was unsure about continuing on to medical school. She realized that her parents would be upset if she told them she wanted to stay at home and raise a family. But her biggest fear as a Muslim and a mother (someday) was based on the dangers she perceived in the world. "I find there's a lot of dangers and there's more things that, I think kids are tested so much more than they should be and there's so much burden to put on kids. And, I don't know, I just, I really like the idea of staying home with my kids and you know, being there for them, being like, whenever they need me, I'll be there."

When asked how Islam affected other parts of her life, Irshad acknowledged that she would not vote in an election if she felt that the parties did not reflect her religious convictions (gay marriage was one example discussed). She would only marry a Muslim man, a Sunni Muslim man, because "like I said, Islam is based on Qur'an, Sunna, and anybody who deviates from that, I don't want it." And her children would be raised Muslim. Her views of male–female relations were also religiously swayed.

Women have to cover, from the head to toe. You have to cover your body. And men don't … We're equal but we're not the same thing, and I think that, like the woman's body is attractive, you know what I mean? It's very attractive, in a way that men's bodies aren't. And we have to acknowledge that and like, know that there is a difference. And this is, that's one of the big differences between men and women … Others would include, like I said, it's better for a woman to stay home so that she can ensure that the family life goes smoothly and make sure that the family is safe and taken care of.

Irshad's idea of motherhood was strongly influenced by the example of the Prophet, who was very playful with his children and protected them like a mother. Therefore, Irshad considered the idea of staying at home and raising children as an emulation of the Prophet. She realized that not many Muslim youths shared her ideas on the roles of men and women in Islam, but she attributed this to fear and a lack of understanding about their faith.

At the same time, Irshad believed that Canada was a wonderful place to live in and that multiculturalism was an asset to Canadian culture. It allowed people "to practise whatever belief they have and whatever belief they bring from their own country, so long as it does not endanger anybody's life or doesn't pollute the society." But Irshad acknowledged that there were segments of Canadian society that didn't accept certain types of immigrants, particularly Muslims, especially in smaller towns. She had contemplated wearing the niqab "where you would just cover your face and just like show your eyes. I know that I've considered that and my parents would never allow it … They won't allow a lot of things just out of fear you know, of what would happen to us." In fact, friends of hers who decided to don the niqab found that they were treated very differently by the same people – their identity was constantly being called into question. She would still like to wear it if her parents permitted it, even though she might be treated differently. Although she considered it a choice and not a religious requirement, Irshad believed that wearing the niqab would make her feel more "complete." It would also help to create a stronger barrier between her and the men around her. Irshad did not share her parents' fears about being outwardly Muslim in Canada, because "I'm Canadian, these are my peers."

For Irshad, Islam was a complete way of life. Aisha and Irshad were both devout Muslims. But for Irshad, the way she understood her faith was more narrowly orthodox. There was no acceptance of the other interpretations of Islam that fell outside her Salafi understanding of Islam. Her conflicts did not lie with being Canadian and Muslim but rather with trying to be more Islamic in a way that went against her parents' wishes. She did not go to the mosque or to the local imam for her faith. She turned to the Internet, because there were many scholars to access. But again, she chose these scholars with the utmost care: "I have to listen to the one that I know will not lead me to any other path, you know, that will lead me to pure, the way Islam is, pure Islam basically."

Living in Canada was comforting to Irshad. Although she had met intolerance, it was rare, and she found Canada the most tolerant country in which to live. For Irshad, living among people from other religious traditions meant following the example set by the Prophet in that he lived peacefully among Christians and Jews and showed respect for other beliefs. Islam fit in Canada, because it was the "most tolerant of religions." Irshad did not find that she had to fit in to live in Canada. In fact, she considered herself (and her sister) more religious than her parents. For Irshad, there were two types of Muslims growing up in Canada: "the Muslim youth, we're either religious or not. And the religious ones, they're mostly at odds with their parents." Her cousins and her friends were all more religious than their parents. She corrected her parents when they brought culture into the conversation or when they tried to make their children "downplay" their faith in public. For instance, her parents recommended that she just wear baggy clothes instead of the ankle-length skirt, but according to Irshad, women could not wear pants, "because in Islam, you can't look like the opposite gender." Irshad's relationship with her parents had become problematic because of her increasing faith. She conceded that her parents wanted her to have a career in order to be financially stable. They did not want her to wear the niqab. In this sense, Irshad recognized that she was very much like the religious Muslim youths she associated with: "And it's very funny, because I find the Muslim youth, you know, the religious ones, we tend to be sometimes at odds with our parents." In fact, both her older sister and younger brother wished to be more "religious" and had met resistance from their parents. Irshad's brother was 16 years old, and he wanted to grow a beard.

Like, in Islam it's something, growing a beard is something that is very encouraged, and some people say it's even obligatory. And I know he really wants to grow a beard. And my parents, they would never let him because they, they're like, "you know, this is a time when Muslims are under attack, and if they see you wearing a beard, especially you being a Muslim male with a beard, you're, you know they're gonna maybe label you a terrorist." So it's like out of fear, like I can completely understand where my parents are coming from, you know, like they fear for their children.

The most interesting cultural division Irshad had with her parents concerned the concept of tolerance. She did not see race in Islam: she had Muslim friends from China and Bosnia and all over the world. They were sisters in faith. The same was true for men, according to Irshad. She would have no qualms marrying a Muslim from China or Africa. But her parents believed that she must marry someone from Somalia. She had what she would consider "cultural" differences with her parents. "I don't care what the race of the man is. It makes no difference to me." Although extremely orthodox in her practice of Islam, she was also fully Canadian and happy to live in a diverse society.

CONCLUSION

The religiously minded women in this study shaped and nurtured their religious identities: many participated in local religious organizations, such as Muslim students associations, and had easy access to local and transnational religious sources via the Internet, satellite television, and publications. Yet none of their contact zones, be it family, friends, the mosque, or the Internet, dominated as the source of their religious orientations. Each contact zone did, however, contribute to how these women constructed their religion and their religious identities. At the same time, these women, whether or not they were religious, displayed a similar standardized perspective as to what Islam entailed as a religion. This globalized "orthodox" model of Islam almost always included the so-called five pillars of Islam but also encompassed a religiously founded moral orientation that incorporated the standard dietary regulations (no pork or alcohol), strict restrictions regarding sexual contact with men, and a variety of other virtues, such as respect for others, humbleness, politeness, having good manners, and striving to improve oneself and make the world a better place. Lina (MF14), a 19-year-old female born in Kuwait, was not raised with any understanding of Islam. Her father was an atheist, and her mother did not practise the faith. A close friend passed away when she was 16, and she turned to Islam for solace. Having taught herself about the Islamic faith, she succinctly stated the core beliefs in Islam found among the women included in this study: "Belief in Allah, the ultimate creator; belief in Muhammad; his messenger; belief in basically praying regularly, practising regular charity, and showing compassion and doing good deeds towards other human beings, any moment that you can."

Their understanding of Islam is noteworthy, because it also represents a global notion of Islam as a faith, a model that has become extremely widespread around the world. As just discussed, a great many of the Muslim participants in the study conducted their personal searches about Islam, relying not only on sources in Canada (especially their parents, relatives, and friends) but also on globalized sources, particularly through the Internet. Authentic Islam for them could be found anywhere.

In addition to the dominance of this global model of systemic Islam, which was just as dominant among the Muslim men (see chapter 5), most of these women, like Lina, also went about arriving at their understanding of Islam in very individual and quite multi-dimensional ways in which no influence or, as noted, "contact zone" was particularly dominant. Those who did not choose to adopt orthodox Islam as their religion also did not, by and large, turn to a different religion; they were either not religious at all or in a few cases adopted a kind of "spiritual but not religious" stand, as did some of those in the non-religious categories. In this, the women were somewhat different from the men, among whom only a very few took this "spiritual" direction. In terms of the lived religion approach, therefore, the vast majority of the Muslims of both genders lived their religion mostly inside the boundaries of systemic Islam or predominantly outside it. In this regard, they displayed another aspect of that contrast between those among our participants who came from Muslim backgrounds and those within the other two religious identity categories, the Hindus and Buddhists. It is this contrast that is important to keep in mind as we examine the rather different way of "doing religion" that these latter two groups exhibited. The first of these are the Hindu women.

7

Perpetuating Religion and Culture: Hindu Women

NANCY NASON-CLARK AND CATHY HOLTMANN

FOUR INTRODUCTORY PROFILES

Born in southern India, Leela arrived in Canada with her mother and younger brother when she was 9 years old. At the time of the interview she was 19 years old. When the family first left India, they immigrated to Saudi Arabia and stayed there for three years. During their early days in Canada, the father died, leaving Leela's mother, Smeeta, alone to raise her two children. Since Smeeta had obtained university-level commerce training in India many years before, she was able to find employment working for an accountant. A few years ago, the maternal grandparents moved to Canada, and all five family members were living together in the Toronto area.

Leela (HF27) was studying commerce – in her second year – and planned to work in accounting or the human resources field in her future. She was a student on the St George Campus of the University of Toronto. Getting a good education was important to Leela and especially important to her mother. Sometimes they disagreed over whether or not she was putting enough effort into her university courses.

Identifying as a Hindu, Leela indicated that she practised regularly but laughed when asked if that meant daily. "See, that's the beauty of Hinduism … you don't have to practise all the time. My grandparents and mom pretty much follow it every day, and I'm, uh, not that regular." Speaking of religion, Leela said, "it's something that you believe in, to make your days go by easier maybe." She did not think there was a difference between religion and spirituality, but she was quite clear that both were distinct from superstition – something she expressed no interest in and some disdain for.

Leela had become more aware of her own religious practices and beliefs recently: "So, I like hear my friend talking about going to church every Sunday. And I'm like, 'Why am I not going to temple every week, or whatever?' It's made me want to understand my religion a little more." As part of this quest for more knowledge about Hinduism, Leela took a religion course at university last year.

She also asked her mother on a regular basis to drive her to the temple: "I like going to the temple and I like praying to God, and I wish I could do it more often ... Honestly, I would love to go to the temple every single day. That would be the greatest thing for me." Yet, ironically, when she would get to the temple, she would not be sure what to do. She questioned her grandparents about this. They actually said prayers there, but since Leela did not know any of those prayers, she just went there and talked quietly. For her this was enough. This alone was meaningful. She did not understand any of the Sanskrit prayers that were said in the temple, and she doubted that her mother or grandparents did either. But this did not seem to matter to them or to her. For Leela, going to the temple offered tranquillity, a sense of calm in a life filled with all the busyness and stress of student life. She said, "I find peace. I really do. I feel so calm every time I go there. There's like no stress. Like, oh exams are coming, whatever, whatever. There's nothing. Just go there and sit." She found religion comforting, and although she did not practise it as regularly as she thought she should, it was always with her – in the back of her mind. "Personally speaking, for me, it's always been there. It's always been comforting for me. So, it's nice to believe in something like that. Therefore, yeah, it's a good thing." Later, in discussing those who do harm in the name of religion, Leela noted, "religion itself cannot be evil."

From her perspective, religion and ritual were intertwined. "To practise a religion, I guess you have to do the rituals, and when I do the rituals, it's just more in tune with God than anything else." At home, she had her own representations of deities (she calls them idols) in her room, and she would sometimes light a devotional lamp or say a prayer. So that she knew the lines to be said, Leela had them written on a piece of paper, kept in her room. "It's a very flexible religion," she mused. "It's very adaptable to any society." These were things that especially drew Leela to Hinduism. Yet she was aware that there was so much about the faith and its practices that she did not really understand. For questions, she turned to her grandparents, and when they did not know the answers, to the Internet.

When her grandparents came to live with them several years ago, the family began to engage more regularly in Hindu practices. Her grandparents and mother prayed and did *pujas* every morning and evening. They had a particular god that was important to the family: "Venkateswara[1] is my family god," as he was for many Hindus who came from the same region in India that they did. While her grandparents and mother were vegetarians, Leela and her brother ate meat. She spoke of not feeling any pressure from them to abstain from meat, although on special religious or family occasions, Leela and her brother would assume their vegetarian diet.

In terms of religious practices, Leela and her family would get together at home with other Hindu families from the same area to celebrate *pujas* and sing *bhajans*, the traditional songs. Singing had always been an important part of Leela's life, and she still sang in a band that performed a mixture of new and traditional Indian music. Her mother would prefer her to go for classic Indian music, but Leela said, "I'm a mix of both."

Culturally, Leela was quite engaged in her community, especially since her election as a youth director of a cultural group. She said, "I'm very proud of being Indian, of being brown ... I like my culture a lot. So yeah, I would want to preserve it and continue it on." Yet she thought that the traditional emphasis on gender roles did not apply in the Canadian context: "traditionally, it would be like the guy works and the girl sits at home and breeds ... but I don't think that applies anymore." She noted that her mother was modern – in her words, "my mom's pretty much a twenty-first-century woman." Nevertheless, Leela had chosen a rather conservative lifestyle – she did not date or drink alcohol.

Leela was very positive about Canada's multicultural policy, especially since she clearly remembered their life in Saudi Arabia, where she was not allowed to practise Hinduism. Of this she reflected: "So we used to do all of our festivals where no one could see us, like in the kitchen. But here we don't have to do that, we can do it openly." She regarded Canada as socially and culturally very accepting of immigrants, and she appreciated the religious freedom she experienced here.

There are several features of Leela's life that reflected the experiences of the majority of the 39 young Hindu women interviewed as part of this project:

- the centrality of family ties;
- the fluidity of religious expectations and practices;
- the intertwining of cultural and religious boundaries;
- the role of music and food as cultural and religious markers;
- the primacy of educational attainment.

Leela added to this list the importance of religious rituals performed together with others of the Hindu community, but in this she was typical only of a minority in the sense of being among the 6 women of Hindu families that we classified as highly religiously involved. A similar number fell at the other end of the classification, the 8 who were more or less not religiously engaged at all. To illustrate this group, we present the story of Preema, followed by two profiles that represent what might be seen as the majority in between, the 25 we classified as ethnocultural Hindus.

Unlike most of the Hindu women who were interviewed, Preema (HF10) did not feel particularly close to her family or to the religious traditions that were part of her upbringing. She and her younger brother were born in Germany to parents who emigrated from Sri Lanka. Like Leela, she was 9 when they arrived in Canada and 19 at the time of the interview. Her parents took the children to the temple regularly when they lived in Germany and prayed and celebrated various religious ceremonies at home, and Preema took some religious education courses in elementary school. By her teenage years, she had stopped participating in religious rituals and started to question her religious beliefs.

Currently in her second year of university, Preema had chosen to abandon many aspects of her religious background. "Well, I guess I'm associated with Hinduism, but I don't really believe in it." Her parents used to ask her to accompany them when they went to the temple. She stated, "I used to refuse a lot, and then they finally stopped asking me." While her parents still went to the temple, she and her brother had stopped entirely. What was religious for her parents Preema considered a cultural activity for her. While there were times when she would miss activities at the temple, she had never considered going back. She considered herself an atheist.

Most of her friends had different religious backgrounds. "Well, they're usually shocked when I tell them that I don't believe in God." Differentiating herself from her friends, Preema said, "I think that [religion] is important to most of the people I know in my culture, my age. They do take an active role in religion, participating in such activities like celebrating. They usually do that a lot." Preema noted that her parents were probably unaware of her current atheism: "They probably don't really know that I don't believe in any kind of god. I doubt they do." Later, referring to a question about whether her atheism was strong, she noted, "I don't really know what I believe in, really."

Her ambiguity about her beliefs seemed to be linked to other areas of questioning as well. She was not close to her parents and in fact seemed to be actively engaged in keeping them uninformed about her life and choices. They did not know that she was changing her major, had been in relationships, and no longer accepted the broad tenets of Hinduism. In this sense, she was somewhat similar to a few of the Muslim male participants we met in chapter 5. She noted, "I don't really have a relationship with them, we don't really talk about much." Despite this, she continued to live in her parents' home – with all her secrets.

Preema's parents had very high expectations of her, especially when it came to education. They wanted her to be a medical doctor, to live at home, not to date, and eventually come to support them financially. She wanted to study philosophy and come to "know the truth." When asked, Preema stated that her parents would probably be "shocked, disappointed, and angry" with her decision to leave biology as an area of study. Her main criticism of Canadian culture was that it was too materialistic.

Leela and Preema offer us a case example of a religiously engaged and a religiously unengaged young Hindu woman in Canada. Yet within this research sample, the majority lay between these two poles of religiously engaged and religiously unengaged. To illustrate, we offer the stories of Akuti and Jaya, two women whose lives reveal some of the nuances of the interplay between ethnic, cultural, and religious factors.

Akuti (HF06) was born in Sri Lanka and immigrated to Canada with her parents just after her third birthday. When the family first came to Canada, both parents had to work for pay while they were upgrading their education to meet Canadian standards. There was little time for going to the temple. She said, "It was tough, because they had to start all over from scratch. I don't think they were too concerned about going to temples, because they were working 16-, 17-hour shifts in factories just in order to support the family, because their education isn't qualified here." Once they became financially secure, her mother and father became more active in the temple and the Tamil community. With two parents who are Hindu, Akuti considered her family religious – there was a shrine in the home and daily prayers: "being religious for them was the fact that they prayed." Her father, but not her mother, observed dietary laws. Both parents told Akuti religious stories while she was growing up, and they encouraged her to pray daily. My father "emphasized the importance of it. I remember him offering me, he said, 'I will give you a dollar every day if you pray' … eventually I started praying every day."

Akuti and her mother lived together, a result of the recent divorce of her parents. Since divorce is frowned upon within the Tamil community in Canada, Akuti said that she and her mother felt ostracized. This had a profound impact on her religious journey. Her mother seemed to have rejected formal Hinduism as a result of her experiences related to the marriage and its dissolution. Akuti worried about being judged by members of the Tamil community, and as a consequence she did not participate in events. "So, personally, I don't really get too involved with the culture or get involved with the Tamil Students Association, because I am afraid of what they might find out." While most of Akuti's friends were Tamil, they were not Hindu. However, her boyfriend often went to the temple.

For Akuti, religion was "moral faith," something that was directly related to how you acted. It was a way of living that connected people to something bigger than themselves. She believed in karma and reincarnation and considered herself very religious. Yet she no longer went to the temple herself. She thought that culture was linked to religion but that it had more to do with geography. From her point of view, Hinduism was like other religions in that it taught you to do good and not to harm others. "I'd never be allowed to waste any food. I would have to eat every scrap of rice off my plate, because they would say, 'You're wasting food. There are kids from Sri Lanka, kids from across the world who don't have this. So eat for them.' And so that's what I would have to do. Just be very thankful. Just be very grateful." She believed in heaven but not hell – earth is hell. "I'd really like to think there is a heaven where I could go and just sort of frolic around and have nothing to worry about. No exams, no hardships in life."

And how had religion affected her life? "I think I am a very good person … I don't do negative things. I don't do things to maliciously hurt other people. If anything, I go out of my way to help other people."

Jaya (HF15) presented as a relatively unengaged Hindu exploring religious pluralism. Her family came to Canada from Kenya when she was 11, but they originated in India where she was born. The family moves were linked to career opportunities for her father, yet at the same time the family thought the children would have a better life in Canada. She was 24 and studying for a graduate degree in epidemiology. Her father was more religious than her mother, practising daily within their home. They only went to temple on special occasions. She described her family and herself as secular Hindus: "Yeah, like I don't think I would shy away from saying I am religious. But I wouldn't necessarily say that I am spiritual."

While Jaya valued aspects of the Hindu world view, in her mind she separated world view from practice and considered that the two separated at some time in history. "I don't think the rituals are necessarily based on tradition." For Jaya, science was very important, and she thought that science and religion described two different views of the universe – science being verifiable and religion non-verifiable. Yet she did not see them as opposed to each other. "The basic distinction between religion and science is how you get your world view, and science tends to be backed up by evidence and experiments and, you know, reliability and so forth, religion is more faith-based. But I think that in science there is also room for having that faith, and that's what theory is about. So I don't think they are necessarily two distinct parts."

Jaya described her own practice as being interfaith-based:

> By definition Hinduism is just an amalgamation of some different beliefs through time, and it evolved that way … I consider myself a Hindu, but it's more by birth a Hindu. I make that distinction, by culture a Hindu, but I don't know if I ascribe to traditional Hindu beliefs. Traditional. Because by definition I think there is room to – how do I put this? – to have that interfaith aspect and consider myself a Hindu and like no one can really challenge that. I think it would be different if I was from a Christian or Islam perspective.

She had read about Christianity and Hinduism, some Sufi and esoteric literature, as well as Wicca and native religions: "So I am comfortable with calling myself a Hindu, and I've never really felt inclined to say I am not Hindu or anything like that, although many people may think I am agnostic, or maybe atheist, or something like that." Part of her religious practice was writing. She did light incense and had a Krishna statue. She practised certain breathing techniques as well as yoga. She took meditative walks and reflected on prayers. She considered dance to be religious practice, because it focused her mind and her whole body, giving her a sense of empowerment, release, and achievement. For Jaya, all religions had a common thread through their focus on compassion and being good. She thought that there were many paths to the same goal: "There is a common thread, generally most religions through their whatever, code of ethics ... to guide you into being a moral person ... They all have that common focus on how to help people get along with each other and not just get along, but how to have meaningful deep relationships and that sort of thing."

HINDUISM

The scholarly task of categorizing Hindu religiosity and identity is complex, given the nature of Hinduism, its historical development, and its relationship to Western colonization (Anderson and Dickey Young 2004; Frykenberg 1989; Kurien 2007; Orsi 2005). Hinduism involves a wide range of religious beliefs, practices, and texts, including the worship of gods and goddesses, and because of this diversity the very definition of Hinduism has been contested (Madan 2006). In fact, tolerance for religious differences is a deeply held value for many Hindus. Within the systemic religion framework applied in these chapters, Hinduism does not have the kind of clear global model that Islam appears to have and most of the Muslim participants were actively helping to form and reproduce. Although Hinduism describes the religious identity of the majority of people in India, it is from this perspective not a centrally organized religion, and a significant proportion of the Indian population practises more than one religion (Narayanan 2006; Purkayastha 2005). Growing up forty or fifty years ago in India or in other countries where Hindus were either the religious majority or where they comprised significant portions of the regional population such as Sri Lanka, East Africa, or the Caribbean, the parents of today's immigrant youths were likely not concerned about deliberately constructing a religious identity. In their youth and in their homelands, their religious identity was primarily ascribed (Kurien 1998; Vertovec 1992). In moving to Canada, Hindu immigrants became part of a racial, cultural, and religious minority that has changed the face of Canadian society, at least in large urban centres (Beyer 2005b; Bramadat and Seljak 2005). However, in this new context and present age, 1.5- and second-generation Hindu women are confronted with the challenge and option of choosing how they will construct their particular religious and cultural identities.

In terms of their religious identities, the women confront particular challenges, given the variety and complexity of Hindu beliefs and practices coupled with a lack of any sort of centralized religious authority structure either in Canada or in their countries of origin. What counts as validly religious or validly Hindu, therefore, perhaps much more easily comes to be determined by the experiences of the women themselves. The lived religious orientation takes precedence, because ideas of what are considered normative Hindu religious practices and/or beliefs are not as clearly available from any institutional authority (McGuire 2008). Therefore, it is the efficacy of Hindu practices in the lives of 1.5- and second-generation Canadian women, rather than the determination of whether or not they are authentically Hindu, that moves to the fore for this segment of the participants, more so than for the Muslims and perhaps even the Buddhists.

Similar to Joshi's study of Hindus in the United States, we were more interested in asking "how is she Hindu?" rather than in asking "how Hindu is she?" (Joshi 2006, 20). What emerged was a complex, yet vivid, portrayal of identity construction – together with its ideological and behavioural components. This construction involved choices, strategies, and resignations, sometimes made in isolation from others, often in the "contact zones" of a faith community or an educational cohort or others who shared a similar experience of having grown up in a country that for their parents might be a different world. Thus, as we shall see, religious identity for the Hindu women in the study was resisted, embraced, celebrated, despised, and altered. But for the clear majority of them, it seems that it had not been abandoned, forgotten, or lost.

THE IMPORTANCE OF FAMILY

For the women in our interviews, the religious, ethnic, and cultural aspects of their families of origin were among the foundation stones upon which their identity was built. According to the students interviewed, ritual participation and food were the primary ways that their families sought to maintain that heritage and pass it on to their children. Like the Jewish grandmothers in Janet Jacobs's book, *Hidden Heritage*, or the orthodox women of Lynn Davidman's research, *Tradition in a Rootless World*, the Hindu mothers in particular made every effort to cook their way into the hearts of their children (Davidman 1993; Jacobs 2002). Prayer, food, music, and dance grew out of their family traditions, creating webs of connection with their lived experience of religion.

All of the young women in the study indicated that what they knew about Hindu practices and beliefs they had learned primarily from their family. Although few were completely satisfied with the explanations they had received as to the specific meaning of, or beliefs behind, Hindu practices, strong bonds were forged between family members through shared religious and cultural practices. For example, most of the participants had been raised in homes with some sort of shrine that included pictures or statues of a variety of Hindu gods and goddesses for whom *pujas* were offered. Parents and grandparents regularly engaged in *pujas* at the shrine and invited (or forced) the children to also take part. The ritual practice of most of the young women waned as they grew older and became more preoccupied with their university studies, something that parents did not seem to resist. Devotion to the gods and goddesses varied, as did beliefs in the purpose or effects of prayer and *pujas*. Many young women indicated that, even as university students, they maintained some form of a prayer life. For example, one Punjabi woman, Rubina, who was doing graduate work in neuroscience, described her ritual practices and prayers as a form of meditation that helped her to remain focused.

> When I do perform them I do treat them as like, as just a … a form of meditation. Just like when you're really focused at doing … like at the lab that I work at, as a grad student. I do lab work day in and day out, and if I need to be focused on that, you know? … I was working with radiation today. I had to kill some rats today and stuff like that, and you really need to be focused on what you are doing or else you can be very distracted like by killing an animal or if you're [working with] things that have radiation. You don't want to contaminate everything – it can hurt someone and yourself. And doing your prayer is another form of meditation in that you are very focused on it … and … and it's … it's just a practice that you do. (HF01)

The interview data reveals that dietary practices are a prominent feature of many Canadian Hindu households. A number of women in the study, among them Rubina, talked about how the practice of fasting helped them to stay in touch with their bodies and pay attention to their health. In developing a level of self-awareness, they were also able to forego fasting when they felt they needed more energy to pursue their studies. They had learned this from their parents, whose own vegetarianism was often dependent on their level of activity in relation to their work lives. Antal spoke freely of her religious practice, noting that for her religion was a way she had learned to live. "I see religion as more of a sort of way of living. A way of life … not rituals but just different practices … some days you don't eat meat or you fast. Things like that." Referring to her parents and extended relatives, she said, "They followed Hinduism. That was sort of their way of life, but they weren't very strict with it. It looked pretty relaxed … except on Tuesdays" (HF09). At this point she broke into a laugh. "I get tired of peanut butter sandwiches," she said, still laughing, referring to times when her mother was observing dietary restrictions for religious reasons. Other women spoke about the importance of the unity of body, mind, and nature as part of their Hindu practice. In response to a question about practices that kept her spiritually connected, Ratna said:

Yeah, I think there are, and I don't necessarily think they are connected with any religious tradition, just things I have picked up ... Well, you know just always going outdoors and just being in nature and being with trees and streams and just like breathing. I say breathing and it goes back to my yoga background. I do practise certain breathing techniques to, just if I am experiencing stress or things like that. I meditate on my breath maybe, or going outdoors. (HF15)

One notes in this quote that what appear to be Hindu practices are not always necessarily attributed to Hinduism, an aspect, in this case, of the fluidity of boundaries in Ratna's religion.

While home-based Hindu practices were central to the religious identities of the families, they were not confined to the nuclear family. Our participants regularly spoke of how many families would gather in homes to either perform *pujas* or *bhajans*, the performance of devotional music. Through these celebrations, the women could develop strong bonds with people in their particular Hindu community, and some looked forward to breaks from university when they could go home and reconnect with extended family and friends through religio-cultural practices, which always included sharing meals. This was particularly important for Baruna, a woman whose parents were separated. She said:

BARUNA: There's a sense of closeness just because you've known these people for so long. So you don't know them – but you know them, and it's something that's familiar and regular, which is nice. And just the smell of the incense, and I can't throw the flowers anymore because it's Canada and we have to clean up and it's too hard to clean up, so ... You used to be able to chuck flowers at your uncles and aim for people! And now it's just put it in the basket. But it's still nice. There's that cutting up the fruit. It's just ... I try to go early so I can help out or else it's ... if you don't participate in helping out, then you're just pretty much – it's another party; it's not a religious thing then. It's just socializing 'cause everyone talks during the *puja* and everything so ...
INTERVIEWER: So it makes it religious for you?
BARUNA: Yeah. For me it's as close as I'm gonna get to anything considering my culture 'cause it's religious and cultural, which Hinduism has always [been]. (HF34)

Baruna's explanation of her participation in communal events shows that for her, the religious and cultural aspects of being a Hindu were intertwined, a typical feature of those we classified as ethnocultural Hindus. Yet she made the point that what made the event religious was the fact that she was participating in the preparation of the fruit offering for the *puja*. For her, being an active participant in preparing the ritual food was what made the *puja* a religious experience, more so, it seems, than taking part in the *puja* itself.

As mentioned, each Hindu family seemed to have a particular blend of gods and goddesses to whom they were devoted, often depending on the birthplace of the parents or grandparents. Families literally brought their gods and goddesses with them. Yet even families that were devoted to the same gods and goddesses practised their devotion in different ways and took from these practices unique meanings. Temple attendance varied widely among the families in our sample. Hindus typically go to the temple, either as families or individuals, for special festivals or to pray for personal needs (Bannerjee and Coward 2005; Kurien 1998; Pearson 2004). The Canadian temples that the families of these Hindu women frequented often included a combination of gods and goddesses, depending on the devotional practices of the founding members. This highlights the tremendous variety within Hindu religious practice in Canada and underscores the fact that immigrants are engaged in the process of recreating their religion in their new home (Bramadat 2005).

The women's families embodied the religious diversity within the bounds of what they considered to be Hindu. Several of the women had experiences of inter-religious marriages in their families of origin. Often their fathers' religious devotions differed from their mothers', largely because of regional religious customs, and the families had adopted some blend of Hindu traditions. Stories of their families' religious practices also included the presence of symbols from other religions, such as having pictures of Mary and Jesus and holy water from Lourdes included with the pictures and statues of Hindu gods and goddesses in the household shrine. One woman spoke about how her grandmother, upon first coming to Canada, went to a Christian church and had even joined the choir (HF04).

The religious fluidity within the Canadian Hindu families can be further explained by what Beyer refers to as their "heartland" experiences (Beyer 2007). He employs the notion of heartland as a conceptual tool rather than the more often used "homeland." In so doing, he highlights the fact that its explanatory currency extends to those for whom the region or country of reference is not – and never was – home. The women in our study considered Canada their home, yet there was often also an identification with another country that tugged on the young adults' heartstrings. There were boundaries and barriers, religious and cultural in nature that shaped a young person's life experience here in Canada and could not be reduced to present circumstances or even current loyalties. Through the process of globalization, religious values have become multi-centred or transnational, their "core" or "centre" of authenticity something to be negotiated. Authority, authenticity, ambiguity, diversity, and transnational ties help us to understand some of the features of the religious journey that was described by the 1.5- and second-generation Hindus of this study.

Of the 39 women interviewed, 26 were born in Canada, making them second-generation Hindus. The remaining 13 were born either in India, Sri Lanka, the Caribbean, Europe, or Africa but moved to Canada at the age of 11 or younger – hence the designation of generation 1.5. This is not only indicative of the diversity among Hindus in Canada but shows that these women came from families that had experienced significant changes in their lived religion. The women had witnessed their parents adapt to the changing circumstances of their lives in which home-based religious practices were central, not only because they were portable but also because they were not dependent on the availability of temples or religious leaders and did not require the sanction of external authorities. Several women said that the level of outward religiosity of their parents had fluctuated depending on what was going on in their lives, most often affected by the work of providing for family in a new land. Adjusting to the gender norms of Canadian society in terms of juggling the responsibilities for both work outside the home and care of the children without the help of an extended family or servants was particularly evident in the stories they related about their mothers. For these women, religious change was in fact normative. In particular, those of generation 1.5 who had memories of participating in Hindu communities outside of Canada, like Leela, whom we met at the beginning of the chapter, were very aware of the differences in religious practices within their own tradition depending on the context.

The connection of Hindu women in this study to Canadian society was mediated in large measure by the strength and vitality of family ties. For most, it was the extended family – or at least some members of their extended family – that encouraged and then brokered the initial move to Canada. Relatives brought them here, often provided some temporary respite upon arrival, and emotionally, as well as practically, ensured that the Canadian welcome mat had been set in place. It is not surprising, then, that as these 20-something women talked about life in this country, it was replete with images of family gatherings and high respect for their relatives.

The young women recounted, with fondness and sometimes emotion, stories of how hard their parents worked to get to this country, the menial jobs their highly educated fathers and mothers took here, and their long climb toward economic prosperity and social integration. They credited their parents for working hard to establish and then maintain a vibrant cultural community for Hindu Canadians. In terms of strategy, mothers did this through the home environment, while fathers sought its creation outside the domestic sphere. In the early days of their lives in Canada, the mothers had to learn where to shop, how to cook with different vegetables, how to translate their skills to a different labour market, and how to ensure a smooth transition for their children. Com-

mensurate with these activities, most mothers also took responsibility for creating a religious shrine within the home – presumably because most often they
were the ones the young women described as being more religiously devout.
However, there were several examples of fathers and grandparents – like those
of Akuti and Jaya, whose lives we highlighted earlier – taking an active role in
modelling religious practice for the children. In many ways, the women's stories of close-knit families persevering despite challenges confirms the "model
minority" status assigned to many South Asian families in North America by
the majority (Joshi 2006; Purkayastha 2005) as well as the ethnic stereotypes
that influence perceptions of Hindu women (Pearson 2004). Traditionally for
Hindus, the home was the first temple, and since women had been primarily
associated with the home, domestic religious practices were women's domain.
With the adaptation to Canadian society, where the majority of women work
outside the home for pay, Hindu women's roles are changing. Nevertheless,
the women in our study assumed that they would be largely responsible for
their children's religious education, particularly if they were to marry a non-
Hindu, although religious in this case often meant as much "Hindu" culture as
"Hindu" religion. The following exchange with Debjani (HF22), a 19-year-old
from Ottawa, nicely shows the complexity:

DEBJANI: I would definitely want to expose them … to Hinduism. Like,
they are Hindu [laughs] right, like, you know what I mean … I can definitely see myself wanting to instill it into them … When it comes to the
point where I have to decide if I want my children to know this, like, I
definitely would for sure.
INTERVIEWER: Do you think it would be a problem, say, if you married
someone who was non-Hindu, do you think you could raise your kids
both in Hinduism and [another religion]?
DEBJANI: I would expose them to both for sure. Because I mean if I
feel so strongly about this, I can't say to my husband [laughs] you know,
like your religion doesn't matter … Because it does. If it matters to me,
it should matter to them. And if they, if you know they're not religious
at all and they don't really practise anything, then maybe they, I'm not
going to say, you have to practise Hinduism, but at least be open to it …
And that's what I would want to instill in my children, like, more of the
community than the actual, like, religion.

Their mothers had all received some form of post-secondary education or
training and in most cases worked for pay outside the home. Yet their mothers
were also primarily responsible for feeding the family, taking care of the household, and teaching domestic religious practices to their children. Following
their mothers' examples, all of the women were enrolled in post-secondary

education, and many of them indicated that they too would take responsibility for their future children's religious and cultural education. Several of them made reference to what they felt a woman's duty was: to provide a nurturing atmosphere in family life. Yet, as Pooja said, "my mother has always tried to tell me I should make sure my career is sort of going places and make sure I can take care of myself" (HF07). It was evident that the young women in this study were figuring out how to deal with the Canadian secular ideal of women's equality in relation to traditional Hindu gender hierarchies (Bannerjee and Coward 2005; Pearson 2004).

Two of the women had parents who were divorced, and another woman's parents had been separated for most of her life. In all three instances, these women lived with their mothers. In one case, Akuti said that she felt ostracized from the Tamil community as a result of the divorce. She spoke of a disconnect between her life and her Hindu identity. She was adrift in the community. For her, the markers of a religious identity were closely tied to family togetherness, and in her case that was ripped asunder (HF06). In the other case, the woman's mother had come to Canada as part of an arranged marriage that fell apart, and her parents were divorced when she was young. As a result of the divorce, her mother became very religious, and the Hindu faith was a source of strength for her and her children. Influenced by her mother's religiosity and self-reliance, this woman described herself as very spiritual and had served as president of her university's Hindu Student Association (HF18).

It is obvious from the interview data that the young Hindu women found themselves engaged in the processes of selecting and/or rejecting aspects of their familial religious and cultural heritage. But this was not entirely a straightforward process of "seamless compartmentalization" (Beyer 2007). Seams were apparent in the tension between the worlds of their home-based Hindu ethno-religious culture, the Canadian culture of their friends, and the context of their current educational pursuits. At this stage of their lives, the young Hindu women were negotiating choices within and between these aspects of their lives.

SOCIAL NETWORKS OUTSIDE THE FAMILY

As with almost everyone else in their generation in Canada, it was largely within the social world of their friends that the women were navigating their integration within Canadian culture. Ebaugh and Chafetz found that second-generation youth who encounter identity challenges in the US are most likely to discuss them with their peers, especially those who are also of immigrant families, regardless of their cultural and religious backgrounds (Ebaugh and Chafetz 2000). The women in our study did not speak about having primarily Indian or Hindu friends but rather had a mixture of native-born and immigrant friends. Those of the Hindu women who considered themselves religious were sometimes critical of other Hindu youth associated with temples, because they saw them as more committed to socializing than to the deepening of their faith. Their friends generally tended to be those with whom they were in school. As immigrants, the families of the women in the study had mobile histories, and even within Canada the women had experienced relocation because of career opportunities for their parents. Some spoke of moving in order to get closer to relatives or because of educational opportunities for themselves. With each move came a readjustment in terms of friends, neighbourhoods, and proximity to extended family.

All but a few of the women in our sample were still living at home with their parents. However, when questioned, many of the women said they disagreed with their parents regarding certain religio-cultural aspects of their lives. There was a range of strategies of negotiation that the women chose in order to deal with this clash of values. Few of them spoke of openly arguing or challenging their parents' values. Several of them spoke of participating in religious observances with their parents out of respect rather than belief. They disagreed with their parents about some Hindu orientations and practices, such as whether or not they should date or abstain from meat on particular days, but they had not told their parents. Some of these differences are probably part of a normal process of maturation, influenced by the women's relations with the Canadian cultural world of their friends.

One interesting strategy employed by these women in negotiating the boundary between the worlds of their families and friends was silence. Purkayastha refers to this strategy as typical for the majority of American South Asian immigrant families, illustrating patterns of bounded ethnicity (Purkayastha 2005). Several women mentioned that they had boyfriends, but few of them had spoken openly to their parents about this. This finding parallels those for many Muslims in our study, as discussed in the previous two chapters. "Don't tell, and they won't ask" seemed to be the operating rule in many of these families. Perhaps this was because the women felt that the gulf between the traditional Hindu culture of their parents and Canadian popular culture was too wide to negotiate safely. Perhaps, like many adolescents and young adults, these were just things that one didn't talk about with one's parents in order to avoid conflict. While the parents would not willingly approve of their daughters dating, they knew (as did their daughters) that there was little they could do to stop them. Both sides were complicit in pretending that certain things were not happening.

For example, Tenuja said that she was secretly dating a boy she had known since elementary school. She figured that her parents assumed they were still "just friends." Her boyfriend's family was more strictly religious than she had been raised to be, and she was trying to become more devout. Tenuja mentioned that she wore a red *bindi*/dot on her forehead – it is supposed to be a black dot for a single woman and a red dot for a married woman.

INTERVIEWER: And your parents? Do they know you're wearing a red one?

TENUJA: They know I'm wearing one, but they haven't said anything, like, "What? You're wearing a red one?" [laughs] I didn't say anything to them ...

INTERVIEWER: Did you start wearing it because you were getting serious with your boyfriend or you kinda wanted to tell your parents you were dating somebody?

TENUJA: Um ... not both ... I guess like in a way, like ... like for safety reasons, like when you wear the black one, y'know? They know you're still young and not married and stuff, right? So this kind of keeps me safe, and I dunno, I'm happy wearing it, so ... (HF16)

Tenuja's reasoning, in which she simultaneously resists her parents and engages her religious-cultural tradition, is similar to the strategy used by young Canadian Muslim women in a study conducted by Hoodfar (Hoodfar 2006). She describes how Muslim women, whose immigrant mothers were not veiled, chose to wear the veil as a non-verbal religious symbol that gave them social power among their families and friends (see chapter 6).

In marked contrast to other women in our study, Sonya talked about addressing a situation of conflict with her parents openly. Sonya told the interviewer that her parents had said, "Well, ok, this guy that you're dating has to be the one that you're going to marry, because otherwise you can't date, because Indian people don't date" (HF30). But she felt that this meant that her parents did not trust her, and she told them that she was hurt because they were more concerned about what it would look like in the Indian community than how she felt. Sonya thought her parents believed that she would do what "Canadian, in quotations, girls would do when they're dating. Like particularly promiscuous, or like date seven thousand people at the same time, or go out with somebody who's not Indian or ... something like that." In the process of working this out with her parents, Sonya felt that she had come to a better understanding of her parents' values and that this had helped her to establish her own personal values and beliefs. In Sonya's case, open discussion led to a deepening of her ethno-religiosity rather than an outright rejection of her parents' beliefs.

THE ROLE OF EDUCATIONAL CONTEXT

For the young women in this study, the other social world that intersected with the world of Hindu ethno-religious culture and the world of their friends was Canadian education. It was here that the participants in our study experienced the shortcomings of multiculturalism. For example, in preparing to become a schoolteacher, Sonya had become acutely aware that even though she had grown up in the ethnically diverse city of Toronto, all of her teachers had been white. She said of her university cohort:

With my class of 42 people, there is me and there are two other ladies that are – one's Gujarati or no, one's Punjabi and the other one is north Indian, I think. I'm not quite sure where she's from, Delhi maybe. We're the only three coloured people in the whole class – everyone else is white. And if you come out of your class and you're walking through the halls – everybody is white again. And if you go to big group sessions where, like, all the sections come together and we have, like, assemblies – you can count the brown people on your hands. (HF30)

Sonya told the interviewer that she had made it a point in her field place-ment to introduce Grade 2 students to Diwali in the context of a class on cele-brations around the world. She said that she had dressed in Indian clothes and had brought pictures and home videos and that this had really impressed the children. Sonya was attempting to fill a gap that she had found in her own public education experience, one that was spoken of by other women in the study, particularly as it pertained to the recognition of only Christian holidays during the school year, with all other religious holidays ignored. Critiques of the public education system in Canada have pointed out that the seculariza-tion of schools has led to religious illiteracy among the majority and a "mis-recognition" of minority religious groups (Seljak 2005, 192).

Some of the women in this study mentioned that their Hindu religious holi-days were not recognized by mainstream Canadian institutions, while others spoke about their educational experience leading them to question the validity of the beliefs and practices they had learned at home. Several of the partici-pants mentioned that their education had brought them beyond the religious naïveté of their youth. Parveen said:

I would ask my parents questions and stuff, but they didn't really have all the answers, so I think that kind of led us to um ... to being sceptical about the religion and the religion as a whole, not just Hinduism, sort of thing ... We weren't as educated then as we are now ... I just started asking more questions and nobody really had the answers and it just kind of like ... I don't know, I came up with my own conclusions, and then events in my life were kind of supported by them and what other people would say to me or my teachers. You know? (HF20)

These women said they preferred scientific answers to life's mysteries. Nei-ther their parents nor their teachers could help them construct a positive relationship between science and religion when some of the young women were questioning the validity and sense of their Hindu practices and beliefs. Researchers have pointed out that the so-called value-free secular education provided in Canadian public schools actually promotes the liberal values of the dominant society and remains protective of Eurocentric and Christian values. It does this to the detriment of minority groups who hold a different set of world views and attitudes and have had different experiences (Mahmood 2001; Seljak 2005).

The 39 women in our study were in university and preparing for careers. Most of them had chosen science, engineering, or business as their fields of study. They felt strong pressure to succeed academically – first and foremost from their highly educated parents. Education took precedence over regular religious practice in their families. The women said that in supporting their daughters' educational pursuits, their parents understood that it left them little time to attend the temple and often prevented them from fasting. Yet for some, ensuring success in education had religious value. Amita mentioned that her Hindu identity influenced her attitudes toward education:

> AMITA: That's the way I was really taught about our religion that, you know, if you go and step on books – you've got to give respect to that book.
> INTERVIEWER: It's bad luck?
> AMITA: Oh, I wouldn't call it bad luck, it's just more that … if you're not giving respect to that book or to education in general – education won't come to you, [so] how are you supposed to get smarter or, like, be educated when you don't ever give respect to that? (HF14)

Several of the women said that when they did find time to pray, it was often during exams. Some of the participants mentioned having Saraswati, the goddess of education, in their household shrine. By word and example the message rang out: advanced education brings choices in the future and economic freedom.

For the most part, the women shared their parents' belief that educational attainment would lead to labour market success. Since they reported little evidence of direct discrimination in their lives – and offered isolated examples of it within the lives of their parents – these young adults believed that they would experience the transition to jobs and careers much the way they perceived Canadian society as a whole – open, pluralistic, and welcoming of diversity. Only time will tell whether or not the dreams of the Hindu women under study are matched by the reality of their lived experience.

While these Hindu families placed a great deal of faith in the opportunities that the Canadian education system would provide for their children, there were signs that this system was eroding their Hindu identities. Some of the women had learned about world religions while attending high schools in Ontario, and a few had taken religious studies courses during their undergraduate years at university. This had heightened their curiosity about their own Hindu religion, and some were in the process of learning more. However, Smita said that at university she had learned that her parents were not following Hinduism correctly – she said, "I don't even think they know what Hinduism is. Like I took, um, I took religion before and then what I learned in religion is, like, drastically different from what they practise at home, so my book … so if this is true Hinduism, we deviate so much, it's no longer Hinduism, right?" (HF21). Like others in our study, Smita was disappointed that her parents did not have better answers for her questions about Hindu myths and rituals. Some women were critical of what they perceived as a lack of depth in their family's religious practice. In their opinion, if they did not really understand what they were doing, how authentic could it be?

While all of the women interviewed had learned about Hinduism primarily at home, none of them mentioned the pandits at their local temples as sources of information. This is similar to what we discussed for the Muslim participants in previous chapters. The Hindu women did not see pandits or temple priests as reliable authorities on Hinduism. Some of them described the Hindu religious leaders as relics of a traditional culture who were more interested in their own economic well-being than that of the Canadian Hindu community they supposedly served. More reliable sources of information on Hinduism for them were university undergraduate courses, books, and the Internet. This is interesting in that they believed that professors and texts were more accurate sources of information about Hinduism than the older generation that actually practised the religion in Canada. In this respect, they were not unlike their non-Hindu peers, since many youths today prefer to fashion their own religious identities rather than simply following the particular practices of their parents or elders (Putmam 2007).

These factors do have implications for the future. If a significant proportion of the 39 women who took part in the study were only moderately engaged or unengaged in their Hindu religious world but indicated that later on, perhaps once they get married and have children, they would become more engaged and interested in teaching their children about the faith – where would they turn for answers and guidance? Based on their present practices and attitudes, it appears that they would turn to texts, scholarly and online, rather than to the Hindu communities established by their parents' generation. In this they would again parallel the Muslims in our study, except that the latter had to a large extent already embarked on the road to reconstructing their religious heritage for themselves, whereas only a few among the Hindu women (and, as we shall see, even fewer among the Hindu men) had done so. This has the potential to transform Hindu religion in Canada from one that has been passed on by a community of "doers" to a religion more informed by texts and individual interpretations of those texts. Books and the Internet might be gaining an authoritative edge over the lived experience of the vivid colours, sensual textures, rich tastes, sensual bodily gestures, intriguing music, and interesting smells of their Hindu world. The religious and cultural world of their families is emotionally complex and seems messier than the world of texts. To the extent that our sample is indicative of what the future holds, it seems that Hinduism in Canada, which has largely been influenced by the adaptation of communal heartland practices, could become increasingly influenced among the second generation (and third?) by much more rationalistic and individualistic models of relating and reconstructing religious tradition.

In a study of a Hindu temple in Houston, Texas, the parents of Hindu youth there were not concerned that their teenaged children were not very religious, and they felt that they would become more religious later in life when they married and had children of their own (Jacob and Thaku 2000). According to one woman in our study, Hinduism views life in a series of stages, with later stages being devoted to more spiritual pursuits. Therefore, the notion among parents that their youth will become more religiously engaged in Hinduism as they mature could be viewed as in accordance with their religious beliefs. On the other hand, mainline Protestants and Catholics in North America, who make up the religious majority today and who are themselves descendants of immigrants, are sometimes quite concerned about the lack of institutional participation among their youth. Young adults from these groups are described by sociologists as "good enough" Christians because of their minimal institutional involvement and their views that all religions are equally legitimate (Hoge et al. 2001). Waning reliance on communal and embodied forms of religiosity among the second generation could have significant consequences not only for the Hindu community but also for an increasing religiously illiterate Canadian society as a whole.

CONCLUSION

Currently, the glue that holds the Hindu Canadian communities together is located in the first generation's social world. The parents of the second-generation women in our study have participated in establishing the ethno-religious communal activities and institutions, and their daughters have largely benefited from them. The young women have been enveloped by religious and cultural traditions without having to actively support them in order for them to continue. But while they have benefited from the work of their parents, their participation in the social worlds of their friends and Canadian education has made many of them somewhat critical of their heritage, although most of the Hindu women in no sense rejected it outright. Many valued it highly. Their knowledge of authentic religious practice was not derived from simply imitating what their parents did but rather from their own personal searches and decisions, often based on external sources such as the Internet, academic courses, and books. It is difficult to say where they will finally arrive, but it is certain that most of them did not reject their heritage and definitely wanted to perpetuate at least selected portions of it. Twenty-four-year-old Sonya, quoted above, who grew up in Scarborough and described herself as "not quite prac-tising but sort of in the middle," could speak for many when she said:

> I think that because I like to read, I think that I will probably get around
> to reading more of the texts eventually. Part of my concern is by the time
> I have children, will I be able to teach them enough about the Hindu
> religion that will allow them to pass it on? It's the same thing with lan-
> guage. That's my big concern. If I have kids, someday, I will want them
> to know something about the place that they came from or that their
> family has roots in. And I guess it also depends on who I marry, but like,
> I would like whoever that person might be, I would like them to learn
> about anything and everything that they can know. And so, for that pur-
> pose, I will probably read something more. And I hope that by the time
> that I have children, I will be able to give them, like, pretty much the
> same sort of education, if you want to say, that my parents gave me. And
> I would definitely do it the same way … So it's sort of up to us to decide
> how much we want to learn in order to teach our kids. I think that I will
> have the capacity to teach my children enough to continue it on. As for
> the rest of the generation, I don't know. (HF30)

In this context, there are several things that are quite clear to us. Based on this analysis of interviews with 39 young Hindu women enrolled in universi-ties in Canada, we have learned that they were engaged in identity work that involved choices, strategies, boundary maintenance, and emotion. It involved the world of their families of origin, the broad parameters of Canadian cul-ture, and university life. Woven through these sometimes distinct – but often overlapping – social worlds were themes of ethnicity, religion, gender, and cul-ture. Sometimes the navigation between and within their multiple identities brought the women into conflict with others. Sometimes it caused them to question core assumptions. Often it pushed the young women to make choices that were different from those of their parents or their friends at university who did not share either their religious or ethnic identities. Interestingly, the web of connections drew the young women into deliberate, sustained, and chal-lenging negotiations that had the potential to make them personally stronger and as a result strengthen the country their parents had chosen to call home.

Comparing our Hindu female participants to those with Buddhist or Muslim backgrounds, one notes a kind of in-between position, one that is perhaps again well represented by Sonya as just quoted. Unlike so many of the Muslims, both men and women, leading an authentically and religiously Hindu life was not as important as maintaining Hindu religious and cultural identity, along with an array of practices and orientations that concretized that identity. But for most of these women, maintaining that identity was indeed important. Unlike the Buddhist participants, as we shall see in chapters 9 and 10, the religious elements of that identity were usually of some importance and certainly not as marginal. In the theoretical terms we are using, Hinduism as religion appeared in the lived religion of these women, but it did not dominate, and their contribution to systemic Hinduism in the Canadian context remains uncertain, even by their own admission. In both these latter respects, however, they differed markedly from their Hindu male counterparts, for whom even the identity, let alone the religion, for the most part did not appear to be that important. It is to a more detailed look at this subgroup that we turn in the next chapter.

A Dominance of Marginal Relations:
Hindu Men

SHANDIP SAHA AND PETER BEYER

A DEMOGRAPHIC PROFILE OF 18 MEN
FROM HINDU BACKGROUNDS

As is evident from the very low numbers in comparison with the other sub-groups, Hindu men were difficult to recruit for this project, and this is a direct reflection of their comparative lack of interest or involvement in matters Hindu and, for many, even religious or spiritual. The Buddhist men, it will be noted, were similar in this regard, and the parallels between the two groups are remarkable, including in the sense that few if any were strongly involved in the religion of their family background, in this case Hinduism. Some had what one might call "spiritual" interests, but they were the minority in both groups. In terms of their demographic profile, the Hindu male group was somewhat at odds with the overall Canadian Hindu population, especially in the sense that a relatively high number of our sample had family origins in Trinidad or Guyana: 7 out of the 18 came from families with these origins. Another 2 came from Sri Lankan families, and 5 came from families in which both parents were born in India. Of the remaining 4, 2 were from mixed Indian/Euro-Canadian families, 1 from a family that originated in Bangladesh, and 1 had an ethnically Indian father from Kenya and an English mother. This distribution contrasts markedly with the overall Hindu population: in 2001, of the roughly 225,000 immigrant Canadians who said they were Hindu, about 150,000 were born in South Asian countries, and only about 39,000 were born in Trinidad or Guyana. Of the approximately 76,000 Hindus born in Canada, about 5,000 declared their origins as the Caribbean or Latin America, whereas 65,000 declared themselves as having South Asian origins. This significant skewing did not, however, correlate with any obvious differences among the 18 in terms of their relation to Hinduism, their cultural profiles, or their orientation to broader questions such as how they felt about Canada and living in this country. Unlike with the Buddhists (male and female) in our sample, country of family origin or ethnicity appeared to bear no consistent relation to any of these questions. Moreover, these 18 Hindu-background men, like their female counterparts (see chapter 7) were also heavily Canada-born: 11 were of the second generation, and only 7 were of the 1.5 generation. This difference as well did not manifest itself in any noticeable way in their religious and cultural orientations and practices.

With this demographic profile in mind, we move now to a general analysis of all 18 interviews with the purpose of trying to identify certain patterns and themes that emerged as the interviewees talked about their families, their exposure to their parents' culture and religion, and the formation of their own religious identities while growing up in a multicultural society. On this basis, we will in a subsequent section analyze in greater detail the interviews of four participants whose experiences best reflected the themes that emerged from the entire set of 18 interviews. A strong overall conclusion is that these youth neither felt caught between two cultures nor felt any pressure to assimilate into Canadian society. On the contrary, they preferred to fashion their own religious identities based on what they considered appropriate for them without seeking any recourse to any sort of external religious authority.

THE HISTORY AND COMPOSITION OF THE FAMILIES

The majority of the participants' parents exhibited very similar family histories, and – even if it wasn't explicitly stated – parental attitudes were influenced by the *ashrama* system of Hinduism in which a religious life is actively pursued after one has received a proper education and discharged one's duties to society and family by working and supporting one's immediate and extended family members (compare the discussion with respect to the Hindu women participants at the end of the previous chapter). Thus, while shrines and godrooms may have been plentiful in their homes, religion was not a predominant force in the lives of the interviewees' parents; rather, their lives were structured around the concerns of maintaining an extended family. In some cases, parents and other family members went to temple on special occasions when families gathered for Hindu holidays, while in others religious practice was a private affair, with parents and grandparents offering prayers every morning in front of a small shrine within the home.

Past scholarship on the Hindu diaspora has rightly emphasized how temples and community associations are crucial in maintaining religious and cultural identity in a foreign land. Appadurai (1996) argues that when Indian immigrants settle in North America, they do not completely assimilate but construct what he calls "ethnoscapes" or landscapes of group identities. Immigrants and their families, according to Appadurai, maintain religious practices that create an ethnic identity based on an imagined relationship to their homeland. It is difficult to say with certainty just how well the life histories of our interviewees' parents conformed to this thesis. The Hindu men rarely mentioned how their parents felt about their homelands in relation to Canada, but from what they did reveal, their parents' life histories did not quite support Appadurai's thesis. Religious centres were not necessarily the only area in which social or religious activities took place for the interviewees' parents. Parents focused on recreating the tightly knit family and social networks of their homelands by building ties with family already settled in Canada and with other members of the immigrant community to which they belonged. This meant that the pattern of religious practice of the parents tended to be replicated within Canada and not with primary reference to the country of origin. While a small minority of interviewees described their parents as devout Hindus who visited their local Hindu temple regularly, the majority tended to describe their parents either as going to temple on a semi-regular basis to mark major religious festivals or as practising home rituals and singing devotional songs at home in front of a domestic shrine, either individually or with family friends. In other words, both temples and homes were the focus of social and religious activities for parents and a means by which they could preserve the culture in which they grew up (Bannerjee and Coward 2005; Coward, Hinells, and Williams 2000; for a US comparison, Min 2010).

There were certain exceptions to these patterns. In some instances, both parents were raised as Hindus in their homelands but neither inherited the religiosity of their households nor made an effort to practise Hinduism when they came to Canada. This pattern of (non-)religiosity was retained when the parents immigrated to Canada, with the parents distancing themselves completely from their religious and cultural backgrounds or restricting their participation to cultural events. The case of Arvind (HM01), who is profiled in some detail below, exemplifies this pattern. A variation can be found in the case of Raj, a Canada-born 19-year-old whose family came from Guyana. His parents were raised in Hindu families, but they gradually drifted toward Christianity when they came to Canada, although they did not by that token abandon their Hinduism. Raj, therefore, grew up attending various Christian churches, but he and his family also occasionally attended Hindu temples. Their and Raj's construction of religion was not exclusive, or at least one might say that their construction of Hinduism included the possibility of incorporating other religions. Raj expressed his and assumedly his family orientation like this: "I mean the way I see it, you don't have to restrict yourself to just one … religion. I mean other religions say [that you do] … or you'll go to hell, y'know. I don't see it like that. The way I see it is if you could just get a bit of that god in you, y'know what I'm saying, a little bit of those things that teach you how to live life better, better principles, that's fine" (HM14).

The more complicated variation on this last instance is to be found in the case of participants whose parents might have been raised in Hindu households but whose extended family members consisted of individuals who converted to Christianity. This seems to explain why the parents eventually converted to

Christianity and had their children baptized. Suraj (HM15), also profiled below in some detail, exemplifies this pattern. The only major exception to the backgrounds mentioned above can be seen in the cases of participants who came from mixed religious backgrounds, with one parent being Hindu while the other was either Christian or Muslim. There were 4 such cases among the 18. In these instances, the parents both practised their religion independently and did not seem to be involved in the practices of their spouses. Consequently, as will be outlined below, the participants who came from this background had very little exposure to the religious and cultural heritages of their parents.

DEGREES OF PARTICIPANT RELIGIOUS AND CULTURAL PRACTICE

In sum, most of the families sought to build a new life in Canada by recreating, as much as possible, the closely knit family and social networks of their homelands. This prevailing strategy may help to explain why many of the interviewees' parents visited their former homes only infrequently; then again, several others did visit with some regularity. Some were twice migrants, having settled in other countries before moving to Canada. Many extended family members had resettled in North America or Europe, thus rendering trips to the country of origin less necessary. In addition, the formation of cultural associations and the establishment of numerous Indian grocery and clothing stores meant that the interviewees' parents could experience their culture without having to travel back home. In some cases, parents had become so distanced from their homelands that they did not exhibit a strong desire to revisit them again. This was the case with Arvind, who is profiled below. In other cases, such as that of Anil (HM09) and one or two others who came from twice-migrant families, the parents were sufficiently transnational in their working lives that the sense of "here" and "back home" was not that sharply distinguished.

In this context of relative distance, many of the interviewees inherited or developed a certain distancing from their parental culture and religion. In the case of participants whose parents came from different religious and cultural backgrounds, there was no focused socialization in one religion/culture or the other, both being as often as not seen as issues of personal choice. Consequently, these participants had little, if any, consistent exposure to their parents' religious and cultural heritage. Sanjiv, for instance, grew up in a mixed Indian Hindu and Euro-Canadian Christian family in Oakville, a city near Toronto that he described as "fairly white." He said that he never felt "caught between two cultures," or, as he put it, "I didn't see that as a problem. My parents did a good job in that aspect. There is no real conflict or anything like that" (HM02). Yet the few attempts by his Indian mother to immerse him in her culture failed miserably, because he felt that he just didn't fit in with people who lived more uniformly in one cultural environment. In fact, all four of the participants who came from mixed cultural or religious families were non-religious and did not have a strong relation to the culture of their Hindu parent. One notes, however, that mixed parentage does not always have this result, as, for instance, several of the Muslim and a few of the Buddhist participants discussed in other chapters demonstrate.

The outcome among participants whose parents were both Hindus showed a significantly greater degree of variation. For some of these individuals, their exposure to Hinduism and the culture of their parents was limited, because their parents confined their practice of Hinduism to the occasional trip to the local temple and perhaps morning prayer at home shrines or because they put little emphasis on explaining much about Hinduism and Indian culture to their children. As with the Hindu women, a good number of parents seemed to have been more concerned with ensuring that their children focused on their education and integrated properly into Canadian society. Overall, but for various reasons, very few of the participants were actively involved in religious and cultural organizations associated with their parents' heritage, nor did they exhibit a desire to limit their social network to those sharing their ethnicity. They chose their friends on the basis of shared common interests, with the result that they cut across both religious and ethnic lines, often including few other Hindus or people of South Asian descent. In this they were similar to many others among the Buddhist and Muslim interviewees, as well as the Hindu women.

The participants who came from family backgrounds in which both parents were Hindus tended, however, to have very different views toward Hinduism. There were those who rejected Hinduism: they tended to fall into three categories. First, there were those who continued to practise Hinduism out of obligation rather than out of conviction. These were participants who either rejected religion or were agnostic but still continued to practise Hinduism with their parents in order to avoid family conflict or because it was a tradition that had to be respected while they were living at home with their parents. An example is Sajan, a 21-year-old whose parents came from northern India. He had this exchange:

INTERVIEWER: Okay, do your parents know you're agnostic?
SAJAN: … uh … I dunno.
INTERVIEWER: Okay, 'cause you say you continue to still pray with them and go to festivals. Do they just assume that you still follow?
SAJAN: They know I don't care [laughs]. They know I'm just doing it for them.
INTERVIEWER: [laughs] Okay. So you do it basically to make them happy?
SAJAN: Well, I mean, I don't wanna, y'know, start a fight [laughs] – not to make them happy but to – I guess you could say to avoid a conflict.

INTERVIEWER: Keep the peace.

SAJAN: Keep the peace, okay, it doesn't trouble me to, y'know, if they want, once a month, go to the temple or something ... it's not a problem, so ... (HM05)

A second category consisted of those who drifted away from Hinduism but considered themselves to be spiritual or at least not against religion. They often believed in some sort of power greater than themselves. Sometimes, as in the case of Vikram (HM11), who was born in Madras and came to Canada at the age of 5, there was nothing in particular that triggered their movement away from Hinduism; it was something that occurred over time as they grew older and more mature. We saw this in a couple of the cases of the non-religious Muslim men as well (see chapter 5). For others, such as 22-year-old Jimmy who was from a Trinidadian family, it was specific questioning that initiated the drift. Here is how he put it:

I just started to question some of the teachings, like I didn't really know too much about Hinduism, but I had a rough idea, and I just started to think more for myself and kind of ask myself well, is this realistic? Like, is this the way things are supposed to be, or does God really exist? And then when I look around and you see, you look at society, and I'd ask myself, well, there realistically could be some sort of power involved, but whether or not it's what I'm being taught, I don't think so, plus I don't know if Hinduism would really fit into my life. (HM16)

In a third category were those few, like some of their counterparts among the Buddhist and Muslim interviewees, for whom Hinduism and religion more broadly had never held much attraction. Prakash, a 22-year-old born in England whose parents originated from Guyana, put this position quite clearly in the following exchange:

INTERVIEWER: Would you say there was a reason why you didn't identify with your childhood religion?

PRAKASH: Well, I never identified with it. All of it seemed pretty clearly manifestly false to begin with.

INTERVIEWER: Would you consider [Hinduism] to be inadequate, or would you consider all religions to be inadequate?

PRAKASH: I think all. (HM17)

There were other participants whose parents were Hindus and who still identified themselves as practising Hindus. The majority of them, however, learned about Hinduism mainly by imitating what their parents did at home in front of their altars, mostly without any great understanding for what these practices meant and why one did them. Religion was indeed emphasized by the parents of these participants, but again, it also often took second place to education, because the parents wanted their children to build a secure future for themselves. Thus, while these participants definitely identified themselves as Hindus, they exhibited very little concrete knowledge of Hindu theology and ritual. The extent of their knowledge about Hinduism was limited to the concepts of karma, reincarnation, and living an ethical life. They still, however, practised whatever it was they considered to be Hinduism, because it was a family tradition that needed to be continued and because it helped the participants maintain a certain connection to their family heritage. As Balendra, a 19-year-old from a Bengali family, put it, "I don't truly believe in the religion [i.e., Hinduism], but I believe it is important to have an association with it so that you can understand your parents and your relatives" (HM08). Mathavan, a 19-year-old born in Canada, from a Sri Lankan Tamil family, was more definite about his Hindu identity: "I'm more Hindu because of my parents and my family and whatnot, because the culture, especially, back in Sri Lanka my grandparents had temples and whatnot. So I'm Hindu" (HM10). Exceedingly rare were those who not only considered themselves Hindu but also practising Hindus. Only one of the 18 was unequivocal in this regard. Ravi, at 26, was the oldest of the group. He came to Canada with his family from Guyana when he was 3 years old. Like quite a few of the Muslim participants, he had started taking his religion seriously again only recently after being fairly blasé about his Hindu identity throughout his earlier years. He described his religiousness and his level of involvement in the following exchange:

INTERVIEWER: What would you say is your religion?
RAVI: If I had to pick one, I'd say Hinduism.
INTERVIEWER: Would you say that you practise Hinduism regularly?
RAVI: Yes.
INTERVIEWER: What does that entail?
RAVI: I go to service, I go to temple every Sunday, and every morning and evening I do a chant. I chant mantras ...
INTERVIEWER: Is there an altar in your home?
RAVI: Yes ... throughout my upbringing [the altar] has always been there for you to use as you feel the need to ... It was not a very religious home at all. At this point in time, I'm by far the most religious member of the household, perhaps the only religious member of the household ... I suspect if anything was to change at the altar, they probably would go to me or ask me, because they know that I use it the most ...
INTERVIEWER: Is there a particular god or goddess that you have there?

RAVI: There are various deities.

INTERVIEWER: So there's no one that you worship more often than the others?

RAVI: My interface with Hinduism is different than some. I have specific deities that … resonate with me, for example Ganesha or Shiva, but when I interface with my altar, it's usually through chanting, meditation, vibration. It's a very abstract interface, this is not quite my conception of the divine. (HM12)

The prevailing lack of knowledge about Hinduism among these participants tends to underline how the majority of them had made only one or two trips to their parents' homelands when they were young and did not seem to be interested in returning to directly experience the culture and religion of their parents. The participants whose parents were born in India usually did not exhibit any attachment to or particular interest in visiting their parents' spiritual and cultural home, and this was equally the case with the participants whose parents were Trinidadian or Guyanese. India may have been the origin of their spiritual and cultural heritage, but it never figured in the discourse of the Trinidadian and Guyanese participants during the course of the interviews. Once Indian migrants settled in the West Indies to work as indentured labourers for the British, they adapted Indian culture and Hinduism to the local culture and, in the process, created their own cultural and religious traditions that were very distinct from those in India (see Vertovec 1992). These were the traditions in which the participants' parents were raised, and it was these traditions that were brought by West Indian immigrants to Canada. This did not mean, however, that the West Indian participants exhibited a greater attachment to their parents' homelands. The identities of the West Indian participants were, like their East Indian counterparts, not shaped in any way by encounters with their parents' places of origin. The basis for their national solidarity was Canada, where they lived the life of the average Canadian youth but with the added challenge of negotiating and defining how large a part their parents' religious and cultural heritage was to play in their lives.

CLASSIFYING THE HINDU MALES

The diverse nature of the participants' family and religious histories makes it quite difficult to develop categories that can meaningfully express the sorts of relationship these men of Hindu background had to their religious and cultural heritages. It is quite clear that, unlike the situation with the Muslims but very much like that with the Buddhist participants, adopting a scheme centred on degree of religious involvement would only serve to miss the main axes of variation, since few if any of these men were what one might call religiously involved: they did not espouse much of anything that is usually encompassed under the vast panoply of what in most people's eyes counts as Hinduism, and they did not engage with any regularity or seriousness in corresponding religious practices such as prayer, *puja*, meditation, service (*sevak*), devotional singing, reading of sacred writings, and so forth. In this regard, the 18 men were much more clearly outside such criteria of involvement than their female Hindu counterparts. Accordingly, when it came to situating them on the scale that emerged from the overall analysis of the Hindu interviews (see chapter 4), most of the men demonstrated characteristics that allowed us to classify them either as non-practising (essentially non-religious) Hindus or as ethno-cultural Hindus, the latter designating those who related positively to Hindu as a cultural category and mostly only in that context as a religious one. Of the 18 men, 11 could be classified as non-practising, another 5 as ethnocultural. That left 2 who could from one perspective be classified as practising except that their practice was only in one case self-identified as Hindu; that was the case of Ravi, who was just discussed and quoted. Even here, however, his level of practice could only be described as rather moderate and in some respects quite idiosyncratic. The other exception is Anand, who is profiled below. He was highly practising, but he also had composed his own religion or spirit-uality that bore only passing resemblance to what most observers would be willing to call Hindu. The unity of his practice was in his own lived religion, not in terms of a systemic tradition. Together, these two men showed just how difficult it was with this sample of 18 to convincingly classify them at all. One thing is fairly evident, however: to whatever degree this small group repre-sented young male adults from Hindu families in Canada more generally, they were at this stage in their lives not going to be contributing meaningfully to the reconstruction of Hinduism in this country, at least not as a systemic religion. One could, perhaps, argue that they thereby manifested the Hindu *ashrama* system wherein pursuing religious practice and goals is not a priority at their stage in life and especially not for their gender, but that would be rather thin speculation, given that none of them mentioned that this was how they them-selves interpreted their present lives, attitudes, and behaviours.

Eleven Non-practising or Non-religious Hindus

The participants who fell into the category of non-practising Hindus all ac-knowledged that they were quite distant from the religious and cultural herit-age of their Hindu parents and expressed little to no interest in wanting to discover more about their religious and cultural inheritance. Most tended to define religion in terms of relating to a higher power within an ethical and moral system that was personally suited to an individual, but the non-practising Hindus replaced their rejection of Hinduism with either an alternative form of spirituality or with nothing at all. Thus, marrying only someone who was of Indian background and raising their children in Hinduism was of little consequence to these interviewees. They refused to let their choice of a marriage partner be dictated by purely religious or cultural concerns, nor did they want their children's future dictated by these concerns. It was more important that they expose their children to a wide variety of ideas and cultures and then let them decide what was right for them.

The non-practising Hindus are well represented by Arvind (HM01) and Michel (HM03). Michel was a 20-year-old biological and social sciences major at the University of Toronto whose Hindu father and Catholic mother practised their religion on a very private and highly individual basis. Michel's father practised Hinduism by making regular trips to his local temple where he prayed to various Hindu deities. In describing the nature of his father's religiosity and his relationship to it, Michel stated, "Yes. He prays every morning. I mean he goes to *mandir* [temple] … I go to *mandir* now. I don't go to church now, but I will go to the *mandir* with my father. Even though I am not Hindu … No … Even though I don't pray to the gods … it's still … I don't know … I enjoy it. It's a good time for me and my dad also" (HM03).

When describing the religiosity of his mother, Michel stated that her disagreements with the politics of the church hierarchy had changed her into a lapsed Catholic who nonetheless had built her own individual form of spirituality around her firm belief in God: the lived religious style that she had developed, he said, had a certain influence on his own orientations. When describing his mother's religious beliefs, Michel stated, "I think she believes in God, but I don't think that she agrees with all the politics of the system … the Catholic system … the hierarchy and all that … She's a more naturalistic person … she believes in a more holistic … way of looking at life … in terms of nature … the balance of nature … I think that I got a lot of that from her."

Raised in Montreal, Michel was placed in the Catholic school system where his exposure to Catholicism left no more impression upon him than his occasional trips to the temple with his father. Michel saw his trips to the temple, as noted in the quotation above, as a way to spend some quality time with his father, but his exploration of Hindu scriptures seemed to have left him rather bewildered. When asked about the books he read on Hinduism, Michel stated, "The gods and the stories of the gods, you know? Hanuman and all that and Ganesha. It was more about the mythology behind it. I didn't really understand how it affects the way you live or what you believe … I used to say that I am not even sure what Hinduism is. I just stopped thinking about what religions are, and I just said they all believe the same thing." This distance between Michel and Hinduism was reinforced by the fact that none of his school friends growing up were Hindu or Indian and he had no contact with his father's family. Michel's father was alienated from his parents and extended family in India after he chose to reject an arranged marriage and married Michel's mother instead. Michel only started to learn more about Indian culture in university through some of his newly found South Asian friends who took him to cultural events organized by Indian students associations. Here again, the Canadian university environment provided an important context, not to meet "others" but to meet "one's own." These experiences helped Michel at some level to become a bit more connected to his father's heritage, yet that level was rather superficial and not enough for him to feel that he could fully identify with Indian values and culture. Michel described his feelings after being exposed to Indian culture in the following terms: "Yes ... I am connected. I feel it. I understand it. I've been there ... seen it. I am basically connected. When it comes to my day-to-day life, there is no real connection ... I don't have my dad's values ... There is a father-son thing, but I don't see myself taking his values upon myself."

The experience of 21-year-old Arvind was somewhat similar to Michel's. Arvind's parents were raised in South Indian Brahmin households, but they never seemed to have gravitated towards Hinduism. Arvind's father never exhibited an interest in Hinduism, while his mother was educated in a Catholic missionary school in India. English, consequently, was spoken in the home instead of the family's mother tongue of Telugu. Here is how Arvind described his parents' religious upbringing:

> I never got the impression that their religious upbringing was very religious. My mom went to an English school run by Italian missionaries when she was younger, and she spoke English in her household. Hinduism wasn't always very big in their house. It was like ... my father ... I think ... it was more important, but still ... he never really clicked with them ... He never talks about religion, he never goes to temple. (HM01)

This pattern of religiosity seems to have been retained when Arvind's parents came to Canada. Arvind's mother is still involved in the South Indian community, but his father has all but distanced himself from everything to do with the Indian community because of the internal politics and cliquishness, which he found distasteful. Thus, after living in Canada for years, Arvind's father had become so distanced from his faith and culture that he no longer felt any strong desire even to visit India. The only individual who seemed to exhibit any overt Hindu religiosity was Arvind's grandmother, who came from India to live with her children in Canada. Arvind, however, did not seem to have much contact with his grandmother. She lived in Toronto, while Arvind and his family lived in Montreal.

Thus, given his parents' lack of religious involvement with Hinduism and the lack of contact with his grandmother, Arvind was, from an early age, already quite distanced from his Hindu heritage, and this distance became even greater while he was in elementary and secondary school. Arvind stated that he had only a few friends of Indian descent, because he was raised in a predominantly Jewish neighbourhood. He said that he knew more about Judaism and Jewish culture than he did about Indian culture and Hinduism and that his contact with Indian culture decreased even more over time because his circle of friends in elementary and high school were primarily made up of Jews and Christians. Arvind described his exposure to Hinduism growing up in Montreal by stating, "I knew more about Judaism than I knew about Hinduism at the time ... I was very influenced by Judaism and then Christianity, because it was all around me." Unlike Michel's experience, the composition of his social network did not change at all when he went to university, and this explains why Arvind had difficulties identifying with Hinduism and Indian culture. By the time Arvind began studying engineering when he moved to Ottawa for university, he admitted that he did not know anything about being Indian and felt that he was neither Indian nor Hindu but Canadian and agnostic. He stated: "I did a little bit [of Hinduism] in first year Carleton. It was an elective, and then I dropped the class because I didn't have to take it ... I don't know all the names of the gods or the major ones even, but there is a caste system ... but that's pretty much all that I know about it ... Really, I don't know anything about being Indian other than I was born from Indian parents." It was not surprising, then, that Arvind had no interest in marrying someone from within the Indian community and that if he were to have children, they would have the right to choose their own religious faith.

Ethnocultural Hindus

The interviewees who could be described as ethnocultural Hindus were in many ways not that different from their non-practising counterparts. These participants were raised in families where either one or both parents were Hindus; the participants' circle of friends crossed cultural boundaries; their knowledge of Hinduism was rather rudimentary, with their exposure to it limited to the occasional trip to a temple or watching their parents practise Hinduism at home. What, then, makes the participants identified as ethnocultural Hindus different from their non-practising counterparts? The principal difference is that they considered themselves to be practising Hindus, yet their practice was not necessarily done out of religious conviction, nor was it built upon a strong and thorough knowledge of the ritual, philosophical, and historical dimensions of Hinduism. The basis for their knowledge was imitating the practices of their Hindu family members because it was part of the culture and tradition in which they were raised. In other words, they identified with Hinduism more in cultural than in specifically religious terms (cf. Min 2010, whose findings for the US were both similar and different).

The ethnocultural category is well exemplified by Gopal (HM07) and Suraj (HM15). Gopal was a 22-year-old participant whose Trinidadian parents immigrated to Toronto in search of better economic conditions. Gopal's experience of Hinduism was very typical of this group. When describing what he believed were the traditional practices of Hindus, he responded by stating, "[w]ell, we celebrate things like Diwali ... Every year, in West Indian culture, for Hindus, we do at least one prayer, one *puja* ... at your home ... at least once a year. I think that's important" (HM07). Gopal's parents and extended family members visited their temple only twice a year but practised more regularly at home in front of the family altar. Thus, Gopal learned about Hinduism mostly by watching his parents at home praying in front of their altar and described his childhood experience of Hinduism in the following terms: "When we were younger at home, we'd normally sit in the back and watch our parents, and now as we got older and more responsible, we've taken a bit more of a role and participated when we can."

As was so common across the sample of Hindu participants, Gopal explained that his parents' generation did not place much emphasis on teaching religion to their children, because they wanted their children to focus on their education and bettering their lives. The influence of religion in Gopal's home was, however, enough that he definitely considered himself a Hindu even though he could hardly articulate anything about Hindu ritual practice. Gopal never mentioned the names of specific Hindu texts as sources of religious authority, nor did he mention the names of specific deities, doctrines, and rituals. When asked to describe the main teachings of Hinduism, Gopal answered the question in the following manner: "[A Hindu] ... is someone who is understanding of all religions, not just critical, not just looking at their own religion and thinking it's the best ... [It] is a way how to live your life, I think that's an important thing."

Gopal admitted that he did not visit his local Hindu temple more than twice a year, but it was clear that these visits did at some level shape his understanding of Hinduism. These temple visits may explain the emphasis he placed on the observance of *pujas* and major religious holidays as being the core feature of Hinduism and why temple priests were the key sources of religious authority for him, while important texts in Hinduism like the Vedas, Upanishads, or the Bhagavad Gita were never mentioned. These temple visits also heightened his awareness of the differences between Hinduism as practised in West Indian and Canadian temples, although he was barely able to articulate the differences he noticed. His understanding of these differences was articulated in the following terms: "Well ... uh ... certain things we can't do here, like certain things you need to use, like mango leaves … You can't get that here unless you ship it in and stuff like that that you use … different things to substitute for that, right? … So I think that's one of the big differences because of where you live, we're living in a cold climate."

Regardless of the influence that his sporadic visits to the local Hindu temple had upon Gopal's views of Hinduism, temple worship far from defined his conception of Hinduism. Temple priests, Gopal stated, were knowledgeable, but their value as religious authorities seemed to be undermined by their inability to communicate in a way that was relevant to youth of his generation. This, along with growing up in a home where domestic worship was common, might help to explain why Gopal did not see temple worship as essential to a Hindu's identity. When asked about the necessity of visiting a temple, Gopal said, "I would only go if it's one of the special days or occasions, um … The way I see it necessarily as a Hindu, you do not actually have to go to temple all the time … Mainly the reason would be if it's a special occasion."

Gopal's knowledge of other branches within Hinduism was limited to his vague awareness of the differences he observed between West Indian and East Indian Hinduism, and while he stated that he did regular prayers, he never mentioned what they were, nor did he talk about Hindu deities or any theological position to which he might have been attached. On the contrary, he seemed not to have placed any particular emphasis on strictly observing Hinduism: "We're supposed to be a vegetarian, and um … I do observe that every Thursday. I don't eat meat or any egg or anything … umm … I think that's important, to live a healthy life and to be aware of God just every day." For Gopal, the biggest strength of Hinduism was its accepting nature, and this formed the basis for building a strong community. When asked about the principal strengths of Hinduism, Gopal stated, "Main strengths? … It creates a community … um … When you're there, no one's judging you, you don't have to present yourself in any way, you just go there, everyone's welcoming, and I think that's a good thing." What Gopal meant in this quote by "there" was not clear, especially since he placed very little priority on temple Hinduism, but it was very clear that for Gopal, being a Hindu had very little to do with the traditional Hindu goal of achieving spiritual liberation (moksha) or advancing a particular religious agenda specific to a particular stream of religiosity within Hinduism. For Gopal, the practice of Hinduism was first and foremost a private practice that was meant to build an ethical, open-minded, and tolerant community of family and friends.

In the case of 23-year-old Suraj, both of his parents were raised in Guyanese Hindu families, but their households were shaped by a complicated religious history. Suraj stated that the majority of members in the family of his maternal great-grandfather were Christians, which explains why Suraj's maternal grandparents were married under Hindu rites but attended an Anglican church on a regular basis. Suraj's paternal grandmother was a practising Hindu, and while Suraj did not exactly detail much about his father's religious life, it seems that Suraj's mother was the reason that his father eventually converted to Christianity and married in a Methodist church, where Suraj was baptized as a baby. In Suraj's own words:

> Well, my parents were born Hindus, my mom's father was a mix of black and Portuguese, so there's a lot of Christian influence there. My grandmother, she was Hindu, but my mom's parents are married under Hindu rites, but they attended an Anglican church, so she had Christian influence there. Plus on her father's side of the family, most of them were Christian, but on my dad's side they were pure Hindu, but they married ... My mom's first husband was actually Muslim, so my big brother's Muslim and his wife is Muslim and um ... when she married my father, they married in a Methodist church. And they were baptized Methodist and so was I ... Well, my parents were Hindu, and they converted to Christianity. One of my dad's sisters who is Hindu married a pastor's son, so she converted to Christianity, which is primarily the reason my parents converted, because when they were in New York, they lived with her and they went to a Christian church with her and I think that's about it. (HM15)

Unlike Michel, Suraj's exposure to Christianity was not at the expense of Hinduism, even though his parents and many other family members were Guyanese Hindus who had converted to Christianity. Suraj retained the influence of Hinduism from his paternal grandmother, who still practised Hinduism. He stated that while his grandmother did not teach him formally about Hinduism, he gradually absorbed some of her religious practice through his close contact with her. Suraj described his initial exposure to Hinduism in the following manner:

> My grandmother, my dad's side, her brother died, and we went to his one-year ceremony, and they had a singer there, and after the ceremony, he was selling cassettes, and she bought one and I took it and I was listening to it ... so she was telling me about what the [Hanuman] Chalisa[1] was and I just ... She told me it was something good to read, and I started reading it on my own, and I tried memorizing [it].

Along with the Hanuman Chalisa, Suraj began to learn Hindu prayers and devotional songs, even though he did not understand Hindi. He read romanized versions of the Hindu texts, relied on English translations, and read these prayers along with Christian prayers while he was growing up. Initially, this caused a certain amount of tension between him and his father, who would have preferred that Suraj stay within the fold of Christianity. Suraj stated:

> My mom didn't have a problem with it at first. My dad ... kind of told me it was okay to respect the Hindu religion but kind of emphasized the fact that I was baptized a Christian and, although he wouldn't say it, I think he didn't like the idea, but after he saw it was more like something, not a phase I was going through, that I actually believed in it a lot, he said it was better I follow something instead of disregarding all religious beliefs entirely.

Suraj stated that his practice of Hinduism began to wane considerably after the death of his paternal grandmother, and he continued with Christianity until he began university. When his interest in Hinduism was rekindled after taking a course on Hinduism in first-year university, however, he did not turn to the religious leaders in his temple for guidance, and this was for two reasons. The first was that Suraj did not see temple Hinduism as central in the lives of Guyanese Hindus. When asked if members of the Guyanese Hindu community went to temples for significant events such as birthdays, anniversaries, or death rites, Suraj stated, "Very rarely, they're usually done at home. Birthdays are usually done at home, because we're Guyanese so we eat a lot of chicken and duck so we can't do that in a temple. Anniversaries are usually done at home too. The only thing I find Guyanese people use the temple for is just for services. They usually do everything else at home."

The second reason Suraj did not turn to his local temple was that he had difficulty accepting the authority of the temple priests. He was more willing to consult the Internet for his knowledge of Hinduism and use temple priests as a last resort if he needed to know something. In this respect, he had a lot in common with several of the Muslim participants we discussed in previous chapters. The information he would get from the Internet, however, tended to be more general in nature and might help to explain why Suraj's knowledge of Hinduism tended at times to be rather vague. When asked about the main characteristics of a Hindu, Suraj answered, "I'd say that they don't eat meat. I don't eat meat or pork, so at least if they eat meat, not to consume those ... But now I just find that it doesn't really matter what you consume once you truly believe it and follow some basic principles of it." His reliance on the Internet for general information on Hinduism may also explain the rather improvised nature of his religiosity. Suraj stated that he prayed to his images of gods and goddesses in his bedroom before he went to bed, and then he went on to state, "Yeah, sometimes I sing to myself ... Monday I fast all day, I didn't eat anything ... I don't know how to do the prayers properly, so I kind of just ... do my own little thing, and I made sweets and I distributed them." What becomes evident from these descriptions is that Suraj was constructing his Hinduism in a kind of personal way that had little necessary reference to any sort of "orthodox/ orthopraxy" model, whether from his family, the temple, the Internet, or even his university course. He was practising his lived religion much more than he was contributing to the construction of a systemic Hinduism.

Suraj was also careful to not talk about his Hindu religious life when he was at the church he went to every Sunday with his family. The congregants were of the same generation as his family members and would have been quite resistant to the idea that one could claim to be both Hindu and Christian. For Suraj, this was not a problem, any more that his idiosyncratic construction of his own lived religion was a problem. All the deities he prayed to at home were manifestations of one supreme being, and consequently, he was worshipping the same God regardless of whether or not it was in a Christian or Hindu context. However, did Suraj tend to favour or identify with one religion more than the other? At one level, it is difficult to say. Suraj's levels of church and temple attendance were roughly the same; his knowledge of Hinduism was just as limited as his knowledge of Christianity, which he boiled down to following the Ten Commandments. And he had no religious preference when it came to choosing a possible marriage partner. On another level, however, his description of his current religious practice would make one think that Suraj felt a bit more attached to Christianity than he did to Hinduism:

I try and attend the Christian church every Sunday, but with work and school, it's a bit more difficult to do. More during the summer when I have a better chance, I try and go every Sunday. The Hindu church I don't go to very often, I haven't been in a long time, but daily, it's not … a formal set of prayers that I'll say out, but throughout the day, I'll just catch myself saying something … to myself.

It would be more accurate to say, however, that Suraj continued to identify with Christianity and Hinduism because each religion provided him with something the other lacked. For Suraj, Christianity provided him with a sense of community, which he just didn't feel with Hinduism. When asked about the strengths of Christianity, Suraj stated:

I think it's the sense of community, because when you're baptized, the minister asks the priest if the congregation will make an effort to help raise the child under a good Christian way of living, and I find that the church community in Christianity is very supportive … Well, among Hindu Caribbeans at least is that the community may seem very strong, but I don't think it is just because um … When we were in New York for my grandmother's funeral, the Pundit said at one of the services –

this is what I heard, I wasn't at the service, it was at the temple – that those who don't care about making an effort in Hinduism, he won't really make an effort to um … if you don't care, he doesn't care kind of thing. But I find in Christianity that if you don't care, there's a lot more support, and I find that my mom gets a lot of support sometimes. If she doesn't attend church for one Sunday then there's about three or four people calling, asking if she's okay.

What Hinduism, on the other hand, provided for Suraj was something much more personal. The prayers recited by Suraj, his affinity for the monkey god, Hanuman, and his emphasis on personal worship at home all were the result of his grandmother's influence. Thus, while Christianity gave Suraj the ability to build social networks, his practice of Hinduism was more rooted in maintaining his connection to his late grandmother.

INDIVIDUALISTIC ORIENTATIONS AMONG
THE HINDU MALES: TWO PROFILES

An aspect that emerges from some of the Hindu male interviews but that is somewhat hidden when we focus on general characteristics and on the relation to Hinduism specifically is the degree to which some of the participants had fashioned their own particular religious or spiritual paths. There were some who were not non-religious, they were not Hindus, and they in fact did not identify with any institutional religion. They had a positive religious orientation not captured by such categories. Like some of the Buddhist and Muslim participants, such interviewees displayed a highly individualistic and idiosyncratic construction of religion, one that participants and other observers have often labelled as spirituality rather than religion in order to underscore the difference. Here we profile two of them to demonstrate the variety of orientations among the participants but also to highlight the more general insight that emerged from the data as a whole: the generally accepted categories of "the religions" (including "no religion") does not capture much that, by most definitions of religion, should be included in the domain of religion in Canadian society (McGuire 2008).

Darren (HM04)

Another of the participants from a Trinidadian family, 18-year-old Darren was born in Canada into a religiously mixed household. His mother was a practising Muslim, whereas his father was a practising Hindu. Neither identity was successfully passed on to their son. With such a background, one might suspect that Darren would be quite conflicted, effectively straddling several worlds: the Trinidadian and the Canadian, the Muslim and the Hindu, the Christian and the non-Christian, for instance. Such was not the case, however. The way that Darren has emerged with a clear sense of himself in terms of religion, a positive orientation to his life, and an optimistic view of his future is perhaps instructive of how the vast majority of the Hindu male participants in this research might well be Desis, but they were not confused, caught between two (or more) worlds.[2]

On first flush, Darren impressed one as just another non-religious young man of Hindu parentage. When asked to define religion, he said that it was "[a] societal construct based on controlling the population" (HM04). Yet when the interviewer asked him about the relation of religion to spirituality, Darren made what can only be called the classic distinction. He declared that "belief in God and spirituality [are] just completely different from religion." The difference was a matter of a meaningful and personal orientation for one's own benefit versus a collective form of control based on unquestionable tradition. Here is how he put it:

> Spirituality's more personal ... My dad's Hindu and my mom's Muslim and I went to a Christian school for a few years, so I had quite an interesting spectrum. But from what I've seen, religion is all about ... things that you shouldn't do, or things that, if you do, you'll be rewarded; things that, if you do, you'll be punished ... But aside from that, why are you doing it, they can't provide a concrete answer. It's more, "we're doing it because it's tradition" rather than "I'm going to give you an actual answer why are we doing this" ... Whereas in spirituality, it's for your own benefit. It's a personal journey that you take, and it's something that you have to be comfortable with, not the people around you. Nobody else can sit in judgment over your spirituality. It's your personal decision.

Implicit in this quote is his attitude toward his parents' religions. Growing up, he participated in both Hindu and Muslim practices, such as visiting temple, celebrating Diwali, or fasting during Ramadan. At the time of the interview, he avoided pork, alcohol, and beef, the latter in deference to his Hindu side, the former out of habit from his Muslim side. Neither parent, however, was all that insistent; until Darren reached high school, the two parents agreed that they would be neutral between the two religious backgrounds as far as raising their children was concerned; no one was to be forced to one side or the other, although Darren said that he was exposed to far more things Hindu than Muslim. The parental agreement broke down later, but it was apparently too late to make a difference. As a result, he almost absorbed more about Christianity (note the reference to a few years in Christian school in the quote above) than he did about his parental religions. The outcome of this socialization was not a yearning to learn more about one or both parental traditions or even more about other religions. He also did not reject any of them out of hand. He wanted neither to distance himself nor to become closer. Rather, he constructed a personal spiritual orientation that eclectically borrowed whatever was meaningful from whatever religion. An almost "classic SBNR" (spiritual but not religious [Chandler 2008]), he engaged in a complex and individualistic negotiation of his own identity that had elements from all the influences to which he was exposed without explicitly identifying with any of them. Here is one revealing exchange in that regard:

> INTERVIEWER: Have you found ... the religions that you've been influenced by ... inadequate for yourself?
> DARREN: I did until I came into that whole spiritual thing, awakening ... Yeah ... I did feel like they were kind of inadequate 'cause they weren't giving me the explanations I wanted, and a lot of it was, "do this because this is the way it's always been done" ... If they can actually come back and say, oh, well, it was done this way because so-and-so and so-and-so, and that answer made sense to me, I'd say okay, I'll do it, but when I can't be given that kind of answer, I ... y'know, it's difficult for me to accept it blindly.
> INTERVIEWER: OK, now that you've found your own spiritual path, how do you feel about following the traditions of your parents still? Do you think it's something that you're going to stop, or do you just do it out of tradition or respect?
> DARREN: I do it out of a mixture of tradition and respect ... I don't believe that there is anything wrong with what they're doing to communicate with God, and I still believe that if I was to go to Muslim prayers and pray to God, then I would still be praying to God, 'cause it's a personal connection. And if I was to go by my dad's side and do the Hindu prayers, I'd still be communicating with God, so I still do it, and I'm still ... It's tradition and respect, but it's also that I don't find that there's ... any reason why I shouldn't.

The success with which Darren reconciled diverse strands on his religious or spiritual side had its parallel on the cultural side. When asked about his cultural identity, he declared himself "proud to be a Canadian but ... also proud of the West Indian descent." He related that during his high school years, his circle of friends was dominated by Trinidadians, mostly of the first generation; he felt more comfortable and accepted among them. Since then, that circle had widened again, correlating with his greater security in his own identity. Not surprisingly, he was also quite positive about Canadian multiculturalism, felt that religious freedom was a reality in this country and that Canada was very welcoming to immigrants and even a land of opportunity. He declared that he felt he was a full and equal member of Canadian society, and even though, like the majority of interviewees, he had occasionally encountered discrimination as he was growing up, he felt that he could be optimistic about his own future in this country. When asked whether the prejudice he had faced was a bad indicator for his career prospects, he responded with this practical observation: "I don't think so, because most of the jobs I've seen, people are multicultural, different backgrounds, so I don't think it'd be too much of a difference."

Anand (HM13)

One of two participants from a Sri Lankan Tamil Hindu family, Anand was born in East Africa, his parents having fled their native land in the early 1980s because of the civil war there. He grew up and lived in Toronto. Like that of so many other interviewees in the group of 18, his relation to the cultural and religious heritage of his parents was complex but also in some ways tenuous. Anand did not consider himself to be a Hindu religiously, and yet he still participated in family religious practices, and his spiritual journey included much that he and others considered Hindu. From early childhood he remembered having "dialogues with God"; he loved going to temple, enjoying the environment: "I would feel vibrations … and … peace in mind … and maybe it was the scent of incense or whatever it was, but it was a soothing atmosphere that I liked, it was very soothing to the heart."

Anand's curiosity about religious subjects was nonetheless not restricted to or even all that much centred in the Hinduism of his family. Rather, he showed himself from an early age to be a religious seeker. Even in elementary school, he would ask his religiously diverse friends about their religious traditions: "I would ask my Muslim friends, well, why do women have to wear hijab? And I would ask my Christian friends, why is Sunday the Sabbath?" Typically, when it came to the Hinduism of his own family, he was dissatisfied with the inability of his parents to answer his questions:

ANAND: I would ask my parents, but they would never give me a clear answer, and I would ask my relatives and they wouldn't know. There's so much tradition in Hinduism, and so many people don't know the doctrine, they mostly know the [rituals], and maybe that's just my family, but …

INTERVIEWER: And so when you say they don't know, would they know the stories?

ANAND: They would know the stories, but I would want to … know
why more in depth, why do we have to do a certain ritual … That's what
interested me, the origins of such rituals.
INTERVIEWER: OK, and they didn't have answers?
ANAND: They didn't have answers.

Although Anand was unusual in his level of lifelong interest in religious
and spiritual questions, like so many other participants, regardless of religious
background, when it came to religion, he required explanations, a discursive
rationale for religious beliefs and practices; following tradition because "that's
what we do" was not enough. In his case, he ended up channelling his religious
and spiritual sensibilities into a fairly complex spiritual and religious journey.

When he was in high school, Anand became very involved in Christianity.
His description of his encounter with Jesus is again both typical for such experiences and yet highly individualistic:

I was interested in this character Jesus … And I remember watching
Jesus videos … Jesus as a boy, and those always fascinated me, like how
this man is god. That whole concept is fascinating. So yes, when I was 13
[my brother] barged into my room and he handed me a small Bible and
he said, read this, I want you to read this and he opened to the book of
John, and I read it and I found it fascinating. And I don't know if you'd
believe me, but I felt something burst into my heart. It was like an explosion and it was a fantastic feeling and I knelt by my bed … and I prayed
to God and I prayed, "I feel you and I know you're real, please show
me the way." And I felt something lift from my shoulders. It was like all
this time I was weighted down by something and then something just
came and lifted it away and I felt so free and so alive, it was an amazing
feeling.

Anand joined the Christian club at school that his brother had founded; he
eventually became its leader; he went to church regularly. Toward the end of
high school, however, he reached a point of dissatisfaction again. He wanted
something more: "I felt there was something missing … I wanted something
more in-depth." The Christian direction of his teen years, it turned out, was
not so much a conversion as a lengthy exploration that ran its course.[3]

Not surprisingly, perhaps, Anand's quest toward the end of high school took
a less tradition-specific and mystical turn. He claimed that he had never lost
interest in other religions and so resumed his search:

I spent a lot of time on the Net, numerous hours at night searching the
Net for various religions, for various faiths, because I felt that something

had to be more united, had to be more personal, more mystical … I came across several books, [but one in particular] that … just revolutionized the way I looked at it … Basically it was the eastern flux … which ultimately says we are all part and parcel of the one god. We are all one; there is no divisions; the mind creates the divisions.

Anand felt a resonance with what he labelled "the cultures and concepts of eastern mysticism." He started meditating. He began practising yoga. His eastern direction had him "reading about these energy portals in your body, the chakras … I had experiences with opening them and feeling the energy pull through, and then after those experiences there was no turning back." Anand admitted that his journey was, in a way, bringing him back to Hinduism, and that is certainly how his parents approvingly interpreted it. Yet when asked whether he felt more Hindu or Christian, he said, "neither, I'm just being what I feel, an evolution, I'm just climbing the ladder right now." Indeed, he had joined the SUBUD organization of Indonesian origin and found himself attracted to the teachings of alchemy, with its emphasis on limitless discovery of oneself.

In all these features of his religious personality, Anand showed himself to be highly individualistic and even idiosyncratic, but at the same time his journey can be seen as in continuity with the Hindu traditions of his family. That continuity, however, is also rather accidental: if we didn't know about his family background, if we just took his description of his spiritual quest at face value, he could have come from any number of backgrounds. If things Hindu came up in his narrative, there appeared to be little that was Sri Lankan Tamil Hindu about them. Indeed, Anand said very little about his cultural background, although nothing would indicate that he felt in the least bit alienated from it. At the time of the interview, he was about to make his first visit to Sri Lanka, and his girlfriend was Sri Lankan Hindu. Still, in neither case did he consider that they had anything to do with his religious or spiritual side. He made no claim to be carrying on or reinterpreting his heritage. His lived religion certainly contained Hindu elements, but one can hardly claim that he was thereby contributing to the construction of systemic Hinduism, in Canada or elsewhere.

CONCLUSION

It has been suggested that this process of negotiation and definition for second-generation Indian youths has been one of "change, resistance, and adaptation." In her study on second-generation Indo-Canadians, Vanaja Dhruvarajan (2003) argues that because racism is an ideology inherent in institutional structures that then manifest themselves in social practices, second-generation Indo-Canadians still find themselves struggling with issues of identity and religion in a country where they have been raised from birth. Dhruvarajan describes how many of these participants still find themselves caught between two cultures and feel they face enormous pressure to succeed in a society where they don't feel accepted, to the point that they would rather renounce their heritage to fit into Canadian society. The interviewees' responses do not fully support Dhruvarajan's conclusions.[4] All the participants supported Canada's multicultural policies and did not mention that they were the victims of institutionalized racism. None of them felt that they were being forced to capitulate to Canadian culture or to any other culture for that matter. It might seem odd, for example, when Suraj referred to a temple as a Hindu church or Gopal eschewed the authority of Hindu priests at his local temple, but this points to how so many of these participants felt they could create their own sense of being and identity without feeling that they had to appeal to the authority of scriptural texts or a particular religious leader. The interviewees instead tended to juxtapose diverse elements of their cultural and religious experience to create unique religious and cultural identities, which made them feel comfortable in their social circumstances. In other words, all of these interviewees refused to accept any other basis for shaping their religious and cultural identities than their own personal experience. One nonetheless senses that the interviewees understood that their religious identities were fluid and would always be in the process of being defined and redefined with the changing circumstances in their lives. It is impossible to determine for the moment what future religious trajectories these interviewees will take, but charting and interpreting them would be a fascinating task that will have to be a research project for another time.

Summarizing, the Hindu men in our sample were not particularly religious, if by that we mean immersed in the Hindu (or other) religion of their family heritages and actively contributing to the reconstruction of that religion in the Canadian context. One could rightly call the relatively few who were religious "spiritual but not religious" precisely in this sense of not living their religious identities within an institutional religious tradition, here Hinduism, but nonetheless living a coherent religious identity of their own making and of variable and fluid contours. The Hindu men were similar to the Hindu women in this regard, except that they were less immersed in their families' religious and cultural traditions; their religious and spiritual practices revolved more around their own personal quests rather than in the context of a social network, above all of their families (see the discussion on gender differences in chapter 11). From another perspective, these Hindu men bore more than a passing resemblance to some of the Muslim men and women, albeit only those on the lower end of the Muslim 10-point scale we used in chapters 5 and 6: from about category 2 to category 5. There as well we found participants who put together their own lived religious identities, which included elements from their family traditions – for them, Islam – but not exclusively or dominantly centred on them. From a lived religion perspective, their reconstructions make sense, for them. From the perspective of systemic religion, here Hinduism, however, they are at the moment contributing little. Things will have to change if the future of institutional and systemic Hinduism is going to depend on them in the future. In that regard, they are similar to the third religious tradition group represented in our study, those of Buddhist background, and it is to them that we turn in the next two chapters.

9

Maybe, in the Future:
Buddhist Men

PETER BEYER

A DEMOGRAPHIC PROFILE OF 19 BUDDHIST MALES

In Canada at the time of the 2001 census, almost 79% of the about 1,100 Buddhist males born in Canada and aged 21 to 30 had some form of post-secondary schooling. This represents a lower figure than for any of the other five religion/gender combinations, 5% lower than for the Muslim males and fully 10% lower than for Hindu males with the same characteristics (Beyer 2005c). It is from this segment of the Buddhist population that our sample of 19 Buddhist males was drawn; all of them were, at the time of their interviews, enrolled in university. Of significance, however, is that the proportion of Canada's Buddhists who are in this gender and age group is much smaller than it is for the corresponding Muslims or Hindus: only about 0.4% of Buddhists were men born in Canada and between 21 and 30 years old. That figure for the Muslims is about 1% and for Hindus about 1.6%. As we will see, these figures do not mean that Buddhists are somehow lagging behind Muslims or Hindus in terms of levels of educational attainment; rather, it reflects the fact that men from demographic groups in which Buddhism is a dominant religious identity are less likely to identify as Buddhists and with Buddhism. This is also, no doubt, one of the reasons that our research project was comparatively unsuccessful in recruiting Buddhists, and Buddhist men in particular.

In age, the Buddhist men ranged from 18 to 29, with an average age of 21.3 years. Only 3 of them were 25 years or older, whereas 11 were 20 years old or younger. As such, they were on average a very young group. In light of their young age, the Buddhist male participants, for the most part, would likely not have settled into a definitive adult identity, including quite possibly as concerns religion. None of them was married (although one, the 29-year-old, had children and a common-law spouse), and few had full-time jobs or were already actively engaged in pursuing careers.

The Buddhist males were mostly born in Canada. Of the 19, 12 were born in Canada, and only 7 immigrated as children and were therefore part of the 1.5 generation. As anticipated, there was no detectable difference between the two subgroups, especially as concerns their relationship to Buddhism. The Buddhist men or their families had their origins in a number of mostly East Asian countries: 2 had origins in Cambodia, although the mother of one of them was French-Canadian from Quebec. Two were ethnically Japanese, and another had a Japanese mother and a British father. One was of Sri Lankan background, 2 of Vietnamese. The remaining 11 were ethnically Chinese from Taiwan, Hong Kong, and the People's Republic of China, including various combinations. One had a Chinese father and a Euro-Canadian mother; 2 were ethnically Chinese but had one parent who was second-generation Chinese born in Canada and one parent who arrived in Canada at a young age. These two might already be considered third-generation. Ethnic background did not seem to make much of a difference in how these men situated themselves in Canadian society; they all had little difficulty in this regard. As we shall see, however, there was a fairly strong correlation between ethnic background and how these participants related to Buddhism; in essence, people with origins in Southeast Asia were more likely to have a stronger relation to Buddhism than those with Chinese ethnicity, even though this difference was not extreme. This result corresponds rather well with the religious identity characteristics of the general Canadian Buddhist population: whereas about 48% of people of Southeast Asian origin declared themselves to be Buddhist in 2001, only about 15% of those of Chinese origin did so. Looking at the specific demographic of interest here, the difference is just as striking, as is the fact that so few young men identify with Buddhism. Of men born in Canada and between the ages of 21 and 30, a little less than 5% of those with Chinese ethnicity declared themselves Buddhist, whereas 15.5% of those with Southeast Asian origin did so (Beyer 2006a).

With regard to type of Buddhism, few of the male Buddhist participants were aware of subcategories within Buddhism, say between Mahayana and Theravada or between Pure Land and Chan/Zen Buddhism. In fact, most of them had little specific knowledge about Buddhism at all. Therefore, such internal divisions and distinctions did not often enter the picture in any meaningful way. Again, however, there was a meaningful difference among them that correlated with culture: those who grew up in ethnically Chinese families almost all drew little distinction between what they considered Buddhist and what one might call a general Chinese religious culture (see Crowe 2010; Thompson 1996; Yang 1967). They did not, for instance, make any or at least no consistent distinction between rituals and practices relating to the Buddha(s) and rituals and practices related to ancestors. Many, in fact, showed that relatively widespread East Asian association of Buddhism with matters related to death, dying, and the dead. Ancestors, the graves of relatives, and related matters were therefore often considered part of Buddhism, an understanding that came almost from a combination of the fact that their parents saw things this way and the participants' lack of knowledge about Buddhism as a distinct religion or even a distinct philosophy and world view.

CLASSIFYING THE BUDDHIST MALES

As discussed in several of the previous chapters, the classifications we are using for the three religious subgroups derive from the data themselves, and in light of the very significant differences from one to the other, we could not use the same classification scheme for all three groups. Doing so would have meant losing the particularities of each. The Buddhist classification includes four broad categories, only two of which were represented in the Buddhist male group of 19. There were no practising Christians among them, nor were there any that we could reasonably classify as imitative traditionalists. All of them either were religio-culturally based religious seekers or had such a minimal or tenuous relation to Buddhism that they fell into the "little bit Buddhist" category. The clear majority, 12 of 19, were in the latter group and only 7 in the former. As we shall see, however, among those in the religio-culturally based religious seeker category, there were some who might eventually make somewhat of a contribution to the reconstruction of Buddhism in Canada. On the other hand, virtually none of these participants could be regarded as anything but thoroughly integrated and generally comfortable in Canadian society. They were in that sense by all appearances mostly "like anyone else" in their generation, whether of immigrant families or not.

None of the Buddhist men was what one might call typically involved in religion, whether Buddhist or otherwise. This was especially the case with the 12 classified as "a little bit Buddhist," meaning that they had Buddhist identity and practice in their family background but that was about as far as their association with Buddhism went. Moreover, none of them were self-identified Christians, even though two of them came from families in which many members had adopted Christianity and they had been exposed to the Christian religion as they were growing up. No other religion came into consideration, even in their families. Although the 7 men whom we categorized as religio-culturally based religious seekers were by that token more positively inclined towards religious/spiritual questions and in several cases considered themselves Buddhists, they generally engaged in few, if any, identifiably Buddhist practices and in large part had little knowledge about Buddhist teachings, writings, and practices.[1] For instance, meditative practices, studying sutras and other Buddhist texts, chanting, going to temples, listening to dharma talks, engaging in meritorious acts, having a shrine in their home, being concerned about the karmic consequences of their actions – the 7 men engaged in very little of such activity (cf. McLellan 2009, especially 164ff).

Religio-culturally Based Religious Seekers

The label applied to this group of 7 men in our sample may be somewhat misleading, if one imagines people for whom the "seeker" aspect is a constant and central aspect of their lives. That was not the case for any of them, unlike for some of the Hindu men. Rather, as indicated, the label points to the fact that these participants saw Buddhism, as they understood the term, to be at least an important aspect of their identities or they considered religious/spiritual questions as important ones for which they honestly sought answers. Four of the 7 did both, meaning that 3 of them did not even identify as Buddhists. Here is how Brandon put it: "I don't really know what label I would give to myself because I don't know what I am ... If one defined religion as 'religion' in the everyday sense of that word, I would say that I'm an atheist, but on the other hand there is a spiritual aspect that I have, that I work on, and that I believe in" (BM03). David, one of those who identified as Buddhist, was equally as vague: "I can identify with Buddhism pretty well, and I think it's not really believing in ... God or whatever, it's like looking within yourself and then choosing to live your life by being true to yourself and others. And I guess that's sort of spirituality and it's also a religion" (BM13).

The four who identified themselves more or less as Buddhist saw their Buddhism more in terms of a moral orientation or a philosophy that did not require any particular sort of ritual or other practice. Anzan, a 19-year-old from a Vietnamese family, said that he went "through the general rituals" but actually did not engage in any kind of practice that he could identify. Yet he also said that being Buddhist was "becoming more important because it helps me realize ... Buddhism, it's more a meditative, more of a relaxed philosophy of thinking and investigation than following rules" (BM10). When asked what then was most important about being Buddhist, he expanded: "It's that ... questioning, the aspect of trying to understand a situation fully, from all perspectives without influence" and felt that this was what was meant by meditation. In the process of explaining, he also mentioned the importance of compassion and the idea that everything was impermanent. Others of the four put more emphasis on values and ethical questions. As Peter put it when asked what it was to practise his religion:

Practise is to practise the rules of Buddhism. It's to respect others, to take the time to be good ... it's the values, the values that advocate the good. What I want to say is that I don't think that one day I would be able to do harm to anyone voluntarily, because I know that's not good, because of religion, or what my mother taught me. But I don't think one has to be between four walls and pray every day and light incense in order to practise religion. (BM01)

The seekership aspect for these men, as indicated above, was not particularly strong; they were not spiritual seekers in the sense of experimenting with or engaging in a variety of practices, testing out different beliefs or religions, or having the "big questions" or life's meaning and purpose, death, afterlife, or the existence of a spiritual/transcendent reality occupy them in a more or less constant fashion. They were not "spiritual but not religious" like the two Hindus we profiled in the previous chapter. Instead, what they exhibited, in comparison with the Buddhist men that could at best be called "a little bit Buddhist," was an ongoing interest in such matters and an openness toward religious/spiritual involvement on what they saw as a Buddhist basis, if only in the future. The quotes just cited give some indication of what was involved. Two of the 7 men gave very concrete indications of what their modest seekership might involve – namely, becoming at some point initiated as a Buddhist monk, if only for a brief period. Here is how Brandon contextualized this intention:

> Y'know, before I started my undergraduate studies, I travelled a bit in
> western Canada … but once I've finished my BA, I'd like to travel across
> Canada by bicycle and then take a plane to Cambodia. I said to myself
> that it would fun also to go and get myself initiated as a monk … maybe
> just for a year, just to learn and see what I have to offer, because my
> [Cambodian] father didn't teach me anything about Buddhism, just the
> family rituals … So I want to see for myself, firsthand, that's the thing.
> (BM03)

One notes that this motivation was both cultural and religious; he wanted to go to Cambodia to do this, not to the Buddhist centre down the road in the city where he lived. Brian, a 24-year-old of Hong Kong origin, was less specific but expressed almost exactly the same wish. Here is a revealing exchange that came right at the end of the interview:

> INTERVIEWER: Do you think religion is a good force?
> BRIAN: … I think it's good to have religion. If you don't, people don't
> have a place to turn to. They don't have a place to look for the unknown
> questions. It's a place where they can find closure and answers.
> INTERVIEWER: Do you see yourself, sometime in the future, reading
> more about Buddhism, learning about basic Buddhist teaching? [Note:
> the participant had indicated that he knew next to nothing about this
> subject.]
> BRIAN: I'll be honest with you. I would love to maybe spend a year or
> two as a monk, just to experience it, y'know, just to really experience
> it. Give everything up, just to see what it is really like to commit to a
> religion. So for myself it is more of an experiential thing, more so than
> religious. But hopefully in that time, I learned something new. And,

because I have been exposed to so many religions, different cultures and religions, it's all about the learning process for myself. (BM12)

Taking into consideration these various characteristics of the religio-culturally based seekers among the Buddhist men, one would be hard-pressed to predict what, if any, contribution the population they represent will eventually make to the reconstruction of Buddhism as systemic religion in the Canadian context. Given the lack of in-depth knowledge of Buddhist teachings and tradition, it seems likely that this contribution will remain minimal until such time as some of them undertake greater involvement, such as that suggested in the last two quotes. In the meantime, however, these participants showed a far closer relation to Buddhism than did the rest of the male sample, those we classified, sometimes charitably, as merely "a little bit Buddhist."

Buddhist Family Background: "A Little Bit Buddhist"

The 12 men in this category, the remainder of the Buddhist male participants, all had some exposure to what they understood as Buddhist practice and teaching during their upbringing. Some participated in family Buddhist rituals as children; almost none did so at the time of the interview. Some came from families that were now predominantly Christian, although, as already noted, none of the participants considered themselves Christian or engaged in Christian practices beyond the occasional gesture to please one's parents. In comparison to the 7 men in the previous category, those in the little-bit-Buddhist group were disproportionately of ethnically Chinese backgrounds: 9 of 12 in the latter as opposed to only 3 of 7 in the former. The dominance of this ethnic origin was reflected in the understanding, such as it was, that these 12 participants had of Buddhism and its relation to their cultural heritage.

Almost without exception, those of Chinese ethnic origin saw Buddhism as a partial religious identity: Buddhism was an aspect of what their families did religiously, or it was the dominant religious identity of only one parent or of one or two grandparents. It was not an exclusive religious identity. They did things Buddhist, or their relatives did, but they were not just Buddhists. In addition, and as an aspect of this partiality, Buddhism, for them, concerned only certain matters, such as those related to death and thereby the ancestors (cf. Yang 1967). For many, the line between matters Buddhist and other strands of Chinese popular religious tradition was from fuzzy to practically non-existent. To give some examples of how this relation was expressed, William, a 19-year-old who was born in Hong Kong, when asked about his parents' Buddhism, mentioned that they followed the rules of feng shui (which the participant called superstition) and encouraged their son to wear amulets, about which he said that "it's supposed to be like Buddha is protecting me in that way" (BM16). Another, Christopher, had this exchange:

INTERVIEWER: You mentioned that your grandparents are here [in Canada]; have you ever seen them practise Buddhism?
CHRISTOPHER: Well my grandmother does Tai Chi; my grandfather I don't think I've ever seen him ... well, he comes to the cemetery with us, but that's about it. (BM19)

Alex, a 20-year-old whose parents were Vietnamese refugees but of Chinese ethnicity, described his family's tenuous relation to Buddhism this way:

We don't practise any religion at all, other than when my grandparents died; that's when I first saw our religion in reality, because we practised Buddhist kind of traditions during the funeral. My grandparents were cremated, they were put into little urns and taken to a Buddhist temple. They had incense, they were burning those tall candle-y things ... and say prayers and stuff. I have to say that was very strange to me, because I had never done that before ... After that we didn't practise anything at all, not Buddhist at all. (BM04)

Finally, Shane, a 21-year-old who considered his mother a practising Buddhist, had this to say about what counted as such Buddhist practice in his family:

When someone died, we went to a Buddhist temple and we ate with the monks. My mom ... at a point during the lunar calendar, she lights incense whenever it's my grandmother's birth date or her death date ... I remember at a point in her funeral where we would burn like fake dollar bills and ... fake animals, just so when my grandmother goes up to heaven, she has an abundance of wealth and a lot to eat. I guess that would be the aspects of Buddhism. (BM17)

There were, however, as one might expect, one or two participants who did draw a sharper boundary around Buddhism. One of them, Jamie, another 19-year-old born in Hong Kong whose mother considered herself an express and devout Buddhist, used the difference between culture and religion to make the distinction and thereby also expressed the common East Asian idea that religion is a matter that concerns only particular subgroups of society.[2] Here is how he explained the difference between religion and culture:

Hmmm, relate religion to culture. Well, there's a big difference. I think religion ... I mean you can still see different cultures today even though religion is pretty much fading. I mean, like Asian kids, they have their own culture, although Asian kids aren't practising any religion at all ... I think culture equals lifestyle and religion is a category of a different group. I mean people believe in this religion, they have their own life-style; it's a different group. (BM09)

As these quotes also indicate, the relation of this group of 12 participants to what they saw as religion of any kind was rather tenuous. Most described themselves as atheists or agnostics; one or two admitted to being spiritual but not religious, although not in a way connected to their understanding of Buddhism. One declared himself to be a Buddhist but also said he was non-religious and knew and practised next to nothing related to Buddhism. This distanced relation to religion, including Buddhism, was not usually negative: some thought that religion was a bad thing; most thought it was good – at least if kept within bounds – but not something that had much importance for them. A good example, which resonates with the last quote from Jamie, was from a participant who related religion specifically to certain groups, certain group practices and ways of living, but who also distanced himself explicitly from it. Here is what Matthew, a 20-year-old from a Cantonese family that had converted almost entirely to Roman Catholicism, had to say:

> I see religion right now as large groups of people who have a …
> common faith base … like Buddhism, like Catholicism, like people
> who are Hindu or Muslim … there's a lot of religions out there … So, I
> guess my view of religion is pretty similar to other people's, except …
> it's gotten very out of hand I think … It has to be an organized group
> of people with a set of beliefs that never change … people that always
> come together in a place of gathering like a church or a temple, and they
> have to offer thanks to this god, or the ancestors, or the past. I mean, for
> some people that's a way of living. I guess you could say it's not my way
> of living. (BM05)

The tenuous relation to Buddhism of these participants was most evident in their lack of knowledge about Buddhism beyond what they absorbed and interpreted from their family experiences. Even when they displayed some knowledge of specifically Buddhist teaching, this was vague and often already forgotten. Christopher admitted to this tenuousness in a somewhat amus-ing way. In answer to a question about whether he had ever tried to find out about Buddhism, he said, "Uh, no. I've been given pamphlets when I was at the temple, just about the history of Buddhism. I don't remember. I think ori-ginally it's from India, and then a person with a pretty long last name, he went on a journey, all across Asia or something. I think there was a tree involved. I hardly remember anything" (BM04).

The marginal knowledge and tenuous relation to Buddhism of these partici-pants – and for this purpose including the religio-culturally based seekers – raises the question of what sort of religious socialization these participants typically received. As noted in the chapters on the Muslim participants, it is arguable that explicitly religious socialization is a necessary but not sufficient condition in most cases for a religiously engaged adult. In the case of the Buddhist participants, it is evident that many of them were exposed to, broadly speaking, Buddhist ritual practices and, to some extent, Buddhist teachings as they were growing up. Yet two aspects of this socialization are of note. First, very few of them experienced this socialization as an exclusively or clearly delimited Buddhist one; rather, the Buddhist elements were but aspects of what one might more accurately call socialization into the Chinese, Japanese, Cambodian, Vietnamese, or Sri Lankan culture of their families. Glen, a 21-year-old man whose parents came from Japan, put this relation and its consequences for religious identity and knowledge in a clear and concrete way. In the course of describing a ritual performance with his aunt at a Buddhist temple in Japan, the following exchange occurred:

INTERVIEWER: Did you feel like you were participating in religion at that time?
GLEN: I was participating in religion but not as part of that religion. This was probably something she did every time she walked past these kinds of temples ... The fact that she did it and when she was doing it, I think it was very much ... more part of the culture, like that's the way it's done and there's not much explanation needed if it's just, that's the way things are done over there.
INTERVIEWER: So, would you characterize yourself as a religious person?
GLEN: No, I wouldn't ... because I'm not really practising; I'm not really acknowledging any spiritual or philosophical group ... I wouldn't call myself Buddhist. (BM14)

Second, even in cases where Buddhism constituted the exclusive and complete religious identity of the family, or at least of one of the parents, these parents either did not engage in expressly teaching their children Buddhism or did not to any great extent insist that their children follow them on their religious path. Shane, whose mother was a practising Buddhist, related how his parents had made a deliberate choice not to socialize their children religiously:

INTERVIEWER: Did your mother ever try to give you and your siblings a religious education of some sort?
SHANE: No, because I have talked about that with my dad before. I've asked him ... why we've never gone to church or been practising Buddhism, and he and my mom have discussed that they didn't really feel the need to implement religion into our lives. So that's why me and my

sisters aren't practising at all. They decided that we should choose the path we want to go. (BM17)

Zhan injected a different but related idea. He averred that Buddhism itself was not as insistent – one might say as proselytizing or as exclusivist, but these are not the words he used – as other religions. To some extent as an explanation of why he did nothing Buddhist and knew little about Buddhist teaching, he stated that

> more than anything else, I think Buddhists accept more things than some other religions and cultures, and that, you know, that's the advantage. I find more than anything else, as a Buddhist, we don't judge people … We don't have a rigid standard of morals and ethics that, you know, that you're going to hell if you're doing something and not doing something. Buddhism is a very laid-back religion. (BM15)

Resonating somewhat with this statement, Jimmy, an 18-year-old who was born in Taiwan, ventured the opinion that even those in his local Taiwanese community who were practising Buddhists had in common with those who were not that "they don't tell people they are Buddhist or they really don't show it" (BM02).

One does not have to accept such statements as accurate assessments of contemporary Buddhism to see that their general tenor accorded with the attitudes expressed by several others: the Buddhism that these participants knew was largely a cultural, partial, and in that sense optional inheritance from their parents without clear boundaries and definition; for none of them was it, as Islam was for many of the Muslim men and women who participated in this study, a coherent and complete system of belief and practice or a way of life, except perhaps in a very vague and general way and then only for a very few of them. Buddhism had not been transferred to them, nor did they live it as a distinct religion. It was more of a vaguely understood resource than a clear identity. As such, if these young adults are ever to engage in reproducing Buddhism for their Canadian context, they will first have to (re)appropriate it as religion, and even if this happens, it is unlikely to be the way that their parents know this tradition. It is almost as if they will have to discover Buddhism anew.[3]

MULTICULTURALISM AND BELONGING

While some of the Buddhist men actually self-identified as Buddhists, most would probably fall under the general heading of having "no religion." As such, if one follows Canadian census data, they were part of the second most numerous religious identity in Canada, after Roman Catholic Christians or

Christians overall. They were for the most part not members of a *religious* minority in quite the same sense as their expressly Buddhist, Muslim, and Hindu fellow citizens. The question that can then be posed is whether this situation was reflected in their attitude toward Canadian society – to what degree they felt, as our question asked, "full and equal members" of that society and, in that context, their opinions about Canada as a multicultural society. As one might suspect from what was said about Muslims in previous chapters, there was no detectable effect at all, because the Buddhist men in our sample, like all the subgroups by religion and gender, in great majority felt comfortable and approved of Canada's multicultural character, although, again, not uncritically and not without sometimes having negative experiences of discrimination at some point in their lives.

The attitude toward Canadian multiculturalism among the Buddhist men was complex but generally positive. Referring specifically to religious diversity in Canada and whether he found that important, Anzan, whose family came from Vietnam, used the frequently heard idea of a Canadian mosaic: "Yes, I believe [religious diversity] is [important] because it's like a mosaic; it's a mosaic of the rest of the world if … some religions, most of them, every religion actually is accepted. You learn to understand the rest of the world more because you live in a microcosm of the rest of the world itself" (BM10).

In a slightly different vein and with reference specifically to the Toronto region, Zhan said that "[Toronto] is the most multicultural city in the world, and I think there's a much higher tolerance in Toronto for different cultures and different religions here than anywhere else in the world" (BM15) (see the more extended discussion in chapter 12). Not all of them were quite so unequivocally positive, pointing out a range of actual or potential problems. One ventured that Canada was trying very hard but that achieving a truly accepting and multicultural society was in fact quite difficult. Matthew put this idea concretely in terms of the potential for second-generation people like himself finding themselves adrift. He felt that the Canadian government was doing its best "to make people feel more at home" in Canada and that it was a worthwhile effort. Yet he also asked:

> Would I be better off being in China … amongst people that … look
> the same, [who] might have that common background? But then I
> have a couple of friends who returned to their home countries … well,
> they're kind of outcasted there too … So, it's almost as if you have no
> home now … like you have no roots really; your roots are really light
> and everywhere, so you're kind of just drifting here and there. And I
> think it's gonna be a problem among many people my age, for second-
> generation immigrants. Like, they may feel at home here, but not
> really, fully comfortable, and there's really not much you can do about
> that. (BM05)

Peter, who arrived at the age of 3 from Cambodia, expressed this in terms of the idea of being caught between two worlds: "I live between two totally different cultures ... In terms of myself, I can deal with both, [but] in terms of my family, it's more difficult, because ... between the need to respect myself as a human being, as an individual, and what others want me to be, it's for sure that there are always going to be conflicts" (BM01).

Yet another declared that multiculturalism was fine but thought that outright assimilation of newcomers to the dominant culture was just as good. In other words, the assessment of the ideal of multiculturalism was not always completely positive. On the other hand, no one suggested that Buddhism was either positively or negatively associated with this question in spite of the insistence of some, as noted, that Buddhism was inherently open and tolerant.

SOME DETAILED LIVES

Given the clustering of the 19 Buddhist men into only two of the four broad categories and the dominance among them of people from Chinese ethnic background, the selection of representative profiles for a more detailed look was relatively straightforward. In what follows, we will discuss some of the lived reality of three people, one from among the religio-culturally based seekers (Michael, BM18) and two from among those deemed "a little bit Buddhist" (Christopher, BM19, and Takahiro, BM06). Of these, the first two are of Chinese ethnic background, the latter not of Chinese background, in this case Japanese. These three, of course, do not actually cover the full range of variation in the sample; that would require profiling almost all of them. But it should be noted that two types of ethnic profile and one type of religious profile are being left out – namely, two Buddhist males who were respectively from an ethnically Vietnamese and an ethnically Sri Lankan family and two who grew up in families that were mostly Christian but who themselves were not. Analysis of the data, however, shows that most of the variation that these four show is also captured in the profiles of the three on whom we do focus.

Michael (BM18)

Michael did not consider himself a Buddhist, either exclusively or even religiously. He described the religious and cultural aspects of his upbringing in a way that rendered explicit what may well have been implicit in the descriptions of several of the others of Chinese background: "Religiously, I guess I was raised in a kind of progressive, traditional Chinese household; we were, I guess, Confucian, Daoist, and Buddhist at the same time, because the three religions or philosophies are very compatible and it's been – it's very Chinese."

At the time of the interview, he was 27 years old; he was born in Hong Kong and arrived in Canada with his parents when he was 5 years old. His exposure to religion was not, however, limited to his family experience; his parents sent him to a Christian high school, because they felt that a public high school would not teach him good morals whereas a Christian one would. Michael, however, responded to the experience in a way that he considered consistent with his Chinese identity:

> We went to chapel on Wednesdays to sing Praise the Lord and stuff like that; we took Bible class every grade from Grade 9 'til OAC.[4] Um, yeah, I sang the carols and we sang [in] the praise band and stuff, but I just did it because it was part of the school curriculum; I didn't really believe in it or anything ... but I do accept the morals, because I believe all religions teach people a sense of goodness ... So even though I was trad-itionally Chinese ... I took in that Christianity ethic, and I fused it with my own culture because I thought it was compatible.

The description Michael gives here corresponds in many ways to what can be called his "typically Chinese" way of understanding religion. He referred to the ancestral altars, statues of various Buddhist and Chinese gods, and the practice of feng shui in his parental home as aspects of superstition, not as religion. Asked to then define religion, he stated that it was "something that somebody or a group of people believe in that is beyond comprehension, beyond understanding" and which requires "a leap of faith." Superstition was "traditional Chinese folklore" or any "traditional folklore." Yet religion was also something that "gives you strength and at the same time it makes you feel very childish and weak." Religion, he said,

> helps people explain things that they can't explain ... It's philosophy for the masses. I would say [that] an enlightened person would believe in philosophy. A less enlightened person would believe in religion ... because philosophy is – you try to think through things for yourself; you don't have to alienate your thoughts and say oh, okay, God said so. You're using reason and rationality to understand things, or in our modern world, using science to understand things.

This evaluation did not, however, mean that Michael eschewed things Bud-dhist, Daoist, or Confucian. Rather, he separated what he saw as their philo-sophical from their religious aspects. He occasionally went with his mother to a Buddhist temple in Toronto and participated in the rituals there with her but not as religion. Here is how he put it: "I go with her [to the temple]. I do everything ... but I don't really pray for anything or focus or concentrate. I just do it ... to please my mom. Because ... I approach Buddhism as a philosophy, not as a religion, which is how she approaches it, as a religion. She actually worships the statue, whereas I read the scriptures and learn from the stories."

Later in the interview, he discussed more precisely what he meant by the last phrase, noting that he read mostly academic books on Chinese, Buddhist, Daoist, and Confucian philosophy, that he had taken university courses on these topics. When asked what he took from these readings, his response again began with this distinction:

Honestly, going to the temple and offering incense and all of that, I think it's a bunch of crap. Because, like I said, Buddhism, Daoism, and Confucianism, you can approach all three from a religious perspective; at the same time, you can approach all three from a philosophical perspective, and believe it or not, it's in Confucian texts, Confucius himself vouches against idol worship. So, yeah, even the monks, they don't bow to a Buddha, they just meditate.

Not surprisingly, when asked if he was religious, Michael replied, "spiritual and philosophical" and stated that he considered the Buddha and Confucius to be like Plato, Aristotle, or Hegel. When asked how then he dealt with the grand questions such as why there is so much suffering in the world – a central Buddhist question, after all – he said, "How do I deal with it? I just accept it." A little later he added, "I think my approach to life would be very Daoist, because I just take things as they are; I just go with the flow."

As noted, Michael considered himself and his orientation to be very Chinese, and this as a result of his upbringing. In his attitude toward his eventual spouse and children, however, he made a clear distinction between religion and culture. He stated that the ethnicity, religion, or colour of an eventual spouse did not matter to him – his current girlfriend at the time was Latin American and apparently Christian – but that he would not want his children raised religiously. He was open to his children becoming religious if that was what they ended up choosing. As he put it, "I want my child to discover things himself instead of it being enforced on him ... Let the kid discover himself. If he decided to be a Christian, let him be Christian. If he decides to be Muslim, let him be Muslim, and I don't want to enforce anything." At the same time, he also felt that his children would certainly receive a Chinese cultural upbringing: "that's inevitable, because I'm Chinese. You can never escape from your own culture, so I guess if I raise my kids, there would be a heavy Chinese bias." This aspect of his orientation, in turn, pointed to his assessment of Canadian society and its supposed multiculturalism.

Michael thought multiculturalism was more rhetoric than reality; the policy, he felt, was a political strategy. By contrast, he considered Canadian society to be "very white" and Christian. Not only that, speaking about both American and Canadian society, he considered North American society relatively more religious, and this was not a good thing. Here is how he put his understanding:

> It's still a very Christian country that we live in and south of the border
> … As North Americans I think we are more religious than Europeans
> and Asians, even though a lot of people consider North America to be
> the most advanced society in the world. But when it comes to religion,
> we are actually quite religious when compared to other countries … and
> being religious is actually regression, I think personally … I think the
> more you step away from religion, the more enlightened you are.

In spite of this judgment, Michael nonetheless insisted that religion was not necessarily a bad thing. As he put it, "if it pleases your soul, it's good. If it corrupts your soul, it's not good."

As these last quotes indicate, the words that Michael used to express himself, like "soul" or "enlightened," often had quasi-religious overtones in keeping with his self-image as someone who sought constantly to improve himself. He called this orientation philosophical and spiritual, and he made a consistent distinction between this orientation and a relatively, in his mind, inferior one that he called religious and superstitious. One could understand this attitude as quite Chinese in a certain way, Michael styling himself somewhat as in quest of the Confucian "superior man" (*junzi*) in contrast with the "inferior man" (*xiaoren*). He himself connected it with his being Chinese. And as such, he was perhaps more articulate and, being older, somewhat more mature than many of his fellow Chinese Buddhists in the sample. At the same time, he did represent quite a number of the latter in both the partial way that they related to Buddhism and the ambiguous attitude they had toward religion more generally. If, for the sake of argument, he could be considered farther along the road to what the younger participants might become as they get older, then what his profile portends for (Chinese) Buddhism in Canada is quite specific: little contribution will come from the second and subsequent generations toward the development of Buddhism as religion in this country. Institutionally religious Buddhism will have to depend on the continued renewal of the first generation through immigration. Moreover, the fact that the other religio-culturally based seekers, while different in details, had an orientation quite consonant with Michael's on this question, indicates that his case was not even limited to those of ethnically Chinese people with Buddhist backgrounds. That conclusion, in the current context, applies only to the men in the sample. As detailed in the next chapter, the situation is somewhat, although not that much, different for the women.

Jason (BM19)

For Michael, Buddhism was an aspect of being Chinese, and it was in the context of a strong and articulated Chinese cultural identity that matters Buddhist had the place that they did. Especially among several of those designated "a little bit Buddhist," this relation was even more tenuous and Buddhism significantly more vestigial, because the Chinese cultural factor itself was weak. Jason offers a representative example. He was born in the Greater Toronto Area to a second-generation Chinese mother and a father who came to Canada from China when he was only 10 years old. Both parents are ethnically Chinese. He could therefore be looked upon as almost a member of the third generation (or, perhaps, 2.5 generation). At the time of the interview he was 23 years old and pursuing an undergraduate degree at the University of Toronto with a humanities specialization.

Jason did not consider himself to be religious or spiritual. When asked what his religion was, he replied, probably half in jest, "post-modern madness"; for his parents, he offered "consumerism." Like several others, he identified his parents' Buddhism with traditional Chinese practices associated with the immediate ancestors. Visiting graves and performing ceremonies like burning incense and fake money, offering food and paying respect by bowing was what came to mind, and even on these gestures he was vague as to what exactly was involved even though he often went along. He had never been to a temple of any kind and had never met a Buddhist monk in his life. Not surprisingly, he did not consider himself a Buddhist, except "in the most superficial way that there is." He was not interested in looking further into Buddhism even though he had "read a bunch of Buddhist texts and interpretations of Buddhist texts." On the other hand, he did express an interest in creating his own "system of religious thought," his own lived religion, one might say. Yet sharing this with anyone else was not important; he did not like "organized groups" and therefore was not interested in joining anything collective.

Jason displayed a common – although by no means unanimous – attitude among the participants who were non-religious in that he considered religion to be a good thing, just not for him. He felt that religion could be a good foundation for morality and that it did people good to be able to share their faith. Yet, perhaps again reflecting a widespread East Asian cultural distrust of religion as somehow fundamentally sectarian in nature, he also made this statement: "There was an event at the University of Toronto. I like going to those things, like an Islamic thing or a Judaic thing. It's … just a lot of fun 'cause it's like 'We're Jewish, look at us!' It's like 'We're Islamic, look at us!' So it's like, yeah, I gaze and I'm like, y'know, you're so cool, you're so like into your religion that it … cuts you off from other people."

This sense of not belonging and not wanting to belong extended to other collective categories besides religious ones, including being Canadian and being Chinese. Jason admitted to being Canadian and being Chinese, because that was what he was born into, but he had no strong sense of identity with either. On the other hand, as the words just quoted indicate, he thought the problem with religious and cultural belonging was that they cut one off from other people. He was not looking to belong to any kind of a group, but the sense of human connection was important to him.

Listening to Jason's interview, there are several moments when he appeared to express a rather profound alienation. Quite a few of his answers to questions had a flippant air to them. He felt that chaos was a predominant condition of the world but that this was more part of the human condition than it was anything peculiar about the time and the place in which he was living. The world around him he saw as full of horror, and yet he himself was not dissatisfied and even considered himself lucky. He was not in any sense depressed, although he did confess that he was not sure what he actually believed, only that he couldn't believe in anything absolute. The following exchange is perhaps indicative of a mood that pervaded his responses:

INTERVIEWER: Do you feel that you're an accepted and equal member of Canadian society?
JASON: Not always, no.
INTERVIEWER: Why not?
JASON: I don't know, sometimes I just get the feeling that nobody cares, or that everybody cares, which is about equal to the same thing … There seems to be this aura of indifference everywhere, so it's like it doesn't really matter whether I'm part of it or not.

Overall, Jason was in certain ways representative of many in the "little bit Buddhist" category. He had no real relation to anything that, from most perspectives, could be called religion, let alone Buddhist religion. His upbringing exposed him, to some extent, to both but not enough to have made a difference or even to constitute something that he felt he had to reject, unlike, for instance, some of the second-generation Khmer Buddhists in McLellan's study of Cambodians in Ontario (McLellan 2009, 164–9). As he stated, he "wouldn't join a religion," he hadn't "lost religion," and he felt no need to "find religion." Unlike Michael, he did not dismiss religion simply as superstition, but neither did he see in it much that was positive for him and for society more broadly. His attitude, however, was also in some senses on the extreme side: other participants exhibited it to some extent but not usually to the extent that he did. The third person profiled here shows this rather well.

Takahiro (BM06)

At the time of his interview, Takahiro was 20 years old, studying biological sciences at the University of Toronto. He was born in Canada of immigrant Japanese parents who initially came to this country because his father had been transferred here by his Japanese employer. One result was that he had no extended family in Canada, although he visited his relatives in Japan on a fairly regular basis. In this respect, his experience was quite different from that of the vast majority of the other Buddhist men. Takahiro's parents did not make a great effort to involve their son in their own regular Buddhist practice as he was growing up, exemplifying even more clearly the pattern evident among all the Buddhist male participants. He was not much exposed to Buddhism and therefore knew relatively little about it in terms of belief, philosophy, or practice.

Himself having religious parents, it is perhaps not surprising that, in contrast to many of the other Buddhist men, his opinion of religion was straightforwardly positive. As he put it quite clearly, "I would say that in general [religion] is a good thing. My parents are religious, and I find that they are great people. A lot of people who are religious, I find, have had a positive influence on my life and my peers ... In general it has a really good impact, especially in my life. I'm not sure about how it has affected other people's lives."

On the other hand, as someone familiar with recent Japanese history, Takahiro also felt that religion could have negative manifestations; in this context, he mentioned Aum Shinrikyo and the sarin gas attacks in the Tokyo subway in particular (see Kisala and Mullins 2001). Accompanying this generally positive orientation to religion was an openness "to the possibility of accepting religion in my life." This was not going to happen any time soon, however, and he insisted that when it did, he would construct his religion himself rather than simply adopting the traditions of his heritage – as we have seen, a very typical response on the part of virtually all our participants regardless of religious background. As he put the matter,

> I want to figure it out myself, as opposed to being something that, because my parents believed in it, I believe in it as well ... Personally, I haven't really dedicated enough time to this side, to form my opinions on it. Because that takes a lot of time, dedication, and to really want to figure out what's out there. But I'm at that stage right now where I'm very busy with school.

This interest but lack of urgency or priority prevented us from considering him a religio-culturally based seeker, and indeed, Takahiro declared himself to be neither religious nor even spiritual. That said, his openness was likely serious, because he did mention a summer when he was still in high school during which "I was really believing in God," but then "things just drifted away ... maybe my faith died." If there was a particular religion at issue during his "summer of faith," it was more Christianity than Buddhism, yet Takahiro had also previously shown interest in Buddhism, reading books on his own that he thought "were quite interesting." The sources that he mentioned, however, were "Western" Buddhists, not Buddhist texts as such or those written by Japanese or even East Asian Buddhists. Like that of most others in this sample, his knowledge of actual Buddhist teaching, such as it was, did not come through his parents or through other aspects of his upbringing such as, for instance, visiting temples, attending classes at temples, or listening to talks by Japanese monks. For some of them, such knowledge came from high school or university courses; for Takahiro, it was independent reading, the content of which he had mostly forgotten by the time of the interview.

The way that Takahiro related to Buddhism was, not surprisingly, linked to the way he related to being Japanese. He felt himself to be more Japanese than Canadian but also stated that this balance was changing insofar as he was realizing that he had more in common with other Canadians than with people who were Japanese. Indeed, he did not feel as comfortable around people born in Japan as around those of Japanese origin born in Canada or other Canadians. This was not a language issue, since he spoke Japanese fluently. It was more a cultural one. For instance, he thought that Japanese people were more materialistic than Canadians and that he resonated with the latter. He had little desire to go back to Japan even though he had, as noted, visited there many times. He did, however, lament the fact that there was not a sufficiently large community of Japanese Canadians in his Toronto environment and that therefore he had very few Japanese friends.[5] In other words, Takahiro in no way rejected his Japanese-ness, but he realized that it was of a particular, Canadian kind. Here is how he expressed much of this:

> I consider myself more Japanese than Canadian, even though I was born here, but slowly I'm beginning to realize that maybe that was just a kind of infatuation with Japan because I don't really know Japan too much ... At the same time ... I wanted to consider myself Japanese ... because I didn't want that part of me to die away, but now I accept myself for being Canadian and more multicultural, I'd say. I've become really used to Canada in the way Canada is and I guess I accept that, but at the same time I do miss Japan and I still do consider myself Japanese.

That melding of Japanese and Canadian in his identity, in his image of himself, was reflected in his attitude to Canada as a society and to the place of religion in that society. He thought Canada welcomed immigrants and that it allowed religion to have a strong influence in the lives of immigrants. As he put it in response to a question about the influence of religion in Canadian society:

> I think that [for] Canadian Canadians, the non-immigrants, [the influence is] not so much but for immigrants, definitely. They bring their own religion to Canada ... I think it's a good thing because that's what defines it, right? Multiculturalism. If they don't bring their religious backgrounds, that'd be like them forgetting who they are and their roots, so I think it's a good thing.

Not surprisingly, Takahiro felt that he was an accepted and equal member of Canadian society, that he fit in, even though he would have liked more people of Japanese origin in the country with whom he could be friends. The one experience of intolerance that he related came during high school and involved some Korean fellow students who held him responsible for Japanese imperialist atrocities in the first half of the twentieth century.

CONCLUSION

In projections released in early 2010, Statistics Canada (Caron Malenfant, Lebel, and Martel 2010) considered that from 2006 to 2031, Buddhism in Canada would likely grow much more slowly than any of the other major non-Christian religious identities with the exception of Judaism, and this in spite of continued high projected immigration from East and Southeast Asia. It remains to be seen, of course, how much these projections will correspond with reality, but the profiles of the men in our sample who declared themselves to be of Buddhist background indicate rather clearly one factor that might support this conclusion. To the extent that Buddhism constitutes the religious identity of a good minority of those arriving in Canada from these parts of the world, they will contribute to the growth of Buddhism in Canada, at least in terms of religious identification. Yet to the extent that our small sample of Buddhist men is any indication, these immigrant Buddhists may not be overly successful at passing on this identity to their Canadian-born or -raised children, and indeed, statistically, Buddhist parents in Canada are the least likely to pass their religious identity on to their children (Beyer and Martin 2010). Even if our sample of Buddhist women was not so unequivocal in this regard, the men did constitute about half of these children, and they were not adopting a Buddhist religious identity, let alone being engaged in Buddhist practice, to any great degree. That may change, of course, as this on average quite young second generation gets older, founds families, and pursues careers, but this, if at all, again only to a degree. What is more, as indicated by the Buddhist-background men in our sample, to the extent that they do adopt a more positively religious profile in the future, this will only in some cases result in a specific identification with Buddhism. Without socialization into Buddhism as religion and as a particular religion, the prospects of this segment of the population contributing to the growth and elaboration of Buddhism as a systemic religion in Canada are minimal. At most it may eventually contribute elements to the later-adult lived religion of these participants.

The same cannot, however, be said for their cultural identification, and this in two respects: the culture of their parental regions of origin and Canadian culture. Very few of the 19 Buddhist men did not continue to have a strong relation to the Chinese, Japanese, Vietnamese, Sri Lankan, or Cambodian culture of their parents. Jason and one other may be the exceptions. In a great many cases, as discussed, this cultural orientation manifested itself in, among other ways, their very understanding of religion. Yet parallel to this continued "ethnic" identification was an almost equally strong identification with Canada, at least in terms of a sense of belonging and/or comfort in living in this country. None of the 19 wanted to live anywhere else or felt that they were to any significant degree excluded from the mainstream society. Their attachment to the culture of their parents and their lack of attachment to Buddhism or any other religion did not seem to be determinative of the extent to which they were at ease in the country of their upbringing. To be sure, two or three of the participants thought that challenges lay ahead in this regard. Living "between two cultures" or, perhaps better, simultaneously in more than one culture was not necessarily without its problems, whether for personal relations or for one's sense of self, but these issues were also considered comparatively minor. One could say that, to the extent that this small sample may be representative, those of immigrant families and Buddhist background will go into the future as quite Canadian, quite "Asian" (in whatever particular idiom), and perhaps just a little bit Buddhist.

In these respects, of course, this group of 19 contrast markedly with the other major subgroups in our sample, with the exception of the Hindu men, as we saw in the previous chapter. However, what is thus far missing from the Buddhist men is the presence of people who take religion/spirituality seriously enough that in spite of not contributing to the construction and reproduction of systemic religion – here Buddhism – in Canada, they will elaborate individual lived religious identities that they and others will identify as such. In this respect, they contrast somewhat with the Buddhist women in our sample. As with the two gender groups among those of Hindu background, the differences between the men and women Buddhists, while not enormous, are nonetheless well worth emphasizing. It is to a consideration of this group what we now turn.

Fluid Boundaries of a Tolerant Religion:
Buddhist Women

MARIE-PAULE MARTEL-RENY AND PETER BEYER

The previous chapter examined the Buddhist male participants in the study; in this chapter, we look at data from the Buddhist female segment of the study and how they compare with the Buddhist males, as well as with the Hindu and Muslim female participants. While Buddhist participants were, for reasons that will be explored later in this chapter, the most difficult to recruit, female Buddhists were somewhat more forthcoming in their participation than their male counterparts, with 28 young Buddhist women participating in the study against 19 young Buddhist men.

A DEMOGRAPHIC PROFILE OF 28 BUDDHIST WOMEN

The Buddhist women in our sample were between 18 and 25 years old at the time of the interviews, with an average age of 20.8 years. The majority of them were in the middle and lower end of the age continuum: 11 were between the ages of 18 and 20, 9 between 21 and 22, and 3 between 23 and 25. As with the Buddhist males, this implies that they were still in the process of forging their identities, including religious identity. Yet as we will see, for many of them this did not preclude reflection on religious questions.

All female Buddhist participants were enrolled in university at the time of the study: three were psychology students; 8 majored in other humanities and social sciences such as political science, history, and anthropology. Another 7 were science majors in programs such as mathematics, computer engineering, and biology. The rest were in diverse fields like law, management, and architecture, or they did not specify their area of concentration. The diversity of concentrations was typical of all the subgroups examined in these chapters.

The majority of Buddhist women participants were born outside Canada, 16 of the 28. These proportions are the reverse of those for the Buddhist men. Many of those born outside the country, however, immigrated before the age of 5 and thus had few memories of their lives in their country of origin. Of the 16 participants who were born outside Canada, 1 was born in China, 5 in Hong Kong, 1 in Taiwan, and 1 in Macau. Two were born in Vietnam, 1 in Laos, and 2 in Thailand. Finally, 2 were born in Sri Lanka and 1 in Dubai from parents who were originally from Sri Lanka. Twelve of them grew up in Ontario, either in Ottawa or Toronto, 2 in British Columbia, and 1 in Nova Scotia. One participant, whose father worked abroad, grew up in various Asian countries. Eleven of the 12 participants born in Canada grew up in Ontario, most in the Greater Toronto Area but others in cities such as Ottawa, Hamilton, and Oshawa, with the remaining participant being from Montreal. As anticipated, there was no detectable difference between the two subgroups as concerns their relationship to Buddhism.

Our participants' parents emigrated for many reasons, which can be classified in three main categories. First, some were refugees, such as the so-called "boat people" who fled after the Vietnam War in the late 1970s and early 1980s or the armed conflict in Sri Lanka. Ten Buddhist female participants mentioned this as the main reason for their parents' emigration. Second, three left their home country because of other kinds of political instability. This reason was mentioned in relation to Hong Kong's retrocession to the People's Republic of China in 1997. Finally, some families decided to come to Canada seeking better economic opportunities and especially better education for their children; this was the case for 9 of our participants. Two participants did not mention why their parents came to Canada.

An interesting correlation between the parents' religion in relation to the participants' religion emerged from the data. Female Buddhists described their mothers (whether Buddhist or Christian) as more religious than their fathers. Indeed, 18 mothers were said to be religious compared to 12 fathers. Furthermore, in seven cases there was a discrepancy between the father's and the mother's religious affiliation; in six of these cases, the participant's religious affiliation was the same as her mother's. This suggests that, for this group at least, gender is an important factor in the transmission of religious identity.

THE CLUSTERING OF RELATIONS TO BUDDHISM
IN 28 FEMALE PARTICIPANTS

As discussed in the previous chapter, the 19 Buddhist men tended to cluster in the "little bit Buddhist" and the religio-culturally based seeker categories; the 28 Buddhist women were nearly as clustered but with two important differences. First, a small number of the female participants were classified as imitative traditionalists – they practised the Buddhism of their parent(s) without significant personal appropriation or reconstruction – or were self-identified and practising Christians. Second, there were somewhat more seekers than those with a marginal connection to Buddhism. Figure 10.1 presents the comparative categories in graphic form.

Even more than the Buddhist men, the women showed a marked concentration in categories depending on the ethnic identity and region of origin of

Figure 10.1   Classification of female (28) and male (19) participants of Buddhist background

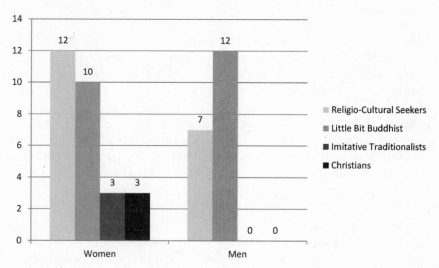

the families. Thus none of those who were ethnically Chinese and whose families came from Hong Kong, Taiwan, or the People's Republic of China were religio-culturally based religious seekers, and all those who were Christians had this ethnic origin. By contrast, 4 of the 5 who were ethnically Chinese but whose families migrated from Southeast Asia were seekers. Conversely, of those in the "little bit Buddhist" category, 6 of 8 were ethnically Chinese, and the families of all seekers came to Canada from Sri Lanka, Southeast Asia, or Japan. While one should not make too much of this correlation between the relation to Buddhism and family origins, it does correspond reasonably well to a similar, if not quite so stark, pattern among the Buddhist men and therefore is likely indicative of how Buddhism is enmeshed differently in the cultures dominant in these various regions.

Religio-culturally Based Religious Seekers

To repeat the description provided in the previous chapter on the Buddhist male participants, "seekers" are those who take religious or spiritual questions seriously in their own lives, whether they actually consider themselves Buddhists or not. The category reflects the fact that very few of the participants from Buddhist backgrounds were actually practising Buddhists but that Buddhism played a more important role for some than it did for others. We call them religio-culturally based seekers, because the way that they take these questions seriously bears in each case a clear relation to the religion of their families, Buddhism, but sometimes with an admixture of another religion like Christianity, Shinto, or Hinduism, to the culture of their families, or both. The category of course includes a fair amount of internal variety. There were those who had a modest connection in their seeking to the religion and culture of their families and those who understood Buddhism primarily in diffuse moral as opposed to specific belief or practice terms. But there were also a few who were in their own terms practising Buddhists and had undertaken to appropriate Buddhism for themselves – who had, like so many of the Muslim participants, set about to carry on the Buddhism of their parents but in such a way as to reconstruct that Buddhism with relation to their own religio-spiritual searches, their own experiences, and their different lives in Canada. These few could be seen as contributing to the construction of systemic Buddhism in Canada; Buddhism was an integral part of their lived religious lives.

Inasmuch as the men in this category were dominated by people who treated Buddhism as the moral basis of their outlook on life or simply considered religious/spiritual questions seriously, the women showed a different subgrouping: the majority of them actually engaged in some form of what they saw as Buddhist practice, with a smaller group engaging in a less tradition-specific quest. In terms of religious identification, all but one of them considered herself to be Buddhist, although not always exclusively so. There was, in fact, a general openness to other religions, notably but by no means exclusively the Christianity to which almost all of them had had some meaningful exposure as they were growing up, whether through relatives (including parents) who were practising Christians, Christian friends with whom they went to church, or education in explicitly Christian schools. This closer relation to Buddhism and to religions more generally is worth examining in greater detail, because it is illustrative of how Buddhism might be operating differently as a religion for these young women than was Hinduism for the Hindu participants and Islam for the Muslim participants.

For the most part, the seeker women rejected closed, exclusive, authoritative, and especially "pushy" or proselytizing religion and were more attracted to religion that was open, flexible, and non-exclusive. Not surprisingly, then, they also tended to conceive their Buddhism in these terms. This perceived flexibility, openness, or non-exclusivity of Buddhism manifested itself in a number of ways and paralleled similar ideas expressed by the Buddhist men. Eileen, a 25-year-old of Chinese-Vietnamese origin, was particularly clear in this regard: "The strengths of Buddhism ... I think that it's a very flexible religion, so we don't exclude like some religions that think people who aren't of their religion aren't human, that they're not good people. I think that we are more open; I think that the strength [of Buddhism] is that we are more open, and we integrate more easily, that's what I think" (BF06). Correspondingly, she rejected interpretations of Buddhism that negated this understanding: "What I don't like is when people say – I don't like strictness, for example when people say, 'if you're Buddhist you have to do this, this, this, and this.' From what I understand, that's not essential in Buddhism. For me, what's essential is that you understand and that you have a thirst, a curiosity for learning and to do your best."

Others came at the question from different angles. Sanuthi, a 23-year-old 1.5-generation participant from Sri Lanka, admitted that she took whatever she wanted from different religions to create her own personal religion, but she also identified herself as Buddhist, which she clearly considered, as another participant put it, "laid back." Here is what she said about what Buddhism required: "It's basically the same things, like honour your parents and no killing, no stealing, no real drinking. But it's not so much if you don't do this you go to hell, or if you don't do this something bad happens to you. It's just these are things that people should follow so everyone can get along well, but if you don't do it you just keep being born again, so whatever you want is fine" (BF15).

Yet a third person in this seeker group, Nuveena, another 1.5er from Sri Lanka, looked upon her Buddhist upbringing as providing her with a resource upon which she could draw when needed: "I think that was the whole thing with my dad where he wanted us to learn … the actual sutras and stuff just so that if we came to a point in our lives where we needed something, we needed some answers, that we'd have them and we'd know where to go to look for them. And that if we wanted to figure it out for ourselves that it would be there in raw form" (BF22).

Buddhism was not necessarily the only religion understood in this way. Kalaina, a 20-year-old who came from Laos as a child, felt that Buddhism's flexibility was actually characteristic of all religions. When asked if she thought that one form of Buddhism was more authentic than others, she said that "religion is so interpretive; what you interpret as authentic may not be authentic to other people. Religion is what you make it, it's definitely not concrete and stable as people might want it to be" (BF03). Nancy, a 23-year-old second-generation Japanese Canadian, melded Buddhism with Shinto in her life. She saw the former as a "very compassionate religion" and on that basis attractive. With regard to the latter, she had this to say:

Shinto is a religion that doesn't have so much structure and doesn't bind you into believing, you know, "it's the Buddha or nothing" or it's "Christ or nothing." So I just like that openness, that it's very easy. You don't always have to keep the gods satisfied by praying six times a day; you could just whenever and they'll always, you know, it's the feeling that they'll always be there, and you don't have to make any great sacrifice for them. (BF16)

One might suspect on the basis of what we learned from the Muslim sample that the greater involvement of these women in actual Buddhist belief and practice might reflect a more explicit Buddhist socialization as they were growing up. As it happens, this is only partially the case; some of the women Buddhist seekers, such as one of the ones just quoted, received a more religiously focused Buddhist upbringing, but others undertook their own education in the face of their parents' inability or unwillingness to do so. A very clear example of the latter is Kalaina. Her interest in religion and in her own religion, Buddhism, was sparked while she was already at university, but to pursue this interest she relied on her own research and reading. She could not draw on her upbringing, to some extent because of a generational and cultural difference from her parents. Here is what she said in that context:

> I find that I definitely have to look at books, because if I ask my mom something about Buddhism, I think it's very hard for her to explain it, because I don't think it was formally taught to her. It was just, she learned it from what she saw. It was just the way in which that's passed down more verbally or orally or through actions rather than through written form or stuff like that. But I find myself gravitating towards books and stuff, because that's the way I've been taught to learn. (BF03)

Mai, a 23-year-old 1.5er from neighbouring Vietnam, related a very similar situation when she described how she came to develop an interest in knowing more about her family's religion:

> When I was about 12 or 13, my parents started doing the Buddhist thing again, and then I've sort of been exposed to that, but I find that my parents … don't explain it to me … And it's like they do it because that's all they know how to do, they don't really know why they're doing it, kind of thing. So maybe it's because they didn't translate to me the meaning or the significance of things, but from what I grew up with, the Buddhism part, I didn't really understand it, it's just a whole set of things I didn't know. And then recently we've started going to the temple. One of my parents' friends became a Buddhist monk about six or seven years ago, and we go up and visit him at the temple every once in a while. So last summer I started reading some books on it, and I've sort of been self-educating myself on that. (BF04)

As both these quotes also indicate, part of the issue is that these seeker participants often found their religious socialization inappropriate or, put another way, that the Buddhist religion to which their parents and elders exposed them was too culturally specific and too unreflected, much as several of the Muslim participants complained that their parents mixed particularistic cultural practices with their Islam. Mai, for instance, labelled the Buddhist practice of her parents as "just ritual and superstition" (BF04). Eileen, a highly practising 25-year-old for whom Buddhism was very important, described a difference in orientation between her and her mother in terms of what each sought from religious practice. Here is what she said:

> For my mother, she practises Buddhism, and she says to herself, "I'm going to have a better karma in my future life." She does things because of her future karma, she does things because "oh, this will be good for me" ... As for myself, that bothers me a bit, this idea of doing something for the sake of a better reincarnation, doing something in order to live with the gods above. That bugs me ... It's a point of disagreement between us, and sometimes a little frustration, 'cause what I want, I want to understand, I want to know *why*. As for the next life, I don't know, I don't see it, I don't want to know anything [about it] ... Yes, I suppose it's important, but it's not a proof for me, to do something so that my next life will be better. I want something here and now. (BF06)

What might, from a Southeast Asian perspective, be interpreted as a difference between a "lay" Buddhist attitude and a more "monastic" one Eileen saw explicitly as a matter of cultural difference between her and her mother. Her mother had lived a difficult life during the Vietnam War and therefore saw things differently. In somewhat similar fashion, Nuveena saw the temple-oriented Buddhism to which her parents exposed her in Canada as inadequate, again from the perspective of not making proper sense to her. She said that,

> There came a point where I just didn't want to be Buddhist because the way that they were teaching it here. I didn't like it. Like when I went to the temple they'd say all these things and it was like, I don't believe that [laughs]. And I was really frustrated until I went to Sri Lanka, and my grandmother basically went through everything and she went about it in a more scientific manner ... and then my dad gave me a book, and that explained a lot of what the teachings were ... Like it gave me more answers and it made it, I didn't feel as like, I just don't want to do this. Not do this, but I just, what I saw in the religion was sort of like, you just have to go the temple and you have to pray and you have to do this thing and that thing and this is how it is, and the priests would be like "oh you have to believe this." Where it's really not like that, and it frustrated me because I didn't agree with that, and my questions that I had for the

priests, they couldn't answer it. Whereas my grandmother was able to answer it, like ... more scientifically as well as, like, philosophically and in terms of Buddhism itself. (BF22)

These contrasts with the Buddhism of the parents points directly to the fact that most of the religio-culturally based seekers also actively constructed their own Buddhism, based on their own experience, inclinations, and research. Katherine, a second-generation 23-year-old from a Chinese-Vietnamese family, began her effort to take Buddhism more seriously toward the end of high school. She undertook a conscious quest, as much for herself as for being able to "pass on the tradition." She put it like this:

[I started wanting to learn more about Buddhism] sometime in high school ... There was a time when I was just trying to figure out what the different religions were, and I figured I might as well start off with Buddhism, because that's what I grew up with ... I thought it was really important that I kind of got serious about it especially if, y'know, if I had kids, and I was thinking that maybe I'd want my kids to know what my parents were about, and that was an important part of my parents' life. (BF13)

This participant shared the rejection of Buddhism that was ritualistic without explanation, stating that "Buddhism sort of started off as a philosophy or way of life" and then was culturally pushed toward what she called "ceremonies and sacrifices" for gods, which she labelled as "sort of silly." Some of the seekers could be quite concrete about the contents of their Buddhism. Mai had this less than confident rendition of the Buddhist ideas of nirvana, anatta, and reincarnation:

Well, I may have really twisted it in my head, but I believe in a oneness with the universe kind of thing. And that everybody is a part of it, but there's not a real god ... If you can transcend and you can reach that nirvana or whatever, and then you become one with everything. And then you're sort of like truth in itself ... [When you reincarnate] it's not like a new entity, but it's not like an old entity either. It's sort of something within itself. I don't know [laughs]. See, I get so messed up, and sometimes I'm like, "what the hell am I saying?" But like, it's how I put it, it's what I've gathered, that you get reincarnated but it's not like it's you, it's like, your totally, your true Buddha nature, like something inherent in you but it's not really you, it's just something, like we sort of like associate like an ego or a personality with this entity but there's really nothing there. (BF04)

Mai also undertook a specific search on her own to discover her Buddhism. She said, that

It's only been recently in the last year that I keep wanting to find out more about Buddhism. And I think it's about the self-searching, like sort of self-enlightenment. Nobody can do it for you, it's not prescribed. You have to do it on your own terms, and you question everything, you question reality, you question truth, and that really appeals to me, I don't really know why. (BF04)

Although many of these women thus had a positive relation to Buddhism and had undertaken or begun to undertake its appropriation for themselves, it was still the case that very few of the seekers actually engaged in explicitly Buddhist ritual and practice and even fewer were exclusively Buddhist in doing so. Eileen was one of these few. Here is what she related when asked in what sort of practices she engaged: "Regular practices, let's see. I'm not consistent, but when I can, I do meditation, I also recite mantras and – I don't know what you call it – it's [reciting] the names of the Buddhas with a string of 108 beads. Yes, I do things like that when I can. When there's a retreat, I go on it. And if a Buddhist monk is giving a teaching, like last week when Hsing Yun[1] came, [I went there]" (BF06).

Eileen also had a guru, a woman who was herself a follower of Hsing Yun. Yet her level of practice and involvement, including by her own admission – "I feel kind of alone" – was rare in her generation as it was rare in the sample of women who participated in this research project. As she herself said, most people she knew in her generation were, at best, Buddhist in name only, because their parents were Buddhist. And, as another indicator, Katherine, who, as we saw, had only begun to try to learn more about Buddhism at the time of the interview, felt that her minimal level of practice already put her at the 7 to 8 level out of 10 when it came to how important Buddhism was to her. Among the reasons for this, as we have seen, was the lack of an explicit Buddhist socialization, the failure of the parents to effectively pass on their Buddhism, and the flexible, even optional character of the Buddhist belief and practice that was passed on, something that the Buddhist women participants had internalized and almost always saw as a positive feature of this religion in contrast to the "pushiness" that they perceived in others, notably certain forms of Christianity.

The relation of culture to religion that many of these young women portrayed presents yet another variation when compared to what was happening among the Muslim and Hindu participants. If many Muslims drew a clear line and saw themselves as purifying their Islam from the cultural accretions of their parents, if the prevailing orientation among the Hindus was more or less the opposite in that they drew no consistent line between what was culturally and religiously Hindu, a good number of the Buddhist women in this religio-cultural seeker grouping did both: they drew a distinct line between what was Buddhism and what was their parental ethnic culture, but they also saw the two as quite closely associated. Eileen represents one version of this in that she practised in some senses a kind of "Western" Buddhism with its stress on individual responsibility, but she did this in a recognizably "Chinese" Buddhist frame with her Fo Guang Shan–style Buddhism (cf. Verchery 2010). Like others, she considered that her mother (parent) practised what one might almost call a "less enlightened" Buddhism, one that the parents did more out of cultural or traditional habit than out of real understanding.

Another variation was presented by Chamika, an 18-year-old 1.5-generation Sinhalese Buddhist. She had a very strong sense of what proper Buddhism was and explained it rather directly with reference to the Four Noble Truths and the Eightfold Path:

> Buddhists believe that there is no "you," there is no "me," and there is no "I." And that the way to end suffering is through the Four Noble Truths: understanding where suffering comes from; knowing that there is suffering; and then you have to follow the Eightfold Path ... So it's basically knowing that there is suffering and so that the Buddha taught how to get rid of suffering, which basically means being more aware of your thoughts and your feelings. That's the simplest way that I can put it. (BF25)

Meditative practice was the heart of Buddhist practice for her; the rest, such as annual celebrations, temple ritual, and caring for monks – features of traditional Sinhalese lay Buddhism – were secondary. And yet she was very insistent that what she practised was not just specifically Theravada Buddhism but Sinhala Buddhism as well. Her Sinhala cultural and Theravada Buddhist identities were distinct but in her mind intimately linked to the point of being inseparable. She said, for instance, that "our culture is based on the religion ... there's no real separation between the two." Yet the most important practice of her Buddhism, meditation, was according to her open to anyone, Buddhist or not: "you don't have to be Buddhist to reach nirvana; anyone can ... Meditation and all that isn't restricted to Buddhism; anyone can do it." In brief, Chamika's Buddhism was universal, but that universal Buddhism was for her an inseparable and essential aspect of Sri Lankan Sinhalese culture (cf. Mitra Bhikkhu 2010), so much so that she claimed that if any of her eventual children married someone who was not both Sinhala and Buddhist, she would disown them: "Tough luck, no way. You marry them, you're not my kid anymore" (BF25).

Buddhist Family Background: A Little Bit Buddhist

The title for this subcategory is actually a quote from one of the Buddhist women participants. When asked what she felt her religion was, Susan answered "Hmmm … I guess I believe I'm a little bit Buddhist, because I do believe in a lot of the things that they teach" (BF08). Characteristically perhaps, she only had a very vague idea of what those teachings were.

As noted above, of the 8 participants in this category, all but 2 were from ethnically Chinese families, and like the corresponding men, they tended to draw very imprecise lines around what counted as Buddhism, more often than not identifying it with whatever religious practices prevailed in their household as they were growing up – that is, with the exception of Christianity. One of the more remarkable consistencies across the 8 participants is that all of them had significant exposure to Christianity as they were growing up, yet none of them considered themselves Christian.[2] In fact, Christianity was more often than not the prime reference when many of them, like several of the seekers, decried "pushy," proselytizing religion.

This combination of exposure to Christianity and rejection of proselytizing religion did not always mean that the participants were negatively disposed to Christianity or religion, although that was indeed sometimes the case. Tylanni, a 19-year-old whose family came from Hong Kong when she was 3, said that "my mom is registered as a Christian, and my dad has a Catholic certificate," indicating that Christianity had a certain presence in the family, but she also thought that, as religion, both[3] were dangerous:

TYLANNI: I study in history. I really believe – Christianity and
Catholicism is really dangerous.
INTERVIEWER: How come?
TYLANNI: Well, um – in like political ways, they're really influential
and – I mean they're the cause of a lot of wars in Europe, so I think it's
really dangerous. (BF24)

Selina, an 18-year-old second-generation Chinese-Vietnamese Canadian, related how some of her high school friends were constantly trying to convert her to Christianity, even saying she would go to hell if she didn't. At the end of the interview, she had this to say: "a big problem I know that I have is people who preach their religion. It's great that they believe in it and, if I ask and I'm interested, for them to tell me, but like my friend who would come over and tell me, 'you're going to hell,' like, I don't like that kind of thing" (BF01).

Susan was also among the majority in this category who demonstrated this critical stance toward Christianity but extended it to other religions as well.

She attended a mainline Christian high school but felt that religions were the cause of many wars and decried adherents to religions that were "overbearing, pushing a lot" (BF08). On a slightly different note, Gladys, a 20-year-old who emigrated from Hong Kong when she was 2 years old, accused religion of causing more harm than it did good and was especially critical of religion that excluded those outside the fold:

> I think it's created a lot of problems, like in history and around the
> world. Like in Ireland with the Catholics and the Protestants. You know,
> like, if you all believe in the same God, why are you still fighting? So I
> think it's caused more problems than it's helped people, personally ...
> And [some religious groups] *shun* members of their *own* community
> and their own religion. Where, like, I thought you were supposed to be
> accepting of all people. So I just see it as being kind of contradictory.
> You know, just sort of like, you say you're supposed to love and accept
> everybody, but then here you are just doing the opposite to this person.
> (BF02)

It is perhaps indicative and not that surprising in this context that the attitude toward things Buddhist was generally much more positive. Tylanni contrasted Buddhism with "other faiths" as specifically tolerant: "it's not as narrow, I think it's really highly tolerant among the faiths because we celebrate everything else too, right?" (BF24). Susan, when asked what part of Buddhism she thought that she followed, answered that "people have told me that I'm pretty open and tolerant of almost anything, so, that's part of it ... and yeah, generally I try not to be prejudiced" (BF08). Yet in conjunction with this orientation, as the title of the category indicates, these participants also had only a vague idea of what Buddhism was, what it included. There was mention of particular items, such as the doctrine of karma or vegetarianism, of Buddhism being a basis for morality and virtue, but none of the 8 could go beyond such general characteristics to talk about specific forms of practice or coherent sets of belief. Buddhism was, as noted, an element of the general culture bequeathed to them in strong or weak form through their families and not something all that distinct, unlike the much more clearly delimited and often negatively evaluated Christianity. Correspondingly, the majority of the women in this category had a very positive orientation toward their inherited (Chinese) culture, but again in many cases were not able to pinpoint precisely what that meant beyond one or two representative details.

Jennifer, who arrived from Hong Kong when she was 9, had a great deal of difficulty sorting out her orientation to religion and to the Christianity and Buddhism of her upbringing in particular. She said she sometimes felt that she was Christian, sometimes Buddhist, generally neither, but that she was definitely not a religious person. On the question of culture, however, she was unequivocal and positive. She was proud of being from a "traditional Chinese family" and singled out the respect of elders as a particularly characteristic feature:

JENNIFER: Our family is [a] ... Chinese traditional family ... [with] strict rules ... I think maybe because I believe in Chinese culture, I think I would even raise my kids that way, so I don't object to it, even though I'm raised here.
INTERVIEWER: What would you consider Chinese culture? Give me some examples.
JENNIFER: The way you respect your elders; not to say white people don't respect their elders, but I think, like, here, y'know, working in a white-person society, everybody refers to each other [by] their first name and stuff, and even now I still find that rude, because like at home or like even like in the Chinese community, [when] you ... refer to anybody older than you, [it's] never by their first name ... So things like that, um ... it's hard to pinpoint exactly ... I never thought about it yet. It's just like when I think about it, I think I would want to raise my children that way. (BF12)

In a similar vein, Gladys stated that the cultural identity of her eventual marriage partner was important and that there was an important difference between her culture and that of many of her non-Chinese friends:

GLADYS: My culture's really important to me ... It's a large part of who I am, obviously, so I would like to be able to share that with someone who already has some understanding of what that is. And also just the communication between two families ... because when I get married I'd want our families to be really close.
INTERVIEWER: When you say like your culture's really important to you ... what comes to mind?
GLADYS: ... I've kind of noticed that in Asian families the parents sort of tend to still like look after your kid even, like as they're growing up still. You know? I know a lot of my friends, once they've reached 18, their parents like, "yeah, OK, you're on your own" ... find your own way through school and stuff like that. Which is good for independence, I suppose. Like it's good, but then like my parents are, you know, still helping me out with school. And they're still very much like involved in my life. Which I think is, which I like right now, personally ... yeah, I picture myself doing that when I'm a parent. So, I kind of notice that difference. (BF02)

Nor were the ethnically Chinese the only Buddhists in the category that valorized culture. Nevinka, whose Sri Lankan family came to Canada when she was 3 years old, actually had only a very indistinct idea of what it meant to be Buddhist or Sinhalese, and yet she felt it was important to pass both on to her eventual children and very much in the combined form in which she experienced it. She put it this way:

> If I do have kids, I would like them to be somewhat exposed to Sri Lankan culture and to Buddhism, just because it's gonna be so sad if it just stops. Like if there were no more generations that knew anything about any of it. Like your actual roots, where you descend from. So yeah, if I did have kids I would tell them – like I have to learn about it first, before I can [pass it on] or give them information about Buddhism or the Sri Lankan culture and stuff. (BF09)

The generally positive orientation toward culture in combination with the relatively low knowledge and awareness of Buddhism as a distinctly observable religion corresponds to a similar orientation among the religio-culturally based seekers discussed in the previous section: the difference is the greater distinctiveness that Buddhism had for the former, the more explicit identification with it, and the greater openness to and importance of religious/spiritual questions and answers. This pattern compares and contrasts with the relatively few women in the last two categories, the imitative traditionalists and those who were Christians with Buddhist family background.

Imitative Traditionalists: Carrying Forth the Religious Heritage

Although there were only three women in this category, it represents an important possibility for the relation to Buddhism among our participants, because here we have something close to the carrying on of religious traditions in the relatively unreflected style of most of the parents: they do what they have been taught while growing up but do not concern themselves overly with appropriating and understanding – that is, reconstructing – Buddhism for themselves on the basis of their own efforts. Imitative traditionalists were like those who were "a little bit Buddhist" in their level of understanding but exhibited much higher levels of practice and considered that practice important, not just something they did to please their parents. In reverse, they were also like the religio-culturally based seekers, or at least those who had appropriated Buddhism for themselves, but precisely without this active and self-described reconstruction.

Of the three participants in this category, one was far more reflective than the others and therefore could be clearer about why she "imitated" rather than appropriated. Dana was a 19-year-old woman of mixed Thai and Anglo-

Canadian parentage who felt closely tied to the culture and identity of her Thai mother, although she by no means therefore felt distanced from many of the cultural aspects that she inherited from her Protestant Canadian father. Highly indicative of her orientation was that she refused to differentiate Thai culture from Thai religion – that is, Thai Buddhism. Her position reinforced and in its own way made much clearer what was the case for many of the other participants that we have slotted into the two categories already discussed: Buddhism was a differentiated religion for relatively few and a descriptive category for aspects of certain "ethnic" cultures for most others. Here is how Dana put it in one particularly revealing exchange:

DANA: I have a hard time defining the distinction between Thai cultural practice and customs and Thai religion ... because I don't see that there is a clear line between them ... Thai culture and its customs and traditions and stuff is a direct result of religion, so, I think that, you know I can't touch someone's head, you can't put your feet up there; it's a question of respect. And I think that comes from religion ... Thailand [is] really hierarchical ... it's very respect- and prestige-oriented, and you know you can't talk back to elders, and that's very, you know that's not only Thai, but I think all of the traditions and customs that I am familiar with are religious-based. Like I am sure if I looked into it I could tie it into religion somewhere in history.
INTERVIEWER: How do you define religion?
DANA: Well that's interesting 'cause when we did it in class I didn't ... I didn't agree with what [the] professor ... had said, but I think there's more to it. For me ... I think it actually runs through my blood. I feel it ... Religion to me is an explanation for how I think. How I feel a lot of the time, but it's religion within culture, within Thai cultural customs and traditions. (BF19)

What Dana said next is what really marked her orientation as different: she was not a practising Buddhist so much as culturally Thai:

DANA: I mean it doesn't govern my life, I don't wake up and pray every morning, I don't go to bed and pray every night. I pray when I remember to. I pray when I think I need to. I pray when I know it will make me feel better.
INTERVIEWER: So how does that contrast with the definition that you were getting in class?
DANA: You know, it was just rituals and worship and it's a way of organizing humanity and chaos and there was a bunch of just broad terms. But ... I don't agree with it. They all make sense, when you're studying it from like an outside perspective ... Religion to me is different; like,

when I'm dancing I'm praying to cultural mentors, cultural teachers, cultural anything, Thai culture and Buddha also. Like, I am praying to anything and anybody who I view with respect, in terms of dance and culture and, Thai everything ... I can't define [religion and culture] as being completely separate from each other. I don't think there is a difference. I think religion makes culture. And culture makes religion ... you can't have one without the other. And what makes ... different religion[s] ... is that they all have different cultures to them. (BF19)

Dana's attitude in fact bears a strong resemblance to what many of those Hindus we classified as ethnocultural Hindus did with respect to their Indian culture and Hindu religion: they practised them as of a piece, and that included, as was to some extent the case with Dana, the comparative irrelevance of questions of understanding and even such core issues as to whether or not the "gods," or karma, or reincarnation, or enlightenment were real or important. Not surprisingly, in this and most other respects, all the women in the three categories discussed thus far contrasted with the attitudes and orientations of those with Buddhist background who were in fact self-identified Christians but not entirely. Something of the "tolerant Buddhist" attitude was to be found even among them.

Christians with Buddhist Family Backgrounds

What is perhaps most intriguing about the three Christians with Buddhist backgrounds is that each of them presented a rather different way of relating their Christianity to the Buddhism in their families. Arlene, an 18-year-old from a Taiwanese family, arrived in Canada at the age of 9; she was brought up Christian in her country of birth. A third-generation Christian from her mother's side, she had actually had very little exposure to things Buddhist; none of her Buddhist relatives lived in Canada. She rejected what she knew about Buddhism, which she identified with ancestor worship, monks, and vegetarianism, regarding it as superstition. Yet her Christianity was precisely not of the sort that others in the sample considered objectionable: she was fairly low-key about her faith and gave no indication of wanting to evangelize at all, certainly not aggressively. Even more accepting was Lilly, a 20-year-old whose ethnically Chinese parents were both atheists but who was close to her Christian grandmother, had little contact with the Buddhist side of the family, and was expressly non-exclusive when it came to religion: she considered herself more Christian than Buddhist, but the Christian aspect was not particularly ardent. Here is how she put it at two different times in the interview: "[I consider myself] more ... Christian because I still go to church. Personally, I go to church because my boyfriend goes a lot. I don't think there is one religion that's superior to any of them, I think that we should have the right to take whatever we want from each religion and make a personal thing" (BF11).

The only one of the three for whom her Christian faith was both exclusive and personally very important was Joanne, a 25-year-old born in Canada to a Hong Kong family that had immigrated in the 1970s. She rejected other religions, including the Buddhism of her grandparents and the Islam once practised by her husband, in favour of her own form of Christianity:

> JOANNE: The God that I believe in is an all-loving God ... and doesn't impose for you to pray 10 times a day and, y'know, shake money in a can and light incense around the house ... I'd say that my God is a pretty proactive God and pragmatic, he'd say, well, y'know, "love me, make sure you devote your time to me and that you've really practised the words I'm saying, but please don't trouble me with your prayers all day long" ...
> INTERVIEWER: So what then do you think is the relationship between Christianity and other religious traditions? Hinduism? Buddhism? Islam?
> JOANNE: Personally, I feel like Christianity comes out over and above all of them. (BF10)

Even here, however, Joanne's Christianity was not of the aggressive, proselytizing sort, and her criticism of other religions, and indeed certain interpretations of Christianity, was that they wasted their time on useless ritual practices instead of devoting themselves to making God's earth a better place in which to live.

These three participants in all likelihood do not represent the religious orientations and habits of most ethnically Chinese Christians; it is the points of continuity between them and the "little bit Buddhist" and seeker Buddhists that may be more significant. Religion on a Buddhist background, when it is at all important, is more likely to meld with culture or be judged in terms of how it meshes with the practical concerns of life. It is personal; it should be optional and therefore certainly not necessary. Where there is some urgency, it is generally, with a few exceptions, on the cultural side: it is that, if any part of the family heritage, that should be carried on and preserved.

SOME INDIVIDUAL PROFILES

Ahn (BF21)

Ahn is an excellent example of someone who was a "seeker" but ended up with her parents' religion, and as such she was a "traditionalist" without being "imitative." An only child, Ahn was born in Canada and grew up in Toronto with her parents, who emigrated from Vietnam in 1979 just after the war. Her father, a mechanic, came to Canada as a boat person; he sponsored his own mother's immigration to Canada and then his wife's. While both of Ahn's parents were Vietnamese, her father's family was originally from China, and he maintained a strong Chinese identity, although Vietnamese was spoken at home and was Ahn's mother tongue. Both of her parents were Buddhist, but Ahn's father brought Chinese cultural and religious elements to the family, and Ahn's mother, while raised as a Buddhist, attended a Catholic school as a child. This made for a rich religious background out of which Ahn emerged with a Buddhist identity.

While her parents never forced their religious beliefs on her, Ahn said that "they were so into it … that every time I had something important going on in my life they would go and consult the deities. So then I don't know, it just kind of rubbed off on me." She saw religion as "a secure faith [that] replenishes your hopes. Something that just keeps you going forward when really there's nothing else to look or hold on to." Another important aspect of religion to her was to instill good morals: doing good, following a righteous path. Furthermore, she perceived religion as something positive that gave meaning to situations that would otherwise make no sense. While belief in a higher power was not mandatory in her definition of religion, Ahn spoke at length of the deities that were found in what she considered her branch of Buddhism, including the goddess of mercy Guan Yin, the kitchen god Ong Tao, the historical Buddha, and the War General. Ahn had a little altar at home with statues of these deities, and she consulted them, through divination, whenever there was something important going on in her life. Hers was clearly a very Chinese Buddhism.

To Ahn, culture and religion were connected but different: "Culture to me are things more like traditions, like marriage in certain ways … But then religion is more like the belief." However, she saw religion and spirituality as the same and superstition as a consequence of religion. Ahn herself identified as a Buddhist, but that was not an identity she simply accepted from her parents without questioning it. Rather, she explained that in her teenage years, she eagerly researched many different religious traditions through books borrowed from the library. She especially liked paganism but found out she did not know anyone who practised it; she then looked at Christianity but did not like it as much as paganism. In the end, it was her science tutor who brought her what she calls "moral Buddhist training":

I had a tutor, a spiritual tutor, and he was more with the Zen Buddhism, so there's no deity. Like he, he did that kind of religion also, where he would bring, you know, food to sacrifice and stuff like that. But he gave me, like, teachings from the moral side of it. So, with that from that side, Buddha was seen just as a moral person. It wasn't like a deity or a God or anything like that.

Ahn recalls how her tutor's teachings came at a point where she was wondering about the authenticity of her parents' religion:

> I was already exposed to [Buddhism] from my parents a bit, but they
> just seemed too spiritual for me at that point because I was just like,
> "well are they [the gods] really there? Like, is this just effortless praying
> that [my parents] are doing? Is anyone even listening?" So I wanted
> something more solid. And he kind of brought me that, my spiritual
> trainer … And I decided, well, I have my faith. After I got over the skep-
> ticism … I realized [that] everybody needs their faith because that was
> one of [my mentor's] teachings … So then I realized [that] my parents, I
> should really continue their thing. And then afterwards I just got into it.

The description Ahn gave of her own religious evolution marked her as
somewhat of a hybrid between the religio-culturally based religious seeker
and the imitative traditionalist types: while her personal exploration of different religions put her in the former category, the way in which she finally
integrated her parents' form of Buddhism marked her as a traditionalist, albeit
a "non-imitative" one, since she actually questioned her parents' traditions
before adopting them. The important role played by her science tutor as a religious mentor was also quite unique in our sample, that of an adult who was
not a family member but acted as a resource the youths could go to in order to
get answers to their religious questions.

At the time of the interview, Ahn was 21 and in her fourth year at the University of Toronto. She was studying psychology and neuroscience and planned
to go into rehabilitation science. Pursuing higher education was important to
Ahn, as for many children of immigrants. During the interview, she said that
she initially wanted to become a medical doctor, something that was strongly
encouraged by her parents. She explained in much detail the academic pressure faced by many immigrant children: "I know how much sacrifice they're
giving me. Especially … given that they were stuck in the whole Vietnam War,
so I feel pressure from that just because of me. And [from] them indirectly."
Despite her efforts, however, Ahn did not have high enough grades to become
a doctor, but she continued her university studies in another branch.

Cathy (BF18)

We chose Cathy as an example of the "little bit Buddhist" type. Cathy was 22
at the time of the interview, an English major at the University of Toronto. She
was born in Toronto to parents who migrated from Korea with their families
while still in their teenage years. In that respect, Cathy can also be seen as a
"2.5er," in some respects closer to the third generation of immigrants than to
the second. Cathy has one younger brother and two younger half-sisters. She

grew up in different towns in Ontario, including Hamilton and Scarborough, as her family moved around to follow work opportunities.

Cathy's story was unique in that her parents, who are both Korean immigrants but met after coming to Canada, separated when she was 8 years old. Cathy had since been estranged from her biological father, and her mother, who works as an administrator in a hospital, was remarried to a Canadian Caucasian man of Christian heritage. She was also exposed to Christianity through her grandmother, who converted upon her arrival in Canada.

Despite this peculiar family history (compared to other "little bit Buddhist" participants whose parents were both Asian and still married), Cathy's upbringing showed characteristics that were common across the sample of "little bit Buddhists." She described herself and both her parents as non-religious, stating that she "wasn't really brought up in a very religious household." Cathy was raised mostly by her maternal grandparents, since her parents, and especially her mother, were busy working and going to school when she was a child. Though she described her upbringing as religiously neutral, some Buddhist elements were present: she recalled listening to her grandparents' stories about Korean festivals, "like the Lantern Festival and the Lotus Festival." Some Korean traditions were carried on in her family, such as the Day of the Dead and the Lunar New Year ceremony, but Cathy said she and her siblings were not brought up as Buddhists. There were no altars or religious pictures and objects in their house, and Cathy did not discuss religion with her mother until her first visit to Korea at the age of 17. Her family never engaged much with the Asian community when Cathy was a child, and for her that explained in part why her relation to her Asian background was rather tenuous.

Despite the scarcity of religious lore available in her family, Cathy remembered the Lunar New Year as "a time of excitement but again a little puzzling," because she did not understand the full meaning of the ritual and her impression of it was that "it was very mysterious, because it was so different from anything else outside of the home." Yet she also recalled the excitement of preparing for it, which involved the cooking and offering of food, of which a portion would be offered to the ancestors: "everything would be set up so that there were two separate tables. One was the main table, where the ceremony took place, and then one was a smaller table to the side that was reserved just for our ancestors."

The ritual itself included Cathy's participation: dressed in traditional Korean costume, she and her maternal uncle would, after dark, open the front door to welcome the spirits of the ancestors into the house. The spirits were then invited to sit at the little table and partake in the offerings the family had laid out for them. Interestingly, Cathy thought that this ritual should normally have been performed by the eldest son of the family. However, since she was the eldest by quite a few years, the tradition was, as she put it, "bent a little," and the responsibility became hers.

For Cathy, this religiously neutral upbringing was a positive thing, and she found that it allowed her to remain open and to take whatever religious element she was drawn to, "without a commitment, without obligation, without guilt." In high school, she read books about Eastern religious traditions such as Zen Buddhism, Daoism, and Hinduism and was fascinated by them. She stressed that this endeavour was purely intellectual rather than a search for wisdom. For her, education and knowledge took the place of religion, and she explained that she had "always been a little bit cynical about faith and belief." She added, "I don't know if it's a product of growing up in a home where we didn't really have a religion, but ... my family was always very critical about the world around us. I guess we were taught to always really question [things]."

In Cathy's views, religion was part of culture, a belief system centred around faith. She also drew a distinction between religion, which she saw as "an organized group insurance to some sort of doctrine," and spirituality, which for her was "something beyond the physical. Whether it's ... nature or it's a god or gods." She also saw spirituality as something that could be done more privately and in a less regulated way than religion, though she did not see herself as having a spiritual life any more than a religious one.

One aspect of Korean culture to which Cathy felt attached was hierarchy based on age, whereby every family member had a title based on their position and role in the family. Younger members owed respect to older ones, and older members must in turn carry their authority responsibly. For Cathy, this made sense, and it was something she would maintain when she had children. As we have seen, this sort of attitude was not that uncommon among these Buddhist women. Nonetheless, although she liked this element, she also agreed that Korean culture had repressive aspects. For this reason, she would prefer to marry someone who was not raised with a strong Korean background, because she felt this would clash with parts of her personality.

CONCLUSION

In comparing the Buddhist women to their male counterparts, one is struck by the greater seriousness with which most of these women took religion – by whatever definition – in comparison with the men, and this even if they were only "a little bit Buddhist." By seriousness, we do not just or even necessarily mean "greater religious belief and practice." That was generally quite low among these women, although on average higher than among the Buddhist (or Hindu) men. Seriousness also means that these women were more likely to have thought about religious questions, might have done a greater amount and depth of questioning and research, even if, in the end, they decided that religion and spirituality were not for them. These and other gender differences receive focused attention in the next chapter.

That said, as with the Muslims and the Hindus of whatever gender, the male and female Buddhist participants in this study also showed some distinctive features with regard to our central question in comparison to the Muslims and Hindus. After having looked in some depth at their responses in this and the previous chapter, it is worth underlining and repeating some of the characteristics of that distinctiveness. The first is the broad opinion that religion is more of a "there when you need it" affair than it is a "way of life." Although for most of them there was significant intertwining of matters Buddhist with their respective family cultures, with few exceptions – and we profiled one or two of them – Buddhist religion was more optional than that culture. If one of these terms referred to their way of life, then it was more the cultural designation (Chinese, Korean, Thai, Vietnamese, Japanese, and so on) than the religious one. While thus optional, very few indeed therefore judged what they understood as Buddhist to be negative, as for instance mere superstition, habit, or crutch – the most notable, but not the only, exception being one of the Christians. Buddhism was by and large good, tolerant, flexible, and not a "pushy" religion, but by that token, what exactly Buddhism was in concrete terms often appeared to be very vague. It may be that as these young adults get older, found families, and embark on careers, they will become less vague and more engaged with whatever they decide Buddhism positively is – this especially among the religio-culturally based religious seekers and probably especially among the women. The constructive efforts may lie in the future, as they may with our Hindu participants. Although that may seem like a clear contrast with the bulk of the Muslim participants in this study – people who had often been active and even ardent in such constructive efforts with respect to Islam – it might actually not be so much. After all, we know no more about the longitudinal outcome among the Muslims than we do about that among the Buddhists and Hindus. As we saw above, much had changed in the lives of these young adults since they were children and since they were in their teens. That process is likely not yet at an end for most of them. Putting this conclusion in terms of lived religion, as the two just profiled women showed with some clarity, being religious or not, being Buddhist or not, was more often woven into an ongoing process of identity construction – who am I, and what does that mean for what I value and do? – which includes rather imprecise boundaries between what is religious, cultural, Buddhist, Chinese, Korean, or what have you. What kind of Buddhism will emerge out of such lived religious processes is, of course, difficult to say.

The Difference that Gender Makes

LORI BEAMAN, NANCY NASON-CLARK, AND RUBINA RAMJI

INTRODUCTION

In the previous six chapters, we looked in some detail at the three religious background groups, each divided according to the gender of the participants. The logic of this division rested in the assumption that gender difference is sufficiently salient that grouping according to this criterion would allow patterns of response to emerge that otherwise would remain implicit or even invisible, patterns such as those demonstrated by the rather different ways the women and the men were located within our overall classification systems for the three religions. In this chapter, we focus more specifically on this issue, examining differences that the separate analyses of each chapter could not make clear separately and on their own.

To set up this task, we first introduce six young people: Anzan and Tylanni, who are Buddhists; Vaanika and Balram, who are Hindus; and Sabirah and Aasim, who are Muslims. We tell their stories in some length in order to highlight ways in which gender, religion, and culture manifest both opportunities to be harnessed and challenges to be overcome as these young people journey through early adulthood in Canadian society. There are many overlapping features to their lives, such as the importance of family, friends, freedom, and educational pursuits. There are ways that their experiences – and their religious expressions – differ. Sometimes this is revealed in choices of food, clothing, or leisure activities. Sometimes it is expressed in values, or goals, or dreams. As you read their stories here and observe the role of religion and culture as it manifested itself in their daily lives, we draw your attention to the difference that gender makes.

Anzan (BM10) was born in Canada to parents who had migrated from Vietnam. We met him briefly in chapter 9 above. At 19, he attended university and still lived at home with his parents and a younger sister. He grew up in a multicultural, low-income neighbourhood in Toronto, the son of working-class parents. Anzan's mother was a factory worker, and his father worked as a cook in a restaurant. His older sister had moved away, but Anzan was not sure what she was doing at that point. In fact, Anzan was vague about many aspects of his life, and his knowledge of Buddhism was rather vague as well.

Anzan experienced some difficulty defining religion, culture, and spirituality, yet he seemed clear that, for him, being spiritual was taking an aspect of a religion and having an entirely personal goal attached to it. In this way, he saw religion and culture as intertwined. He identified as Buddhist, yet he made no claims to practising Buddhism regularly. When questioned further, he was unable to clarify exactly what being Buddhist meant for him, but it was connected to a "meditative, more of a relaxed philosophy, of thinking and investigation." Then, as if to correct a possible confusion, Anzan stated, "I wouldn't say I'm too religious, no, I'm not too entirely religious."

From Anzan's perspective, a Buddhist was "someone who's always relaxed in a positive way. I guess light and compassion ... always calm ... you argue among yourself about a certain situation." Later on, he stated, "it's more scientific in a way ... it's more of a uniform energy."

Anzan did not meditate, and his knowledge of the rituals in which his mother participated was scant. Referring to his mother's daily use of incense as a form of respect for the ancestors, he mused, "I don't really know what it's used for, but it's for communication and ... yeah, it's ... respect, I guess."

Yet despite his cursory knowledge of Buddhism, Anzan appeared firm in his belief that the main strength of Buddhism today was its "ability to adapt through time." He reported that the philosophy of Buddhism helped him "to relax more, especially through the midterm times right now, with studying, and it helps me think more critically and analytically about subjects." But Anzan did not meditate – the most clarity he was able to offer about practice referred to a "thought process."

Anzan was taking a university course that he believed would help him to discover his personal identity, his life goals, and his future:

Yes, I think at the moment it's part of being unsure of my own personal identity at the moment, so I decided to look back at what I had before or what is neglected in the past going through Chinese class and learning my basic language culture, and I found it was getting interesting ... Like this is going to be your set goal, your set future life, and I need a strong base to support it, so I almost need to define or roughly define where I stand at the moment so I can know where I can go.

The bond that Anzan had with his friends was linked to the fact that "we're all from immigrant families, we're all, I guess, from low-income neighbourhoods, so that's what's the same between us." After talking about friends, he reflected on the country as a whole. He described Canada as like a mosaic: "it's a mosaic of the rest of the world" in terms of the "acceptance and the openness of some religions, most of them, every religion actually is accepted; you learn to understand the rest of the world more because you live in a microcosm of the result of the world itself." Anzan was comfortable with both the vagueness of his religious identity and a diffuse notion that Canada offered him and his friends a place where they could grow and develop.

Anzan's story helps to draw attention to the ways in which boundaries and identity co-mingle in the life of a young person who is attempting to sort out all the complexities of religion, culture, family, and education. As we will discuss more fully in the pages to follow, some of the themes that can be identified in Anzan's story relate to his religious heritage – the subject of chapter 9. Others are observed most poignantly in the ways in which gender and Buddhism manifested in the lives of young people who were part of this study. What interest will men, like Anzan, have in passing along their religious identity to their children? And how are messages regarding what it means to be Canadian and Buddhist learned at home, at school, and within the broader culture? These are questions we pick up later in this chapter. But first we turn to the story of Tylanni, a young Buddhist woman.

Tylanni (BF24) came to Canada with her parents when she was 3, left when she was 7 to go back to Hong Kong, and then returned and remained in Canada from the age of 11. We met her briefly in chapter 10. She bonded with Hong Kong during those formative years there, and Tylanni hoped to move to the country of her birth at some point in the future. Its fast-paced lifestyle was her primary motivation.

Studying history and economics at the University of Toronto, Tylanni was decisive when it came to differentiating religion and spirituality: "spirituality is more of a personal thing whereas religion is more of a group." Her distinctions between religion and superstition are more nuanced: "my grandparents aren't really that superstitious, but they believe in the Buddhist religion, while on the other hand, my dad is really superstitious but doesn't really believe in the Buddhist religion." From her perspective, religion was a good thing "if it doesn't influence too much of the daily life, like if religion isn't like your whole life, then I think it's a good thing."

Religious pluralism characterized Tylanni's nuclear family. "My grandparents are both Buddhists from both my mother's and father's side, but apparently my mom is registered as a Christian, and my dad has a Catholic certificate." Speaking of her own faith, she said:

> I used to do things that were Buddhist because when my grandmother was alive and they used to – on the first or the fifteenth day of the month, we used to burn all these things for the ancestors and be a

vegetarian for the day. We don't really do that anymore unless it was on occasion, and we'd go to the temple and have vegetarian food ... I'd do that back in Hong Kong ... Well, considering that I don't really have a religion, it's not that important, but I think you should have some sort of faith.

During her life, Tylanni had vacillated between some form of practice related to Buddhism and some form of practice related to Christianity. In Hong Kong, she would go to the temple with her grandmother. By 10, when she was back in Canada, she "went back to my Christian beliefs." Interestingly, as a child she compared religions and felt that Christianity suited her more fully.

As a late teen, she reported that she had adopted some of the main teachings of Buddhism – like virtue and self-control – and left behind those aspects of Christianity that she once had practised. She preferred notions of karma and reincarnation to Christian beliefs in heaven and hell: "I think reincarnation is more appealing." Tylanni referred frequently to the notion of virtue, something she clearly identified with her Buddhist background.

She wore a necklace from her grandmother that identified Buddhist symbols: "most of the time I wear it." It was meant to "fend off bad spirits." With a laugh in her voice, Tylanni said she wore it when she had nightmares.

If she had a question about Buddhism, she would ask her dad and then consult the Internet. "Google is my best friend," she confessed. Tylanni and her father discussed religion from time to time, especially Christianity and the Bible, but she said her mother did not really care about her religious beliefs. Her father seemed to want to ensure that she had not adopted a Christian world view.

As parents – especially Asian parents who had immigrated to Canada – Tylanni's mother and father were rather liberal. Her father suggested that she find a partner, "but my mom keeps telling me not until after university." She would bring her friends home when they had been drinking, and her mother's only comment was: "Don't mess up the carpet." Comparing her parents to those of her friends, Tylanni said, "I really like my parents." Her younger brother, on the other hand, whom Tylanni described as "more Canadian," argued all the time with her parents. She claimed that he did not have the Buddhist teachings, having been so very young when they lived in Hong Kong. "He kinda left behind all of the culture," she concluded. But with friends who still lived in Hong Kong, and the Buddhist virtue living in her head, Tylanni reflected, "I'm working my best trying to move back."

Throughout Tylanni's story, you can see various markers of the difference gender made between the young men and women in our study whose religious heritage related to Buddhism. In ways that we will develop more fully below,

Tylanni's family played an important role in both how Buddhism was constructed and why it made a difference. In particular, the overlapping of cultural traditions with liberal notions of parenting drew her even closer to her parents and also to Buddhist concepts of virtue. Gendered ideas of morality and personal goodness were pivotal to her self-understanding, revealing the important interweaving of religious and gender ideology in the social construction of what it meant to be a person identified with a spiritual quest. Tylanni lived her Buddhism differently from Anzan. Later in this chapter, we hint at factors that may help us to understand why this was the case. We turn next, however, to the ways in which gender and Hinduism interface. And here we focus on the stories of Vaanika and Balram.

Vaanika's family arrived in Canada a couple of decades ago from northern India. Both she and her younger brother were in university in different cities; Vaanika (HF02) was in her second year of a master's program in the social sciences, while her brother was completing his studies in computer systems. The family had lived all of their Canadian lives in Ottawa. She spoke and wrote both Hindi and Punjabi – languages that they spoke at home. Vaanika's parents were both university-educated and employed: "my dad works in the government, and my mom works in hi-tech."

Hinduism permeated Vaanika's life: she was a vegetarian; her decisions were made through Hindu morals and values; and she prayed and meditated every day. In fact, she reflected, "I think a religion is a way of life, it always guides me on how to become a better person, and whenever I have to make a decision, it [is] something I can fall back on and not worry about it ... Sooner or later it will be a framework from which I will make all my decisions." Defining spirituality as the inner passion for God, Vaanika reflected on the fact that her entire family network was practising Hindus. "Spirituality is acting out your devotion to God," she said. Sometimes this was done as a collective, and other times one acted on one's own – this was how she lived her religious passion.

For Vaanika, women's responsibility centred around their duties in the home and the well-being of their family – irrespective of whether or not the women worked in the labour force. As she mused about her future, she mentioned that it was doubtful that her prospective family would be able to survive economically without her employment income, yet she believed that it would be her second duty to raise the children and contribute to their upbringing. Reflecting on her own mother, Vaanika concluded, "she wanted to work, and she totally pulled off everything. So, I think it worked really well for my parents and still is ... I find it is something I learned from [them] for sure."

Occasionally, Vaanika and her family would go to temple and participate in the rituals there. The entire family were Ram devotees, and both parents and children had been initiated. Sometimes other relatives would join them on

Sunday for readings and meditation, and sometimes it was Vaanika's family alone. Meditation occurred on a daily basis. Vaanika said that family religious devotion was obligatory when she was a child. In her words:

> When I was younger, I definitely felt ... uh ... I felt forced. I felt obligated and that, you know, at a certain time when we would meditate I had to sit there and meditate, and so it was, um, I got turned off a little bit and very frustrated. And then when I went away to university, um, almost six years ago, I was kind of on my own, and I didn't have any friends there. I used to sit there and meditate, but there wasn't that structure for me anymore ... and then I actually came back, which was really nice, when I came home, I would actually look forward to going to prayer on Sunday, which was really nice and then, now it's all from me ... it comes from within. And, um, I meditate on a daily basis and, um, every Sunday, you know, I like, look forward to prayer.

Reflecting on her own religious practices, Vaanika noted that it brought "a lot of peace and guidance." When she was lonely, it was to these religious practices that she turned. In an interesting way, it was her parents' way of practising their religion that helped Vaanika with the transition to her own religious practices at university. She said, "My parents didn't instill that idea of always going to the temple and praying, or needing to go somewhere or [be] with other people to pray. You can do it on your own time. It doesn't matter what you're wearing, where you are, what you are doing, where you are sitting, um, you can sit in the middle of the street in New York and pray."

While none of her friends were Ram devotees, Vaanika did not see that as an issue. Yet most of her friends were Indian Hindus – even though many did not practise the way Vaanika did. For guidance, she turned to her parents' guru, with whom she kept in touch through email and letter-writing. Her brothers, cousins, and extended family were also a source of support religiously, answering the day-to-day questions for which she sometimes needed answers. However, as she was quick to note, not all of her extended family were Ram devotees or even religious.

Vaanika did not really feel that she had experienced much in the way of religious or cultural discrimination:

> I guess I haven't, and, um, from what I know, I know my parents haven't had that as well. We have been fortunate that there has been a respect and admiration for our, maybe more for our culture than our religion. I guess people, you know, take a look at the colour, and the music, the sounds and the smells and think that's part of our religion and, um, they have really appreciated that ... but then there's always that, you know,

"you guys believe in a hundred gods or goddesses"... kind of attitude ...
But other than that, there hasn't been any prejudice or discrimination.

Vaanika believed in karma and reincarnation: "for every action that's negative, there will be a negative karma-related consequence." For her, religion was
about sacred texts and morals, and spirituality was about practice and devotion. While she did not have a clear definition of Hinduism, Vaanika was clear
that Hindus, no matter what their particular beliefs and practice, respected the
diversity in their religion. She respected the faiths of others.

Thinking of her future, Vaanika said, "I am spiritual and I am religious ...
It's important enough for me to have that in my children ... that's a passion
you want to teach your children about." As a result, she would like to marry
a man who enabled her to stay in tune with her culture and her traditions –
and for Vaanika, it was important that he be Hindu as well. She was open to
the involvement of her parents in the choice of her partner, but she noted, "I
mean it's never going to be like arranged the way my parents were in India."
For Vaanika, she existed between two cultures, and her life was a balancing act
in a way. Of this she reflected: "I have a balance of both types of friends which
means that ... I watch both, you know, Hollywood and Bollywood, and, now
more than ever, I am more into, with Indian culture than I am, um, into the
North American culture ... I have been really fortunate to have a balance even
through my parents ... I cook both Indian and, um, you know, North American food, and I listen to both types of music." Balance was a central theme in
Vaanika's life, with her friends and with her family. And her religious identity
was interwoven through it all.

Vaanika was very clear on how she lived her religious identity. It was very
important to her, and it permeated her understanding of family, of gender,
and of labour – both paid work and unpaid work completed in the domestic
sphere. As a young woman, she saw it as her role – as her mother did before
her – to translate both cultural and religious traditions to her family through
home-based activities. The embodied nature of her religious quest could be
seen in what she did and how she did it. As she said of herself, balance was
important – and included in that balance were notions of Canada and India,
religion and culture, gender and work. These are all themes that were central
to the lives of the young women and men identified with various religious
traditions. But Vaanika, perhaps more than most, talked about them easily and
revealed some of the strategies that she developed to maintain that balance
she saw as so important. In contrast to Vaanika, Balram was moving away
from the Hindu tradition of his upbringing. Yet he appreciated the important
role it offered his family – and perhaps especially now with the health issues
his father had faced. Like her, Balram was close to his family and maintained
strong connections to his broader family network in southern India.

Balram (HM18) was a 25-year-old university student who came to Canada with his parents when he was 9 years old. The family left southern India in search of better opportunities for his father's academic research program. Both of Balram's parents were well-educated, and his two siblings were in university. The family had visited India several times since their move to Canada, most recently for a period of six months when Balram's father was receiving health care treatment there. Both of Balram's parents were Hindus, and their religious and cultural traditions were important to them. This explained, in part, Balram's willingness to accompany his parents to the temple and eat only vegetarian food when he was living with or visiting them.

For Balram, there was a distinction between being religious and being spiritual: "religious is very much, it's a social thing, whereas spiritual can be independent. You can be spiritual alone, while religion is generally, you're with a group of people." The communal, or collective, part of being religious was something that Balram understood well. Even though he no longer considered himself a Hindu – except by the tradition of his family – he still enjoyed the serenity of a visit to the temple or the sights and sounds of its surroundings.

Balram also drew a distinction between religion and culture. He noted that in southern India where he grew up as a small child, religion and culture were tightly integrated – in the Canadian context, less so. Yet for many people, religion offered some form of help, particularly in a time of need. But from Balram's perspective, "it doesn't give me what it gives other people." Yet he realized that "because I grew up in a Hindu household, I'm sure it's influenced me quite a bit."

Family was important to Balram, and in this sense, the persistent poor health of his father had caused him to question notions of karma: "I think something that's unique in my household has been that because of my father's illness ... things you've done will come back to you ... past lives can come back and affect you in your current life. And to me, that doesn't make sense, so I think that would probably be the start of separating from my parents' culture." Yet they were not in open conflict about these matters. Rather, Balram concluded, "they would rather that I believed what they believed, but they understand that I don't."

It was very important to him that his friends had an open mind, that they were accepting of other people's views, and that they tried to understand differences. Understanding religious differences, according to Balram, was critical, "especially now with Islam being in the limelight." He didn't want, nor did he have, friends who were "fundamentalist" in their beliefs.

Regarding Hinduism, Balram was especially appreciative of its flexible nature. "That's what's really attractive about Hinduism is that it's not very strict. They have morals that you can follow, but it's very open to interpretation for yourself." When prompted to identify what teachings he believed were most important, Balram referred to the "importance of family ... helping out in society ... celebrating together." He contrasted Hinduism with other world religions and said, "there are really no books or scriptures that go 'This is written in stone.' It's very much teachings, and they're open to interpretation, and you can say, 'Oh I disagree with it, or I agree with it' and still be a Hindu."

Respecting the religion of his parents, and respecting all faiths, was something that just seemed right to Balram. Later in the interview, he referred to this as the "Golden Rule in Christianity," which he believes is common across all religions. He thought that "by and large most religious people are good people who are living the way they think is best to live," with a strong sense of morality and how to treat others.

From this perspective, Canadian society, he said, was welcoming of diversity. Our policy, which he described as a "mosaic," was open, but Balram believed that Canada needed to do more to make sure that Canadians continued to be unique, accepting, and welcoming of different cultures and to ensure that there was room for integration and acceptance. "I've found that Canadians are very respectful of different people and skin colour and language." But he believed that over the next five to ten years, we would begin to see "more testing of Canada's tolerance for different religions."

For Balram, like other Hindus interviewed, being part of the Canadian mosaic was important and his experience of Canadian society welcoming. As a Hindu male, his religious identity and practice was framed in part by his family of origin, but he was seeking new ways to think about his spiritual practices and ideology in a broader framework. The gendered experience of being a young Hindu in Canada separated women and men along lines that related to the centrality of family traditions and practices. Like other Hindus, he appreciated the flexibility of Hinduism; like many other Hindu males, he had not adopted as many tenets of the religious tradition as his parents might have hoped. Like Vaanika, he was constructing personal boundaries, but his appeared more fluid, less dependent on the way his family practised Hinduism, yet retaining, like her, deep respect for his parents.

In some ways, the patterns observed between Hindu and Buddhist youths – both young men and young women – compel us to draw some parallels, which we do below. But before we turn to them, we look at two stories from our Muslim interviews. For those young people linked to the Islamic faith, daily life was constructed by a variety of religious practices, many of which were visible to other co-religionists as well as to those of other faiths (or no faith at all) with whom they interacted. For the purposes of this chapter, we deliberately chose two Muslims who were very much at the highly involved end of our scale. Sabirah was the lone female in category 9; Aasim was the lone male in category 10 (see table 5.1 above).

Sabirah (MF13) was 20, a young Muslim woman who thought about God constantly and saw Islam as a "way of life." She stated, "Islam ... is like a debt to God ... What I feel, it's just like a way of life, not really like an every week kind of thing." She was born in Canada, and her father came from Kenya, her mother from Pakistan. She had two older siblings, a brother and a sister, both also born in Canada. Her father was an electrical engineer, and her mother stayed at home full-time, although she had a university diploma in early childhood education. Her parents lived in England for a while after getting married and then moved to Canada for her father's job. Sabirah was in her first year of university, majoring in biomedical science.

Sabirah differentiated between religion and culture: "culture is more of a binding of people who live in the same area, whereas religion can be from people from all over the world ... can bring them together. So you can have religion in common or you can have culture in common." She also saw religion and spirituality differently, as highlighted by other individuals: "spirituality just means that you've found your place in the world. And I think religion, you find it with others as well." Religion was of utmost importance to Sabirah: "I believe it's the truth, so I have to put that before anything else. So I believe that that will fulfill my purpose, if I put that first." At the same time, she had a mixture of friends, both Muslim and non-Muslim: all female. She considered herself to be of a higher level of practice than other Muslims in her generation, including her friends. Religion became more significant to Sabirah as she grew up:

> As a young girl ... I used to practise when I was younger, but I didn't know why. So I think when I got older it was more that I knew what I was doing then, and I had a reason behind it. Otherwise it was just, you know, doing what your parents tell you. But when you get older, you look into the sources more, and you say, "okay why are we doing this?" And you kind of try to understand things. So it's a different kind of practising than ... more with your own enthusiasm.

She became more interested in understanding her faith in her early teens, and then in high school Sabirah began reading and learning about Islam herself. She did this by going on the Internet and listening to online lectures or going to lectures that were delivered in the community. While surfing the Internet, Sabirah did not feel the need to ask questions, because "I found that annoying, I'm like, I have to know the basics first. Because I find people start asking questions when they don't have, like, any belief, because it's just an excuse. They start asking questions so that they can avoid it." When she had questions, she searched articles that discussed the understanding of the Qur'an and Hadith. She might search out information from past authorities but did not consider today's imams to be valid sources of authority: "Yeah, like from the past times, like from maybe 200, 300 years ago or before that. Like, most of those imams are authorities, because they're pretty well-known. And their ideas weren't ... they were consistent with the Qur'an and Hadith."

In describing the ideal characteristics of a Muslim, Sabirah included such concepts as being sincere, having a good character and good manners, and being trustworthy. This was done out of fear of God. The most important practice to Sabirah was prayer: "I think like trying to schedule your ... like what you're going to do with the prayer times, that's more important. So that you don't have problems, like 'okay if I go there, when will I, like how will I pray?' Instead say 'okay this is when I'm going to pray and then I'll go here.'" Sabirah held to the global five-pillars model of Islam in her other practices. She prayed five times a day, gave to charity, fasted during Ramadan, and wanted to perform *hajj*. She began fasting around the age of 8. She learned to pray regularly from her parents, in the morning, afternoon, and evening. By the age of 13, Sabirah began performing all five daily prayers by herself. She did not pray at the mosque, because it was not mandatory for women to attend. But she believed it was important for men to attend regularly – she even persuaded her father to attend lectures at the mosque. Sabirah would go to the mosque for social functions, such as Eid celebrations, Ramadan evening prayers, marriages, and funerals. She did not see the mosque as a necessity for female youth, because "the girls, they can find fun things to do themselves. Like they'll get together and you know, they'll just talk ... but it helps create a space for young men."

Sabirah wore the hijab for religious reasons: "I think it's obligatory, but because we live here you get so used to not wearing it. So then it feels like a challenge, but otherwise it's like, it should be something normal that like when you get older you start covering, you know, more." She began wearing the hijab at the age of 13. At the interview, Sabirah was wearing a black hijab, a long-sleeved coat, and a long skirt, dressing in a highly modest way. She stated that it is mandatory for a woman to cover everything except her hands and her face. In Pakistan, Sabirah's mother wore the hijab and covered her face but stopped the practice in England because there were very few immigrants there and she felt unsafe. She began wearing the hijab again in Canada when her first daughter began wearing the veil. After 9/11, Sabirah's father became worried and told his daughters and wife to stop wearing the hijab. Sabirah talked to her brother, who convinced their father that it was still safe to wear it in Ottawa. "I think my brother, like he knows more about the society, you know, how to live here. So he kind of helped explain that to my dad, you know, you don't need to do that, like stop following your religion because you're scared or something."

At times, Sabirah disagreed with her parents, but she was careful to respect them, something that she believed was integral to the teachings of Islam. She tended to differ in opinion from them regarding cultural issues (Pakistani culture): "Yeah, because uh, like our culture is very um, un-Islamic [laughs], and that's a problem at like weddings and, 'okay do you play Indian songs or do you not?' I think there are a lot of things like that. But not disagreements, but we have ... we just discuss it. Like, is this right or wrong?" When it came to religion, she did not have any disagreements. She might go to them when she had a question but did not expect answers from them. At that point, each of them would find their own answers through the sources of Islam. She believed that as long as both children and parents were religious, they would have fewer problems. Jokingly, she stated that "if you're religious, then you know you have to listen to them too, unless they're saying something wrong. So you just listen [laughs]."

Sabirah was critical of Western media for its representation of Muslims. She said that Muslims had become the new enemy. Although she had not outwardly experienced any discrimination living in Canada, she believed that the negative images of Muslims in society would affect her ability to get a job.

In comparison to other countries, Sabirah thought Canada was doing a good job with multiculturalism. Like other Muslims we interviewed, she saw Canada as a religiously tolerant society. "Like, I noticed in the States with my cousins, they're more American-like. And in Canada they, you know, people are ... they're Canadian but they still have their ways. And they're not looked down upon because of that. I think that's the difference." Even though there were negative images of Muslims in Canada, Sabirah felt free to practise her faith freely. "That's a frustrating thing, that people are scared of you or ... That, I think that's the frustrating thing, but practising is fine. There's no problem in that."

For Sabirah, Islam affected every aspect of her life. She found that it was important to always read prayers in many places or events in her life, during any spare moment she might have: "like, you know, if you're going on the bus, you can read a prayer. Or getting up in the morning or going to the washroom, you read something before you go. Waking up, you read a prayer. Like all the time." Islam affected the type of academic career she hoped to pursue, veering away from studying music or drama because it was not "encouraged" in Islam. It affected which political party she would vote for (the NDP are "for gays," so she would not vote for them). She would only marry a Muslim with a Pakistani background, and her parents would arrange the marriage, but she would have the right to accept or deny their choices. She maintained a sexually segregated boundary around herself. She was not allowed to hang out in public places with her female friends, such as the mall or restaurants, because it might lead to inappropriate contact with men. She did not go "out" with friends but might go over to their houses to spend time together and talk. Like many other highly involved female Muslim youths in our study, Sabirah believed that it was important to contribute to society and wanted to be a good role model. She taught children between the ages of 6 and 8 at Muslim Community Services Ottawa.

Negotiating the boundaries of her life as a young Muslim woman was something that Sabirah took very seriously. She was especially thoughtful about her practice of Islam, and this permeated almost every facet of her daily life. In a fashion similar to that of other children of immigrants, she well understood her parents' religious beliefs and practices, but she felt at times torn between the accompanying social and cultural pressures. The embodied nature of her spiritual expression – a theme we develop below – could be seen in the various ways that Sabirah thought about, and lived out, her passion for Islam. While the story of Aasim, to which we now turn, is similarly focused on religious devotion, some of his struggles – and his responses – differed from hers. Here too the interplay between culture, gender, and religion can be seen, very close to the surface.

Aasim (MM03) would turn 25 on his next birthday. He was working on a second degree at the University of Ottawa – in one of the "helping" professions. After working for a short period of time as a personal trainer, using some of the skills learned from his kinesiology background, he had decided that this career path was not really in keeping with his Muslim spiritual identity.

His father, originally from India, and his mother, from an island off the coast of Africa, decided to settle in the Toronto area after moving to Canada. Like many other immigrant families, Aasim's father was in search of better employment opportunities, and both of his parents wanted to see what life was like in a different country. "I guess he must have been successful in finding what he was looking for, because he decided to stay."

Aasim spoke with certainty about his identity as a Muslim and how it was differentiated from his cultural background.

> I can only speak from my perspective, and as a Muslim, that religion is something which is based on hard facts and beliefs based on our holy text and what we believe to be divine instruction. Whereas culture is something which is evolving, changing, based … based on your ethnicity, language, other factors that are, I guess … distinct from religion. The two can merge, but culture can be very different from religion … I believe there is a truth in the world and a person must subscribe to those truths. So religion is not only good, but it's necessary.

From Aasim's point of view, religion gave people values and morals. He practised his Islamic faith regularly, which for him meant "practising the basics, the fundamentals on a regular basis … there's a few things that you can't neglect on a day-to-day basis. They have to be done consistently, like praying five times a day." He expounded the five basic principles of Islam and then identified some of the behaviours he tried to avoid, such as drinking alcohol, eating pork, and "fraternizing with the opposite sex."

On Fridays, Aasim would go to the mosque for congregational prayers, or when he was on campus, he would attend the communal gathering of Muslim students there. He liked to "pray with the gathering," listen to lectures, read the texts, and talk and socialize with other men of similar faith. He said that on campus, doing so was extremely convenient. "See, we have the same values and the same needs, so we try and cater to those needs on campus and help each other, help facilitate the practice of religion away from home on campus."

The biggest challenge for Aasim as a Muslim was linked to the Islamic rules associated with the sexual segregation of society. In the Canadian context it was difficult to adhere to the Islamic ways that men and women should interact with each other.

> So I've found it difficult to kind of adopt these rules that I know are binding on me into my lifestyle just because of the context of the society we live in, where society is not based on these same principles, these same structures. So I find it, not that I don't like them, it's that it's extremely difficult, and I think that's what most Muslims would probably tell you … You constantly have to fight to try and uphold those principles in your own life.

For Aasim, education was the key to dispelling misunderstandings about the Islamic faith or Muslims in general. He believed that the majority of people, Muslims included, were very uneducated as to what Islam actually teaches. He wanted to change that. For him, culture could dilute religion in people's lives, and he felt that the way to address this challenge was for Muslims to practise their faith openly. "Because of the recent backlash and whatnot, people have become a lot more secretive, and people have become hesitant to practise Islam openly and let people know what Islam actually is, because of fear, of further backlash and repercussion."

During the years he spent at the University of Ottawa studying for his first degree, Aasim was quite involved in the Muslim Students Association. He aided in any way he could, offering a helping hand, organizing events, and negotiating with the university administration. This activity was important in terms of his religious development:

> Being given that responsibility I found really pushed me to develop spiritually at a much faster rate than otherwise would have happened. Just knowing that you're responsible for so many people, and having to represent Islam so openly, it forces you to really question your beliefs, question whether you feel comfortable with this, whether it's something you want to be doing or not. And I found that it was extremely beneficial for me.

As he grew stronger in his identity as a Muslim, Aasim began to question and challenge his parents. When he started to educate himself about Islam, he realized that his parents, like many immigrant parents, brought a lot of "cultural baggage" with them from their countries of origin. "I came to a point where I just rejected all of that, and I felt I started from a clean slate, where I threw everything [out] that I was told, threw much off to the side, and learned the basics all over again."

Aasim and his parents discussed matters of faith, but they did not disagree to the point where it became a problem or a strain in their relationship. Yet he felt that his mother "still doesn't feel the importance of the basic things in Islam that we believe women should do, like wearing the hijab ... They're just not values that we share ... She just feels that it's too difficult for her to change at this point in her life." He also disagreed with his parents about the primary importance of education and the extravagance of cultural celebrations like marriages. "I feel like the way it is done culturally goes against Islamic principles."

Aasim wanted to live his life in a way that would "conform to Islamic principles." That was why, a couple of years ago, he left the "whole fitness club atmosphere." It was "not conducive to my spirituality ... and especially with the gender relations, I found that it was not appropriate for me. So ... I decided to come back to school."

Aasim socialized almost exclusively with Muslim friends who thought along the same lines that he did, shared the same values, and tried to uphold the principles of the Islamic faith. In the university environment, he found a lot of support for doing just this. He credited Canadian society for its openness to multiculturalism and a plurality of faith traditions. Even so, there was a lot of conflict between his understanding of Muslim ideals and the Western way of life. Aasim was trying to negotiate these delicate waters and to help other Muslim students do likewise.

The pursuit of truth, as it related to his Muslim identity, was very important to Aasim. In fact, this pursuit in many ways differentiated a large portion of the young people associated with Islam in our study from those who were linked to Hinduism or Buddhism. It marked the boundaries around their lives – how the day was divided between secular and sacred activities – but also how men and women thought about – and experienced – their dreams and goals. Both Aasim and Sabirah wished their parents were as religiously committed as they both found themselves at this point in their lives.

THE DIFFERENCE THAT GENDER MAKES

Exploring the difference that gender makes in our discussion of religion is a tricky business. We don't want to exaggerate gender as a category, and yet as we worked through the data, it was apparent that there were patterns of gender difference that emerged and were worth exploring in some detail on a comparative basis. Behavioural norms, dress codes, social expectations, family duties, permissible roles, and responsibilities within religious organizations are often worked through in gendered ways. Some of these patterns can be summarized under the general heading of the "embodied" nature of religion, to which we will turn in the next section.

One of the challenges in sorting through gender issues is assessing how gendered patterns relate to religion and culture. The interrelation between culture and religion is difficult, if not impossible, to disentangle. Thus, we cannot always accurately assess whether a gendered pattern is religious or cultural. What we can do, however, is rely on the voices of our participants to understand how they themselves linked their religious practices and gender roles, although this too is complicated by the fact that there was no definitive answer from our participants about the relationship between religion and culture. So, for example, one area in which this culture–religion mix was particularly difficult to decipher is dating: for all of the groups we interviewed, women seemed to be less free to date in the usual manner of young people in the North American context. Yet whether this was a cultural norm or a religious one was not always clear. Perhaps more "religious" in this context is the idea that it was okay for Muslim men but not for women to marry outside of the faith (but within the bounds of the People of the Book). Yet as we saw with Aasim above, rules about gender contact were taken seriously by some of the young men as well. For Aasim, working in a fitness club eventually came too close to violating Islamic norms of gender contact.

As we will see later in this chapter, gender plays an important role in the transmission of religion, or, in other words, in religious socialization. Women play a key role in laying the groundwork for the religious practices of their children, being the keepers of home-based rituals and sometimes the initiators of more public forms of practice. Both mothers and grandmothers were influential in our participants' lives and, like Vaanika and Sabirah above, imagined part of their roles as women to include passing on their religious tradition to their children.

The general pattern in North America – and indeed in most parts of the world – is that women are more religiously involved than men are: "existing measures continue to find that women's religious involvement exceeds men's across different nations, religions and types of society" (Vincett, Sharma, and Aune 2008, 5). This seemed to hold true in this study as well, so, for example, among our Buddhist participants there were no male imitative traditionalists, but we found three females in this category. Although this is too small a number to make any generalizations, we would simply note that it follows the general pattern in North America. Perhaps more telling is the relatively low participation rates in the study, and somewhat lacklustre involvement, of both Buddhist and Hindu males. While not as clear in the Muslim group, women in the highly involved categories comprised 50% of all women, and men in those categories comprised 43% of all men. Three out of the 4 (including Aasim and Sabira) in the highest categories of orthopraxis and belief were women. And fewer women than men were in the non-religious categories.

We want to be clear that the patterns we have identified, as the issues we have discussed above, are not without exceptions. Thus, recall Cathy, a Korean Buddhist woman who as a child participated in a ritual with her uncle to welcome spirits of ancestors into the home – a ritual traditionally reserved for the eldest son. And through a number of the previous chapters, we heard stories of fathers and grandfathers providing the foundation on which their sons and grandsons based their religious knowledge and practices. While there were some fairly restrictive rules about dating and gender roles, our female participants were also encouraged by their families to seek an education and to have careers. Ultimately, our point here is that while we have made some observations about gendered patterns, it is important to remember that there is a rich texture to the interview data we collected and that therefore sweeping generalizations are inappropriate. We include below some of our observations about gendered goals and socialization, focusing specifically on the ways our participants both learn to become Hindu, for example, as well as the ways in which they frame their goals in gendered ways. We then turn to the embodied nature of the religious practice and experience of our participants, for it is here that we most often saw gendered patterns emerge.

GENDERED GOALS/SOCIALIZATION
ASSOCIATED WITH SPIRITUAL QUEST

For Buddhist males like Anzan, the concept of identifying with religion is in itself a goal. The identification incorporates the idea of following the philosophy of Buddhism without any particular ritual involved. It involves being moral but also includes being compassionate, calm, and positive. It is one's outlook that makes one Buddhist. The spiritual quest of male Buddhists tends to focus on building a religious identity, through thinking rather than actions. This thought process is further developed through learning – learning about one's culture and language.

Female Buddhists, on the other hand, like Tylanni, also strive for a spiritual understanding of faith, which influences their daily life. These youths search for meaning in Buddhism as well, but it incorporates the values of virtue and self-control with religious consequences: karma and reincarnation. Female Buddhists also seem to associate these Buddhist values with the relationships they have with their parents – following the Buddhist teachings means that familial bonds will remain strong. A main difference between Buddhist males and females is the notion of community: females seem to bond with others who carry the same Buddhist concepts of religious identity. Therefore, their socialization is more than a personal quest: it is a communal goal.

When we contrast the story of Tylanni with Sabirah's, we see clearly that the religious goal for Muslim females is to remember God in all things – although here we are referring mainly to the highly involved. Thus, religion plays a large role in the socialization of Muslim women. The concept of a complete life that revolves around Islam is a strong message found among these female youths. To follow this spiritual quest, female Muslims create delineated boundaries between religious goals versus cultural behaviour. Women should avoid friendships with men, dress modestly, and marry only a Muslim. These goals place limits on their own socialization – Muslim women, like the young women we interviewed, prefer to spend time with other Muslim women. They feel no pressure when they are with each other, since they have all chosen to express their spirituality through action. These actions, in turn, are offered as ideal models for younger Muslim girls. Free time is devoted to the better understanding of Islam and deciding for themselves what is required of a "pure" Muslim, without the influence of culture (both the culture of their parents and Canadian culture). The goal for these women is to immerse themselves into Islam completely, while at the same time making sure that they are able to pass down these same goals to the next generation of young Muslim girls. Yet this immersion does not take place at the mosque with the larger (male) Muslim community but is rather an individual identity, nurtured privately, and is expressed in the way they articulate their faith through daily actions.

Muslim males like Aasim make a strong stand to maintain an Islamic identity within the secular culture that surrounds them (within Canada and the culture of their parents). From this perspective, knowing the truth of faith provides people with values and morals. And so the practices that are performed by Muslim men are based on the principles expounded by Islam: to avoid alcohol and pork and not to fraternize with the opposite sex. Interestingly, the concept of only same-sex socialization seems a much easier quest for women than for men. As they interact with Canadian society, they are constantly feeling infringed upon to mingle with the opposite sex. Here Aasim's words above ring clear. Yet men have a larger socialization structure – through the mosque and the Muslim students associations on campus. Like Aasim, many young Muslim men begin to associate with other young men of like faith once they reach the university campus, with its greater availability of the religiously and culturally like-minded. Rather than physically act as role models, many Muslim men believe that it is through "religious" education that the truth of Islam can be understood and properly followed. The very act of openly being Muslim is in itself the goal, because it develops one's own sense of religious identity and it also acts as a way for others to learn the true teachings of Islam. The same responsibility is echoed by female Muslims, but it seems that women have an unproblematic time being openly Islamic in comparison to Muslim men.

Hindu females like Vaanika see religion as a way of living – all decisions can be made through religious morals and values. Not only is it a way of thinking but a way of behaving. Quite a few are vegetarians and meditate daily. Like her, they wish to pass on these Hindu values and morals to their children. Many Hindu females acknowledge that their actions are influenced by the notions of karma and reincarnation – therefore, practice is as important as devotion. Although religion is a spiritual quest, it also offers social support. Therefore, the desire to maintain these religious goals includes marrying a fellow Hindu so that children will be raised with the same religious passion.

Hindu males seem to understand the communal aspect of religion as well, as they often accompany parents to temples and eat vegetarian food to show respect to their parents. This is the collective expression of the spiritual quest, similar to what was mentioned by Balram. But what seems to be of more importance is the understanding of the concepts that are the foundation of the faith. Even though Hinduism expounds moral values, the idea of interpretive flexibility seems to play a more important role in religious identification – by attending festivities and respecting parents, one can be a good Hindu. Therefore, the action of respect – respect of other views and cultures and religions – is the goal of the male Hindu quest. Although it is a daily quest, it is less defined by "religious" actions than it is for Hindu females. Hindu women seem concerned with passing along the actions and customs or rituals associated with Hinduism to the next generation, while Hindu males seem content with fulfilling the spiritual quest of their faith by the way they see and treat those around them.

The spiritual quest of religion has many overlapping goals within all three religious traditions, but a clear pattern that has emerged is that the women have taken on the responsibility for maintaining spiritual goals through actions, which they hope to pass on to the next generation. Women wish to be role models in order to help the younger generation to follow the same spiritual quest. At the same time, the men all quest for the goal of being virtuous and moral, but these goals are often expressed more through thoughts and outlook rather than through specific actions. Muslim men appear to take the concept of being moral one step further – they must look and act in a way that expresses the truth of their faith.

The way in which a person affiliates with a religious tradition can be considered unique in each instance. Yet at the same time, patterns emerge from the numerous analyses in which people choose to live their lives and construct their religious or non-religious identities. Gender has a role to play in the way men and women are religious. Furthermore, the way women and men transmit their religious identity through practice varies in particular ways, a theme to which we now turn.

Buddhist males tend to identify as being Buddhist, like Anzan, making it a part of their personal moral gauge, but do very little in terms of practice. It is more of a philosophy for the way one lives than a physical expression. The fact that mothers perform rituals does not seem to concern the male youths – they see it as more of a physical expression of the philosophy that they carry with them: to show respect, be positive, and be calm. The way they see themselves as Buddhist is to "think" Buddhist. Thus, religious identity is linked to understanding one's culture. If one can understand where one comes from, one can be "religious."

Female Buddhists also express a desire to be linked to a Buddhist culture. Moral concepts such as virtue and self-control are definitely important – they help to guide one's actions. But to be Buddhist also requires them to incorporate it somehow into their lives, as we saw in Tylanni's story. Faith is not just a thought process but the physical acknowledgement of performing Buddhist rituals, even if just on special occasions. These processes could include going to the temple or being vegetarian for a day. One further identity boundary is raised by female Buddhists: the desire to wear or carry a marker that represents Buddhism. Some wear necklaces to ward off bad spirits, others carry cards of the image of Guan Yin in their wallets. In Tylanni's case, she wore her necklace when she had nightmares.

Practising Muslim youths tend to have stronger boundaries as to what is religious and what is not. Female youths think of God constantly, because their religious beliefs are heavily linked to the way in which they live their lives. Sabirah spoke of this directly. Rather than identifying as being Muslim by what one does weekly or at festivals, for female youth the concept of knowing and remembering God is there at all times and influences many daily decisions. To be Muslim is to "live" Islam. Therefore, physical boundaries are just as important as moral ones. For instance, females do not mix with males, they do not marry people of different faiths, and they do not go against parental wishes.

Religious dictates override those of the cultures in which they are being raised, to the point where these females limit their interactions with non-Muslims as friends and all males in general. One might assume that these females are pressured by parents and other family members to maintain these boundaries, but many of them have come to find their own religious identities themselves, even going so far as to don the veil without parental coercion and in some instances against parental wishes (but always with respect). In fact, many of these young women take issue with the way their parents practise their faith – some mothers do not wear the veil, and if they do, they do not do it properly, according to their daughters. Some fathers fear for their daughters in the way they may be treated in public if they wear the veil. Yet the veil helps to maintain their religious identities, because it helps them to maintain their "modesty" in Canadian culture. They do not exclude themselves from society, because the veil has created a natural barrier in the way they interact with men and non-Muslims.

These practices are further transmitted by young females in that they wish to be role models to younger Muslims in their communities. They take on volunteer positions in camps and focus on professions that will allow them to work with the younger generation of Muslims growing up in Canada. In a sense, they are trying to counter the "Canadian culture" in which they are surrounded, because this culture, through various sources such as the media, often criticizes "Islamic" practices as oppressive (such as wearing the veil for women or wearing a beard for men). In essence, they are becoming the transmitters of religious identity and practice to the younger generation through their behaviour and through their words.

Muslim males are also strongly driven to maintain a boundary between religion and Canadian culture. Many believe that they must maintain a physical barrier between themselves and females in society, even to the extent of leaving their chosen profession. But while Muslim males avoid fraternizing with the opposite sex, they do have a sense of religious community that does not seem to be as important to the women. Following the command to attend mosque on Fridays, males gather with other males, whereas females tend to pray at home or with their female friends in the domestic sphere. Yet at the same time, both genders also reiterate the fact that being Muslim is a constant remembrance. It is not only about praying five times a day or avoiding pork and alcohol; being Muslim is about values and morals. For women, these values are expressed in the way they respect their parents and wish to instill these values in the younger generation. In contrast, the males share their values and morals through community – a male community. Of importance to note is that both Muslim males and females feel that, living in a secular culture that does not understand Islam, it becomes their responsibility to educate and represent Islam to others – for women it is to the younger generation, and for men it is to the general public. Both genders are willing to challenge parental wishes in order to practise Islam in a "purer" way, without what they interpret as their parents' cultural baggage and fears.

Although it has been argued that one can be a Hindu without doing anything, the idea of what it means to be a Hindu to women incorporates the same elements that have been found in both Buddhism and Islam. The way in which one lives is a function of religiosity. Hindu females perform Hinduism through their decisions: they carry strong Hindu morals and values. These values, they believe, make them better people. From this perspective, to show one's devotion to a god is through expression. This is often transmitted through practices in the home but also communally. These physical practices, such as meditation and prayer, are sources of peace and guidance – something they feel can be found through their parents' way of practising Hinduism. Friends supply a strong religious support system as well. There is also an urgent desire to transmit these religious values to future generations – through their own children. The fact that culture is part of religious tradition is important in understanding how Hindu belief is maintained in host countries – Indian culture is an important element for maintaining religiosity.

In comparison, Hindu males understand religiosity as communal activities in large part – eating vegetarian foods and going to the temple. But there is more of a distinction between culture and religion among Hindu males, because religion is more of a physical action than a way of living and thinking. Hindu males seem to straddle the concept of living in two cultures in a clearcut fashion – being Hindu is to perform certain acts, but it is not something that enters into cultural life. Morals that dictate behaviour are considered interpretative rather than definitive. But family continues to play a large role in the way both Hindu males and Hindu females live – respect for family is of utmost importance, as we saw in the lives of Vaanika and Balram.

Both genders in all three religious traditions have built their religious identities upon the firm foundation that respect for family and familial practices are of utmost importance. Each religious tradition is performed in different ways: some are transmitted through the concept of morality and virtue, while others are transmitted through physical rituals. Both men and women show generational differences in the way they understand the rituals they perform, but women seem to be the defining group to transmit these values and rituals to the next generation growing up in Canada. As we have seen from the above discussion, much of the gender differences and patterns reside, perhaps not unexpectedly, in the body. We will therefore turn our attention a bit more fully to that aspect of the gendered patterns we observed.

THE EMBODIED NATURE OF RELIGION

The notion of religion as embodied draws on a range of perspectives that intertwine to help us understand the relationship between body, space, and religious practice. Here we read embodiment in a broad fashion, from ritual practices to clothing to geographic location. Scholars like Robert Orsi and Meredith McGuire have paid particular attention to the idea of lived religion, which we use as a main framework in this book and which focuses on the ways in which people practise their religion in day-to-day life. As McGuire points out, though, lived religion should not be understood as a purely subjective, individual concept: "rather people construct their religious worlds together, often sharing varied experiences of that intersubjective reality" (McGuire 2008, 12). Orsi emphasizes the public nature of "private" religious practice, thus calling us to understand the fluidity of those boundaries and the importance of studying and understanding what people do (Orsi 2005). Both shift attention from belief to practice. Kim Knott further complicates the picture by drawing to our attention the geographies of religious practices (Knott 2005). Thus, we see the clothes one wears, the food one eats (or does not), and the places one practises one's religion as all being within the rubric of "embodiment." We may consider involvement in ritual, commitment to dietary rules and restrictions, or the creation of sacred spaces as related to the ways in which religion is practised and, for the purposes of this chapter, the ways in which gender intersects with that embodiment.

Among those we interviewed we might see the Buddhist men as least "embodied" and more cerebral. As we noted in chapter 9, Buddhist men were not engaged in rituals or practices in a consistent manner, if at all. Yet when we look more closely, we can see mention of "general rituals" and descriptions of Buddhism as "meditative," comments that lend support to the notion that there is in fact an embodied element to their lives that links to their (sometime) self-identification as Buddhists. For the seekers, the idea of returning to a homeland and living as a monk was mentioned, a project that would clearly contain a significant shift in embodied reality. But there were more subtle comments that point to an embodied Buddhist approach that was articulated as "relaxed" or "open."

Buddhist women were similarly cerebral, although they were more likely to engage in rituals and practices, like Tylanni in our opening story. A number of the Buddhist youth expressed dissatisfaction with ritual and practice without a concomitant understanding of why they were engaging in a particular ritual or practice. For Tylanni, the concept of virtue was very important. It seemed that the Buddhism that was transmitted to them was not in fact cerebral enough, and for those inclined to identify as Buddhist there was a need to move past "mere" ritual to a deeper understanding that many seemed to feel could only come through the intellect. For Tylanni and others, culture had not been left behind – it was living in their heads. Another young Buddhist woman, Eileen (BF06), as we saw in the previous chapter, expressed it this way: "What I don't like is when people say – I don't like strictness, for example when people say, 'if you're Buddhist you have to do this, this, this, and this.' From what I understand, that's not essential in Buddhism. For me, what's essential is that you understand and that you have a thirst, a curiosity for learning and to do your best."

While there was occasional mention of the wearing of pieces of jewellery by some of the Buddhist women, which was, for them, linked to religious or spiritual practice, there was nothing that would "mark" their bodies as being linked to any particular religious practice to an outsider. This, of course, is in contrast to both Muslims and Hindus.

For the more observant Muslim men and women at the higher end of our 10-point scale, daily prayer, five times each day, constituted a core religious practice. This practice is embodied geographically by being performed in relation to the location of Mecca and by using the body as an instrument of ritual. However, where, exactly, prayer is performed, especially in relation to the mosque, can be different for men and for women. As one of our participants noted, "but, like the mosque is not really somewhere that ... Men go every Friday, to pray, but women don't really have to, they could if they want, but going to the mosque is not a big deal for Muslims, for women especially." We saw a similar public/private divide between Hindu men and women. For the women, ritual practice was much more likely to be situated in the home than in the temple, which was seen as largely irrelevant to their religious practice.

On the other hand, many of the Hindu males seemed to embody their faith through extended family networks: their Hindu identity was constructed in the way they understood Indian culture. Rather than performing rituals to frame their religious identities, they placed value on family connections.

Muslim men and women also share modesty of dress as an outward symbol of their religious commitment, although there are great variations in the translation of this ideal. Nowhere is it more complex than the wearing of hijab by Muslim women, like Sabirah in our opening stories, a practice that has taken on disproportionate significance and garnered an inordinate amount of attention in the non-Muslim world. Although Muslim men may wear a beard (and our higher-on-the-scale male participants mentioned this as desirable), it does not distinguish them in the same way that Muslim women are distinguished through the "veil." A variety of studies have affirmed the wide range of reasons that Muslim women cover their heads (Hoodfar 2006) and the disproportionate and alarmist attention this practice receives (Bakht 2008).

As observed in chapter 5, the two "orthodox" women we interviewed both wore hijab and saw it in terms of religious observance. Not all of our "highly involved" women wore the veil, but the majority saw it as an ideal worth reaching as a way of fully embodying the tenets of their faith. Of those who did, our findings bear repeating. The 12 of the highly involved women who did wear the hijab gave a variety of reasons for donning the veil. One woman felt that it was part of her identity, another for reasons of modesty. A few of them met with parental opposition to wearing the veil. One woman said that her father considered it "backward-minded for women to wear it." Another woman stated that her mother believed that by wearing the veil, she was losing her rights as a woman and a Canadian. Another woman began wearing the veil because her aunt bought it for her, even though her mother felt it too restrictive. 9/11 also played an important role in her desire to identify as a Muslim in Canada (see chapter 6, 119–20). Our study confirms, yet again, that the issue of head covering is complex, is often expressive of women's agency rather than their oppression, and, in short, cannot be simplistically categorized or understood.

Of note is the fact that the women who did veil did not mention any fixed method of veiling, but they held the concept of veiling as a personification of the purity of Islam. It was their way of being "better Muslims."

Food plays an important role in each of the religious groups we studied, whether in the form of dietary restrictions, special meals during holidays and festivals, or as part of ritual offerings. It is here that we see one of the more pronounced and sustained gendered divides that carries across the groups who participated in this research and indeed could be identified as something that women across many religious groups have in common: without a doubt, it is predominantly women who labour in the kitchens and men who enjoy the fruits of those labours. As Holtmann and Nason-Clark put it in chapter 7, Hindu mothers have cooked their way into the hearts of their children and communities.

Food also plays a central role in Islam: not just in the foods that are acceptable and prohibited (pork and alcohol) but also through fasting during the month of Ramadan. Although the Muslim women were highly individualistic in the practice of their faith, breaking fast during Ramadan allowed them entry into and an opportunity to partake in the larger Muslim community, since many of them went to the mosque with their families during these occasions. These communitarian events seemed to augment a sense of group identity, with a majority of the Muslim women maintaining that a major aspect of Islam as a religion was the idea of global community.

As with food, it is most often women who manage the physical home space related to religious practice. For Hindu women, this may mean the creation and maintenance of a home shrine and engaging in *pujas*. Among our participants, Hindu women were much more likely to maintain some sort of ritual practice than were the Hindu males. Many Muslim women noted that a significant role of Muslim women was to raise children and take care of the home, even if they had jobs. Although the Muslim women in this study were pursuing higher education, the majority still lived with their families and did not talk about living on their own – that would happen with marriage. In many instances for highly involved Muslim women, the home played the role of a sanctuary, because it helped to maintain the boundary of sexual segregation and also allowed them to pursue their own investigations into their faith. Home space is a much understudied geographic location of religious ritual that requires more research to fully appreciate the pivotal role it plays among religious groups and for individuals.

For Muslim women, there is an interesting generational split, which we observed among some of our participants. Somewhat surprisingly, it was sometimes the younger generation (our participants) who were more religiously observant or conservative than their mothers. This took the form of more regularly observing prayers or wearing hijab and more modest dress. As we saw in chapter 6, for Irshad, for example, career took second place to the idea of having a Muslim husband and family, a prioritization that was in direct contravention of her parents' wishes that she be a career woman. Thus, not only gender but generation (including social and cultural context) had an impact on the ways in which religion was practised by some of our participants.

At the same time, there was mention that fathers were sometimes less practising. For instance, Sabirah found that her father used to be considered "the cool dad," because he let his children listen to music and watch inappropriate movies. But as each of our participants began their own individual searches into their religion, they found ways of seeing how their parents differed from them in practice. The most important aspect among all our participants in the way they formed their religious identity (apart from what they learned from their family) was the personal investigation they undertook to better learn about their religious traditions, whether to become more practising or to leave certain aspects of the faith behind.

CONCLUSION

We return to the stories of the six young people we introduced at the beginning of the chapter: Anzan and Tylanni, who are Buddhists; Vaanika and Balram, who are Hindus; and Sabirah and Aasim, who are Muslims. In each of their lives, there are themes that arise out of the interviews. These themes include the way they saw themselves as religious or as spiritual. Anzan's story reveals how challenging it will be for young men to pass along a specific and systemic religious heritage to the next generation if their own identity is rather porous and their commitment to it remains mostly cerebral. For Tylanni, on the other hand, Buddhism was tied to what she did, particularly in the context of family living. While morality and personal goodness interweave both their stories, it was Tylanni who explicated this more clearly as part of her spiritual quest. Her lived religion included systemic religion in clearer fashion than did Anzan's. The two Hindu youths whom we highlighted revealed the gendered intermingling of culture and religion as it is experienced within the generation of young people whose parents have chosen Canada as their new home. Vaanika, like a good number of the other Hindu women in our sample, was already thinking about how she would be engaged in translating her culture and her religion to her children. And for her balance was important – balance of both a religious and a practical nature. In many ways, she embodied the quest for balance between her own dreams and the dreams of her parents for her successful career. Although Balram, the young Hindu male we highlighted, was in the process of moving away from his religious heritage, he will almost always be connected to it at some level through his family network – parents and extended relatives here and in India whom he respects and cares for deeply. The flexibility he saw in Hinduism will, no doubt, enable him to continue to live in a way that allows him to harness some of the strength of family and faith when the ideal of Canadian multiculturalism meets with the reality of daily living.

While fluidity and flexibility are central features of both Buddhist and Hindu identities, for the two Muslim youth we highlighted, Islam presented a stricter way of translating the faith into everyday life, which permeated, at least ideally, every dimension of life. For Sabirah and Aasim, their beliefs and practices as Muslims sometimes presented challenges to their lives at university and at work. Boundary negotiation was thus a prominent feature of the lives of these Muslim youths. For Sabirah, this boundary maintenance and negotiation was predominantly a private issue, although she shared it with her girlfriends (both Muslim and non-Muslim). For Aasim, boundary maintenance involved both private struggles and sharing in community at mosque and through the Muslim students association to which he had belonged on campus. It was associated with many practices as well as rather stringent beliefs. Some of the practices can make it difficult for young men and women to negotiate the restrictions they have placed upon themselves in order to live an "authentic" form of Islam. Negotiating the boundaries of their personal and religious lives was something that many Muslim youths in this study took very seriously, and although some found it difficult to maintain, they all felt that they were able to practise their level of faith freely in Canada. For women, it was often a private issue, although it would be shared among other young women of Islamic faith (and non-Muslim women who shared the same values and morals). For men, it was often a communal activity – something they did together. But both men and women in this study demonstrated the same level of fluidity and flexibility in deciding how to define "authentic Islam" and how it was to be lived on a daily basis.

Gender matters when it comes to the nexus of religion and cultural boundaries – that is the story that emerged from the interviews that were conducted with young men and women linked to Buddhist, Muslim, and Hindu faith traditions. They each embodied a religious identity in very different ways. As we consider the impact of this, it is imperative to focus on the way men and women are religious, or how they live their religious lives. It is also critical to consider the transmission of religious identity and practice and the ways that this transmission itself is gendered. One can add to that both the gendered socialization of the spiritual quest, the embodied nature of religious belief as well as its practice, and, of course, how boundaries – especially religious and gender ones – are constructed and maintained over time.

Growing Up in Toronto:
Muslims, Hindus, Buddhists

KATHRYN CARRIÈRE

Born and raised in the Greater Toronto Area, I have always had a sense that "my" city is not like the rest of Canada. To be sure, the fact that most of my friends and family live there helps make the city seem particularly welcoming for me. The foods, the sights, the smells – they all give Toronto an exciting and dynamic "vibe" for me. As I walk through neighbourhoods, I see many temples, mosques, churches, and synagogues, each giving its members a place where they can practise their faith. But, when I look at the ways religious devotees relate to one another and peacefully interact outside of their homes and places of worship, something tells me that Toronto is more than just a multicultural urban centre. Even after years of attending university in other regions of Ontario, I return to my hometown feeling that there is something special here. What is it that makes Toronto so special? Why are the people who live there so proud of their religious and cultural backgrounds? Or is this assessment just a product of my imagination?

Perhaps my sentiments are unique to members of my own faith community, Christianity. Maybe I simply see Toronto as an accepting and wonderful place to live in because I, as part of the religious majority, have never experienced anything but institutional and social recognition. Never having to venture too far to find a church to pray in and never having to ask my bosses for permission to take religious holidays off, I would be lying if I said I felt my religious needs were not accommodated by mainstream society. And having been born and raised in the Greater Toronto Area, perhaps I simply "hang out" in Christian-centred neighbourhoods and likely chose to avoid workplaces that neither recognize nor cater to the religious needs of their employees. Or maybe my religious belief system gives me rose-coloured lenses. In fact, it is very possible that people outside of the Christian community or even those who may not be as familiar with the city's urban landscape as someone like me experience greater difficulties when seeking to religiously navigate and integrate into Toronto. Are those who don't celebrate Christmas or Easter given the opportunity to practise and adhere to their religious beliefs? And do they feel any less a part of Toronto than those who fit in the religious majority? Is this city just as special to them as it is to me? These are important questions when one seeks to sketch the cultural and religious landscape of Ontario's capital city.

Put briefly, the research reported here suggests that although I may have a more positive attitude than many and perhaps most, the experience of many young adults from the Toronto area who do not share my religious identity is not overwhelmingly different from my own. Many, in fact, share my sentiments to a significant extent: they also believe that particular institutional, socio-cultural, and religious factors enable them to move relatively easily among various meaningful identities and thus live their lives as they envision them.

Two obvious questions in this context are, of course, whether the Toronto region is peculiar in this regard and whether our results for Toronto are representative of or peculiar to the subgroups we examined. With regard to the first question, could one not come to a similar conclusion about life in other major Canadian cities, not just the other two in which our research project was carried out, Ottawa and Montreal, but the other largest immigrant-receiving cities in the country, Vancouver, Edmonton, Calgary, and Winnipeg? The short answer to this question is "quite possibly." Unfortunately, our project does not permit such a comparison, since we did not have a comparable density of participants even from Ottawa and Montreal and of course next to none who grew up in the other cities. In addition, the participants who did grow up in Montreal or Ottawa did not refer to the environment of their cities nearly as often or in as specific terms as that much larger number from Toronto. Two other studies, however, give at least a partial indication. Paul Eid's study of second-generation Arabs in Montreal (Eid 2007) provides at least some evidence that growing up in Toronto or Montreal may not be vastly different, although his study does not include any direct comparison and therefore significant differences may simply not have had a chance to emerge. Similarly, Kamal Elizabeth Nayar's study of Sikhs in Vancouver (Nayar 2004) includes focus on the second generation, but since her research did not include Sikhs in other cities and ours did not include Sikhs at all, comparison is again not directly possible. With regard to the second question, Janet McLellan's study of Ontario Cambodians (McLellan 2009), which included the second generation, does indicate that what our study reveals about growing up in Toronto probably does not apply equally for all subgroups. What these comparable studies reveal, therefore, is that the analysis we offer in this chapter remains at the level of a contribution to this overall question of city differences; it is anything but conclusive.

The overall sample of our participants, as noted many times already, consisted of male and female university students who came from immigrant families of Hindu, Muslim, or Buddhist background or identity. As in the overall sample, those from Toronto varied greatly in their levels and style of religious involvement and commitment and had roots in a very wide variety of countries. Some were born in Canada, while others migrated as children with their families. They were enrolled in a broad array of academic disciplines and had an assortment of political and social orientations. They often spoke about their lives, beliefs, and plans for the future with a candor that reflected confidence and optimism. Listening to their narratives, we noted how they spoke about Toronto, and the things they knew made their city somewhat different and, according to them, perhaps even exceptional in terms of religion and culture.

One of the questions our research posed concerned multiculturalism and its real-life effects on the religiosity of our participants. It therefore came as no surprise that many of our Toronto informants believed the city's multiculturalism to be one of its key identifying features. Trickling down from the national level, where the policy was first implemented by Prime Minister Pierre Elliott Trudeau in 1971, Toronto's multiculturalism now reaches far beyond the basic coexistence and institutional recognition of diverse people. As one Toronto participant put it, referring to the multiculturalism policy, "I think it had a much different influence on Toronto ... this multicultural place [with] so much noise and activity ... I dunno, like to me, that's one of the coolest things about Canada, that's why my parents came here, y'know, like ... Trudeau, multiculturalism, y'know? Like ... I'm not a hugely nationalistic person, but that's probably the thing that makes me most proud to be Canadian" (HM06). While perhaps exceptional in the way he phrased it, a number of participants, as we saw in previous chapters, shared this broad sentiment.

DENSITY, DIVERSITY, AND ITS CONSEQUENCES

The most obvious "difference" that being in Toronto makes is that it has become a city demographically – if not, of course, politically and economically – dominated by immigrants and their offspring. At the time of the 2006 national census, somewhat more than half of the residents in the Toronto metropolitan area were either immigrants or the children of immigrants. About 44% of the population declared themselves to be members of visible minority groups (Statistics Canada 2007). Recent Statistics Canada projections see this figure surpassing 60% during the next two decades (Caron Malenfant, Lebel, and Martel 2010, 30). Although adherents to non-Christian religions probably constitute no more than about 15% of the population as a whole, they likely constitute close to one-quarter of the immigrant/second generation and visible minority population.[1] Moreover, although these populations are more heavily concentrated residentially than non-visible minority populations, they are still broadly spread across the metropolitan area, with the result that most people "belong to demographic minorities." Religiously, however, Christians, both immigrant and non-immigrant, are still in the clear majority (see Beyer and Martin 2010, 93).

A great many of our participants were well aware of and commented on this demographic difference, and most of them declared that it made a qualitative difference to living as a member of a religious or ethnic minority in Toronto. The meaning of that difference can be gleaned from listening to a small sample of them. Here are some representative statements:

Maybe it's just Toronto, because when I say Canada, I know that the rest of Canada is really different from Toronto ... I've been to other parts of Canada, like Montreal, and I guess I just like Toronto 'cause it's a lot more multicultural, and people are a lot more accepting ... I believe that Toronto is one of the places in the world that's undergoing like ... a really special social experiment where, like, so many people of so many different beliefs and values and cultures come together in this one place and numbers are really highly represented. Like, even minorities are still significant minorities, you know? So, there's a lot of significant minorities in Toronto and stuff like that that [take] up a significant portion of the population, and it's almost never been done in the world before, like in other parts of the world, so it's really ... it makes Toronto sort of special. And I like that. (BM07; 20-year-old ethnically Chinese male)

Canadians on the whole, I think so, yeah. I mean, look at Toronto. That's probably the only city you'll see like that. But it's the most multicultural city in the world, and I think there's a much higher tolerance in Toronto for different cultures and different religions. (BM15; 20-year-old Sri Lankan Buddhist male)

I think ... Canada definitely is more multicultural than some places like ... I mean there's particular cities like Vancouver and Toronto that obviously ... To me, multiculturalism is just having the different cultures all together, y'know, um, the different religions, the different beliefs and all that, it's living in that society where there's Sikhs, there's Muslims, there's Christians, y'know, there's Hindus, whatever, and um ... But it's also just getting along with each other and respecting each other's religions, y'know, that's what a good multicultural society is, so ... (HF19; 23-year-old Indian Hindu female)

It's sort of a tolerance for everybody's individual perspectives, celebrations of their culture and the partaking in that. And I think it's wonderful, especially in the school system where you can do that and people can talk about their traditions, talk about their festivities. And I think Toronto is a wonderful, wonderful, rich example of a city where you can celebrate anything under the sun, publicly or privately, y'know, on the same streetcar, y'know, um someone's passing out sweets 'cause today's Holi, today's a Hindu festival, as chance would happen. (HM12; 26-year-old Guyanese Hindu male)

I'm going on a ramble but I think … Canada's a great country for immigrants, and I think it's important that we foster this multicultural atmosphere that exists here. And I think it's only natural that we will use, or like the Canadian government uses it to their advantage, to sort of sell Canada as this amazing you know, non–melting pot multicultural society. One of the few in the world where you can find every single ethnicity. And in Toronto it's a perfect example, you can find a place to eat for every single culture you can think of, you know. Like, that's pretty incredible and good authentic food, you know … You sit on the subway, and you can really say wow, there's someone of every colour on this train. And I'm like, that's pretty cool. And I think it's a really amazing thing, to be honest. (MF32; 20-year-old Muslim female of mixed South Asian and South American origin)

Of course, not everyone who ventured an opinion was quite so effusive, and some assessed the consequences of this diversity rather differently. Yet widespread was the recognition that although cultural and religious diversity are officially mandated at the national level in Canada, the fact that Toronto's streets are full of people from all over the world makes multiculturalism a real and tangible element of everyday life and thus renders the city extraordinary in comparison to other urban centres. It may, of course, be that, like myself, these participants were seeing their city through rose-coloured glasses and that most of them really had no basis of true comparison with other cities, but this was nonetheless their perception.

Although they in no sense negated these positive attitudes, some participants analyzed the reasons for and consequences of Toronto's "density of diversity" a bit differently. Two examples of such assessments can illustrate the difference. For some, the acceptance of multiculturalism and diversity could at times seem grudging, a fact of life in Toronto whether one liked it or not, and if one didn't, it was difficult to express that publicly. As Hasan, an Ismaili Muslim, put it, "I just feel like in Toronto, it's just … a little more open and not spoken of, because there's just – living in Toronto alone you have to accept other cultures. You can't be – you can't be an explicit racist in Toronto" (MM24). Mehdi, a young man from an Iranian family, said it a bit more harshly: "In Canada, you can associate with everybody, they treat you very well – but they hate your guts. I mean, they don't show it, but … we have such a diverse ethnic background in Toronto, in Canada … that nobody can show their, ah, individual thought patterns" (MM33).

For others, the density had a side that was at times positive and at times negative – namely, it allowed people to follow the human tendency to "stick to their own kind" and not actually mix. Anju, from a Hindu family, put it rather graphically when she said:

> There is also the multiculturalism that is being practised in Toronto …
> You can literally live in your own enclave and have your postman who
> is Indian, you can have your bank teller – actually this is the reality of
> my life – your bank teller can be Indian, and not really have to know
> English almost. Your doctor can be Indian, your dentist is Indian …
> You know what I mean? Seriously … So, in that sense is multicultur-
> alism working, or is there something else that people would find more
> comfort identifying with? There's so much, and I don't know my exact
> thoughts on it. Obviously, as a whole there are problems with this
> notion that we are one big happy family. (HF08)

Krishna, a 25-year-old whose parents migrated from India, said much the same thing but was a bit more negative in his evaluation:

> I find that now, over the past few years, cultures are becoming more
> isolated, so you go to parts of Toronto, and you can meet people who are
> born here, who really don't speak English or don't speak English well,
> or who either came here maybe 15, 20 years ago and they're fine with
> that because they live within their community. But I have a problem
> with that. I think Canada needs to do more to make sure that Canada
> is going to be unique, because Canada accepts and welcomes different
> cultures, but it also has to be unique because we are able to get them to
> integrate well together and so far, we have not been doing a good job in
> that. Hopefully, we will change that. (HM18)

Clearly, Toronto was not utopia for our participants, but overall there were many things that they felt were, if not unique, then certainly special, and that specialness affected how they lived and how they lived their religious lives.

MULTICULTURAL NEIGHBOURHOODS AND FOOD

Even though various respondents talked about multiculturalism at the governmental level and how certain policies encouraged people of all faiths and cultures to coexist peacefully, most participants spoke more about the multiculturalism that they saw and interacted with on a daily basis. Among the multicultural aspects they mentioned were the ethnic neighbourhoods that are scattered across the Greater Toronto Area. From relatively small and clearly delimited neighbourhoods like the Spadina/Dundas Chinatown, the Greek Danforth, College Street's Little Italy and Corso Italia, the Indian Village on Gerrard Street, Dundas West's Little Portugal, and the Christie/Bloor Korea Town (or KBA, Korean Business Area) to great swaths of multicultural territory in Mississauga–Brampton–Bramalea or Scarborough–Markham, the list seems ever growing.

Such ethnic neighbourhoods provide members of particular communities with a variety of stores, restaurants, and services specifically tailored to their tastes and needs. While walking through Toronto's Little India, one notices the many Indian dining establishments and grocery stores, providing their clientele with the opportunity to prepare and consume authentic dishes, which often include many imported ingredients. Accordingly, Little India allows Indian-Canadian migrants to pay tribute to their heritage by facilitating the continuation of meaningful food ways. Rajya, a Hindu female, for example, said: "There are changes … like Indian stores, like Indian restaurants and those new places opening up. There was a time when you had to search high and low for a place. And now, you know, it's booming everywhere, and people are trying Indian cuisine and things like that" (HF28). Rajya recognized that the urban tapestry of the city was not always so multicultural. Now, because of the ever-growing ethnic population and their specific cultural and/or religious preferences, businesses have evolved and diversified to better serve more diverse consumers. Many migrants have opened up ethnic businesses and dining establishments – to earn a living, of course, but also with the intention of introducing a little bit of themselves and their own culture to greater society through a mutual love of food. In fact, quite a number of the participants mentioned that their parents owned or worked in such restaurants. This is, of course, not a unique Toronto development or feature, but it is one of those that seem to make a difference in this as undoubtedly in other large urban areas.

Access to certain types of food also affects the religious practices of some communities. As in our sample as a whole, a large portion of our respondents in Toronto identified either fully or partially as Muslim, and many of these young men and women declared that they followed Islamic halal dietary laws. In the increasing number of Toronto neighbourhoods with pronounced Muslim populations,[2] finding halal grocers, butchers, and/or restaurants is no more difficult than locating a McDonalds or Tim Hortons. Twenty-year-old Laila, for example, claimed that it was easier than ever to keep a halal diet in Toronto. She said, "But you know how Toronto is, on every other corner there is some halal burger shop or halal pizza shop" (MF26). As a busy university student, Laila, like most young adults her age, often had no choice but to eat on the go. Taking time to eat a well-balanced homemade meal was often not an option for her, with her daily commute from Ajax to Scarborough and her large amounts of never-ending schoolwork. But because of the numerous halal fast-food and take-out options available to her, Laila did not need to compromise her religious beliefs for the sake of convenience. The ease with which she could locate restaurants that catered to her dietary restrictions encouraged Laila to continue "being" Muslim outside of the domestic context. Arguably, adhering to such restrictions presents less of a challenge than it might in cities with fewer Muslim residents and fewer such areas of concentration. Still, in this regard as well, Laila might have been reporting a recent development, because others said that it was not always so easy in Toronto.

Even for members of other community groups, visiting Toronto's ethnic neighbourhoods provides them with the chance to experience different cultures and culinary tastes. Nyla, an 18-year-old Muslim whose parents migrated from Guyana, expressed just this when asked about multiculturalism in Toronto. She said, "Multiculturalism? I think there is a lot of it. I like how there's little communities all around Toronto, like Chinatown and yeah, the little Indian area, the Italian area, Korean ... Yeah, you can learn about different cultures by going to that area. You can try their food, and you see their stores and different clothes and everything" (MF06).

Nyla saw Toronto's multicultural environment as a learning opportunity. Being able to experience personally the flavours and food ways of numerous global communities on a local level allows people to interact with other cultures on their own terms, without international or even intercity travel. The kind of interactive multiculturalism that so many of the participants stressed as the only real multiculturalism is comparatively easier in this urban environment.

Beyond satisfying personal dietary needs, the ease with which individuals can access culturally specific ingredients, spices, ready-made meals, and even cooking tools also importantly permits the ongoing practice of particular religious rituals that are dependent on key cultural components. On a very basic level, most religions have "rituals that include some form of feasting, either directly or symbolically" (Lightstone and Bird 1995, 38). A very important component of these rituals are the offerings that worshippers give for their deity(ies). Hindu devotees, for example, present their gods and goddesses with edible offerings, or *prasad*, of fresh fruits and vegetables, grains, dairy products, and oils; Theravada and Mahayana Buddhist worshippers present oil, candy, fruit, mushrooms, and rice at various shrines both inside and outside temples.

Certain spices and foods used for worship, though common in more tropical parts of the world, may be difficult to find in North American contexts. Grocery stores that cater primarily to Christian communities may not stock items that other religious communities require in order to pay tribute to their god(s). Other religious groups, in these instances, are forced to flexibly adapt to their circumstances and make do with whatever items they are able to forage. Hinduism, for example, has "traditionally proven to be flexible about [ceremonial] details" (Parsons 1994, vol. 22, 66). When particular foods are not available to be put forward in worship, presiding priests or celebrants recommend suitable substitutes. While such ritualistic adaptations are a part of life for many religious communities who are minorities in the areas they inhabit, it appears that members of such religious groups in Toronto have more tools available to them to enable the seamless continuity of their rituals.

Tara, an 18-year-old Hindu whose parents migrated to Canada from India, for example, mentioned the importance of *aarti* in her family's worship. *Aarti* is a Hindu ritual that involves lamps, the wicks of which are soaked with ghee (clarified butter) and a plate with flowers, incense, and *akshata* (a special type of unmilled rice blended with turmeric). She said, "there's one gathering, like in Markham, like every month. The family has a gathering; we have prayer, like chanting and then singing of religious songs. And then afterwards they'd have their *aarti* – like the tea lamps and all – and afterwards there'd be food, and then people would eat. So it was a couple of evening gatherings" (HF11).

Although Tara did not explicitly say it, each tiny component of *aarti* interacted with the others to make the ritual comprehensively meaningful and important to her and her family. And the meal that was shared after the people performed their *aarti*, more likely than not, consisted of Indian food that typically required particular *masalas* (ground-up spice mixtures), which, although often made from scratch using imported spices that are easily available in Toronto's wide selection of Indian/Asian stores, can also be purchased premixed and ready-to-go. The convenience of pre-made spice mixtures can save South Asian families a great deal of time, which in an urban landscape can be very precious.

MULTICULTURAL AND MULTI-RELIGIOUS RESOURCES

Besides the food-related ritualistic aspects, many other sorts of supplies are necessary for performing various forms of religious worship. Special types of incense, candles, garments, and even music are required for many of the rites that our Toronto-area participants spoke about. William, who immigrated to Canada from Hong Kong at the age of 3, talked about how easy it was to be Buddhist in Toronto. When asked specifically whether Buddhists were able to fully practise their religion freely in Canada, he replied, "Yeah, I mean, there's been an explosion of Chinese culture in the Markham area where I live and I guess in Toronto too with Chinatown ... So, it's not as if there's an absence of supplies or anything for them" (BM16).

Although William and his family belonged to cultural and religious minorities in both Toronto and Canada, within certain areas of the GTA they were in the majority or at least in the largest subgroup (Beyer and Martin 2010). The many stores and services provided there, as discussed earlier, cater to the particular needs of the East Asian community. And because of the large concentration of Buddhists in Chinatown, various shops there carry common prayer items that might be difficult to find otherwise, such as butter lamps, *tingshas* (metal symbols), and *thangkas* (portable images of the Buddha). The convenience of having such prayer and ritualistic items available not only enables worshippers to practise various elements of their faith more easily but also may serve to reaffirm the validity of their beliefs as well as their belonging within the Greater Toronto Area in that they can interact with others (i.e., the shopkeepers and other customers) who share their world views.

Anita (HF32), who was born in India and arrived in Toronto when she was 6, told us that her sister passed away soon after their entry into Canada. Despite the emotional difficulty of the situation, Anita's family was able to follow through with the expected and appropriate religious rituals. She said, "I know we still followed through with the traditional Hindu rituals ... like we cremate, so [my sister] was cremated here, and the ashes were taken back to India. That was when I went [back to India], when I was 11" (HF32). Following ancient Hindu tradition, Anita and her family most likely took part in the *homa* fire ritual, when a special funeral priest leads specific rites designed to bless brass water-filled pots. Oil lamps are solemnly passed over the body of the departed, and flowers are offered to the gods and goddesses. The water from the brass pots is then used to wash the corpse, while incense is burned. According to Anita, her family did not encounter any difficulties in meeting the appropriate Hindu ritualistic standards. The brass pots, lamps, and incense would all be relatively easy to locate in the very South Asian Brampton community where they lived. In terms of cremation, in India a *homa* (or fire) shelter with a wood-burning funeral pyre is typically used to cremate the body while hymns are sung. In the Greater Toronto Area, however, because burning and disposing of human remains outdoors is illegal, Hindu congregations and the communities they reside in have had to adapt. Many funeral homes in Brampton and Toronto are very familiar with the particular ritualistic needs of Hindus. Some funeral homes permit sacred wood and ghee to be placed inside the coffin with the body, while other homes allow the body to be carried around the cremation chamber (in traditional Hindu fashion) while prayers may be recited. Various funeral homes also permit the cremation switch to be pressed or flipped by the chief mourner, who in Anita's sister's case was likely her husband (if she had been married), father, or eldest brother. Such accommodations by funeral parlours and directors are primarily due to the fact that mainstream society (in both Brampton and Toronto) has so much exposure to and interaction with the very organized Hindu religious community. Their large demographic presence affords the recognition of their voices and the subsequent meeting of their needs. To be sure, adjustments may have to be made, but the accommodation to their different needs is also significant.[3]

Seema, a young Hindu woman who lived in Brampton, also spoke about how effortless it was to continue particular rites and religious practices. She said, "Everything [we require] we have here ... Especially living in Brampton" (HF24). Seema recognized that for members of her community, maintaining congruities between Indian and Canadian religious culture was relatively easy. She was also referring to the many Hindu temples, or *mandirs*, that can be found dotting the landscapes of Brampton and its surrounding areas. These *mandirs* range from liberal to very conservative and from very large with over 5,000 members to very small, some located in family homes. And that is just in the Brampton region. When one factors in how many temples can be found in the Greater Toronto Area, it becomes apparent that Toronto Hindus indeed have a wide variety of choices available to them in their search for a suitable house of worship. Seema informed us that her family did not regularly frequent one particular temple but rather attended various ones throughout the Toronto area on an occasional basis.[4]

The notion of choice when finding a temple or mosque came up very often during our Toronto interviews. Toronto's ethnic neighbourhoods have a large number of culturally specific religious institutions where members of different communities congregate, worship, and socialize. Because levels of zeal and liberalness/conservatism vary from devotee to devotee – in addition to already existing linguistic, cultural, and ritualistic variations in practice – many cultural and/or religious community groups have created worship centres that reflect their particular beliefs and customs. There are so many ethnic, sub-ethnic, and religious communities with significant numbers throughout the Toronto area that members are able to form smaller, personally relevant assemblies much more easily than perhaps would have been the case decades ago when community groups were neither as large nor as organized. Zaina told us that Etobicoke's mosque situation was very different today[5] from the way it was in 1976 when her family first arrived from Iran. She said, "I'm not sure as to the number, but there weren't even half as many as there are now. Like there really wasn't ... Like, I guess people didn't have the incentive to build mosques or like start up mosques" (MF46). Zaina recalled how difficult it had been for her and her family to plant meaningful roots in one of the few-and-far-between mosques.

The existence of such an assortment of temples and mosques, according to our participants, enabled them and their loved ones to participate more easily in the religious community(ies) of their choosing. Anita, a practising Hindu, conveyed this when she said, "I mean there's always new temples popping up everywhere. I mean, I think that way it's like, there is that community. There is that chance for them to have their own religious practice, have their own place to worship; like that we've had that chance to flourish" (HF32). Anita recognized the important role that belonging to a religious congregation had in facilitating personal and communal growth for members of her community.

Because they are able to locate and participate at temples and mosques that they feel better represent their particular beliefs, practices, or needs, many Greater Toronto Area migrants and their families choose and are able to remain loyal to one particular house of worship. Maryam and her family, for example, left Tanzania to come to Canada when she was just 1. Attending the same downtown Toronto mosque, or *jamatkhana* ("gathering place") as she refers to it, since she was a child, Maryam as a 26-year-old adult remained very attached to it today. She claimed:

> Okay, I grew up downtown. And we used to go to this *khana* called Dundas West. And then we moved to the suburbs. But because of, like, our community and our relationships were so strong at Dundas West, when we moved to Mississauga, we didn't go to the *khana* in Mississauga. We kept going to the *khana* on Dundas. So, I go to the *khana* on Dundas on the weekends, and then on the weekdays to the *khana* in Mississauga because it's closer. But I would say I would affiliate with the *khana* on Dundas West. (MF22)

The friends they made and the beliefs they shared, in her family's opinion, were worth the extra effort and commuting time it took to get from Mississauga to Toronto's west end. Only on weekdays, when there was more traffic and less spare time than on weekends, did Maryam choose to attend the more conveniently located suburban *jamatkhana* closer to her Mississauga campus. The main point, however, was that she had the choice.

The convenience and variety afforded by many mosques and temples was something about which a good number of our Toronto-based participants spoke when discussing their faith. Often they chose to attend a variety of such establishments and not just one. For those whose lived religious orientations valued diversity of praxis and beliefs, the coexistence of a variety of establishments allowed them the freedom to nurture their faith as they saw fit.

Within Hinduism, a religious system that features a wide variety of gods and goddesses and an even wider variety of names for these divinities, having many temples spread throughout the Toronto region gives worshippers the choice as to which god or goddess they should focus on at a particular time. For example, a Hindu may choose to attend Mississauga's Lakshmi *mandir*

during the Diwali season but may attend the Ganesha Durga temple for Ganesha's birthday, which typically falls between late August and late September.
Because Hinduism has so many deities and individuals are more or less given
freedom to choose which one(s) to pray to, devotees can potentially run into
quandaries when attempting to celebrate the birthdays of their gods and/or
goddesses as part of a spiritual community. For those living in the Greater
Toronto Area, having so many *mandirs* to choose from reaffirms the spiritual
priorities of Hindus in that they are much more likely to find a suitable *murti*
(or statue) to offer *prasad* to, as well as like-minded devotees with whom to
partake in the rituals. The situation contrasts markedly with settings where the
Hindu population is not thick or rich enough to afford such variety, a situation
that is still largely the case in cities like Ottawa and Montreal (see, e.g., Sekar
2001, admittedly on research that is now more than a decade old).

Lali, a 24-year-old practising Hindu, talked about the importance of commemorating feast days within Hinduism. She told us that she had always been
able to locate and take part in the birthday celebrations of her favourite gods
and goddesses. She said, "Because we have hundreds of gods, every so often
there's a birthday here, a birthday there and celebrations and whatnot. So I
attend all these functions, and I participate actively. I may not be organizing
them, but I definitely do attend" (HF38). Although Lali's school schedule prevented her from having co-ordinating or organizational roles in such festivities, she enthusiastically partook in the events that various temple committees
planned. Because of the wide variety of events available for such devotees to
attend across the city, many Hindus can be fluid and flexible in the ways they
choose to worship.

Rajya also told us how she supported the activities of temples throughout
the city. She said, "I've been to other temples in Toronto and things like that.
I've gone to things that my cousin, might [go to]. If they have a holy show, I'll
go and support her or whatever. If I have family who is doing *puja* at a temple,
I'll go there to support them" (HF28). Rajya's spiritual practices in this sense
were not limited to a particular religious community and the rites they celebrated. She was able to take full advantage of the choices available to her. In
this instance, Rajya visited various temples not only to cultivate her own spiritual beliefs and give herself a broader religious experience but also to convey
her support for the activities and beliefs of her family. And in attending such
functions, she was declaring her belonging within her wider family circle. In
supporting temple functions that were important to her cousins, aunts, and
uncles, for example, Rajya was reasserting the importance of the desired role(s)
that the religious dimension should play in their lives as Hindu adherents.

Our Muslim respondents also spoke about the roles that mosques played in
maintaining community morale. Twenty-six-year-old Maryam said, "I would

say that people go there to talk, to meet, to socialize for sure. And then there's like the whole support system that comes with it" (MF22). Much of the literature on immigrant religion confirms that the purpose of religious communities transcends the strictly religious realm. Advice on child-rearing is shared between mothers, and men discuss politics, the weather, work, and sports. Youths, in the meantime, may gain comfort knowing that they are not the only ones who have to deal with overly strict or old-fashioned parents. People are able to reveal thoughts, ideas, and values that might not be entirely appropriate, relevant, or understood in everyday life outside of their religious community(ies) by those of other backgrounds with different beliefs.

Islam, like Hinduism but not to the same extent, as we have seen, also serves as a kind of "umbrella category" for an assortment of believers from a variety of sects and cultural groups, each with their own ritualistic modifications and interpretations. Sunnis, Shi'is, Ahmadiyyas, and Ismailis (to mention only those found in our sample of participants) all operate within the broad framework of Islam. And because Toronto is such a diverse and heavily populated region, with recognizable numbers of many ethnocultural religious communities, mosques need not cater to the Muslim community at large but rather can represent smaller denominations and ethnic/regional groups. Nyla, for example, told us about how difficult it would be to be part of a mosque that focused on Middle Eastern expressions of Islam, because she and her family had become so used to the Guyanese Muslim congregation that they were a part of. She said, "in my mosque and my family, there's not really anyone from another country that's Muslim, and in my mosque there's no one really from other countries. It is mostly just our family and other Guyanese people" (MF06). Such a specific culturally affiliated mosque is a luxury not all Muslims are afforded, especially those living in regions with lower concentrations of Muslims of any stripe.

A particularly important element of the urban mosques that participants talked about was the role they played in supporting new migrants. Providing a culturally, religiously, and even linguistically familiar context for individuals and families who had recently been uprooted from or simply left their support networks in their homeland, temples, mosques, and other places of worship serve as key locations where religious adaptation and sociocultural integration begins. Maryam, a Muslim whose family came to Canada from Tanzania, a country with a relatively high ratio of Muslims to non-Muslims, told us how the mosque crucially serves as a safety net and morale booster for immigrants: "We also have different, like, you know, tutoring for kids, for newcomers, that kind of support for newcomers. So it's definitely community-based, and it's important to me" (MF22). Because of the high number of migrants entering the Greater Toronto Area, religious institutions have become accustomed to helping with new migrant adaptation through social networking as well as fol-low-up care in order to ensure comfortable living and to help reduce the level of difficulties they might encounter.

Some participants from Buddhist families also told us that their temples had important cultural socializing roles. For example, Anu, a 22-year-old Buddhist who came to Canada from Sri Lanka when she was 5 years old, stated that the Greater Toronto Area had at least two Sinhala Sri Lankan temples that specifically catered to the cultural and religious requirements of the Buddhists of her community. Anu says, "Whereas, I mean, we have ... two Sri Lankan temples. So there's one in Scarborough, and there's the one in Mississauga" (BF22). The presence of such Sri Lankan temples suggests that members of their community recognize the linguistic and cultural differences separating them from East Asian Buddhists. Unlike the majority of Buddhist temples in the Toronto region, the Sri Lankan temples have Sinhalese monks who are able to relate to their congregations on a very personal level because of ethno-cultural similarities. Anu specifically focused on the roles that the monks played in cultivating both spirituality and morality within the next genera-tion of Sri Lankan Canadians. She said, "And [in] the [temple] in Mississauga, the priests are very open with the kids, like the youth, and they're able to get across to the youth much better than the priests here, in Scarborough" (BF22). Serving as a bridge between older, more conservative generations and their often-times Canada-born children, her temple priests used faith as a common tool to close generational gaps. Anu acknowledged the critical importance of connecting the younger generation with their faith and suggested that without such a connection (as apparently was the case with the temple in Scarborough) the temple's close-knit community would deteriorate with time.

SCHOOLS AND EDUCATIONAL CONTEXTS

Also pertaining to migrant youth, many of our informants spoke about the role religious education had for members of their community. A very large portion of our Toronto-area Muslims, in particular, had attended such schools in their childhood, as offered by their mosques and Islamic associations part-time during the school year, on weekends, and full-time in the summer. Almas, a 21-year-old Muslim, explained the purpose of Islamic school. She told us:

> I mean, in the summer we would go to classes [at the mosque] and learn to read the Qur'an and stuff like that. Some mosques do [have Islamic school], some mosques don't. I believe there's a couple that are sort of more youth-based. Generally, [the community teachers] generally over-look the youth sometimes, I think. They sort of overlook the youth, and so some mosques, they realize it as an issue and try to, they sort of, I

guess in terms of trying to respond to youth needs, they don't really address issues that youth are going through. But, sort of like younger kids, they will teach them how to pray, like religious principles and stuff like that, but not sort of [the] issues that people face in school or with peers and stuff. (MF28)

Because Almas attended a multicultural public grade school during the school year, she was unable to receive the Muslim education that her parents wished her to have on a daily basis. By taking part in Islamic school, she was able to familiarize herself with what are considered basic spiritual viewpoints and principles, within a Muslim environment, as taught by Muslim teachers and community leaders. Although particular issues, such as how to deal with non-Muslim peers, are not always addressed in these mosque-based classes, simply having a Muslim education is considered beneficial in a religiously diverse city where religious values can easily go awry. Twenty-six-year-old Maryam also spoke about religious-based education, telling us, "We have our religious schools, and we have seminars and stuff like that, yeah. I mean, there's been a lot of seminars on being a Muslim kid today, [on] Ismaili youth today" (MF22). Maryam attended these classes herself, having immigrated to Canada with her family from Tanzania when she was just 1 year old. In these schools, Maryam learned how to be an Ismaili youth in Canada – something her parents might not have been able to help her with. Among peers her own age, from her own particular stream of Islam, Maryam could openly discuss and question values and beliefs that were communally accepted. Recognizing the importance of having religious educators, Maryam was continuing to volunteer her time, teaching religion at Saturday school to Grade 5 students about twice a month.

Nineteen-year-old Nahla also attended weekend school with other Muslim youth when she was a young girl. She said, "we had a Sunday school, and it was really small but ... there was a lot of community building there" (MF05). And because of the school's effectiveness in capturing the interest of youths and applying Islamic principles to everyday situations, the mosque expanded its educational vision and offered a summer youth program to members of its community. Despite a lack of resources, minimal funding, and relatively small potential enrolment, Nahla's mosque community was able to offer young students a variety of meaningful courses:

It was really crude, but there were only three components which was [sic] the actual rituals, history, and the Arabic language. But it was done well. And the students there, there was like very few of us, like a dozen, maybe two dozen maximum ... of all ages, so like starting from kindergarten to Grade 8, like Grade 8, Grade 9. But it was nice, because the teachers were really passionate about what they were teaching. They were sensitive to our questions. (MF05)

Neena, a 19-year-old female, also attended Muslim school during her child-hood summers. Like Nahla and Maryam, Neena considered her time there very rewarding, both spiritually and socially. Because the area where she lived in Scarborough had a large concentration of Muslims, Neena was able to car-pool with a number of her Muslim public school friends to Islamic day-school during the summer:

I went to summer Islamic school, me and my brothers and my sister, we all went. Yes, we all went to summer Islam school in the mosque in Scar-borough. So I learned a lot from there, like stories and stuff. That was a lot of fun, like it's supposed to be. Islamic school was fun 'cause it was just like, you know ... something to do in the summer, 'cause usually the summers you would have off and you would just play, but that was good. Yeah, like, me and my friends, they were family friends, we used to car-pool to Islamic school. (MF37)

The fact that Scarborough, like many other parts of the Greater Toronto Area, has very large and well-organized Muslim communities meant that young Neena could experience an overlap of her private and public identities. Many of the friendships Neena cultivated existed in both the public school and Muslim school context. With a variety of the same friends in both arenas, Neena had a social continuity that many migrants from less diverse areas might not ex-perience.

The density of Islamic educational opportunities gives parents in the GTA a choice. Many mosques offer their own religious school for the youth of their community; some parents opt to simply send their children to the school af-filiated with or located within their place of worship. Yet in light of the other possibilities and the ease of commuting, other Muslims attend schools that are farther away but more meaningful for a variety of reasons. For some parents, it makes sense to have their children go to a school in which their cousins are enrolled, even if the school is across town, as was the case with Umar, who claimed, "I used to go to like another school out in the west end [of Toronto], 'cause my cousin went there" (MM16). Other parents choose to have their sons and daughters in day-schools known for their orthodoxy or highly educated instructor. And still others enlist their children in religious schools that are closer to their workplaces. And even if students attend a particular school for one session, many are able to switch schools relatively easily for subsequent terms. What is important for this discussion is that Toronto-region Muslims have much more choice than Muslims in other areas do, and this is simply due to the vast number of migrants who live in the city and its suburbs.

Beyond evening, weekend, and summer Islamic schooling, there are also Muslim high schools that some of our Toronto-area informants attended.[6] They range from smaller neighbourhood schools that focus on one particular Muslim group (such as the Ismaili school) to large-scale all-girls and all-boys schools that serve the wider community. Irrespective of their size, however, Toronto Islamic schools provide Muslim youth with the fundamentals of their beliefs in a faith-based environment while concurrently demonstrating their commitment to the provision of a sound education. Math, science, English, history, social science, and physical education are offered alongside Islamic studies and Arabic. Special regulations allow the simultaneous observation of religious rules, such as permitting girls to wear their veils during gym class and separating the genders in certain situations such as swimming. The skill sets cultivated within these religious schools remain flexible enough to permit students' subsequent entry into and easy adaptation within post-secondary educational institutions, as the experiences of some of the university-based Muslims we spoke with indicated.

For the participants who simply attended public elementary and high school in Toronto or its suburbs, not being part of mainstream Christian society was never a big issue in terms of their social acceptance or opportunities available to them. In fact, many individuals told us that because most of their classmates were also ethnic minorities, they felt that much more accepted. Anand, a Hindu male of Sri Lankan background, told us that his urban grade school was so multicultural and religiously diverse that the fact that he was Sri Lankan and Hindu was hardly an issue. He said, "I went to a very multicultural school in Scarborough ... It was just [as diverse as] U of T. Scarborough, that's just how my elementary school was. In my young age there wasn't much distinction of race or religion" (HM13).

Eighteen-year-old Tara, a Hindu, also mentioned her educational experiences but at the Catholic high school she attended. Despite her status as a practising Hindu, her parents chose to send her to a mainstream religious school, because they recognized the shared basic common values between the two faiths. At her Catholic high school, Tara encountered many other Indian Hindus whose parents had sentiments similar to those of her own. And to her surprise, these Indians were what she referred to as "Catholic Hindu" (HF11), meaning they practised the Catholic faith, took part in the prayers and rituals, but simultaneously continued to consider themselves Hindus. Tara said:

[My high school friends] would be Indian, but they wouldn't be like ... I went to a Catholic high school. And there I met Hindu friends who

were Catholic but Catholic Hindu. So they would practise the Catholic
religion, but they were still Hindu. Like, I don't know how to explain
that. They were more like a mixture. I had friends like that ... We used
to pray the rosary every morning and stuff. Like, it was really religious.
And some friends I had were really religious in their beliefs, so that
made me feel like, actually more religious. I think that's another reason I
became more religious – like, seeing them all. They used to go like pray
before an exam and all; that made me think maybe I should do that too.
But I'd do it in my own faith. (HF11)

The religious syncretism Tara encountered, though surprising to her, in fact
is not unusual. For example, scholar Peter W. Williams considers religious syncretism the result of encounters with spiritual and/or religious others. In his
exploration of popular American religion, Williams (1989) finds that when
individuals are transplanted into circumstances where they are no longer surrounded by co-religionists, new and innovative hybridizations, rituals, and interpretations of traditional belief and praxis emerge. Particularly in urban and
immigrant contexts, religious syncretism is a meaningful part of everyday life.
For Tara and her friends, the religious diversity of their high school encouraged them to fuse together traditionally distinct beliefs and reinterpret/re-
negotiate them to form a fresh and personally significant religious framework.
Mixing institutional Catholic symbols with Hindu beliefs (and vice versa) was
not something that rendered them "insincere followers" but rather gave these
young adults an integrated spiritual montage they clearly valued.

A large number of our student participants continued to live with their parents while attending one of the three University of Toronto campuses. This
university is the largest in Canada and yet is far from being the only post-
secondary institution in the Greater Toronto Area. Therefore, participants all
across the region could attend university very locally. Living at home, students
were more able to maintain important family and community ties. Among
participants attending university in Ottawa, more than a few told us that their
level of religious observance had declined considerably because they were
living away from home in another city. The sizable number who stayed at
home in Toronto, however, were far less likely to report a similar change, often
continuing their regular family-based practices without problems or issues.
Beyond this, they preserved their social connections with relatives and community acquaintances, which also served to reinforce the cultural beliefs and
religious practices of their childhood.

Because Toronto is both the most multicultural and most populated city
in Canada, it only makes sense that the University of Toronto's student body
reflects this diverse urban landscape. Many of our respondents commented on
the benefits of going to a school alongside students from all over the world,

with varied religious beliefs and cultural practices, although here we should stress, as we did in chapter 2, that this sort of experience is common on many of the large urban university campuses in Canada. Khalid, a 22-year-old Ismaili, for example, told us:

> I've a lot of friends from like different races and things like that. I have like a group of ... friends that are older than me, they're three years older than me, that I knew from high school ... And yeah, I feel a small sense of community with them. Um, with six or seven of us. We're all very accepting of each other, not necessarily of other people, we don't look down on others or anything like that. (MM24)

Similarly, many of 20-year-old Salima's closest friends did not share her Muslim background. She said, "If anything people are like, 'Wow, you have a lot of white friends!' But, like, I make friends with people I'm comfortable [with]" (MF40). Although Salima did have friends who shared her Pakistani cultural background and had religious beliefs similar to her own, she did not racially, culturally, or religiously discriminate when seeking new friends.

At the University of Toronto, students have a great many campus clubs and associations that they can join if they wish. They include student groups geared toward particular cultural and/or religious communities. And many of our participants discussed the impact these groups have on their religious and/ or cultural identity. Many of the young Muslims we spoke with, in particular, recognized the value of cultural and/or religious campus clubs. This, of course, is not unique to universities in Toronto, but the density of such associations may well be. Muslim students in particular often attributed great importance to the role of Muslim students associations (MSAs) in this regard. Especially in the aftermath of 9/11 but also more generally, a number of the Toronto Muslim students said that they felt themselves to be in a situation of having to justify their beliefs to others. MSAs often played a role in assisting in this task, as well as in allowing Muslims to feel more at home on campus.

Zaina, a second-generation Muslim from a Lebanese family, for example, told us just how important the Muslims Students Association and other associations were to her. She said:

> I think there's a strong Muslim community on campus, that's one of the reasons I chose to come here ... They're very involved with students and with Muslim students and they'll do a lot for you. Like, if you need something, if you have, say, there's an exam and I needed something, they'll contact the – or they'll help you and tell you how to go about, maybe doing it later on, or they're very helpful ... I like the environment here, and you have like a lot of different things you want to get involved

with, 'cause like I'm not only involved with like the MSA. I was involved
with the Arab Student Association, I was involved with the Students
for World Justice. There's different organizations I'm interested in, I get
involved in, so it's not strictly Muslim. (MF46)

For Zaina, the MSA's presence illustrated the established nature of the Muslim
community at the University of Toronto (she was at the large downtown St
George campus). She knew she would be among like-minded others who
shared her cultural values and religious beliefs. Alongside hundreds, perhaps
thousands, of other Muslims, Zaina was able to reach her academic goals while
not compromising her beliefs.

Nineteen-year-old Nahla, also Muslim, spoke similarly of the role of the
Muslim Students Association on the University of Toronto's main downtown
campus. She told us:

Do you remember that this year at St George [the MSA] provided *iftar*,
which is where you eat to break the fast? Every day. And it was excellent.
It wasn't just your regular pizza. They actually had a meal. They would
have good Indian rice, and lamb curry, and chicken and salad and fruits
and vegetables and pop. And it was every day and it was open to anybody. So ... we had a lot of obvious non-Muslims going just for the free
food, but that was really good. (MF05)

Nahla was clearly impressed with the level of organization of the Muslim Students Association as well as with the resources at their disposal. Such multicultural on-campus events serve to draw attention to and educate the general,
non-Muslim student body in some important Islamic beliefs and rituals. Because all students of diverse cultures and religious backgrounds enjoy deli-
cious food, especially when it is free, *iftar* allows Muslims to proudly display
important elements of their identity to interested others. While Muslim student groups at other universities outside the GTA might have similar aims,
they are less likely to have at their disposal the myriad Indian caterers and
restaurants that the MSA at the University of Toronto has. Because of the vast-
ness of Toronto's ethnic communities, this student association was likely able
to search around until they found a caterer that was able to work with their
requirements and budget. In cities where ethnic, here Indian, caterers may be
scarce, costs for events such as the daily *iftar* over the entire month of Ramadan would be much higher than they would be in a diverse, heavily populated
city like Toronto where ethnic businesses competitively lower their prices so
as to gain clientele.

Because of its very large Muslim population, the University of Toronto (at
each of the three locations: downtown, Mississauga, and Scarborough) per-

mits students to use its space for prayer and worship-related purposes. Nahla, who came to Toronto with her family from Bangladesh at the age of 11, told us that she attends *jum'ah* (Friday prayer) with her friends at Hart House, which is the university's cultural and arts centre. She told us: "I don't really need to go to a specific mosque, because I pray *jum'ah* on campus every week. And that sort of fills the community involvement rule of the religion, because it's a huge *jum'ah*. Everybody comes there, and there's about 200 people at least at Hart House" (MF05). Nahla was able to fulfill her religious *jum'ah* requirements on campus instead of having to deal with the inconvenience and bother of commuting to a mosque from downtown. Interestingly, however, Nahla attended the Mississauga campus's *jum'ah*, which she actually preferred:

> When I go to UTM [University of Toronto Mississauga campus], it's even a bigger *jum'ah* there … it's really big. Do you know Spiegel Hall? It's half of Spiegel Hall is filled, and there's two *jum'ah*s. And it's nice. I've made friends with a few people. We hear the *kuthbas*, which is a sermon, before the actual Friday prayer. Sometimes it's students, sometimes they're guest lectures. And I like the ones at UTM better actually because I find the *kuthbas* there are more relevant to student life, whereas the ones here are more generic. But I think it's just, it's not a really big deal. (MF05)

Another benefit of having such a religiously and culturally diverse learning environment is that students, as Nahla mentioned, are able to befriend other members of their community, which can serve to rekindle interest in their own beliefs. In meeting other students with similar values, students are able to convey elements of their faith that are important to them. Likewise, students are able to talk and engage with other students who may share similar experiences with them, such as dealing with overbearing parents or dating, thus providing social support. Noor's friends, for example, decided to wear the hijab at the same time that she did. She said:

> My friends, it's funny 'cause they almost went through the same transition as me a little bit afterwards. So, like, pretty much none of them wore hijab; they all started wearing hijab. They started practising, started looking into and stuff like that … I started wearing hijab like six months ago, not even. And this other girl she started – like she's my good friend – she started wearing it the same day as me, but I didn't even know. (MF04)

Noor's story points to the significance of the substantial friendship networks in matters of religion for these Muslim women. Yet it also indicates the frequency of religious transformations among Muslims in this age group (especially ages 18 to 23) and that these decisions are personal: each of these women came to the decision to wear hijab somewhat independently, although peer support is obviously an important part of the picture. The decision to wear the hijab in an environment where there are few Muslims, and few Muslims one's own age, can be very difficult, but Noor's rendition gave no hint of such difficulty. Toronto has a very large Muslim community; a great many of the women wear hijab in various forms. The presence of these women may be comforting and even inspiring to young Muslim women, such as Noor and her friends, who are considering wearing the hijab.

Many of the Hindus we spoke with also talked about the large portion of their friends who shared their cultural and religious beliefs. As with the Muslim youth we spoke with, these students had available to them Hindu students associations that served as an on-campus support system and social network. Lali told us: "I was part of the Hindu Students Association ... The associations are mainly built because most of us in university [have ceased] residing with our parents. So it's just a way to keep in touch with our religion so that we continue to celebrate those auspicious days, um, without missing them to the excuse of school" (HF38). Lali recognized that she would have more contact with the Hindu faith if she chose or was able to live with her parents at home. Yet living downtown, nearer to the University of Toronto, Lali was able to continue observing auspicious days in the Hindu calendar through her connection with the Hindu Students Association. Furthermore, Lali claimed that the vast majority of her friends had comparable beliefs, which served to further cultivate her religiosity:

> I'll start by saying that 90% of my friends are Hindu, and I think my experience was, uh, is pretty representative of quite a few people raised in Ontario, where most of us have gone to public school. And Canada, being a very multicultural country, there were all cultures around me, and I had the choice to be friends with whomever I pleased. But you naturally migrate towards those of your own culture and religion just because of the ease of making that friendship and keeping that friendship. It's not more of ... it's not a discrimination at all, it's more of just a comfort level. So yeah ever since I can remember, 90% of my friends have been Indian and Hindu just for the pure sake of comfort and ease. (HF38)

For Lali, it had always been easier to make friends with those who shared her religious values and philosophies. Within the university context, she was able to attend religious feast days and academic events with the same people, providing her with a continuity not afforded to the entire multicultural and religiously diverse student population in Canada. Lali could cultivate her spirituality and her friendships simultaneously, which is a reality that most students at the University of Toronto experience on a regular basis thanks to the presence of more than 100 recognized religious and cultural student groups and clubs on all three campuses.

In the scope of our interviews, there were a variety of other factors that seemed to render the Greater Toronto Area unique in enabling individuals to combine or switch among various cultural and religious identities. For example, many of our informants were heavily involved in culturally and religiously specific events. Many of them took part in various cultural and religious art forms at the University of Toronto and cited student groups to which they belonged, events they helped to organize, and fundraisers in which they took part. Because Toronto is such a multicultural and multi-religious city, it is no wonder that its largest post-secondary institution works to support various student clubs and organizations that reflect the academic, professional, cultural, religious, and social diversity of its student body.

Twenty-two-year-old Buddhist Nuveena, for example, talked about a Sri Lankan Buddhist art event at the University of Toronto at which she volunteered. She said:

> I did help out last May ... with a Sri Lankan art and Sri Lankan Buddhist art [event]. And it was at U of T, that's how I actually found out about this thing, my friend who was working with that, she sent me the contact ... And it was more like a historical aspect about how the different ones, certain periods of time during the changing of the kingdoms and how ... Buddhism and its artwork changed accordingly. (BF22)

Although the event did not seem to have been focused specifically on Sinhalese Buddhist practices or beliefs, it did allow Nuveena to bring particular elements of her cultural self to the forefront in her academic life. She was able to show her support for her community and serve as a cultural representative of sorts – a role that she might not have been allowed to play within her or her family's Buddhist temple because of her age, gender, and even relative lack of life experience when compared to her communal elders.

MEDIA, MULTICULTURALISM, AND RELIGIOUS DIVERSITY

Participants also reported having easy access to religious and cultural forms of media because they resided in such a multicultural region, where so many other members of their community lived. Because of the large and often concentrated migrant populations in the Greater Toronto Area, there are many services that recognize their needs and rent, broadcast, and/or sell ethnic films, music, and literature. Eighteen-year-old Tara, who was born in India, said, "well, from here, from where I live, there's like a five-minute drive. Like, there's a place we rent movies and I also buy movies from. So it's nearby, and then I usually get [Indian films] from there" (HF11). Unlike Indian migrants living in regions where there are very few other members of their community and accordingly have no access to cultural media, Indians living in Toronto and its suburbs have countless ethnic resources available to them, including specialty channels and shops that make accessible even the most dated of Indian films. In that vein, Rajya told us:

> Before, there was never a time on TV when you'd be able to watch an Indian movie or turn on the TV and see an Indian show. Now they have all-Indian TV, they have like the whole Sunday … There was never a time that I could imagine turning on the TV and seeing an Indian program, because before it was never like that. Saturdays and Sundays came, and there was nothing like Indian viewing of any type. (HF28)

Rajya was referring to the multicultural films and music videos that many cable networks include in their programming. Within some regions of Ontario and all parts of the Greater Toronto Area, two particular channels, Omni 1 and Omni 2, have gained attention for their diverse programming that caters to more than twenty-two ethnocultural groups (http://www.omnitv.ca/ontario/info). Omni 1 and Omni 2 regularly air broadcasts in a variety of languages, including Bengali, Urdu, Hindi, Tamil, and Punjabi. Viewers from many ethnic backgrounds can tune in to movies, documentaries, music videos, news broadcasts, and even commercials. Such television networks, in addition to the shops that stock imported international films, not only work to aid migrants in their Canadian adaptation through media acknowledgement and the edification of culture but also concurrently serve to increase their cultural exposure to non-migrant Canadians.

Accordingly, ethnic families are able to participate in culturally meaningful media from the comfort of their own couches. Balendra's family, for example, paid tribute to their cultural heritage by tuning into Bollywood entertainment shows 24/7. He said, "[My parents] have it on TV all the time. Of course, they'll be into it a lot more, into it than I am" (HM08). The fact that Balendra's parents found such media more personally relevant than he did was likely due to the fact that they were born and raised in India, where Indian television is mainstream. Reminding them of "home" on a very tangible level, such Indian broadcasts serve to provide an emotional haven for migrants and consequently help to preserve their cultural identity.

Very interesting additions to Omni's broadcasting are the religious programs and segments that include lectures, religious music, recordings of religious ceremonies, and religious-themed debates. Although Omni itself is not a religiously affiliated or based network, its producers recognize the importance of its viewers' beliefs. And although religion may not be one of the key motivating factors influencing a large portion of mainstream Canadian society's media choices, for many migrant communities religion and spiritual concerns are at the forefront of their identity and thus affect their consumer patterns. Rajya told us about a swami (a guru/spiritual master) whom she has seen on TV:

> They have one who is actually [based] in Toronto, right now. He's always on TV. He is located in the Toronto area ... He is directly from India ... [and] he usually speaks Hindi. But he knows English. He's not very [fluent], but he tries. His words are really, like, not at the university level, but he's confident, he knows what he's talking [about]. His accent is so strong sometimes that he's hard to understand. But he's very smart. (HF28)

Although not a regular viewer of his show, Rajya recognized the importance of his televised presence. For disabled members of the Hindu community, senior shut-ins, or those who just are not able to attend temple services, televised religious broadcasts offer the opportunity to reconnect with their spiritual congregation. Listening to the thoughts and ideas of newly migrated revered swamis who are familiar with the Indian context and society, individuals can spiritually cultivate themselves in the comfort of their own homes. Irrespective of the circumstances, Hindu adherents are able to participate in activities beyond the temples and community centres. Although Hindus across Canada are potentially able to access the televised swamis, Toronto-based devotees remain privileged in that these swamis live relatively close to them and the topics discussed and/or commented upon are relevant to them on a local, personal level. Calgary-based Hindus, for instance, likely would not truly have the need or the desire to hear about community centre developments in Toronto's Little India or why more families should support the financially struggling neighbourhood temple. While the wider spiritual topics touched upon by the swami would of course relate to the national, and perhaps even transnational, Hindu community, the local social and political examples used to supplement and/or illustrate his points would not be appreciated and perhaps not even recognized by those outside of the Greater Toronto Area.

Beyond television, there are hundreds of ethnic publications, including newspapers, magazines, and journals that cater to migrant communities from all over the world. Available in cultural community centres, religious buildings, commercial businesses, and even mainstream non-ethnic stores, such as Chapters (a large retail bookstore chain), these publications give people the information they require about global issues as well as migrant perspectives on local issues. Other culturally relevant media tools available to ethnic communities include countless full-length cultural films that are screened in public movie theatres. Bollywood, Arabic, and East Asian feature films are regularly presented in AMC, Silvercity, and Cineplex Odeon theatres in addition to many smaller, independent theatres. These films are usually in a non-English language and usually at the regular admission price. Advertised in both English and cultural newspapers as well as online, they are heavily attended by members of the communities they represent. The fact that Indian migrants can watch the latest Bollywood films and Muslims can watch Arabic films in the same theatres that show Canadian movies suggests that they are a recognized and meaningful part of the urban multicultural montage. Reaffirming the role that culturally relevant media have both in social integration and personal adaptation, these Toronto-area theatres embody the spirit of diversity. Additionally, by listing and screening ethnic films alongside North American ones, theatres transmit narratives of equality and mutual social importance.

CONCLUSION

When looking at the political, educational, and social aspects outlined above, one may recognize that indeed, many other Canadian cities share one or some of them with Toronto. I have been to Vancouver's Chinatown – the largest Chinatown in Canada – and have seen how it serves ethnocultural purposes for its residents similar to those that Toronto's downtown Chinatown does for its East Asian community members. Likewise, Montreal has a relatively small but burgeoning Hindu community that has built temples and opened up ethnic businesses. And Calgary has a very active Buddhist community with its own meditation centres and social events. There is even an annual public Buddhist film series in Calgary, which attracts film critics and views from diverse communities. Indeed, there are countless cultural and religious communities across Canada that, in many ways, are just as active and dynamic as those you will find in the Greater Toronto Area.

But reflecting on the affection that many of the participants and I shared for Toronto and its suburbs, I have come to realize what is characteristic of this urban region: Toronto has "internalized" diversity and most of the bells and whistles that go along with it. In municipal policies and political platforms, in schools and workplaces, on television and in movie theatres, in multicultural communities and in ethnic restaurants, diversity can be seen just about anywhere. In fact, there is so much religious and cultural diversity in the Toronto region that people just seem to take it for granted. The students we spoke with illustrated precisely this through the narratives they shared with us. They truly believed that Toronto is unlike any other Canadian city. In their minds, being part of Toronto's diversity meant that they had the freedom to pursue their education and career ambitions in ways that were important to them. They could be as traditional or liberal as they chose, and they were able to explore other belief systems and values as they desired. These young men and young women, despite belonging to cultural and religious minorities, did not feel excluded but rather saw themselves as meaningful participants in that society: if they were members of minorities, so was almost everyone else. To them, Toronto is a place where tolerance is expected and cultural expression is encouraged.

Growing Up in Canada, the United States, and Western Europe

PETER BEYER

A CROSS-REGIONAL COMPARISON

One of the truisms about research on migrant populations – and indeed on any population – is that it is difficult to impossible to make across-the-board generalizations about many of their experiences, the adaptations that they make, the changes that they introduce to their new places of settlement. What happens depends: it depends on the country or the region/urban area within that country; it depends on social group, however identified (e.g., ethnocultural, racial, religious); it depends on social class; it depends on gender; it depends on period of migration; it depends on the paths of migration and the countries or regions of origin; it depends, quite frankly, on the individual. And, of course, it depends on age and generation. The current research focuses on some very particular subgroups in this regard, and as we have been emphasizing, it is difficult enough to generalize across our specific subgroups – university-educated young adult men and women of the second or 1.5 generation in Canada who came from Hindu, Muslim, or Buddhist family backgrounds – let alone seek to do so in terms of some of these other categories. The attempt in this chapter to engage in a cross-country comparison of these Canadian young adults with their parallels in other countries is therefore quite tentative, and its purpose is rather restrictive. We seek only to adumbrate certain issues having more or less directly to do with our central question: how are these young adults relating to the religious heritages of their families and how, if at all, are they contributing to the reconstruction of those religions in the countries where they were born, where they grew up, and where they live?

For the purposes of comparison, we have chosen two other countries/regions along with the Canadian case. These are the United States and Western Europe. We would have liked to include other regions or countries, notably Australia and New Zealand, but the literature on religion among this demographic is only beginning to appear (see Higgins 2008), likely because those populations in these countries are still quite young, given that both countries opened up their immigration to non-Europeans only during the 1970s. If the Canadian research reported here could not really have been done much earlier, at the moment it is too early to expect this for these two countries (Bouma 1995; Phillips 2009; Vrachnas et al. 2005, 2–12).

Our choice of comparator countries or regions derives from the fact that they are in many ways quite different from Canada and yet share a number of core characteristics that make the comparison meaningful. We know we are comparing apples and oranges, but at least we stay within varieties of fruit. Accordingly, Western Europe and the United States are economically rich and share significant cultural and religious heritage. Like Canada, the population of the United States is today still dominated by people with recent or ancestral origins in Europe. The two settler societies are even more narrowly the outcome of predominantly British (and in the Canadian case, also French) settlement and imperial expansion in past centuries. The dominant, established, quasi-established majority, or culturally prevalent, religion in each case has been one or more denomination of Christianity. More important, in each case it was only in the post–World War II era, that any of them had opened itself up to and received significant immigration from non-European and dominantly non-Christian parts of the world; the subjects of our research are of course a consequence of that change in immigration pattern and policy. The comparison can therefore be with more or less parallel immigrant populations in the other countries.

The similarities among the regions, however, in no way negate the substantial differences. The composition of postwar immigration has been different in the three cases; the cultural, political, and social contexts vary significantly; and the timing of the immigration has been different, with Western Europe already receiving large numbers in the 1950s and early 1960s (Penn and Lambert 2009, 34ff), while such increases in Canada and the United States had to await the early to mid-1970s. In addition, Western Europe, because it is divided into different countries, shows important inter-country variation in immigrant population characteristics, in political and legal frameworks, and in cultural context. This is the case to a certain degree in the other countries – for instance, between Quebec and other regions of Canada – but far less so.

Other important differences among Western Europe, Canada, and the United States are also worth summarizing at the outset of this comparison. In the postwar era, as Great Britain completed the dismantling of most of its former empire, large numbers of migrants arrived from former colonial territories – now Commonwealth countries – but there was no consistent British immigration policy encouraging some forms of immigration rather than others. This had the result of a new immigrant population with almost accidental origins in terms of source countries, social class, and religious composition. The most significant non-European numbers came from former British colonial regions in Africa, the Caribbean, and South Asia. They were for the most part from poor rural areas or middle-class professionals from large cities

(Lucassen, Feldman, and Oltmer 2006; Panayi 2010; Raymond and Modood 2007). Once they were in Great Britain, there was from early on a tendency for especially the poorer new immigrants to end up highly concentrated in certain cities and districts, cities like Wolverhampton and Birmingham and districts like East London. The high residential concentration correlated with a high degree of ethnic concentration, with, for instance, Hindus mostly from Gujarat or East Africa (Burghart 1987) and Muslims mostly from Kashmir or Bangladesh (Lewis 2007b,15ff). In addition, because they started arriving earlier, these immigrant populations were by the beginning of the twenty-first century already into the third generation. All these characteristics contrast markedly with the corresponding Canadian patterns of post-1960s migration. In Canada, although certain country origins are better represented than others – Pakistan and India for Muslims and Hindus, for instance – almost all other major potential source countries for Muslims, Hindus, and Buddhists also have an important immigrant presence in the post-1970 period (the most notable exception is the lack of Muslim immigrants from Indonesia). Canadian immigrants are on average much better educated and not nearly so polarized between poor rural and urban professional migrants. These features, as we detailed in the various chapters, go a long way toward explaining why the results with respect to our major research questions are in significant ways different for Canada from what they are for Britain or, for that matter, for other European countries.

Other countries in Europe display variations on the British pattern. France's immigrant population has been heavily dominated by Maghrebian and African migrants who also arrived in the context of the dismantling of France's colonies and the creation of independent states in those areas. They have been heavily drawn from the poorer classes, not middle-class and professional. They have been heavily Muslim in religion, and they have been even more sharply concentrated in the suburbs of large cities like Paris, Lyon, and Marseilles (Simon 2007). They also have a longer history and are thus into the third generation. Dutch migrants have been of a similar nature, to a large extent arriving from former colonial areas (Rath et al. 2001). Germany's story is a classic case of receiving "guest workers" who then become permanent, in this case a situation exacerbated for the longest time – until 1999, when the laws were changed – by a highly ethnocentric citizenship policy that saw newcomers from Eastern Europe but with ethnically German grandparents being granted immediate citizenship while Turks who had been in Germany for more than a generation had difficulty obtaining it (Thielmann 2008). In other countries around Western Europe, immigrant populations from non-Christian regions are still quite small in absolute numbers but often quite significant in terms of percentage of the population (for Switzerland, Sweden, and Norway as examples, see Baumann and Stolz 2007; Bernhardt et al. 2007; Directorate of Integration and Diversity 2009).

In terms of religious identity, Western European new immigration has been heavily dominated by Muslims, not to the exclusion of other religions but in proportions that, even if it were not for other factors having to do with Islam, would at least make Muslims the most visible and thus the most observed portions of these populations. The one partial exception is Great Britain, where Hindus, Sikhs, and Christians constitute highly significant segments and have received corresponding attention (Bhachu 1985; Burghart 1987; Panayi 2010, 144–62; Parsons 1994).

Migration to the United States has been more similar in origin and composition to that of Canada in a number of ways. It has favoured middle-class, educated, and often professional immigrants rather than poorer rural ones as has happened more often in Europe. The single large exception to that rule is the preponderance in American immigration of people, mostly Christian, from Central and Latin America, above all Mexico (Gerber 2011). Both Canada and the United States have a far weightier presence than Europe of East, South, and Southeast Asian immigrants (with the exception of South Asians in Great Britain). Correspondingly, the non-Christian religious populations of these countries are not nearly as dominated by Muslims as is the case in many European countries, even though in each case Muslims still constitute the single largest religious identity among immigrant groups after Christianity. Above all, both North American countries have pursued deliberate immigration policies that have had the effect of favouring more educated people with a greater average amount of human capital on arrival. Although there are differences in detail, this overall similarity means that the comparative differences in immigrant experiences, including as concerns the question of their relation to religion, are attributable far more to the differences in cultural and political context that each country offers (Bloemraad 2006). What this means will become clearer below.

A significant problem in engaging in a proper comparison of the three cases is that the literature on the religion of the second generation of migrants in particular is often both sparse and uneven. As noted, most of the literature on immigrants and immigrant religion for Europe is about Muslims, although that is not so much the case for Great Britain. For Canada, the literature on these questions is in general rather sparse, irrespective of which religious identity one is considering (see the discussion in chapter 1). By contrast, the best literature is for the situation in the United States, and therefore the most effective comparisons are possible between the two North American neighbours. Even here, however, a disproportionate part of the literature on second generations is about Christians, less about the three religious identities that are the focus here.

THE SECOND GENERATION IN EUROPE

Research on second-generation immigrant youth in Europe is reasonably extensive, but, as noted, it concentrates heavily on Muslims when it pays attention
to religion at all (see, e.g., Entzinger 2003; Frese 2002; Geisser 2003; Khosrokhavar 1997; Vertovec and Rogers 1998). Comparison of our results with
this research shows both striking similarities and some important differences,
suggesting that the Canadian – and more broadly North American – situation
has its specificity but that the Canadian youths are also in many ways quite
typical of their homologues in other Western countries. A useful summary
of the European situation offered in a 1998 publication on Muslim European
youth edited by Steven Vertovec and Alisdair Rogers (Vertovec and Rogers
1998, 10–14) can serve as a scaffolding for structuring a comparison of European and Canadian youth – specifically Muslim youth in this case. This work
surveys the situation in several European countries at the end of the 1990s,
including Great Britain, France, Germany, the Netherlands, and Denmark.
Subsequent literature has not noted a significant shift with regard to our questions during the intervening decade and a half. The editors suggest a series of
common contextual factors and how they manifest themselves in the ways that
these youths are constructing their identities and their Islam.

To begin, they refer to what they call "a sharpening self-consciousness" that
is manifested in "a desire to analyse religious scriptures for themselves" and
in "a revitalisation of belief and practice." European Muslim youth and young
adults feel it incumbent upon themselves to engage in a reconstruction of their
religion for their own circumstances. They may in many respects carry on the
ways and traditions of their parents, but they do so critically, not just repeating
but also seeking to understand and adjust in light of that understanding (see
Fadil 2005 for analysis of the Belgian case among young Muslim women).
A second commonality is "the inculcation of implicit values through Western educational systems," one of the manifestations of which is "particularly
among Muslim university students ... the use of the internet and electronic
discussion groups is pushing the frontiers of Muslim values, practice and organization." The sources of religious reconstruction are not the traditional
ones. Third is "an explicit hardening of the distinction between 'religion' and
'culture'" (cf. Eilers, Seitz, and Hirschler 2008; Geaves 2007). Not only do most
Muslim youth make the distinction, they do so in order to clarify their understanding and practice of religion. A fourth point is that they tend to experience "socialization within an atmosphere of ethnic/religious mobilization" (cf.
Lewis 2007a). The context of their orientation to religion and Islam includes
a number of important movements and organizations, mostly domestic but
also transnational, whose activity influences them and in which they often

participate. In that context, for many, "Islam [is] ... a global symbol of resistance to ... Western political and cultural imperialism, capitalism, racism, and white-dominated bureaucratic states." As Cressey's research on young Kashmiris in Britain makes clear, for instance, this status of Islam is acquired in a context of their own economic, political, and social marginalization within their European countries (Cressey 2006). In that frame, their reconstructive efforts are aided by "the growth of what might be called 'vernacular' Islam [including] sermons, literature, and public discussions ... being conveyed in the local ... language." Nonetheless, these efforts take on different forms in tune with "variance of religiosity in relation to stage of life." Their relation to Islam changes as they grow older; it can increase, decrease, or transform in various ways, but it is not continuous from childhood to adulthood. Vertovec and Rogers also note "a tendency toward compartmentalization and secularization of religion." The overall trend is not toward centrality of religion in people's lives, although that does not mean religion thereby necessarily becomes unimportant. It very often remains, at the very least, a critical identity marker, with or without explicit religious content. Finally, the authors claim "an immersion in American and European youth culture embodied in commodities and consumerism, fashion and other elements of style, modes and expressions of speech, music and other forms of media." Overall, these commonalities point in multiple directions, some of which may even appear contradictory but which together emphasize the fluidity of (religious) reconstruction in this generation in Europe. In this context, it is perhaps important to note that Vertovec and Rogers do not point to commonality in the vision of Islam along a global Islamic model, although nothing in their analysis indicates that such a common model is in fact not present.

Comparing these features with our Canadian results, we begin with the similarities between Canadian and European youth and then consider the differences. A sharpening Muslim and Islamic self-consciousness was very strong among these Canadian youth, among the highly involved (7–10) certainly but also among the somewhat involved (4–6). While a good number of our participants were quite willing to follow the Islam of their parents, and several oriented themselves primarily with respect to their perceived local Muslim community, many of them and the bulk of the remaining majority insisted, and were frequently encouraged by their elders, to learn about Islam through their own efforts, to seek sources of knowledge on their own. They most often sought to interpret the core sources at least to some extent on their own, even if several of them also relied on particular expert sources as well, frequently accessed through the Internet. In many cases, their parents, the imam at the local mosque, and the ulama in general were not considered the primary and most reliable sources of knowledge, and not a few of our participants disagreed with

their elders regularly, often considering the latter's understanding and practice of Islam deficient when compared to their own, a trend most prominent
among some of the highly involved (compare also Karim 2009).

This prevailing independence in their senses of self and of Islam is also
reflective of the degree to which these young adults had absorbed many of
the typical core values that Canadian educational systems seek to impart to
their students. The stress on the individual and her/his fundamental worth
and autonomy was perhaps the strongest among these values. Connected to
this was, as Vertovec and Rogers put it, their "emphasis on argumentation,
critical debate and reflexive questioning." In this context, their use of Internet
expert sources and chat groups has been mentioned more than once in the
preceding chapters on Muslims. The feature of the Canadian Muslim youths
that is particularly relevant in this regard is the degree to which they approved
and sought to further the ideas of equality and diversity that is officially and
popularly enshrined in Canadian notions of a multicultural society. As noted,
among the Muslims, no one expressed anything but approval for this policy,
even though many felt that more – sometimes much more – had to be done
for the country to live up to it. Moreover, it is here perhaps that one should
locate the high level of comfort they felt living in Canadian society, their sense
in most cases of being fully Canadian, many saying that it was a very good,
sometimes the best, country to live in. This prevailing orientation contrasts
markedly with the situation in, for instance, Germany or Britain, where it is
precisely this sense of inclusion and belonging that is relatively absent or at
least significantly weaker among the second-generation Muslims (Bernhardt
et al. 2007; Lewis 2007b). Above all, with few exceptions, our Canadian participants felt that Canada was a place where they could properly live their lives
as Muslims, albeit obviously not without the challenges of a largely secularized
society and the occasional experience of overt or implicit discrimination directly or indirectly because they were Muslims.

Similarly, our Canadian Muslim youths followed the European trend of
making a consistent distinction between religion and culture, all the while
fully recognizing how closely the two were usually tied. The purposes of this
distinction were also, in part, the same: to justify their Islamic selectivity vis-
à-vis their elders, usually rejecting elements of the latter's "culture" in favour
of their "religion." And it was they, not their parents, who decided where the
line between the two was, albeit on their perceived understanding of what the
sources they used said. What was comparatively absent in this regard was the
overt use of Islam and the "purification" of Islam of "cultural" accretions as a
way of declaring independence from parental influence and expectations (see
Geaves 2007).

Moving on to the differences, ethnic/religious mobilization on an Islamic
basis, while certainly not absent from Canada, has been comparatively rare

and low-key. There do exist national and more local Muslim organizations, and some of them have occasionally been involved in specific campaigns, such as, in Ontario for instance, a Jewish/Muslim/Evangelical Protestant consortium to seek government funding for religiously based schools or the effort to allow Shari'a to be the basis of private arbitration procedures that would be recognized by the courts (Boyd 2004; Perrella et al. 2008). Beyond such examples, however, Muslim youth in Canada have not grown up in an atmosphere where such mobilization has been prominent. Indeed, as a group, they do not seem to be highly politically conscious. Of our 93 Muslim participants, none admitted involvement in such mobilization efforts, although several were active in Muslim students associations, volunteering in public (usually Muslim) organizations, and even publishing books on Muslim youth experience in Canada. Like Canadian religion in general, the Islam of these youths was largely privatized rather than overtly public, let alone politicized.

The idea of Islam as a global symbol of resistance was correspondingly also muted, although several of the Muslim youths stressed the degree to which Islam set them off from the secular and permissive society around them and from the popular culture that informed it. Yet such opposition did not seem to be couched explicitly in terms of global systems. Here may be one indicator of their comparative lack of marginalization. Immigrants to Canada very often suffer significant downward mobility with respect to others in Canadian society with comparable levels of education and professional experience, and as discussed in chapter 3, the evidence suggests that this disadvantage narrows greatly but by no means disappears entirely in the second generation. That admitted, such marginalization does not entail high concentration in poorer quarters of cities, although Muslims do seem to be at a consistent income disadvantage compared to those of other religious identities. The large Canadian cities to which most immigrants are attracted have thus far not experienced such significant demographic polarization and comparatively – when compared to European countries – modest economic marginalization, even though Canada is not at all free of racist and discriminatory attitudes on the part of segments of the established populations. In terms of our sample, one of the best concrete indicators of this situation was the high rate of post-secondary exposure of our target populations, a feature that contrasted markedly with Muslims in all European countries (see Penn and Lambert 2009; but see also Ahmad 2001). And indeed, exceedingly few if any of our Muslim participants seemed concerned that their life and career chances would be significantly less than those of their non-immigrant and non-Muslim peers. The expectation and fear of marginalization was not evident, which is not to imply that it might not be simply muted and implicit.

The development of local vernacular Islamic sources was not a particular problem for our Canadian youths; their vernacular language was English (our sample contained no francophone Muslims because of the difficulty in recruiting in Montreal), today the closest thing to a global lingua franca. In combination with their access to worldwide electronic and published sources, these youths had little trouble finding what they needed in a language they could understand. Although many of them spoke their ethnic languages and many had made efforts to learn Arabic, the prevailing language of study and communication was the local vernacular, English. They spoke it the way other locals did; they used it that way too.

The issue of variance in their attitude to and involvement in Islam as they moved through various stages of their lives was relevant for our group only with regard to changes between childhood, adolescence, and early adulthood. Typically, many of the Canadian youths in our study found themselves declining in Islamic involvement during some part of their adolescence, in a great many cases only to pick it up again as they entered university and thereafter. That said, many in our sample also related no such change in the intensity of involvement. The "secularizing" pressures of Canadian society seem to have been inconsistently effective among them, although the issue of this pressure was a constant theme for many of them. In this respect, the fact that our group of participants undoubtedly included a disproportionate number of those for whom religion was important, simply as a result of the recruiting technique, makes this conclusion somewhat uncertain. Other Canadian research in which samples were not similarly skewed, notably that of Paul Eid among second-generation Arabs in Montreal (cf. Eid 2007) might point in the direction of greater similarity with Europeans on this question. In addition, what may be typical for European Muslim youth – that they anticipate becoming "better Muslims" once they found a family – was not strongly present in our Canadian sample, albeit with a number of exceptions, such as represented by the stated desire or intention of some of the highly involved Muslim women to wear hijab in the future.

Correspondingly, compartmentalization was a feature typical only of the somewhat involved Muslims; indeed, it might be said to characterize them as a group. Since we cannot say how representative our small sample is of the Muslim youth population in general, we cannot say how prevalent this tendency is. Certainly, the possibility of not compartmentalizing to any significant degree was also strongly represented in the sample.

The feature of immersion in Canadian or North American popular culture was not strongly present in our sample, although a significant number told us that it had very much been one during their adolescence. It was part of the society in which they found themselves living, one of the pressures with which they had to deal if they wanted to lead properly Islamic lives. A great many claimed that they were successfully resisting these pressures, evidently a critical aspect of the widespread opinion that one could be a proper Muslim in Canadian society.

If we turn now to a comparison of the Canadian Buddhists and Hindus with their European counterparts, we have far less material on the basis of which to make this comparison. Nonetheless, much as the literature on European Muslim youth is substantial, there is at least some on Hindu young people in Great Britain and on Buddhists in Germany. There is virtually none on second-generation Hindus outside Britain or on second-generation Buddhists in any other country.

With regard to British Hindus, comparison is not as straightforward as with British and European Muslims, to a large extent because of ambiguities surrounding terms like Hindu and Hinduism. In part the issue is the lack of a broadly agreed upon understanding among Hindus themselves as to what is and is not included in the category, in part it has to do with the great variety of what is included, and in part it has to do with the fluid boundaries above all between "cultural" categories and religious ones. In particular, as we have seen in previous chapters, whereas young adult Muslims use the distinction between culture and religion to clarify their understanding and practice of their religion, Hindus much more typically live what Hindu identity they have across those categories. Virtually every work on Hindus in Britain and Canada, for instance, begins almost as a matter of necessary formality with a discussion of this issue (see, e.g., Burghart 1987; Jackson and Nesbitt 1993; Nesbitt 1998; Pearson 2004; Rukmani 1999; Sekar 2001; Smith 2000; Sontheimer and Kulke 1989). In that light, it is perhaps unsurprising that a comparison of research in Britain to the project reported here indicates that both groups display a complex identity construction that is far from a simple binary of "reconciling two worlds." Not only are there more contributing components than simply the "home" culture and "Canadian" culture, not only are hybridizations neither problematic nor seamless but usually somewhere in between and depending on circumstances, but Hindu religion plays a highly "cultural" role, meaning that there is generally no strong distinction between Hindu as religion and Hindu as culture (Arweck and Nesbitt 2010; Nesbitt 1998), and cultural markers like Gujarati or Punjabi as well as religious markers like Hindu or Sikh are conceived with some fluidity and not as necessarily clear and exclusive boundaries (Jackson and Nesbitt 1993; Nesbitt 1991; cf. Nayar 2004 for the Sikh case in Canada). All these characteristics, within the theoretical framework used in our analyses, are symptomatic of the very different way that global Hinduism has been constructed in the modern era, especially in contrast to other religions like Islam. What this means concretely is that taking differences in class, education, and other variables into account, British Hindus of the second generation appear to be relating to religion and to Hinduism in ways quite similar to the ways our Canadian sample was doing so. As we shall see, something similar can be said with respect to the situation in the United States.

With respect to notable differences, the most striking appear to be that as with Muslims, compared with the British, the Canadians showed a far lower level of influence and immersion in ethnic/religious mobilization, especially of the politicized kind that in the Hindu case is represented by the Hindu nationalist Hindutva movement. While the absorption of this perspective among young British Hindus appears at least to be significant (Raj 2000), in the Canadian case it seemed to be for the most part absent.[1] As discussed above in various chapters, only one of 57 participants from Hindu families exhibited positive sympathies for politicized Hinduism. Most participants seemed mostly unaware of its existence. The reason for this difference must for the moment remain speculative; it is not traceable to the class or origin differences between British and Canadian Hindu populations, because, as we will discuss shortly, this political mobilization on a Hindu basis is also far more prevalent in the United States, where Hindu populations share class and origin characteristics with their Canadian counterparts.

Although very limited research has been carried out among European second-generation Buddhists, there is at least enough for the German case to make a preliminary comparison. In the late 1990s, Olaf Beuchling began to research the situation of Vietnamese Buddhists in the northern city of Hamburg (Beuchling 2005; 2008; 2011). With respect to the younger generation of these Buddhists, his results again show a combination of strong similarities with our Canadian sample and significant differences. With respect to similarities, we find the same blending of Buddhism into the cultural and the diversely religious characteristics of the home culture and a similar view of Buddhism as a "relaxed" religion that does not insist on strong identification and well-defined and "strict" practice. Beuchling also found a similar stress on Buddhism as a set of value and moral orientations that put an emphasis on peace, tolerance, and acceptance of other religions as equally valid.

The differences in this case may, however, be more important. Whether because of the different institutional context for religion in Germany, one that includes state-supported churches and the integration of religious education in the school system, or for other less clear reasons, Buddhism in Germany (at least in Hamburg) receives stronger institutional expression in a way that has a definite influence on the level of knowledge and perhaps level of participation with respect to Buddhism in the younger generations. This stronger expression includes greater emphasis on Buddhist education of young people in the Vietnamese temples, the inclusion of Buddhist education in the public school curriculum in the context of the teaching of world religions, and the presence of a Vietnamese Buddhist monastery in which some of the young people become novices. Little to none of this was available to those in our Buddhist-background sample, with the possible exception of courses on Buddhism at the high school and university levels to which some of our participants referred explicitly. Most striking, and perhaps exceptional, is the presence of monastic institutions; while one or two Buddhist monasteries exist in Canada, they are run by and for the most part populated by Buddhists of European backgrounds (so-called Western Buddhists) rather than Buddhists who have immigrated or their offspring. Therefore, with regard to our central questions of Buddhist reconstruction in the "diaspora" context and the incorporation of identified Buddhism in the lived religious lives of the second generation, the German situation described by Beuchling may be more conducive to both than that of our Buddhist participants here in Canada. Clearly, however, far more research has to be carried out in both and other places before this conclusion can be anything but tentative and more than merely suggestive.

Summarizing the comparison of Europe and Canada with regard to the central research question of the reconstruction of religions among young adults of Muslim, Hindu, and Buddhist backgrounds, it is possible to conclude at least tentatively that such reconstruction has more points of similarity than of difference. Above all, the reconstructive patterns of Hindus, Buddhists, and Muslims, of Hinduism, Buddhism, and Islam, are very different, corresponding to the broader, global patterns of modern reconstruction of these religions. Within each religious identity, the understandings and practice of Hinduism, Buddhism, and Islam are quite similar in Canada and Europe but with these important possible differences: (ethno-)religious mobilization appears thus far to be more prevalent among Hindus and Muslims of the second generation in European countries than in Canada, above all with respect to the attraction of Hindu and Islamic politicized movements. For Buddhists, this is not even a question. This, of course, is not to say that such movements have no presence among young adults in Canada, just that they have a far more minor presence. Similarly less present but by no means entirely absent in the Canadian population is the construction of Hindu and Muslim/Islamic identity as in some sense an oppositional identity to the dominant Western/white/Christian one. Again, this does not seem to be a question among those of Buddhist backgrounds. What this difference may also mean is the lesser degree to which Canadian Hindus and Muslims locate the centre of gravity of their religions elsewhere than in Canada, something reflected in their seemingly higher sense of belonging in Canada and "being" Canadian (if, more often than not, "hyphenated" Canadian) when compared to the bulk of their European counterparts. One must, however, be careful not to push this contrast too far; it is one of those seeming or suggestive differences that definitely require more research with precisely this question in mind.

THE SECOND GENERATION IN THE UNITED STATES

As noted above, the non-Christian religious composition of more recent immigrant populations and their offspring in Canada is more similar to that in
the United States than it is to that in Western Europe. It is therefore not surprising that with respect to the central question of religious reconstruction
among 1.5 and second generations of Muslim, Hindu, and Buddhist families,
the outcomes in the two North American countries are even more similar.
To the extent that research in both countries has explored this question, we
find the same striking differences according to which religion is at issue: Muslims are generally much more highly involved; they feel it incumbent upon
themselves to take personal responsibility for understanding and practising
Islam; they use the globalized five-pillars Islamic pietistic model to do so;[2]
they draw clear lines between Islam and the ethnic cultures of their family
heritages in order to practise a more "authentic" and "pure" Islam (Schmidt
2002); they have high levels of post-secondary education and correspondingly are as a group highly involved in Muslim students associations and the
like (Peek 2005); and although concentrated in the numerous large American
cities, they come to a large extent from middle-class, often professional, families and do not experience as high levels of marginalization as many of their
European counterparts (Sirin and Fine 2008). Hindus, by and large, show the
same propensity to eschew sharp distinctions between being Hindu culturally and being Hindu religiously and stress the importance above all of Hindu
culture in their lives and in the foreseeable lives of their eventual children.
Overall, however, they are not nearly as much a religiously involved and practising group as their Muslim counterparts, but they are socio-economically
even more highly placed and have very high levels of educational attainment,
this in part as a result of the immigration policies that tend to ensure that in
this respect they are simply carrying forward the characteristics of their parents (Kurien 1998; 2007; Min 2010). On the next generation of Buddhists, as in
Canada, there is exceedingly little research (cf. Suh 2004). A proper comparison for this group is therefore at the moment no more possible than it is for
almost all the European countries.

Staying with the Muslims and Hindus, there are also some broad differences,
which can be seen as a direct reflection of the different political, religious, and
cultural context of the two countries. First, it does seem that race matters more
south than north of the border. This is a somewhat difficult distinction, since
it concerns as much perception as it does lived experience. A great many of
our Canadian participants, even if and when they experienced racist and discriminatory behaviour during their lives, as many did directly or indirectly,
nevertheless usually judged that racism to be not overly severe. When they
made comparisons of Canada with other countries, or simply to explain them-

selves, they often averred that it was not nearly as bad as in the United States or, in some cases when it came to anti-Muslim discrimination, in France – this whether or not they had themselves had any experience in these countries. On the other side, although also ambiguously, research on the corresponding young adults in the United States seems consistently to show that racism is not only a common experience but one that influences behaviour and attitudes – for instance, in a propensity to associate mostly with one's own group because one is not accepted in "white" society (David and Ayouby 2002; Min 2010; cf. Dhruvaraja 2003, who also comes to this conclusion for Hindus in Canada). In addition, the "post-9/11" experience for Muslims appears to have been much harsher, and the negative experience lasted much longer than in Canada.[3] That noted, however, this difference does not seem to have produced notable differences in how second-generation Muslims in the two countries relate to their Islam. In both cases, the dominant answer is that one cannot only be Muslim in either country but there is no contradiction between being Muslim and being either Canadian or American.

A further difference has to do with the place and role of religion in the two societies. In Canada, one notes a quite low level of what one might call religious aggressiveness, what some might want to call "competitiveness" (see Beyer 1997). Culturally, it seems, it is generally considered rather impolite and to that degree unacceptable to promote – "push" – one's religion publicly or even to be too open about showing it publicly, to be "in your face" about religion (cf. Adams 2003; Bibby 2002). This cultural tendency militates against a too overt religiously based mobilization, and the politicization of religion has to be done with great care. To this feature might correspond the fact that openly proselytizing religion, especially evangelizing/evangelical Christian religion, does not now claim and has historically not claimed nearly as large a portion of the Canadian population as has been the case in the United States (Rawlyk 1996). Evangelical Christianity does not serve nearly as much as a model religion in Canada as it does in the United States, and therefore newly present religions, like Islam, Buddhism, and Hinduism, are less likely to follow that model. This might partially explain the relative lack of ethno-religious mobilization among the Muslim and Hindu Canadian participants, whether on an Islamist or Hindutva precedent. In this respect, the much greater presence of politicized Hinduism among the second generation in the United States and its minimal influence in Canada is of particular note (Kurien 2007). A question closely related to the issue of mobilization is a possible difference in the institutional "location" of reconstructed religion among the second generation in the two countries. Certain research in the United States postulates that what may be happening among the second-generation Muslims is not just a reconstruction of Islam but one that is significantly centred in institutions, more specifically in religious organizations, and that it is in this sense

following a typically American way of doing religion and thus is an important aspect of its "Americanization" (Williams 2011; cf. Warner 1993; Yang and
Ebaugh 2001). As is the case for the first generation, much of the research on
second-generation Muslims has been conducted within institutions, whether
mosques or religiously identified organizations like the Muslim students associations (Peek 2005). This strategy is, of course, a common and logical feature
of research design in this area, but one of its limitations is that it cannot gain
that much insight into how, in this case, second-generation Muslims are – or
are not – reconstructing Islam or how they are living their religions outside
these institutional contexts. If American Islam, including in the second generation, is developing in a more "congregational" fashion, then this should mean
that Muslims outside these contexts are less likely to be highly involved, active
contributors to the reproduction of Islam in the United States. Research that
finds its data in the context of religious organization is, however, not going to
be able to address that issue, but that does not mean that such organization-
centred Islam is not in fact stronger in the United States than in Canada, for
instance. Be that as it may, the Canadian research that is the focus of this book
supports the idea that second-generation Islam in Canada is not particularly
strongly focused in organizations: the Muslim participants in our research,
while many of them attended mosque and belonged to Muslim organizations,
did not overly identify with them, and many who did not identify with them at
all were still highly involved and active contributors. Moreover, the features of
their reconstructed and lived Islam, as noted already, was in most ways strik-
ingly similar to the reconstructive efforts of American Muslims recruited from
within Muslim organizations. This result at least suggests the possibility that,
on further research, the American difference in this regard may reveal itself
not to be a difference at all.[4]

Although young adult Hindus in the two countries share a similar way of
fusing religion and culture, there is evidence to suggest that Hindus in the
United States are perhaps more religiously involved than those in Canada. The
relative lack of research on this question means that this conclusion must for
the time being remain tentative, since only Min's work in the United States
seems to have asked this question directly and even there the results are somewhat interpretative (Min 2010). Above, we noted that something similar applies to Canadian Hindus: how religiously involved they appear depends to
some extent on what standards of religious involvement one is using; if any
practice at all constitutes involvement, then that is an easier standard to meet
than if one expects regular practice that the participants do for clearly religious
motivation rather than as part of the cultural family practices. On the whole,
however, the orientation of Canadian and American Hindu second generations to the religion of their heritage appears to be quite similar, much as is the
case among Muslims in the two countries.

CONCLUSION: GROWING UP CANADIAN,
GROWING UP IN CANADA

This very brief comparison of second-generation relations to religious herit-ages in various Western countries has inevitably concluded that there are both similarities and differences. That said, it does appear that with respect to the central question of religious reconstruction, the similarities far outweigh the differences, at least as far as people of Muslim and Hindu families are con-cerned. For Buddhists and Buddhisms, research is still too sparse to be able to come to any proper conclusions in this regard. With respect to the two theoretical directions that have informed our analyses in the preceding chap-ters – the lived religion and global religious system perspectives – this finding is significant in two complementary ways. The comparison supports the thesis that "the religions" exhibit a continuity of construction and reconstruction across localities and other identifications, that they are in this sense globalized religious systems or subsystems. Moreover, this process operates differently according to which religion is at issue: Muslims and Hindus in Canada, the United States, and Europe show strong continuities in the comprehension and putting into practice of Islam and Hinduism, but there is much less continuity in construction between these two religions, even and especially in the same "place." On the other hand, taking the perspective of a lived religion approach, although each of the religions is constructed in distinct and internally con-sistent ways, each is at the same time also the aggregate result of individual constructions, yet these individual constructions do not have to be and are most often not entirely subsumed in this religion construction process. Within the lived, individual constructions of our Canadian participants, as with their contemporaries in other countries, a great deal escapes the reproduction of Hinduism and Islam, but enough does not, with the result that most individ-uals, through their lived religion, contribute to the local, global, and continu-ous reproduction of Hinduism and Islam.

Considering more closely the differences among the second-generation Hindus and Muslims in the three regions, one is further struck by the degree to which the cross-national/regional variations are in fact matched and per-haps exceeded by the differences within each of the national or religious cat-egories. This observation refers not only to the just-mentioned individual differences – as emphasized especially through the individual profiles in the previous chapters – the differences from one person to another, but just as much to the variations within the individual over time. The ways that people in each of the countries live their religions and contribute – or not – to the construction of the religions varies with the life courses of the individuals, a factor that, as noted in previous chapters as well, makes all of our conclusions somewhat provisional. The situation in Canada as in the other countries is not static, even when one focuses only on a set group of individuals. To use Danièle Hervieu-Léger's categories (Hervieu-Léger 1999), already within their lives many of our participants, as with the participants in parallel research carried out in the other countries, have passed from being "regular practitioners" to being "pilgrims" and/or "converts"; not only does the content of their lived religion change, so do the styles and forms that carry the content. In all countries, the situation is fluid because things change all the time but also because the dominant styles and forms for doing religion are changing, very often during an individual life course (cf. Gooren 2010). Thus, more than might otherwise even be the case, the future with respect to our central questions in this book is open; we cannot see clearly where all this is going.

Another way to put this central conclusion is to reemphasize what we have said often in the previous chapters: the reproduction, reconstruction, globalization, and glocalization of systemic religions is continuing in contemporary society and is not particularly giving way to spirituality, meaning a non-systemic, de-institutionalized form of religiosity. Rather, the two forms (or lack of form) perpetuate in the same society, sometimes in complementary, sometimes in contradictory fashion. We cannot appreciate what is happening religiously if we concentrate only on the systemic or lived manifestation, because the systemic is most often an integral aspect of the lived and because the lived is most often more than a simple manifestation of the systemic. As our research participants showed, even in the absence of effective (let alone centralized) religious authorities, a convergent reproduction of systemic religion can occur in and through the individual choices and proclivities of lived religions, of individuals pursuing what is meaningful for them.

To conclude, then, religions in today's societies are in the process of globalization and global reconstruction. Those of the second generation participate – or not – in this process in a unique way given their positions in their societies. In the Canadian case, the young adults of Buddhist and Hindu background are *thus far* minimally involved in this reconstruction, which is not to say that their parents will not "pick up the slack" or that the younger generation will not do so in the future. For the Muslims, many are actively involved in this process, although it is difficult to say how they are doing things differently compared to their counterparts in other countries: they are certainly doing things in a fashion similar to that of their American and European counterparts, with some differences that may not be that significant. With respect to this question as with so many others, however, much research needs to be done, and this book is at best a small contribution to the understanding of very complex and fluid developments.

Religion among Immigrant Youth in Canada
In-Depth Interview Questions

No participant was asked all of the following questions, and the themes did not necessarily arise in the order listed.

THEME I: PERSONAL AND FAMILY RELIGIOUS IDENTIFICATION

1 What would you say is your religion?
2 How important is your religion to you?
3 Would you say that you practise your religion regularly?
4 To what religion or religions do other members of your family belong?
5 Have you changed your religion since you were a child?
6 Have other members of your family changed their religion since they were children?
7 What brought about this change?

THEME II: UNDERSTANDING OF RELIGION

8 If I ask you to define religion, what would you say?
9 Do you think it is possible to belong to more than one religion at the same time?
10 Are you aware of religions that espouse the opposite of what you have just said? If so, which ones?
11 Do you think there is a difference between a person's religion and their culture? If so, what differences are there?
12 Do you think there is a difference between being religious and being spiritual?
13 On the whole, do you think religion is a good thing? Why or why not?
14 Are some religions better than others? If so, which one(s)?
15 Do you think there is a difference between religion and superstition? Between religion and magic?
16 If religion in general is good or neutral, are there some religions that are dangerous or even evil? If so, can you give me an example of a religion that you think might be dangerous?

17   Referring to your own religion, is there a single best version or true version of this religion, or are there several?

THEME III: CHARACTERISTICS OF OWN RELIGION

18   Do you belong to one religion, no religion, or more than one religion?
19   Would you consider yourself to be a religious person? If so, what makes you a religious person?
20   What would you say are the chief characteristics of a person following your religion?
21   What is more important about your religion to you? The beliefs? The religious community? The practice? The overall way of life it enjoins? Another aspect or other aspects?
22   What, in your estimation, are the most important teachings/beliefs of your religion?
23   What, in your estimation, are the most important rituals/practices of your religion?
24   Since when have you been a follower of your religion?
25   What branch or version of this religion do you belong to or follow?
26   What other branches or versions of your religion do you know about? If many, name just a few.
27   What do you think about these other branches or versions? Are they as authentic as yours?
28   Do you think you would ever consider switching to one of these other versions or incorporating features of them into your own belief and practice of your religion?
29   Are there common aspects of your religion, whether teachings or practices, with which you have difficulty or which you reject? If so, can you give me one or two examples?
30   What do you think are some of the main challenges or problems facing your religion and your religious community today?
31   Do you think that followers of your religion, including yourself, are responding well to these challenges or problems?
32   What do you think are the main strengths of your religion today?
33   What, in principle, are the main sources of authority in your religion? Are these the sources that actually have authority in your religion today? If not, who or what does have this authority?
34   Other collectivities:
    a   If you are not a religious person or have no religion, do you have a strong sense of belonging to another group, such as a culture, a nation, a race, or other collectivity?

b Do you have a strong sense of belonging to another group, such as a culture, a nation, a race, or other collectivity besides the religion to which you belong?

35 If so, what makes one a member of that group or collectivity?

36 If you belong to both a religion and another collectivity, which, if any, is the more important one for you?

37 As a non-religious person, do you consider that there are other aspects of your life that take the place of what religion does for religious people? If so, how would you describe these other aspects?

38 Why do you think you are not a religious person?

39 What do you think of religious people?

40 Do you know many religious people?

41 As a non-religious person, do you believe that there is some sort of continued existence after death?

42 As a non-religious person, do you believe in any of the following: ghosts, spirits, astrology, precognition, extra-sensory perception, that some people have the ability to see into the future?

THEME IV: INVOLVEMENT IN OWN RELIGION

43 Would you say that you practise your religion regularly?

44 What practices of your religion are to you the most important to observe as faithfully as possible? Why are these the most important?

45 Do you think that other adherents of your religion share your assessment in this regard?

46 How faithfully would you say that you observe these important practices?

47 Have you changed the type of religious practice you engage in since childhood? If so, how?

48 Have you changed the level of seriousness of your religious practice since childhood? If so, are you more or less practising? Why has this happened?

49 How often do you go to mosque/temple/church?

50 What are the main reasons that you go there?

51 Which mosque(s)/temple(s)/church(es) do you go to when you go?

52 Does it matter which mosque/temple/church you go to? If so, why? If not, why not?

53 Does your temple/mosque/church meet your expectations as concerns how it represents and practises your religion?

54 In this regard, what are some of the main strengths of your temple/mosque/church?

55 What are some of its main weaknesses?

56 Who do you believe has the most say about how things are run at the temple/mosque/church that you most frequently attend? Do you approve of this? If not, who should have more say and why?

57 In your opinion, is your temple/mosque/church well run administratively (organization, physical plant, financially)?

58 When was your mosque/temple/church founded?

59 How many members or regular attendees would you say it has?

60 Do you think that your temple/mosque/church responds well to the needs of young people like yourself? If so, how does it do that? If not, how could it do better?

61 What do you think of the religious leaders at your mosque/temple/church? Do you consider them authorities of your religion for you? Do you ever consult them on religious or other aspects of your life?

62 Are you involved in any religious groups, such as youth groups, campus groups, or other groups, that are not a part of your involvement in your mosque/temple/church? If so, what are they? Describe the level and nature of your involvement.

63 How important is such involvement in these other groups to you?

64 What religious practices outside those associated with your temple/mosque/church do you engage in regularly? How important are these in comparison with temple/mosque/church practice?

65 Do you engage in any religious practices that are not usually considered typical of your religion? If so, which ones?

THEME V: CHANGE IN OWN RELIGION (FOR INTERVIEWEES WHO HAVE CHANGED RELIGION ONLY)

66 What was the religion of your childhood, and what is your religion now? What version or branch of this current religion do you belong to?

67 Have you changed religion more than once?

68 When did this change (your last change) in religion occur?

69 Could you briefly tell me what led to this change?

70 Would you describe your religious change as a religious conversion?

71 Comparing your old religious affiliation (includes "no religion") to your current one, how has this change affected the way you lead your life and your outlook on life?

72 How has your family responded to your conversion/change of religion?

73 Are you closer to your family after your conversion/change of religion, more distant, or about the same?

74 Do you still have the same friends that you did before your conversion/change of religion?

75 How many of your current friends would you say are also followers of your current religion?

76 How important is it to you that your friends share your religious conviction or practice?
77 If you have abandoned your childhood religious affiliation but now have no religion, why do you think this has happened?
78 When did you stop practising your childhood religion?
79 When did you stop identifying with your childhood religion?
80 What, if anything, would you say was inadequate about your childhood religion?
81 How have the members of your family responded to this loss of your childhood religious identity or practice?
82 Would you say that most of your friends are also non-religious?
83 Have any of your friends had a similar experience of abandoning the religion of their childhood?
84 Is it important to you that your friends share your non-religious outlook?

THEME VI: PERCEPTION OF RELIGIOUS INVOLVEMENT AND CHANGE AMONG FELLOW YOUTHFUL ADHERENTS

85 Among people of your generation and religious/cultural background, irrespective of which religion they belong to or practise, would you say that your level of religious involvement/practice is about the norm, or are you rather an exception?
86 If you think you are the exception rather than the rule among people of your generation and religious/cultural background, would you say that others are generally more or less involved/practising?
87 If your level of involvement/practice is common, to what do you attribute this commonality?
88 If you have changed religion since childhood, do you think that such religious conversion/change is common among people of your generation? If so, why? If not, why not?
89 Would you say that people of your generation and religious/cultural background have generally maintained the religion of their childhood, or would you say that many have converted to another religion or ceased adhering to or practising this religion?
90 How do you think that compares to young people of different religious/cultural backgrounds [give concrete examples of comparable groups]?

THEME VII: DIFFERENCES BETWEEN OWN RELIGION AND PARENTAL RELIGION (IF RELIGION IS SAME)

91 Are you more, less, or about as involved in your religion than/as your parents?

92 Do you and your parents have differing opinions about your religion? If so, give me some examples of how you differ.

93 Do your parents practise your religion differently from the way you? If so, how?

94 Do you and your parents have arguments about religion, or are you more or less in accord? If you have arguments, what do you typically argue about?

95 Do you make a distinction between your parents' culture and their religion? If so, do your parents also make such a distinction, and if so, do they make it in the same way that you do?

96 Do you make a distinction between your culture and your religion? If so, give me some examples of what is part of your culture that is not part of your religion or vice versa.

97 If you have significant differences with your parents on important issues, would you say that these disagreements are more cultural, more religious, or both? Or are these differences more simply put down to generational differences, the differences in the kinds of lives you and your parents have led?

98 Do you think it is common among people of your generation and religious/cultural background to have such differences/be in such accord with their parents in questions of their religion?

99 Does your religion affect how you relate to your parents? If so, how?

THEME VIII: RELIGION AND OTHER ASPECTS OF PERSONAL LIFE

100 How does your religion affect the other aspects of your life? Does your religion imbue all aspects of your life or only some aspects of it? If only some, which ones?

101 Does your religion have an effect on how you vote in elections? If so, how?

102 Does your religion have an influence on your choice of career/studies? If so, how?

103 If you are married, was your religion a factor in your choice of a marriage partner? If you are not married, do you think your religion will be an important factor in your eventual choice of a marriage partner?

104 Do you think religiously mixed marriages are a good idea? If so, why? If not, why not?

105 Is it important to you that your children be raised in your religion? In your version of that religion?

106 How do you understand the differences between men and women?

107 Do you believe that women have the same rights as men?

108 Do you think that men and women in your religion are generally treated equally? If not, why not?

109 Does your religion treat men and women differently? If so, how and why do you think this is so?
110 Are there social roles that are more appropriate for men than for women? If so, can you give me examples?
111 Are there social roles that are more appropriate for women than for men? If so, can you give me examples?
112 Do you think other people in your generation and religion share your views on the relations between men and women?
113 How many of your friends also belong to your religion/your branch of this religion?
114 Did you meet any or many of them through your religious involvement?
115 How many of your close friends also belong to your religion/branch of your religion?
116 Do you think religion, cultural background, or other factors are more important in determining who your friends are? What makes you think this?
117 Are many of your friends also the sons or daughters of immigrants/ immigrants themselves?

THEME IX: RELIGION AND WIDER CANADIAN REALITY

118 How many adherents of your religion do you think live in Canada?
119 Many religions are represented in Canada. Do you think this is important for what Canada is as a country? How?
120 Canada has an official policy of encouraging multiculturalism. What do you think this policy means?
121 Do you think it is important for what Canada as a country actually is, or is it just rhetoric?
122 Do you think the people in Canada generally welcome immigrants? Immigrants of your cultural origin or religious background?
123 Have you personally had experiences of intolerance coming from other Canadians because of your religion? Your cultural origin?
124 Do you think some religious or cultural minorities in Canada receive better treatment than others?
125 Do you think religion is an important influence in Canadian society generally?
126 Do you think religion should have more influence in Canadian society? Less?
127 Do you think your religion receives equal treatment in Canada compared with other religions? If not, which other religion(s) do you think is (are) favoured?
128 If other religions are favoured in Canada above yours, what are some of the marks of this favouritism?

129 Do you think adherents of your religion are better off in some parts of Canada than in others? If so, which ones?

130 Do you think that your religion should have a greater influence in Canada than it currently does? If so, how could this greater influence be exercised?

131 Do you think that your religion has too much influence in Canada? If so, what are the symptoms of this excess influence?

132 Are you able to practise your religion as fully as you would like in Canada? If not, what would have to change for this to become possible?

133 Considering the practice of religion in your country of birth/the country of birth of your parents, would you say that one can practise your religion more fully there or here in Canada, or is it about the same?

134 Referring to the previous question, is it the same for other religions?

135 Do you feel accepted as an equal and full member of Canadian society? If not, what would have to change for you to feel that you are an equal and full member?

THEME X: RELIGION AND WIDER WORLD REALITY

136 Compared to other countries in the world, would you say Canada is a good place to live in? Why or why not?

137 Are there other countries in the world where you would like to live? Instead of in Canada? As well as in Canada?

138 How in your opinion does Canada compare with other countries in terms of the level of religious tolerance? Is it better, worse, about the same?

139 Do you think that religion is an important force in the wider world we live in? Is this good, bad, or does it matter? How does this manifest itself?

140 Do you think some religions have more influence in the wider world outside Canada than others? If so, which ones? How does this greater influence manifest itself?

141 Do you think your religion is an important force in the wider world we live in? Is this good, bad, or does it matter? How does this power manifest itself?

142 What, in your opinion, are the most important religious developments in the world today?

143 Do you have significant relations with people in other parts of the world? Family? Friends? Others?

144 If so, in what parts of the world do these people live?

145 Have you visited these places very often?

146 What other forms of communication do you have with people in another part of the world outside Canada? Telephone? Letters? Internet/email?

147 Do you watch television/films that originate in these parts of the world?

148 Do you listen to music/read books/newspapers/magazines that originate in these parts of the world?

149 Does your religion occasion you to have contact with these other parts of the world, whether through publications (including newspapers), films and videos, television, travel, pilgrimage, Internet, other media?

150 What influence do you think adherents of your religion here in Canada have on adherents of your religion in other parts of the world? If there is such influence, how is this influence exerted, for instance, through publications, television, films and videos, travel, missionary activity, Internet, pilgrimage, other means?

151 Have there been events or developments in the wider world, outside Canada, that you think have had a significant effect on your religion, on how you practise your religion, on how you think about your religion? If so, please describe them briefly.

152 What do you think are the three biggest problems or challenges facing the world today?

153 What role do you think religion can or should play in addressing these challenges or problems?

THEME XI: DEMOGRAPHICS AND IMMIGRATION HISTORY

154 How old are you?

155 Where were you born?

156 Where were your parents born?

157 When did your parents/immigrant parent/you come to Canada?

158 Why did your family/immigrant parent choose Canada as their migration goal?

159 Are you a citizen of Canada?

160 Where did you first live/where did your parents/immigrant parent first live upon arrival in Canada?

161 Why did they choose that place?

162 Where is your permanent residence now? If you or your parents moved from one part of Canada to another, why did you or they do that?

163 What level of education do your parents have? Elementary only, secondary, post-secondary?

164 What kind of occupation do your parents have?

165 How many brothers or sisters do you have?

166 Do you have many relatives in Canada? How long have most of them lived in Canada?

167 Would you say that the family income of your parents is less than, about the same as, or higher than the average Canadian household income?

NOTES

CHAPTER ONE

1 The working title of the project was Religion among Immigrant Youth in Canada, funded by the Social Sciences and Humanities Research Council of Canada under its Standard Research Program. The researchers included the authors of the various chapters in this book but also Leslie Laczko at the University of Ottawa and Arlene Macdonald and Carolyn Reimer at the University of Toronto. The data was gathered from the fall of 2004 until the spring of 2006.

2 The highly significant exception, of course, is the migration of large numbers of people from Africa to the "New World" in the context of the seventeenth- to nineteenth-century slave trade perpetrated by Europeans. Although involuntary, this migration has to a greater or lesser extent informed the character of every society in the Americas.

3 For examples of research on this question before the turn of the century in various Western countries, including Canada, see Beiser et al. 1998; Bhatnagar 1984; Geschwender and Guppy 1995; Kallen 1977; Khosrokhavar 1997; Maani 1994; Portes and Zhou 1993; Vertovec and Rogers 1998; Young 1991; Zhou and Bankston III 1998. Only in a minority of cases has this vast literature dealt with religion.

4 Some representative Canadian examples include Beiser 1999; Halli and Driedger 1999; Lam 1994; Li 1998; Pendakur 2000. See, as another example, the bibliography provided in Bramadat and Fisher 2010, the purpose of which is to "list the most relevant research resources related to the role of religious groups in the integration of immigrants, refugees, and guest workers into Canadian society" but which actually contains relatively few such resources for Canada.

5 Some of the more recent work that looks specifically at religion among youth and the second generation includes Dhruvarajan 2003; Eid 2003, 2007; Hanvey and Kunz 2000; Liao 2007; McLellan 2009, ch.6; Moghissi, Rahnema, and Goodman 2009, ch.5; Nayar 2004; Pearson 2004; Verchery 2010; and earlier publications emanating from the present research project. See Beyer 2007, 2009, 2010; Ramji 2008a, 2008b.

6 For discussion of this issue, see, from a vast literature, Beaman 2003; Beyer 2001, 2003; Clarke and Byrne 1993; Greil and Bromley 2003; Peterson and Walhof 2002. When

speaking about religions, but not necessarily religion, the participants in this study almost always referred to one or more of these five religions.

7 As of 2001, the census year in which religious identity was last asked, out of a total population of a little more than 29 million, about 580,000 were Muslim, and around 300,000 each were Hindus, Buddhists, or Sikhs. Those with no religion amounted to about 16% of the population, or about 4.9 million, some 100,000 identified with other religions (e.g., Aboriginal spirituality, paganism/wicca, Zorastrianism, Baha'i, Jainism), and the rest declared themselves Christian. See Statistics Canada 2003a.

8 See the detailed discussion of recruitment in the following chapter. For preliminary results from the second project, see Beyer 2013; Lefebvre and Triki Yamani (forthcoming).

9 A number of versions of sociological theory are relevant here. We refer principally to a version developed by Beyer on the basis of Luhmann. See above all Beyer 2006b; Luhmann 1997, 1998, 2000. It is this version that we outline in the text and to which we refer in subsequent chapters. Other similar approaches include those of Max Weber, Talcott Parsons, and to some degree Clifford Geertz. See Geertz 1966; Parsons 1971; Weber 1946. The main differences include very centrally how social systems are conceived.

10 Much of the literature cited earlier in this chapter provides examples of this focus.

11 As will become clear, the project was not successful enough in recruiting participants who had grown up in Montreal to be able to engage in a Toronto–Montreal comparison. A subsequent research project has been able to look more defensibly at this issue. See Beyer 2013; Lefebvre and Triki Yamani (forthcoming) for preliminary results.

CHAPTER TWO

1 Thus, the University of British Columbia began its life as an outpost branch of McGill University. It was founded by Henry Marshall Tory, a prominent liberal Protestant trained at McGill and with a Bachelor of Divinity degree from its Wesleyan College. He then served as the first president of the University of Alberta and later the first principal of Carleton College, which later became Carleton University, where a good number of our participants were recruited. See Corbett 1992 [1954].

2 The argument in this paragraph follows Gidney 2004.

3 For analysis of the student movement of the 1960s in Canada, see Levitt 1984.

4 The University of Ottawa Act of 1965 contains various clauses indicative of this transition, including that the new university would promote and be run on "Christian principles." The act is available at http://web5.uottawa.ca/admingov/university-act.html.

5 Neutrality regarding religion on university campuses connotes permission or allowance by central administration for any religious tradition to organize voluntary, self-governing groups and claim the use of university space for meetings and so forth. This mode of regulation has led to conflict among students with different perspectives on things that implicate religion. For example, organized Muslim and Jewish students at Concordia University clashed during recent decades over matters pertaining to the Palestinian–Israeli conflict.

6 We should note that not just any "electronic advertising" was effective. Putting notices on electronic bulletin boards, for instance, was just as ineffective as putting them on physical ones.

7 The same story can be told in different contexts, each context framing the story in a different way such that the categories used by an observer to tell his or her version of

the story produce stories that vary according to the context in which the participant's story was told. For example, what a media reporter may select from a story in order to tell his or her story can be quite different from the selections of a scientific observer or a health professional engaged in diagnosis.

8   For one of the more recent discussions of this long-standing issue of gender differences and degree of religiosity, see Collett and Lizardo 2009 and the subsequent comments and reply in that issue of the *Journal for the Scientific Study of Religion*. As the authors note in the first sentence of their article, "The fact that women display higher patterns of religiosity than men is one of the most consistent findings in the sociology of religion" (213).

9   Attempts, in the context of the second phase, to recruit Jewish young adults of immigrant families did not prove successful, and the design of both projects made it unlikely that other religious identities would be represented among the participants. That said, a not insignificant number in both projects showed evidence of having fluid or even multiple religious identities.

CHAPTER THREE

1   For further discussion of the differences in income according to religion, see Model and Lin 2002. The issue of immigrant and above all "visible minority" income disadvantage in Canada has been the subject of much more research. See, as examples, Aydemir, Chen, and Corak 2005; Heisz and McLeod 2004; Pendakur 2000; Piché, Renaud, and Gingras 1999; Picot and Sweetman 2005.

2   It would of course be best to isolate 18- to 26-year-olds who were either of the 1.5 or second generation, looking specifically at how many of them were at that time attending university. This would correspond to the selection criteria of our sample. Unfortunately, Statistics Canada does not give easy access to its data. Complete access to the microdata is possible but requires an elaborate application procedure that excludes minor investigations such as are called for here. Alternatively, one can purchase custom data from Statistics Canada, but again, for such minor investigations, this avenue is prohibitively expensive. We therefore availed ourselves of data to which we have had access in the context of previous research projects and to publicly available data from the Statistics Canada website, www.statcan.gc.ca.

CHAPTER FOUR

1   Portions of this chapter were previously published in Beyer 2010.

2   Interviews were generically coded according to religion, gender, and order of transcription, not the order in which the interviews were conducted. MF14 is therefore the fourteenth Muslim female interview to be transcribed and so on for all other quotations.

3   For discussions of Canadian general attitudes, see Adams 1997, 2007; Biles, Burstein, and Frideres 2008; for Quebec specifically, Bouchard and Taylor 2008.

4   In this context, it is well to point out again that some recent research purports to show that the latter tendency is more important than our data make it look. See the discussion of research by Jeffrey Reitz and Rupa Bannerjee (2007) in chapter 3.

5   More detailed discussion and the presentation of concrete data for all these characteristics of all the sub-categorizations for the three religious groups is reserved for the

following six chapters. Here the intention is to offer a comparative overview so that the reader can appreciate the larger picture that emerged from the interviews.

6 An indicator of this possible overrepresentation can be found in the work of Paul Eid on Arab second-generation people in Montreal (Eid 2007). Eid's sample was recruited on the basis of Arab ethnicity or background and not on religious identity or background, as was the case in our research. It would therefore not have been as easily skewed toward religiously interested people. And indeed, Eid's sample included Muslims and Christians (among others) and found that the Muslims were somewhat less involved in their religion than the Christians. The Christians in Eid's sample, however, did not appear on average to be as highly involved in their religion as did our Muslim sample, indicating a greater presence of our less involved categories in Eid's group of Muslims.

7 In this and many other respects, our results both compare and contrast with those reported by Moghissi, Rahnema, and Goodman, whose sample of Muslim youth was apparently much larger than ours. To our knowledge, it is currently the only other broad study of Muslim young adults in Canada that includes religion. Unfortunately, in their report of their findings, these researchers do not give enough detail about the nature of their sample – including its size, factors such as 1.5/second-generation status, and its ethnic background distribution – to make a proper comparison possible. Given that their "youth" sample consists of 15- to 22-year-olds in the years just slightly before our study (2001–04 rather than 2004–06), it would seem a fairly important comparison, but their sample clearly included many relatively recent arrivals. The ethnic divisions are also uncertain, Iranians being perhaps disproportionately represented. See Moghissi, Rahnema, and Goodman 2009, esp. 111–43.

8 For British and Canadian examples from the first and second generations, see Knott 1996; Pearson 2004; Ralston 1998. What we underscore in the text is, in our sample, the degree of this pattern even in the absence of the understanding of this responsibility as "dharma" – a word that was used by none of our participants – or even as (rarely) a religious responsibility.

9 The literature on this distinction is vast. See as examples, including in the specifically Canadian context, Harding, Hori, and Soucy 2010; Matthews 2006; Prebish and Baumann 2002.

10 The interviewee who used this phrase, when asked what the "little bit" was, responded in somewhat typical fashion: "people have told me that I'm pretty open and tolerant of almost anything, so, that's part of it, and I also believe that, I dunno, what's that saying, that 'if you do something bad, it will come back to you?'" (BF08).

11 For discussions of the "syncretic" aspect of Chinese culture and religion and the sometimes ambiguous character of "Buddhism" in this context, see Crowe 2010; Paper 1995; Thompson 1996; Yang 1967.

12 See Harding, Hori, and Soucy 2010 and Matthews 2006 for various Canadian examples; see also Learman 2005 for some of the same organizations and movements more globally.

CHAPTER FIVE

1 Also known under the heading of Ithna Asheri or Imami Shi'ism.

2 No reliable data exist concerning the proportion of these subgroups in the overall Canadian Muslim population.

3 Grouping the participants into low, medium, and high but counting those in category 6 as among the high yields a similar result: the men would be 31% in low, 9% medium, and 60% high; the women, by contrast, 17% low, 17% medium, and 65% high.

4 There exist no reliable data with which one could compare Muslim, Hindu, and Buddhist "involvement" in Canada, above all because the measures of involvement almost always used are perhaps suitable for Christians (e.g., weekly religious service attendance) but not necessarily for any of these other three identities.

5 This figure is based on 2001 Canadian census data, which are discussed in chapter 3. That the 30% figure for non-religious Muslim males may not be drastically off the mark is supported by combining data from the 2002 Ethnic Diversity Survey, which indicated that about one-quarter of Muslim males showed little interest in their religion, and the Canadian census of 2001, which showed that among people whose ethnic origin is from regions of the world where Islam dominates, about another 5% identify as having "no religion." See Beyer 2005b; Beyer and Martin 2010.

6 This relation is likely reflective of a more general pattern. Following data from the 2001 Canadian census, in families where parents profess no religion, from 92 to 98% of the children in their households also have no religion. In families based on mixed-religious couples in which one parent is Muslim, from half to two-thirds of the children in such households have no religion. See Beyer and Martin 2010.

7 For a recent example of a large literature, both scholarly and from the popular press, see Lieken 2012. Our research clearly contradicts the general conclusion of such analyses as applied to Canada. As noted in the text, this conclusion does not, however, exclude the politicized radicalization of the isolated few, such as the so-called "Toronto 18." See Teotonio and Javed 2010 for profiles.

8 As a follower of Ithna Asheri (12er) Shi'ism, he chose as his religious authority or *marja* ("source of imitation") the Grand Ayatollah Sistani (see www.sistani.org), who lives in Najaf, Iraq, and is considered by many the preeminent Shi'a cleric of that country and even among all contemporary grand ayatollahs.

9 The reference is to the parallel sets of governmental structures of the Islamic Republic of Iran, one republican and including a directly elected president and legislature, the other consisting of appointed Shi'a clerics and including the Council of Guardians, the Council of Experts, and the Supreme Leader (*Faqih*). The latter have veto power over the former and control the armed forces as well as the judiciary.

10 Although it was not really clear from the interview, it is entirely possible that his father was a supporter of Ali Shariati's direction during the revolution (as was the father of one of the other Iranian participants) and likely a member or supporter of the communist Iranian Tudeh Party, which, perhaps paradoxically, survived the longest in the post-revolutionary power struggle. See Bakhash 1990; Keddie 2003. Neither of his parents appears to have experienced direct difficulties with the post-revolutionary regime.

11 The interview took place in early 2005; the reference is to a high-profile romance between actress and singer Jennifer Lopez and actor Ben Affleck, which ended in 2004.

12 Ahmed actually rated himself the same way: "on a scale from 1 to 10, 10 being the most religious, I'd be maybe a 6.5 or 7."

13 Ibrahim sported a beard at the time of the interview.

14 In fact, at the time of the interview, Ibrahim had a cast on one of his arms, the result of a snowboarding accident.

CHAPTER SIX

1 As a second-generation Canadian myself (in the terms of the research reported here, a 1.5er), I am not fond of using the phrase "second-generation immigrant," because it somehow implies that I am an immigrant and not a Canadian. Being a Canadian citizen, I find the use of the term makes me feel that I am either a second-class citizen or not "truly" Canadian, since it is still linked with the idea of belonging somewhere else. As the phrase was used within the confines of the research project, it is used sparingly throughout this chapter.

2 For the purpose of this research, I have termed those in category 10 as "Salafis." Salaf generally refers to the Companions of the Prophet and the first generations of Muslim followers. Salafis are thus people who seek to go back to this original Islam, generally rejecting the normative character of intervening developments. Salafis tend to look at the level of one's Muslimness. The categories for Muslimness include the disobedient (*asi*), the trespasser (*fasiq*), and the hypocrite (*munafiq*). The "disobedient" refers to the shortcomings associated with failing to fulfill the basic Islamic obligations such as prayer and fasting. The "trespasser" refers to the practices that actually commit violence to the Islamic law, such as drinking alcohol or committing adultery. The "hypocrite" is a person whose outward appearance or identity does not correspond to his or her inward attitudes, words, or deeds – includes lying, breaking a promise, betraying someone, behaving in an imprudent, evil, and insulting manner (Roald 2001). Although those classified as Salafis in the text do not necessarily think precisely in this way, this classification gives an idea of the clarity of their perception of Islam and its boundaries.

3 These themes were briefly discussed in Ramji 2008a.

4 This issue is further discussed in the chapter on gender and religion. The roles of the hijab for the women in our sample correlate strongly with what other literature on this issue has concluded, especially as concerns the second generation. See, as examples from non-Canadian contexts, David and Ayouby 2002; Furseth 2011; Naguib 2002; Werbner 2007; Williams and Vashi 2007. For Canada, see Alvi, Hoodfar, and McDonough 2003; Hoodfar 2006.

5 A black, robe-like dress that covers the entire body from head to foot. It is a common form of dress for women in some Arab countries like Saudi Arabia.

6 Irshad did not like the term "mosque," because her History of the Middle East teacher told her it means mosquito from the Spanish and therefore is a derogatory term. She was taught that King Ferdinand and his crusaders were wondering "how could we get rid of the Muslims?" They said "we should step on them like mosquitoes in the place of worship," which is the mosque. It seems that this information comes from *The Complete Idiot's Guide to Understanding Islam* but is now considered a misconception that has been floating around the Internet for a few years. The Spanish word for mosquito is *mosquito*, which means "little fly," *mosca* being "fly" and *-ito* a diminutive suffix. It is now argued that the term mosque entered the English language in the late fourteenth or early fifteenth century from the French *mosquée*, which derived from the Italian *moschea*. The Italians got it from Arabic *masgid*, which derived from the term *sagada*, meaning "to worship."

CHAPTER SEVEN

1 A form of Vishnu.

CHAPTER EIGHT

1 A chalisa is a prayer made up of forty quatrains with a set of opening and closing coup-lets. There are many chalisas to different deities, but the most popular is dedicated to Hanuman and is known as the Hanuman Chalisa.

2 The reference is to a term sometimes used in popular parlance among the first gen-eration about second-generation American South Asians, "American Born Confused Desis," where Desi refers to a person from South Asia.

3 On conversion as an element of a religious/spiritual "career," see Gooren 2010.

4 Dhruvarajan's research was conducted in Winnipeg, probably in the very late 1990s or the first years of the new century. One possible reason for the different results may be the size of the target population: the population of 18- to 25-year-olds in Winnipeg in 2001 was no more than three or four hundred, whereas for the same census, the Toronto metropolitan region registered at least 15,000 and the Ottawa region around 1,000. Many of our participants remarked on the difference it made to be in a small or large urban centre. See below, chapter 12 especially.

CHAPTER NINE

1 Another way of putting this characteristic is to say that the participants did not use re-ligion, whether Christianity, Buddhism, or another, to mark their identity boundaries. Compare, in this regard, and somewhat in contrast, the work on "Asian Americans" in the United States – for example, Carnes and Yang 2004. The more common bound-ary markers they used, as we detail below, were cultural, especially being Chinese or Japanese, for instance.

2 The modern Chinese term for "religion," zongjiao, literally means "group teaching." The modern terms for "religion" in Japanese, Korean, and Vietnamese are particular ver-sions/pronunciations of this same word.

3 McLellan comes to corresponding conclusions among Khmer second-generation youth in Ontario, although with salient differences as well, including that among the youths she studied there appeared to be more of a rejection of parental Buddhism as irrelevant rather than just lack of knowledge (McLellan 2009). See also the discussion of the Buddhist women in the next chapter.

4 A fifth year of high school, formerly known as Grade 13, that was for many years the final year of a high school program in Ontario until it was abolished in 2003.

5 This would not be an unusual experience for Japanese Canadians, since this population is not at all residentially concentrated, in part for historical reasons. See Makabe 1998.

CHAPTER TEN

1 Hsin Yun is the well-known founder of the Taiwanese and transnational Fo Guang Shan Buddhist order and of the equally global Buddha Light International Association.

2 In the entire sample of 197 interviews, no one claimed to be a Christian convert, even though recruitment notices asked only for people from a background of one of the three religions. As will be discussed below, the three women who were Christians with Buddhist family background grew up as Christians.

3 Considering Christianity (i.e., Protestant Christianity) and Catholicism as two different religions, and labelling them as such, is common among people from East Asia.

CHAPTER TWELVE

1 This is an estimate based on the 2001 census figure, which stood at about 13%. The question on religion was not asked in the more recent 2006 census, but there will have been some increase in this percentage, given the source of immigrants after 2001. For various projections in this regard, see Caron Malenfant, Lebel, and Martel 2010. The 2011 census data was not yet available at the time of writing.

2 Although Muslims in the Toronto region are more residentially concentrated than, for instance, the dominant Christian populations, there are several significant areas of such concentration – depending on how one counts, at least ten right across the urban area. See Beyer and Martin 2010, 93.

3 That such accommodation has not always or is not everywhere the case is attested in Coward and Goa 1987; Goa, Coward, and Neufeldt 1984; but see then also Bannerjee and Coward 2005 for a more recent accounting that accords more with our findings.

4 While not necessarily definitive or authoritative, see the list of Canadian Hindu temples in the Wikipedia article "Hindu Temples in Canada" (http://en.wikipedia.org/wiki/List_of_Hindu_temples_in_Canada), noting the number in the GTA and in Brampton, Mississauga, Etobicoke, Scarborough, and Markham specifically. Other sources attest to the same distribution.

5 For mosques in the GTA, see, for instance the list of mosques and Islamic centres provided by the Islamic Supreme Council of Canada website at http://www.islamic supremecouncil.com/canada.htm or the listing for Ontario mosques given at http://www.islamcan.com/masjid/cgi-bin/csvread.pl?stateprovince=Ontario&page=9. While perhaps not entirely reliable, such sources are certainly indicative.

6 A list of Islamic schools in the Toronto region can be found at the website of the Islamic World League at http://www.mwlcanada.org/canada/schools.htm#ontario. Again, one notices just how many more of these schools are available in the Toronto area as compared to any other major urban area in Canada.

CHAPTER THIRTEEN

1 Lele (2003) claims otherwise but offers no real evidence for this claim other than the presence of Hindutva-related organizations in the country.

2 See Peek 2005; Williams and Vashi 2007; Bagby 2007; Cainkar 2004 as examples. A good deal of the literature on Muslims in the US, including as concerns the second generation, focuses on "Muslim" as an aspect of people's identity rather than on "Muslim" as religion. See, as examples, David and Ayouby 2002; Muedini 2009; Sirin and Fine 2008. From this literature it is more difficult to conclude how Islam is being constructed as opposed to what importance Islam has in self-identity and attributed identity.

3 See Sirin and Fine 2008 but also Cesari 2010, which includes United States/Europe comparisons.

4 It is in this context that one can understand Karen Leonard's conclusion (Leonard 2002) that what she calls "Islamization" (the tendency to construct Islam on a global, Islamic pietistic model and consider this as entirely appropriate for the American context) and "Americanization" (taking on certain more commonly American forms and value orientations in that construction) may be happening in the American second generation at the same time and are not contradictory. Leonard does not refer to specific research in making this claim, but it is consistent with the research reported by others already cited.

REFERENCES

Abada, T., F. Hou, and B. Ram. 2008. *Group Differences in Educational Attainment among the Children of Immigrants*. Ottawa: Statistics Canada

Adams, M. 1997. *Sex in the Snow: Canadian Social Values at the End of the Millennium*. Toronto: Penguin

– 2003. *Fire and Ice: The United States, Canada and the Myth of Converging Values*. Toronto: Penguin

– 2007. *Unlikely Utopia: The Surprising Triumph of Canadian Multiculturalism*. Toronto: Penguin

Ahmad, F. 2001. "Modern Traditions? British Muslim Women and Academic Achievement." *Gender and Education* 13(2):137–52

Al-Lami, M. 2009. "Studies of Radicalisation: State of the Field Report." *Politics and International Relations Working Papers* 11 (January). www.rhul.ac.uk/politics-and-IR

Alvi, S.S., H. Hoodfar, and S. McDonough, eds. 2003. *The Muslim Veil in North America: Issues and Debates*. Toronto: Women's Press

Anderson, L., and P. Dickey Young, eds. 2004. *Women and Religious Traditions*. New York: Oxford University Press

Anisef, P., and K.M. Kilbride, eds. 2003. *Managing Two Worlds: The Experiences and Concerns of Immigrant Youth in Ontario*. Toronto: Canadian Scholars Press

Appadurai, A. 1996. *Modernity at Large: Cultural Dimensions of Globalization*. Minneapolis: University of Minnesota Press

Arweck, E., and E. Nesbitt. 2010. "Young People's Identity Formation in Mixed-Faith Families: Continuity and Discontinuity in Religious Traditions." *Journal of Contemporary Religion* 25(1):67–87

Aydemir, A., W.-H. Chen, and M. Corak. 2005. *Intergenerational Earnings Mobility among Children of Canadian Immigrants*. Ottawa: Statistics Canada

Bagby, I.A.-W. 2007. "Second-Generation Muslim Immigrants in Detroit Mosques: The Second Generation's Search for Their Place and Identity in the American Mosque." In *Passing on the Faith: Transforming Traditions for the Next Generation of Jews, Christians, and Muslims*, edited by J.L. Heft, 218–44. New York: Fordham University Press

Bakhash, S. 1990. *The Reign of the Ayatollahs: Iran and the Islamic Revolution*. rev. edn. New York: Basic Books

Bakht, N., ed. 2008. *Belonging and Banishment: Being Muslim in Canada*. Toronto: TSAR Publications

Balagangadhara, S.N. 1994. *"The Heathen in His Blindness ...": Asia, the West, and the Dynamic of Religion*. Leiden: Brill

Bannerjee, S., and H. Coward. 2005. "Hindus in Canada: Negotiating Identity in a 'Different' Homeland." In *Religion and Ethnicity in Canada*, edited by P. Bramadat and D. Seljak, 30–51. Toronto: Pearson Longman

Baumann, M., and J. Stolz, eds. 2007. *Eine Schweiz – Viele Religionen. Risiken un Chancen des Zusammenlebens*. Bielefeld: Transcript Verlag

Beaman, L. 2003. "The Myth of Plurality, Diversity and Vigour: Constitutional Privilege of Protestantism in the United States and Canada." *Journal for the Scientific Study of Religion* 42:311–28

Beiser, M. 1999. *Strangers at the Gate: The "Boat People's" First Ten Years in Canada*. Toronto: University of Toronto Press

– F. Hou, I. Hyman, and M. Tousignant. 1998. *Growing up Canadian: A Study of New Immigrant Children*. Ottawa: Human Resources Development Canada

Bernhardt, E., C. Goldscheider, F. Goldscheider, and G. Bjerén, eds. 2007. *Immigration, Gender, and Family Transitions to Adulthood in Sweden*. Lanham, MD: University Press of America

Berns McGown, R. 1999. *Muslims in the Diaspora: The Somali Communities of London and Toronto*. Toronto: University of Toronto Press

Beuchling, O. 2005. "'Der Jade-Kaiser ist im Exil in Deutschland': Aspekte religiöser Sozialisation in der vietnamesisch-buddhistischen Diaspora." In *Theologie – Pädagogik – Kontext: Zukunftsperspektiven der Religionspädagogik*. Wolfram Weisse zum 60. Geburtstag, edited by U. Günther, M. Gensicke, C. Müller, G. Mitchell, T. Knauth, and R. Bolle, 255–67. Münster: Waxmann

– 2008. "Zur Bedeutung des Buddhismus für Jugendliche mit Migrationshintergrund." In *Dialogischer Religionsunterricht in Hamburg: Positionen, Analysen und Perspektiven im Kontext Europas*, edited by W. Weisse, 117–24. Münster: Waxmann

– 2011. "Sozialisation und Erziehung in der buddhistischen Diaspora: Eine ethnografische Perspektive." In *Buddhismus im Westen: Ein Dialog zwischen Religion und Wissenschaft*, edited by C. Roloff, W. Weisse, and M. Zimmermann, 155–74. Münster: Waxmann

Beyer, P. 1997. "Religious Vitality in Canada: The Complementarity of Religious Market and Secularization Perspectives." *Journal for the Scientific Study of Religion* 36:272–88

– 1998. "The City and beyond as Dialogue: Negotiating Religious Authenticity in Global Society." *Social Compass* 45:61–73

– 2001. "What Counts as Religion in Global Society? From Practice to Theory." In *Religion in the Process of Globalization / Religion im Prozeß der Globalisierung*, edited by P. Beyer, 125–50. Würzburg: Ergon Verlag

– 2003. "Conceptions of Religion: On Distinguishing Scientific, Theological, and 'Official' Meanings." *Social Compass* 50(2):141–60

– 2005a. "Au croisement de l'identité et de la différence : les syncrétismes culturo-religieux dans le contexte de la mondialisation." *Social Compass* 52:417–29

– 2005b. "The Future of Non-Christian Religions in Canada: Patterns of Religious Identification among Recent Immigrants and Their Second Generation, 1981–2001." *Studies in Religion / Sciences religieuses* 34:165–96

- 2005c. "Religious Identity and Educational Attainment among Recent Immigrants to Canada: Gender, Age, and 2nd Generation." *Journal of International Migration and Integration* 6(2):171–99
- 2006a. "Buddhism in Canada: A Statistical Overview from Canadian Censuses, 1981–2001." *Canadian Journal of Buddhist Studies* 2:83–102
- 2006b. *Religions in Global Society.* London: Routledge
- 2007. "Can the Tail Wag the Dog? Diaspora Reconstructions of Religion in a Globalized Society." *Nordic Journal of Religion and Society* 20(1):41–63
- 2009. "Glocalization of Religions: Plural Authenticities at the Centres and at the Margins." In *Sufis in Western Society: Global Networking and Locality*, edited by R. Geaves, M. Dressler, and G. Klinkhammer, 13–25. London: Routledge
- 2010. "Differential Reconstruction of Religions among Second Generation Immigrant Youth in Canada." *Annual Review of the Sociology of Religion* 1:1–28
- 2012. "Socially Engaged Religion in a Post-Westphalian Global Context: Remodeling the Secular/Religious Distinction." *Sociology of Religion* 73(2)
- 2013. "Regional Differences and Continuities at the Intersection of Culture and Religion: A Case Study of Immigrant and Second Generation Young Adults in Canada." In *Religion in the Public Sphere: Interdisciplinary Perspectives across the Canadian Provinces*, edited by S. Lefebvre and L. Beaman. Toronto: University of Toronto Press
- and W.K. Martin. 2010. *The Future of Religious Diversity in Canada.* Ottawa: Citizenship and Immigration Canada
Bhachu, P. 1985. *Twice Migrants: East African Sikh Settlers in Britain.* London: Tavistock
Bhatnagar, J. 1984. "Adjustment and Education of South Asian Children in Canada." In *South Asians in the Canadian Mosaic*, edited by E.b.R.N. Kanungo, 49–66. Montreal: Kala Bharati Foundation
Bibby, R.W. 1987. *Fragmented Gods: The Poverty and Potential of Religion in Canada.* Toronto: Irwin
- 1993. *Unknown Gods: The Ongoing Story of Religion in Canada.* Toronto: Stoddart
- 2002. *Restless Gods: The Renaissance of Religion in Canada.* Toronto: Stoddart
Biles, J., M. Burstein, and J. Frideres, eds. 2008. *Immigration and Integration in Canada in the Twenty-First Century.* Kingston: Queen's School of Policy Studies and McGill-Queen's University Press
Bloemraad, I. 2006. *Becoming a Citizen: Incorporating Immigrants and Refugees in the United States.* Berkeley: Univesity of California Press
Bouchard, G., and C. Taylor. 2008. *Building the Future: A Time for Reconciliation.* Quebec City: Government of Quebec
Bouma, G.D. 1995. "The Emergence of Religious Plurality in Australia: A Multicultural Society." *Sociology of Religion* 56(3):285–302
- 2007. *Australian Soul: Religion and Spirituality in the 21st Century.* New York: Cambridge University Press
Boyd, M. 2004. *Dispute Resolution in Family Law: Protecting Choice, Promoting Inclusion.* Toronto: Ontario Ministry of the Attorney General. http://www.attorneygeneral.jus.gov.on.ca/english/about/pubs/boyd/fullreport.pdf
- and E.M. Grieco. 1998. "Triumphant Transitions: Socioeconomic Achievements of the Second Generation in Canada." *International Migration Review* 32(4):853–76
Bramadat, P. 2000. *The Church on the World's Turf: An Evangelical Christian Group at a Secular University.* New York: Oxford University Press

- 2005. "Religion, Social Capital, and 'the Day That Changed the World.'" *Journal of International Migration and Integration* 2(6):201–17
- and S. Fisher. 2010. *Religious Organizations and the Integration of Immigrants, Refugees, and Temporary Foreign Workers: An Annotated Bibliography and List of Community Organizations*. Vancouver: Metropolis British Columbia

Bramadat, P., and D. Seljak, eds. 2005. *Religion and Ethnicity in Canada*. Toronto: Pearson Longman

Bunt, G.R. 2004. "Rip. Burn. Pray: Islamic Expression Online." In *Religion Online: Finding Faith on the Internet*, edited by L.L. Dawson and D.E. Cowan. New York: Routledge

Burghart, R., ed. 1987. *Hinduism in Great Britain: The Perpetuation of Religion in an Alien Cultural Milieu*. London: Tavistock

Cainkar, L. 2004. "Islamic Revival among Second-Generation Arab-American Muslims: The American Experience and Globlization Intersect." *Bulletin of the Royal Institute for Inter-Faith Studies* 6(2):99–120

Carnes, T., and F. Yang, eds. 2004. *Asian American Religions: The Making and Remaking of Borders and Boundaries*. New York: New York University Press

Caron Malenfant, É., A. Lebel, and L. Martel. 2010. *Projections of the Diversity of the Canadian Population, 2006 to 2031*. Catalogue no. 91-551-X. Ottawa: Statistics Canada, Demography Division. www.statcan.gc.ca

Castles, S., and M.J. Miller. 2003. *The Age of Migration: International Population Movements in the Modern World*. 3rd edn. New York: Guilford Press

Cesari, J., ed. 2010. *Muslims in the West after 9/11: Religion, Politics and Law*. London: Routledge

Chandler, S. 2008. "The Social Ethic of Religiously Unaffiliated Spirituality." *Religion Compass* 2(2):240–56

Clarke, P.B., and P. Byrne. 1993. *Religion Defined and Explained*. London: St Martin's Press

Collett, J.L., and O. Lizardo. 2009. "A Power-Control Theory of Gender and Religiosity." *Journal for the Scientific Study of Religion* 48(2):213–31

Corak, M. 2008. "Immigration in the Long Run: The Education and Earnings Mobility of Second-Generation Canadians." *IRPP Choices* 14(13)

Corbett, E.A. 1992 (1954). *Henry Marshall Tory: A Biography*. Edmonton: University of Alberta Press

Coward, H., and D. Goa. 1987. "Religious Experience of the South Asian Diaspora in Canada." In *The South Asian Diaspora in Canada: Six Essays*, edited by M. Israel, 73–86. Toronto: Multicultural History Society of Ontario and Centre for South Asian Studies

Coward, H., J.R. Hinnells, and R.B. Williams, eds. 2000. *The South Asian Religious Diaspora in Britain, Canada, and the United States*. Albany: SUNY Press

Cressey, G. 2006. *Diaspora Youth and Ancestral Homeland: British Pakistani/Kashmiri Youth Visiting Kin in Pakistan and Kashmir*. Leiden: Brill

Crowe, P. 2010. "Chinese Religions." In *Asian Religions in British Columbia*, edited by L. DeVries, D. Baker, and D. Overmyer, 249–74. Vancouver: University of British Columbia Press

David, G., and K.K. Ayouby. 2002. "Being Arab and Becoming Americanized: Forms of Mediated Assimilation in Metropolitan Detroit." In *Muslim Minorities in the West: Visible and Invisible*, edited by Y.Y. Haddad and J.I. Smith, 125–42. Walnut Creek, CA: Altamira Press

Davidman, L. 1993. *Tradition in a Rootless World: Women Turn to Orthodox Judaism*. Berkeley: University of California Press

DeVries, L., D. Baker, and D. Overmyer, eds. 2010. *Asian Religions in British Columbia*. Vancouver: University of British Columbia Press

Dhruvarajan, V. 2003. "Second Generation Indo-Canadians: Change, Resistance, Adaptation." In *Fractured Identity: The Indian Diaspora in Canada*, edited by S. Varma and R. Seshan, 168–85. Jaipur: Rawat Publishing

Directorate of Integration and Diversity. 2009. *Overview 2008: How Well is Integration Working?* http://www.imdi.no/Documents/Rapporter/Overview_2008_ENGLISH.pdf

Ebaugh, H.R., and J.S. Chafetz, eds. 2000. *Religion and the New Immigrants: Continuities and Adaptations in Immigrant Congregations*. Walnut Creek, CA: Altamira Press

Eickelman, D.F., and J.W. Anderson, eds. 1999. *New Media in the Muslim World: The Emerging Public Sphere*. Bloomington: Indiana University Press

Eid, P. 2003. "The Interplay between Ethnicity, Religion, and Gender among Second-Generation Christian and Muslim Arabs in Montreal." *Canadian Ethnic Studies / Études ethniques au Canada* 35(2):30–60

– 2007. *Being Arab: Ethnic and Religious Identity Building among Second Generation Youth in Montreal*. Montreal and Kingston: McGill-Queen's University Press

Eilers, K., C. Seitz, and K. Hirschler. 2008. "Religiousness among Young Muslims in Germany." In *Islam and Muslims in Germany*, edited by A. Al-Hamarneh and J. Thielmann, 83–115. Leiden: Brill

Entzinger, H. 2003. "Les jeunes musulmans d'un Rotterdam pluriculturel: une vision 'maigre' de la citoyenneté." In *L'avenir de l'islam en France et en Europe*, edited by M. Wieviorka, 101–10. Paris: Éditions Balland

Fadil, N. 2005. "Individualizing Faith, Individualizing Identity: Islam and Young Muslim Women in Belgium." In *European Muslims and the Secular State*, edited by J. Cesari and S. McLoughlin, 85–97. Aldershot, UK: Ashgate

Fitzgerald, T. 1990. "Hinduism and the World Religion Fallacy." *Religion* 20, 101–18

Foley, M.W., and D.R. Hoge. 2007. *Religion and the New Immigrants: How Faith Communities Form our Newest Citizens*. New York: Oxford University Press

Frese, H.-L. 2002. *Den Islam ausleben: Konzepte authentischer Lebensführung junger türkischer Muslime in der Diaspora*. Bielefeld: Transcript

Frykenberg, R.E. 1989. "The Emergence of Modern 'Hinduism' as a Concept and as an Institution: A Reappraisal with Special Reference to South India." In *Hinduism Reconsidered*, edited by G.D. Sontheimer and H. Kulke, 29–49. Delhi: Manohar

Furseth, I. 2011. "The Hijab: Boundary Work and Identity Negotiations among Immigrant Muslim Women in the Los Angeles Area." *Review of Religious Research* 52(4):365–85

Geaves, R. 2007. "A Reassessment of Identity Strategies amongst British South Asian Muslims." In *Religious Reconstruction in the South Asian Diasporas: From One Generation to Another*, edited by J. Hinnells, 13–28. Basingstoke, UK: Palgrave Macmillan

Geertz, C. 1966. "Religion as a Cultural System." In *Anthropological Approaches to the Study of Religion*, edited by M. Bainton, 1–46. London: Tavistock

Geisser, V. 2003. "Collègiens lycéens de culture musulmane: des théroiciens ordinarie de la laïcité?" In *L'avenir de l'islam en France et en Europe*, edited by M. Wieviorka, 79–87. Paris: Éditions Balland

Gerber, D.A. 2011. *American Immigration: A Very Short Introduction*. Oxford: Oxford University Press

Geschwender, J.A., and N. Guppy. 1995. "Ethnicity, Educational Attainment, and Earned Income among Canadian-Born Men and Women." *Canadian Ethnic Studies / Études ethniques au Canada* 27(1):67–83

Gidney, C. 2004. *A Long Eclipse: The Liberal Protestant Establishment and the Canadian University, 1920–1970*. Montreal and Kingston: McGill-Queen's University Press

Goa, D.J., H.G. Coward, and R. Neufeldt. 1984. "Hindus in Alberta: A Study in Religious Continuity and Change." *Canadian Ethnic Studies / Études ethniques au Canada* 16(1):96–113

Gooren, H. 2010. *Religious Conversion and Disaffiliation: Tracing Patterns of Change in Faith Practices*. New York: Palgrave Macmillan

Gosine, K. 2000. "Revisiting the Notion of a "Recast" Vertical Mosaic in Canada: Does a Post Secondary Education Make a Difference?" *Canadian Ethnic Studies / Études ethniques au Canada* 32(3):89–104

Greil, A.L., and D.G. Bromley, eds. 2003. *Defining Religion: Investigating the Boundaries between Sacred and Secular*, vol. 10. London: Elsevier Scientific

Habermas, J. 2010. *An Awareness of What Is Missing: Faith and Reason in a Post-secular Age*. Cambridge: Polity Press

Haddad, Y.Y. 2007. "The Post-9/11 Hijab as Icon." *Sociology of Religion* 68:253–67

Hall, D.D., ed. 1997. *Lived Religion in America: Toward a History of Practice*. Princeton, NJ: Princeton University Press

Halli, S.S., and L. Driedger, eds. 1999. *Immigrant Canada: Demographic, Economic, and Social Challenges*. Toronto: University of Toronto Press

Halli, S.S., and Vedanand. 2007. "The Problem of Second-Generation Decline: Perspectives on Integration in Canada." *Journal of International Migration and Integration* 8:277–87

Hanvey, L., and J.L. Kunz. 2000. *Immigrant Youth in Canada: A Research Report from the Canadian Council on Social Development*. Ottawa: Canadian Council on Social Development

Harding, J.S., V.S. Hori, and A. Soucy, eds. 2010. *Wild Geese: Buddhism in Canada*. Montreal and Kingston: McGill-Queen's University Press

Heisz, A., and L. McLeod. 2004. *Low Income in Census Metropolitan Areas, 1980–2000*. Analytical Paper Series no. 89-613-MIE. Ottawa: Statistics Canada. www.statcan.ca

Helland, C. 2004. "Popular Religions and the World Wide Web: A Match Made in (Cyber) Heaven." In *Religion Online: Finding Faith on the Internet*, edited by L.L. Dawson and D.E. Cowan. New York: Routledge

Hervieu-Léger, D. 1999. *Le pèlerin et le converti: la religion en mouvement*. Paris: Flammarion

Hiebert, D. 2009. "The Economic Integration of Immigrants in Metropolitan Vancouver." *IRPP Choices* 15(7)

Higgins, J. 2008. *Annotated Bibliography of New Zealand Literature on Migrant and Refugee Youth*. Aukland: New Zealand Department of Labour

Hitchcock, G., and D. Hughes. 1989. *Research and the Teacher: A Qualitative Introduction to School-Based Research*. London: Routledge

Hoge, D.R., W.D. Dinges, M. Johnson, and J.L. Gonzalez. 2001. *Young Adult Catholics: Religion in the Culture of Choice*. Notre Dame, IN: University of Notre Dame Press

Hoodfar, H. 2006. "More Than Clothing: Veiling as an Adaptive Strategy." In *Religion and Candian Society: Traditions, Transitions and Innovations*, edited by L. Beaman. Toronto: Canadian Scholars Press

Israel, M., ed. 1987. *The South Asian Diaspora in Canada: Six Essays*. Toronto: Multicultural History Society of Ontario and Centre for South Asian Studies

Jackson, R., and E. Nesbitt. 1993. *Hindu Children in Britain*. Stoke-on-Trent: Trentham Books

Jacob, S., and P. Thaku. 2000. "Jyothi Hindu Temple: One Religion, Many Practices." In *Religion and the New Immigrants: Continuities and Adaptations in Immigrant Congregations*, edited by H.R. Ebaugh and J.S. Chafetz, 229–42. Walnut Creek, CA: Altamira Press

Jacobs, J. 2002. *Hidden Heritage: The Legacy of Crypto-Jews*. Berkeley: University of California Press

Jaffrelot, C., and I. Therwath. 2007. "The Sangh Parivar and Hindu Nationalism in the West: What Kind of 'Long-Distance Nationalism'?" *International Journal of Political Sociology* 1(3):278–95

Janhevich, D., and H. Ibrahim. 2004. "Muslims in Canada: An Illustrative and Demographic Profile." *Our Diverse Cities* 1:49–57

Joshi, K.Y. 2006. *New Roots in America's Sacred Ground: Religion, Race, and Ethnicity in Indian America*. New Brunswick, NJ: Rutgers University Press

Kallen, E. 1977. *Spanning the Generations: A Study in Jewish Identity*. Don Mills, ON: Longman

Karim, J. 2005. "Voices of Faith, Faces of Beauty: Connecting American Women through Azizah." In *Muslim Networks: From Hajj to Hip Hop*, edited by B.B. Lawrence. Chapel Hill: University of North Carolina Press

Karim, K.H. 2009. "Changing Perceptions of Islamic Authority among Muslims in Canada, the United States and the United Kingdom." *IRPP Choices* 15(2)

Keddie, N.R. 2003. *Modern Iran: Roots and Results of Revolution*. New Haven, CT: Yale University Press

Kelley, N., and M. Trebilcock. 2010. *The Making of the Mosaic: A History of Canadian Immigration Policy*. 2nd edn. Toronto: University of Toronto Press

Khosrokhavar, F. 1997. *L'islam des jeunes*. Paris: Flammarion

Kibria, N. 2002. *Becoming Asian American: Second Generation Chinese and Korean American Identities*. Baltimore: Johns Hopkins University Press

Kisala, R.J., and M.R. Mullins, eds. 2001. *Religion and Social Crisis in Japan: Understanding Japanese Society through the Aum Affair*. New York: Palgrave

Knott, K. 1996. "Hindu Women, Destiny and *Stridharma*." *Religion* 26:15–35

– 2005. *The Location of Religion: A Spatial Analysis*. London: Equinox

Kurien, P.A. 1998. "Becoming American by Becoming Hindu: Indian Americans Take Their Place at the Multicultural Table." In *Gatherings in Diaspora: Religious Communities and the New Immigration*, edited by S.A. Warner and J.G. Wittner, 37–70. Philadelphia: Temple University Press

– 2007. *A Place at the Multicultural Table: The Development of an American Hinduism*. New Brunswick, NJ: Rutgers University Press

Lam, L. 1994. "Immigrant Students." In *Learning and Sociological Profiles of Canadian High School Students*, edited by P. Anisef, 121–30. Queenston, NY: Edwin Mellen Press

Learman, L., ed. 2005. *Buddhist Missionaries in the Era of Globalization*. Honolulu: University of Hawai'i Press

Lefebvre, S., and A. Triki Yamani. (forthcoming). "Jeunes adultes immigrés. Dynamiques ethno-religieuses et identitaires." *Études ethniques canadiennes / Canadian Ethnic Studies*

Lele, J. 2003. "Indian Diaspora's Long-Distance Nationalism: The Rise and Proliferation of 'Hindutva' in Canada." In *Fractured Identity: The Indian Diaspora in Canada*, edited by S.J. Varma and R. Seshan, 67–119. Jaipur: Rawat Publishing

Leonard, K. 2002. "South Asian Leadership of American Muslims." In *Muslims in the West: From Sojourners to Citizens*, 233–49. New York: Oxford University Press

Levitt, C. 1984. *Children of Privilege: Student Revolt in the Sixties: A Study of Student Movements in Canada, the United States, and West Germany*. Toronto: University of Toronto Press

Lewis, P. 2007a. "British Muslims and the Search for Religious Guidance." In *Religious Reconstructions in the South Asian Diasporas*, edited by J.R. Hinnells, 29–50. Basingstoke, UK: Palgrave Macmillan

– 2007b. *Young, British and Muslim*. London and New York: Continuum

Li, P.S. 1998. *The Chinese in Canada*. Toronto: Oxford University Press

Liao, L. 2007. *The Role of Immigrant Faith in the Acculturation and Identity Development of Chinese Immigrant Youth*. Unpublished MA thesis, Wilfrid Laurier University, Waterloo, ON

Lieken, R.S. 2012. *Europe's Angry Muslims: The Revolt of the Second Generation*. Oxford: Oxford University Press

Lightstone, J.N., and F.B. Bird. 1995. *Ritual and Ethnic Identity: A Comparative Study of the Social Meaning of Liturgical Ritual in Synagogues*. Waterloo, ON: Wilfrid Laurier University Press

Lucassen, J., D. Feldman, and J. Oltmer. 2006. "Immigrant Integration in Western Europe, Then and Now." In *Paths of Integration: Migrants in Western Europe (1880–2004)*, edited by J. Lucassen, D. Feldman, and J. Oltmer, 7–23. Amsterdam: Amsterdam University Press

Lucassen, J., L. Lucassen, and P. Manning, eds. 2010. *Migration in World History: Multidisciplinary Approaches*. Leiden: Brill

Luhmann, N. 1997. *Die Gesellschaft der Gesellschaft*. Frankfurt/M: Suhrkamp

– 1998. "Religion als Kommunikation." In *Religion als Kommunikation*, edited by H. Tyrell, V. Krech, and H. Knoblauch, 135–45. Würzburg: Ergon Verlag

– 2000. *Die Religion der Gesellschaft*, edited by André Kieserling. Frankfurt/M: Suhrkamp

Maani, S.A. 1994. "Are Young and Second Generation Immigrants at a Disadvantage in the Australian Labor Market?" *International Migration Review* 28(4):865–82

MacDougall, H.A. 1982. "St. Patrick's College (Ottawa) (1929–1979): Ethnicity and the Liberal Arts in Catholic Education." *CCHA Study Sessions* 49:53–71

McGuire, M. 2008. *Lived Religion: Faith and Practice in Everyday Life*. New York: Oxford University Press

McLellan, J. 1999. *Many Petals of the Lotus: Five Asian Buddhist Communities in Toronto*. Toronto: University of Toronto Press

– 2009. *Cambodian Refugees in Ontario: Resettlement, Religion, and Identity*. Toronto: University of Toronto Press

Madan, T.N. 2006. "Thinking Globally about Hinduism." In *Oxford Handbook of Global Religions*, edited by M. Juergensmeyer, 15–24. New York: Oxford University Press

Mahmood, S. 2001. "Feminist Theory, Embodiment, and the Docile Agent: Some Reflections on the Egyptian Islamic Revival." *Cultural Anthropology* 16(2):202–36

Makabe, T. 1998. *The Canadian Sansei*. Toronto: University of Toronto Press

Masuzawa, T. 2005. *The Invention of World Religions*. Chicago: University of Chicago Press

Matthews, B., ed. 2006. *Buddhism in Canada*. New York: Routledge

Min, P.G. 2010. *Preserving Ethnicity through Religion in America*. New York: New York University Press

Mitra Bhikkhu, D. 2010. *Dhamma Education: The Transmission and Reconfiguration of the Sri Lankan Buddhist Tradition in Toronto*. PhD dissertation, Department of Religion and Culture, Wilfrid Laurier University, Waterloo, ON

Model, S., and L. Lin. 2002. "The Cost of Not Being Christian: Hindus, Sikhs and Muslims in Britain and Canada." *International Migration Review* 36(4):1,061–92

Moghissi, H., S. Rahnema, and M.J. Goodman. 2009. *Diaspora by Design: Muslim Immigrants in Canada and Beyond*. Toronto: University of Toronto Press

Muedini, F. 2009. "Muslim American College Youth: Attitudes and Responses Five Years after 9/11." *Muslim World* 99:39–59

Naguib, S.-A. 2002. "The Northern Way: Muslim Communities in Norway. In *Muslim Minorities in the West: Visible and Invisible*, edited by Y.Y. Haddad and J.I. Smith, 161–74. Walnut Creek, CA: Altamira Press

Narayanan, V. 2006. "Hindu Communities Abroad." In *Oxford Handbook of Global Religions*, edited by M. Juergensmeyer, 57–65. New York: Oxford University Press

Nayar, K.E. 2004. *The Sikh Diaspora in Vancouver: Three Generations amid Tradition, Modernity, and Multiculturalism*. Toronto: University of Toronto Press

Nederveen Pieterse, J. 2003. *Globalization and Culture: Global Melange*. Lanham, MD: Rowman and Littlefield

Nesbitt, E. 1991. *"My Dad's Hindu, My Mum's Side Are Sikhs": Issues in Religious Identity*. Charlbury, UK: Research and Curriculum Paper, National Foundation for Arts Education. http://www.casas.org.uk/papers/pdfpapers/identity.pdf

– 1998. "British, Asian and Hindu: Identity, Self-Narration and the Ethnographic Interview." *Journal of Beliefs and Values* 19(2):189–200

Orsi, R.A. 2005. *Between Heaven and Earth: The Religious Worlds People Make and the Scholars Who Study Them*. Princeton, NJ: Princeton University Press

Panayi, P. 2010. *An Immigration History of Britain: Multicultural Racism since 1800*. Harlow, UK: Pearson

Papastergiadis, N. 2000. *The Turbulence of Migration: Globalization, Deterritorialization, and Hybridity*. Cambridge, UK, and Malden, MA: Polity Press and Blackwell

Paper, J. 1995. *The Spirits Are Drunk: Comparative Approaches to Chinese Religion*. Albany, NY: SUNY Press

Parsons, G. 1994. *The Growth of Religious Diversity: Britain from 1945*. London: Routledge

Parsons, T. 1971. *The System of Modern Societies*. Englewood Cliffs, NJ: Prentice-Hall

Pearson, A.M. 2004. "Being Hindu in Canada: Personal Narratives from First and Second Generation Immigrant Hindu Women." *Religious Studies and Theology* 23:55–88

Peek, L. 2005. "Becoming Muslim: The Development of a Religious Identity." *Sociology of Religion* 66(3):215–42

Pendakur, R. 2000. *Immigrants and the Labour Force: Policy, Regulation, and Impact*. Montreal: McGill-Queen's University Press

Penn, R., and P. Lambert. 2009. *Children of International Migrants in Europe: Comparative Perspectives*. London: Palgrave Macmillan

Perrella, A.M.L., S.D. Brown, B.J. Kay, and D.C. Docherty. 2008. "The 2007 Provincial Election and Electoral System Referendum in Ontario." *Canadian Political Science Review* 2(1):78–87

Peterson, D., and D. Walhof, eds. 2002. *The Invention of Religion: Rethinking Belief in Politics and History*. New Brunswick, NJ: Rutgers University Press

Phillips, J. 2009. "History of Immigration." In *Te Ara—The Encyclopedia of New Zealand*. http://www.teara.govt.nz/en/history-of-immigration

Piché, V., J. Renaud, and L. Gingras. 1999. "Comparative Immigrant Economic Integration." In *Immigrant Canada: Demographic, Economic, and Social Challenges*, edited by S.S. Halli and L. Driedger, 185–211. Toronto: University of Toronto Press

Picot, G., and A. Sweetman. 2005. *The Deteriorating Economic Welfare of Immigrants and Possible Causes: Update 2005*. Ottawa: Statistics Canada

Porter, J.A. 1965. *The Vertical Mosaic: An Analysis of Social Class and Power in Canada*. Toronto: University of Toronto Press

Portes, A., and R.G. Rumbaut. 2001. *Legacies: The Story of the Immigrant Second Generation*. Berkeley: University of California Press

Portes, A., and M. Zhou. 1993. "The New Second Generation: Segmented Assimilation and Its Variants." *Annals of the American Academy of Political and Social Science* 530(November):74–96

Pratt, M.L. 2008. *Imperial Eyes: Travel Writing and Transculturalism*. 2nd edn. London: Routledge

Prebish, C.S., and M. Baumann, eds. 2002. *Westward Dharma: Buddhism beyond Asia*. Berkeley: University of California Press

Purkayastha, B. 2005. *Negotiating Ethnicity: Second-Generation South Asian Americans Traverse a Transnational World*. New Brunswick, NJ: Rutgers University Press

Putmam, R.D. 2007. "E Pluribus Unum: Diversity and Community in the Twenty-First Century." *Scandinavian Political Studies* 2(30):137–74

Raj, D.S. 2000. "'Who the Hell Do You Think You Are?' Promoting Religious Identity among Young Hindus in Britain." *Ethnic and Racial Studies* 23(3):535–58

Ralston, H. 1998. "Identity Reconstruction and Empowerment of South Asian Immigrant Women in Canada, Australia, and New Zealand." In *Religion in a Changing World: Comparative Studies in Sociology*, edited by M. Cousineau. Westport, CT: Praeger

Ramji, R. 2008a. "Being Muslim and Being Canadian: How Second Generation Muslim Women create Religious Identities in Two Worlds." In *Women and Religion in the West: Challenging Secularization*, edited by K. Aune, S. Sharma, and G. Vincett, 195–205. Aldershot, UK: Ashgate

– 2008b. "Creating a Genuine Islam: Second Generation Muslims Growing up in Canada." *Canadian Diversity / Diversité canadienne* 6(2):104–9

Rath, J., et al. 2001. *Western Europe and Its Islam*. Leiden: Brill

Rawlyk, G.A. 1996. *Is Jesus Your Personal Saviour? In Search of Canadian Evangelicalism in the 1990s*. Montreal and Kingston: McGill-Queen's University Press

Raymond, G.G., and T. Modood, eds. 2007. *The Construction of Minority Identities in France and Britain*. Basingstoke, UK, and New York: Palgrave Macmillan

Reitz, J., and R. Bannerjee. 2007. "Racial Inequality, Social Cohesion, and Policy Issues in Canada." In *Belonging? Diversity, Recognition, and Shared Citizenship in Canada*, edited by K. Banting, T.J. Courchene, and F.L. Seidle, 489–545. Montreal: Institute for Research on Public Policy

– M. Phan, and J. Thompson. 2009. "Race, Religion, and the Social Integration of New Immigrant Minorities in Canada." *International Migration Review* 43(4):695–726

Roald, A.S. 2001. *Women in Islam: The Western Experience*. London: Routledge

Robertson, R. 1992. *Globalization: Social Theory and Global Culture*. London: Sage

Roy, O. 2004. *Globalized Islam: The Search for a New Ummah*. New York: Columbia University Press

Rukmani, T.S., ed. 1999. *Hindu Diaspora: Global Perspectives*. Montreal: Chair in Hindu Studies, Concordia University

Schmidt, G. 2002. "The Complexity of Belonging: Sunni Muslim Immigrants in Chicago." In *Muslim Minorities in the West: Visible and Invisible*, edited by Y.Y. Haddad and J.I. Smith, 107–23. Walnut Creek, CA: Altamira Press

Sekar, R. 2001. *Global Reconstruction of Hinduism: A Case Study of Sri Lankan Tamils in Canada.* Unpublished PhD dissertation, University of Ottawa

Seljak, D. 2005. "Education, Multiculturalism, and Religion." In *Religion and Ethnicity in Canada*, edited by P. Bramadat and D. Seljak, 178–200. Toronto: Pearson Longman

Shafiry-Funk, M. 2008. *Encountering the Transnational: Women, Islam and the Politics of Interpretation (Gender in a Global/Local World).* Aldershot, UK: Ashgate

Simon, P. 2007. "La question de la seconde génération en France: mobilité sociale et discrimination." In *La 2e génération issue de l'immigration: une comparaison France – Québec*, edited by M. Potvin, P. Eid, and N. Venel, 39–70. Montreal: Anthéna éditions

Sirin, S.R., and M. Fine. 2008. *Muslim American Youth: Understanding Hyphenated Identities through Multiple Methods.* New York: New York University Press

Smith, B.K. 2000. "Who Does, Can, and Should Speak for Hinduism?" *Journal of the American Academy of Religion* 68(4): 741–9

Sontheimer, G.D., and H. Kulke, eds. 1989. *Hinduism Reconsidered.* New Delhi: Manohar

Statistics Canada. 2003a. *1971, 1981, 1991, & 2001 Census Custom Tabulations.* DO0324 (vol. CD-ROM). Ottawa: Statistics Canada, Advisory Services Division

– 2003b. *Religion (95) and Immigrant Status and Period of Immigration (11) for Population for Canada, Provinces, Territories, Census Metropolitan Areas and Census Agglomerations 2001–20% Sample Data.* Catalogue no. 97F00022XCB01004. Ottawa: Statistics Canada

– 2004. *Religion (18), Immigrant Status and Period of Immigration (9), Age (7), Ethnic Origin (15), Ethnic Origin Single/Multiple Response (3), Total Income Groups (9) and Sex (3) for Population for Canada and Selected Census Metropolitan Areas, 2001 Census.* Ottawa: Department of Canadian Heritage

– 2007. *Toronto, Ontario (Code535) (table). 2006 Community Profiles. 2006 Census.* Catalogue no. 92-591-XWE. Ottawa:Statistics Canada. www12.statcan.ca/census-recensement/2006/dp-pd/prof/92-591/index.cfm?Lang=E

Suh, S.A. 2004. *Being Buddhist in a Christian World: Gender and Community in a Korean American Temple.* Seattle: University of Washington Press

Teotonio, I., and N. Javed. 2010. "Toronto 18." *The Toronto Star.* http://www3.thestar.com/static/toronto18/index.html

Thielmann, J. 2008. "Islam and Muslims in Germany: An Introductory Exploration." In *Islam and Muslims in Germany*, edited by A. Al-Hamarneh and J. Thielmann, 1–29. Leiden: Brill

Thompson, L.G. 1996. *Chinese Religion: An Introduction.* Belmont, CA: Wadsworth

Verchery, L. 2010. "The Woodenfish Program: Fo Guang Shan, Canadian Youth, and a New Generation of Buddhist Missionaries." In *Wild Geese: Buddhism in Canada*, edited by J.S. Harding, G.V. Hori, and A. Soucy, 210–35. Montreal and Kingston: McGill-Queen's University Press

Vertovec, S. 1992. *Hindu Trinidad: Religion, Ethnicity and Socio-economic Change.* London: Macmillan Caribbean

– and A. Rogers, eds. 1998. *Muslim European Youth: Reproducing Ethnicity, Religion, Culture.* Aldershot, UK: Ashgate

Vincett, G., S. Sharma, and K. Aune. 2008. "Women, Religion and Secularization: One Size Does Not Fit All." In *Women and Religion in the West: Challenging Secularization*, edited by K. Aune, S. Sharma, and G. Vincett, 1–20. Aldershot, UK: Ashgate

Vrachnas, J., K. Boyd, M. Bagaric, and P. Dimopoulos. 2005. *Migration and Refugee Law: Principles and Practice in Australia.* Cambridge: Cambridge University Press

Warner, S. 1993. "Work in Progress toward a New Paradigm for the Sociological Study of Religion in the United States." *American Journal of Sociology* 98:1,044–93

Weber, M. 1946. "Religious Rejections of the World and Their Directions." In *From Max Weber: Essays in Sociology*, edited by H. Gerth and C.W. Mills, 323–59. New York: Oxford University Press

Weeks, M.F., and R.P. Moore. 1981. "Ethnicity-of-Interviewer Effects on Ethnic Respondents." *Public Opinion Quarterly* 45(2):245–9

Werbner, P. 2007. "Veiled Interventions in Pure Space: Honour, Shame and Embodied Struggles among Muslims in Britain and France." In *The Construction of Minority Identities in France and Britain*, edited by G.G. Raymond and T. Modood, 117–38. Basingstoke, UK, and New York: Palgrave Macmillan

Williams, P.W. 1989. *Popular Religion in America: Symbolic Change and the Modernization Process in Historical Perspective*. Champaign: University of Illinois Press

Williams, R.H. 2011. "Creating an American Islam: Thoughts on Religion, Identity, and Place." *Sociology of Religion* 72(2):127–53

– and G. Vashi. 2007. "Hijab and American Muslim Women: Creating the Space for Autonomous Selves." *Sociology of Religion* 68(3):269–87

Yang, C.K. 1967. *Religion in Chinese Society*. Berkeley: University of California Press

Yang, F., and H.R. Ebaugh. 2001. "Religion and Ethnicity among New Immigrants: The Impact of Majority/Minority Status in Home and Host Countries." *Journal for the Scientific Study of Religion* 40(3):367–78

Young, C.M. 1991. "Changes in the Demographic Behaviour of Migrants in Australia and the Transition between Generations." *Population Studies* 45(1):67–89

Zhou, M. 1997. "Segmented Assimilation: Issues, Controversies, and Recent Research on the New Second Generation." *International Migration Review* 31(4):975–1,007

– and C.L. Bankston III. 1998. *Growing up American: How Vietnamese Children Adapt to Life in the United States*. New York: Russell Sage

CONTRIBUTORS

LORI G. BEAMAN is is the Canada Research Chair in the contextualization of religion in a diverse Canada and professor in the department of classics and religious studies at the University of Ottawa. Her publications include *Defining Harm: Religious Freedom and the Limits of the Law* (UBC Press, 2008); "Is Religious Freedom Impossible in Canada?" *Law, Culture, and the Humanities* 6(3) 2010:1–19; "'It Was All Slightly Unreal': What's Wrong with Tolerance and Accommodation in the Adjudication of Religious Freedom?" *Canadian Journal of Women and Law* 23(2) 2011:442–63; "Religious Freedom and Neoliberalism: From Harm to Cost-Benefit," in *Religion and Neoliberal Policy and Governance*, edited by F. Gauthier and T. Martikainen, 193–210 (Ashgate, 2012); and "Battles over Symbols: The 'Religion' of the Minority versus the 'Culture' of the Majority," *Journal of Law and Religion* 28(1) 2012/13:101–38. She is co-editor, with Peter Beyer, of *Religion and Diversity in Canada* (Leiden: Brill Academic Press, 2008). She is principal investigator of a thirty-seven-member international research team whose focus is religion and diversity (religionanddiversity.ca).

PETER BEYER is professor of religious studies at the University of Ottawa. His work has focused primarily on religion in Canada and on developing sociological theory concerning religion and globalization. His publications include *Religion and Globalization* (Sage, 1994); *Religion in the Process of Globalization* (ed., Ergon, 2001); *Religions in Global Society* (Routledge, 2006); *Religion, Globalization, and Culture* (ed. with Lori Beaman, Leiden: Brill Academic Press, 2007); *Religion and Diversity in Canada* (ed. with Lori Beaman, Leiden: Brill Academic Press, 2008); and *Religion in the Context of Globalization* (Routledge, 2013). Since 2001, he has been conducting research on the religious expression of second-generation immigrant young adults in Canada. Articles from this work have appeared in various journals and collected volumes since 2005.

KATHRYN CARRIÈRE received her PhD in religious studies from the University of Ottawa. She has taught at the University of Ottawa and Carleton University. Kathryn is also a certified diversity trainer/facilitator and regularly gives presentations to post-secondary students and employees. She is currently conducting her own research while being a stay-at-home Mum.

CATHY HOLTMANN is a doctoral student in the sociology department at the University of New Brunswick where her research focuses on immigrant women, social networks, and religion. Prior to this, her work has considered social action among Catholic women and Catholic resources for domestic violence. She has been a graduate research assistant with the RAVE (Religion and Violence e-Learning) Project since 2007 and serves as the student caucus leader for the Religion and Diversity Project. Cathy co-ordinated the organization of the 2012 workshop on the study of religion in Atlantic Canada: Diverse Disciplines, Theories, Methods, and Contexts held at St Mary's University in Halifax.

MARIE-PAULE MARTEL-RENY holds a PhD in religion from Concordia University (Montreal). She holds a bachelor's degree in religious studies and early music performance from McGill University and an MA in educational studies from Concordia University. Her areas of specialization include youth and religion, with a focus on Quebec; the sociology of religion and spirituality; and Japanese religion. Her doctoral thesis investigates Quebec adolescents' spirituality and religiosity and addresses definitions and experiences of spirituality in the Western world, as well as issues of religious and spiritual education and globalization. Publications include "Quebec Adolescents and Religious Diversity" in *Voices: Postgraduate Perspectives on Interdisciplinarity*, edited by Kathryn Vincent and Juan Botero-Garcia (Cambridge Scholars Publishing, 2011), and "Religion et spiritualité chez les adolescents québécois: et eux, qu'en pensent-ils?" in *Jeunes et religion au Québec*, edited by François Gauthier and Jean-Philippe Perreault (Presses de l'Université Laval, 2008).

WENDY K. MARTIN holds a PhD in sociology of religion from the University of Ottawa. Her postdoctoral research with Peter Beyer examined the relationship between the religious diversity of newcomers to Canada and indicators of social and economic integration. She is currently developing a series of manuscripts on religion, consumption, and media, which build on her PhD dissertation, "Seeking through the Small Screen: Television as a Resource for Negotiating and Constructing Personal Spirituality." Additionally, she teaches part-time at the University of Ottawa while working as an applied social researcher in the public sector.

NANCY NASON-CLARK is professor of sociology (and chair of the department) at the University of New Brunswick. She is the principal investigator of the RAVE (Religion and Violence e-Learning) Project, a research initiative funded by the Lilly Endowment. Nason-Clark received her PhD in sociology from the London School of Economics and Political Science in the UK. She is the author or editor of eight books. They include *No Place for Abuse: Biblical and Practical Resources to Counteract Domestic Violence* (2nd edition, 2010; with C. Kroeger); *Responding to Abuse in the Christian Home* (2011; edited with B. Fisher Townsend and C. Kroeger); *Refuge from Abuse: Hope and Healing for Abused Christian Women* (2004; with C. Kroeger); *The Battered Wife: How Christians Confront Family Violence* (1997); *Beyond Abuse in the Christian Home* (2004; edited with B. Fisher Townsend and C. Kroeger); *Feminist Perspectives and Narratives in the Sociology of Religion* (2004; edited with M.J. Neitz); and *Understanding Abuse: Partnering for Change* (2004; edited with M.L. Stirling, C.A. Cameron, and B. Miedema). She has served as president of the Association for the Sociology of Religion (1998–2000) and president of the Religious Research Association (2001–04). Nason-Clark served two terms (2000–06) as editor of *Sociology of Religion: A Quarterly Review*.

RUBINA RAMJI is associate professor of religious studies in the department of philosophy and religious studies at Cape Breton University. She has served as chair for the Religion, Film and Visual Culture Group of the American Academy of Religion and is currently the president of the Canadian Society for the Study of Religion (2012–14). She is also the film editor for the *Journal of Religion and Film*. Her publications focus on understanding the images of Islam in North American mass media and its effects on Muslim identity. Her recent research focuses on the emerging religious identities of second-generation Muslim youth in Canada. She is the author of numerous articles and chapters in books, including *Religion in the Public Sphere: Interdisciplinary Perspectives across the Canadian Provinces*, edited by S. Lefebvre and L. Beaman (University of Toronto Press, forthcoming); *Religion and Canadian Society: Contexts, Identities, and Strategies*, edited by L. Beaman (Canadian Scholars Press, 2012); *The Continuum Companion to Religion and Film*, edited by W.L. Blizek (Continuum Press 2009); *Women and Religion in the West: Challenging Secularization*, edited by K. Aune, S. Sharma, and G. Vincett (Ashgate, 2008); and *Religion, Globalization, and Culture*, edited by P. Beyer and L. Beaman (Leiden: Brill Academic Press, 2007).

SHANDIP SAHA is assistant professor of religious studies at Athabasca University in Athabasca, Alberta. His research focuses on religion and politics in medieval India, religion and immigration in Canada, and globalized forms of

Hinduism. His current research on the history of the Vaiṣṇavite *bhakti* community known as the Puṣṭi Mārga has been published in the *Bulletin of the School of African and Oriental Studies* (2006), *South Asia Review* (2007), *The International Journal of Hindu Studies* (2007), and in the forthcoming volumes *Religious Interactions in Mughal India* (Oxford University Press) and *Introducing Hinduism* (Equinox Press). His research on globalization and immigration has been published in *Religion, Globalization, and Culture* (2007).

JOHN H. SIMPSON was educated at Whitman College, Seattle Pacific University, Princeton Theological Seminary, and Stanford University. He is professor emeritus, department of sociology, University of Toronto. His journal articles and chapters in books on religion span a range of topics, including the appearance of high gods in preliterate societies, the role of the Protestant parish minister, glossolalia, the cultural and political resurgence of Christian fundamentalism in North America, leaving religions, the self and social systems, religion and the body, and religion and globalization. He co-edited *Multiculturalism, Jews, and Identities in Canada* (1996). He is a past president of the Association for the Sociology of Religion.

INDEX

9/11 attacks, 49, 123, 126, 258, 302

Amnesty International, 116

Bannerji, R., 47
beards. *See* hijab/headscarf/beards
Beuchling, O., 300–1
Buddhism: and death, 197–8, 207; global construction of, 54, 70; as not proselytizing, 70, 201, 203, 216, 221, 224, 228–9, 234; as optional, 234, 236; practices of, 194; as systemic religion in Canada, 206, 212
Buddhist classification scheme, 67; Christians, 69, 228–9; distribution of participants within, 215; imitative traditionalists, 68–9, 226–8; "little bit Buddhist," 69, 194, 197–201, 223–6; religio-culturally based religious *seekers*, 67–8, 194–7, 215–22, 229–30, 233
Buddhist knowledge among participants, 67, 210, 220, 222; lack of, 193–4, 224, 235; parental inability to explain, 218–9; sources of, 218–9, 238–9, 276
Buddhist men, 192–212; Buddhist identity among, 192; demographic profile of, 192–3; imitative traditionalists among, lack of, 194; ritual involvement, lack of, 257; similarity to general population, 194
Buddhist participants: attitude to religion among, 199, 206–7, 209, 237; between

two cultures, 203, 212, 236; Buddhism as partial identity, 197, 200–1, 203, 205; Buddhist and cultural identity, 210, 215, 219, 222, 225, 228, 233; Buddhist identity among, 67, 70, 197, 211; Buddhist practice among, 205, 222; Christianity, exposure to, 194, 204, 210, 216, 223, 232, 238; and cultural identity, 212; education, importance of, 214, 231; gender differences among, 69; generation gap with parents, 238; individualistic construction of religious identity, 209, 216–7; religious practices among parents, 214, 222; religious socialization, lack of, 205, 217–8, 221, 230, 232; "Western" Buddhism among, 222
Buddhists, second generation in Germany, 300–1; blending of Buddhism and culture among, 300; Buddhism as "relaxed" among, 300; Buddhist education for, 300; Buddhist monastery, participation in, 301
Buddhists in Canada: demographic characteristics, 36–9; intergenerational identities among, 40; projected growth of, 211
Buddhist women, 213–34; demographic profile of, 213–14; greater religiousness of, 233, 257; place of birth among, 213; refugee families among, 214; rejection of "pushy" religion among, 216, 223–4; responsibility for passing on culture, 214, 220, 226